F

N

FRATERNAL ORGANIZATIONS

To
Carol and the Fraternal
Bond We Share

The Greenwood Encyclopedia of American Institutions

Each work in the *Encyclopedia* is designed to provide concise histories of major voluntary groups and nonprofit organizations that have played significant roles in American civic, cultural, political, and economic life from the colonial era to the present. Previously published:

1. *Labor Unions*
Gary M Fink, Editor-in-Chief

2. *Social Service Organizations*
Peter Romanofsky, Editor-in-Chief

The Greenwood Encyclopedia of American Institutions

Fraternal Organizations

ALVIN J. SCHMIDT

advisory editor NICHOLAS BABCHUK

GREENWOOD PRESS

Westport, Connecticut • London, England

Library of Congress Cataloging in Publication Data

Schmidt, Alvin J
   Fraternal organizations.

   (The Greenwood encyclopedia of American institutions ; 3)
   Includes index.
     1. Friendly societies—United States—History.
2. Friendly societies—Canada—History. 3. Friendly
societies—United States—Directories. 4. Friendly
societies—Canada—Directories. 5. Voluntarism—
United States. 6. Voluntarism—Canada. I. Babchuk,
Nicholas. II. Title. III. Series: Greenwood
encyclopedia of American institutions ; 3.
HS17.S3   366'.00973   79-6187
ISBN 0-313-21436-0

Library of Congress Catalog Card Number: 79-6187
ISBN: 0-313-21436-0

First published in 1980

Greenwood Press
A division of Congressional Information Service, Inc.
88 Post Road West, Westport, Connecticut 06881

Printed in the United States of America

10 9 8 7 6 5 4 3 2 1

Contents

B

C

D _____

E _____

F

G

H

I

J _____

K

L

N

O

P

R

S

T _____

U _____

V

W

FOREWORD

Voluntary associations are an integral part of American society. Millions of persons of all ages and representative of the major religious, racial, and ethnic groups in society belong to fraternal and sororal collectivities, some of which date back to the early history of our country. Such groups, both numerous and diverse, have played a critical role in the emergence and maintenance of the pluralism that characterizes us as a people. A substantial majority of the population belong to at least one organization, and multiple memberships are common. Many individuals initially become affiliated with an association (for example, Job's Daughters, Columbian Squires, Rainbow Girls, Junior Odd Fellows, or De Molay) during early adolescence and later join one or more groups when they become adults.

Voluntary groups have considerable import for the individual. Apart from providing fellowship and diversion, they also offer their members aid in numerous areas by providing an arena for expressive behavior, supplying vital personal services, helping to confer status on individual membes, giving reinforcement and support for important values and desired behavior, acting as agencies and pressure groups on members' behalf, generally informing and educating, and performing a wide array of other functions. Under the circumstances, it is little wonder that persons who are members of such groups, as compared to those who are not affiliated, have a more favorable self-image, are less likely to feel alienated and powerless, and frequently play an active role in the polity.

In societal terms, groups help to distribute power at different levels. Often they are organized either to change the social order or to maintain the status quo; many groups provide resources that make services and products available to a considerable segment of the population.

In the descriptions of the fraternal associations in the present volume, the reader will be struck by the diversity of services that groups provide, not only for their own members but also for the public at large. Some fraternal organizations obviously support questionable objectives, but a far larger number support worthwhile causes, particularly in the spheres of education, public health, and philanthropy. For example, fraternal associations contribute substantial monies that enable thousands of students to attend universities; they support research in mental health, and medical facilities that aid crippled children, the indigent, and the mentally retarded.

This volume will present the reader with detailed information on every major fraternal group in the United States and Canada. Included is a brief history of each association, its sponsor or organizer, the number of its members, membership qualifications, the types of causes supported, the benefits derived from membership, a description of the rituals followed, and reference sources that might be consulted by the interested reader. Such information is valuable in its own right. But even more important, part 1 of the book (The Fraternal Context) provides a framework in which fraternal groups can be understood, compared, and linked, not only to each other but to other types of voluntary associations. Part 1 presents the grand view of organizations with a special emphasis on fraternal groups, their historical emergence, the significance of their rituals, the causes they espouse, the values shared by their members, their ties to religious bodies, and their interrelatedness.

Dr. Schmidt is singularly qualified to bring together, to organize, and to analyze data on fraternal organizations. He has been studying voluntary associations for over a decade, and his specialty is fraternal groups. No sociologist is more knowledgeable on the subject.

The present volume epitomizes the high scholarship that is crucial in a treatise of this kind; this will become evident to all readers, but especially to students of voluntary groups. As a volume it truly represents a signal contribution, a definitive statement on the subject of fraternal organizations.

November 1979
Nicholas Babchuk
Professor of Sociology
The University of Nebraska, Lincoln

PREFACE

This volume in the *Greenwood Encyclopedia of American Institutions* covers fraternal organizations of the United States and Canada. For the most part, a brief summary pertaining to the founding date and place, history and development, goals and activities, membership requirements and size, organizational characteristics such as rituals and emblems, and publications of each society are discussed. In some instances, especially in the case of societies that have been out of existence for some time, some of the details are lacking, primarily because the necessary information was not available to the writer.

To write any book is not an easy task, but to write one that requires the cooperation of a large number of organizations—many of whom believe that they have special secrets—makes the task even more difficult. Most of the information presented on the majority of fraternal organizations in the present volume had to be gathered by contacting the organizations in writing. Some societies responded the first time that they were contacted. Some sent helpful material upon being asked the second time. Others furnished information the third time they were contacted. Still others never responded, even upon being contacted for the third and fourth time.

Why some societies ignored all requests to supply up-to-date information about themselves is difficult to say. Undoubtedly some were uncooperative because they felt some of their "secrets" would be compromised. Others may very well have declined all requests because of their isolationistic posture, not too uncommon among fraternal orders. Yet numerous organizations that make much of their secrecy responded promptly and generously. Many even sent a copy of the ritual. On the other hand, some societies that have discontinued their fraternal secrets failed to furnish any material. They never responded to the author's requests for information.

For the societies that did not provide any data about themselves, the author sought the necessary information by tapping various library sources. Some of these were back issues of the *Fraternal Monitor* and *Statistics Fraternal Societies* (now known as *Statistics, Fraternal Benefit Societies*).

These periodicals are publications of the National Fraternal Congress of America. Other sources were Albert C. Stevens, *Cyclopedia of Fraternities* (1907); Arthur Preuss, *A Dictionary of Secret and Other Societies* (1924); William J. Whalen, *Handbook of Secret Organizations* (1966); Theodore Graebner, *The Secret Empire* (1927); Theodore Graebner, *A Handbook of Organizations* (1948); Harold V. B. Voorhis, *Masonic Organizations and Allied Orders and Degrees* (1952); and The Masonic Service Association, "Allied Masonic Groups and Rites" (mimeographed, 1978). Published convention proceedings were also helpful in many instances for gathering information on groups that did not furnish materials.

While the present volume includes more than 450 fraternal societies, it by no means includes all of the societies that made an appearance on the American scene. It would not be possible to include all fraternal societies, as there probably have been at least 2,000 that made an appearance in North America since the mid-1800s. Some of these societies, even national ones, functioned for only a very short period of time. Most of these societies left few or no historical records behind.

Every attempt was made to include all of the extant fraternal organizations, even those who refused to furnish information about themselves. Even so, it was not feasible to include all societies, primarily because in some instances no addresses were known. The extinct societies that are presented were included only when the date of formation and the primary function of such were known. Rarely were organizations included when the date of a specific fraternal society was not known. The sketches of these organizations are usually very brief. To include the extinct societies, the author had to rely to a large degree on Albert C. Stevens, *Cyclopedia of Fraternities* (1907), and Arthur Preuss, *A Dictionary of Secret and Other Societies* (1924). To give proper credit for employing these two sources, the author uses the abbreviation *Cyc. Frat.* for *Cyclopedia of Fraternities* and *DSOS* for *Dictionary of Secret and Other Societies*. An asterisk (*) following the name of a given fraternal group indicates that the present volume contains a written report on that organization.

The reader may wonder why such organizations as the Daughters of the American Revolution, Veterans of Foreign Wars, and the American Legion are not included in the present volume. These organizations may in many instances have fraternal characteristics, but on the whole they are more accurately classified as patriotic organizations. College fraternities are also excluded. Most college fraternities are included in Baird's *Manual of American College Fraternities*, which has been issued in numerous editions over the years. Finally, it needs to be noted that the present book also does not include such groups as the Kiwanis, Rotary, Lions, or Optimist clubs. Some readers may loosely classify these associations as fraternal. However, given the definition of what constitutes a fraternal organization in the next chapter, these societies cannot be considered to be fraternal. Moreover, the published literature on fraternal orders has never considered these organizations as belonging to the fraternal realm. They have commonly been known as service organizations. The sociological literature on voluntary associations supports the latter assertion.

In presenting discussions on several hundred societies, the author tried to be fair and objective with each and every organization. Wherever possible, serious efforts were made to mention the constructive activities (such as works of charity and philanthropy) of every society. In fact, by surveying each of the societies discussed in the present publication, the author, as a sociologist who has studied fraternal organizations for more than a decade, developed a greater appreciation than he had previously had for the many noteworthy contributions and influences that fraternal organizations have made to the social, political, and economic well-being of their country.

Before going directly to the individual organizational sketches of each fraternal group, the writer thought it helpful to produce an introductory chapter, "The Fraternal Context." This chapter discusses the nature, prevalence, and function of American fraternal orders, beginning with the mid-nineteenth century. By reading that chapter, the reader will gain a more holistic view of the role and function that fraternal associations have played in American life.

The writer wishes to thank all the fraternal benefit and fraternal secret societies—too numerous to mention—that provided materials about themselves. Special gratitude is extended to the National Fraternal Congress for making its library available. The Iowa Masonic Library in Cedar Rapids, Iowa, is another source that provided helpful material to the writer for more than ten years. The material gleaned from its shelves greatly aided the portrayal of the Masonic and Masonically allied others. A special note of appreciation also goes to the Commission on Fraternal Organizations of the Lutheran Church-Missouri Synod in St. Louis, Missouri, which provided information on a number of fraternal groups. R and R Research of Indianapolis, Indiana, freely let the writer make use of the back issues of *Statistics, Fraternal Societies*.

Although the author's two children, Timothy and Mark, provided no information about fraternal groups, they forfeited much of the time that they daily spend with their father. They deserve a big thank you!

Finally, the writer is truly grateful for the labor of love that his wife, Carol, gave so generously by typing and proofreading the entire manuscript. Without her understanding and devoted assistance, the many long days and nights spent in writing this book would have been considerably more tedious.

THE
FRATERNAL
CONTEXT

THE PREVALENCE OF FRATERNAL ORGANIZATIONS

The United States has appropriately been called a nation of joiners. This observation goes back to about 150 years ago when Alexis de Tocqueville on his six-month visit to the United States in 1831 said:

Americans of all ages, all conditions, and all dispositions constantly form associations. . . . Whenever at the head of some new undertaking you see the government in France, or a man of rank in England, in the United States you will be sure to find an association. . . . In the United States associations are established to promote the public safety, commerce, industry, morality, and religion. (*Democracy in America*, 2 vols. (Vintage Books, 2, p. 114.)

Had de Tocqueville visited the United States fifty years later he would have been even more impressed by the great multiplicity of associations. By the 1870s and 1880s fraternal organizations were sprouting all over the American landscape, like mushrooms after a spring rain, by the scores and hundreds. Charles Merz, writing in 1927, estimated that there were 800 different fraternal associations in the United States. He also estimated that 30,000,000 of the 60,000,000 people in the United States (1920 census) held membership in some fraternal group. Most of the American fraternal societies were formed during the later 1800s and the early 1900s, as is indicated by the sketches of the fraternal societies in the present volume.

It should be noted here that the concept "fraternal" carries no sexist connotation to anyone in the fraternal organizational context. In fact, women's societies such as the Order of the Eastern Star,* the Daughters of Penelope,* the Supreme Emblem Club,* and the Pythian Sisters* do not feel that they should refer to their societies as "sororal" organizations. Without exception (as far as the writer knows), the ladies consistently apply the term "fraternal" to themselves, and with pride.

THE NATURE OF FRATERNAL ORGANIZATIONS

For more than a hundred years the entire American fraternal complex has basically consisted of two kinds of fraternal societies, namely, the secret orders and the benefit societies. The former include groups like the Masons,* Odd Fellows,* Elks,* Knights of Pythias,* Shriners,* Eastern Star,* Daughters of Mokanna,* and Daughters of Isis.* The latter are represented by groups such as the Catholic Order of Foresters,* Catholic Knights of America,* Sons of Norway,* Independent Order of Vikings,* Independent Order of Foresters,* and Royal Arcanum.* The fraternal benefit societies are primarily engaged in providing life insurance for their members, whereas insurance as such is not available in the fraternal secret organizations, even though they may provide contributions of charity and benevolence to needy members. The fraternal secret orders see the role and function of their rituals as para- mount. Ritual content is seen not only as secret but as a necessary means of teaching moral values. As a rule, these groups offer more than one degree. The fraternal benefit societies (often referred to as "fraternals") place considerably less emphasis on rituals. In fact, some fraternal benefit groups have over the years dispensed with rituals and secrets.

In choosing to call one segment "fraternal secret societies" and another "fraternal benefit societies," the writer has adopted a distinction that has existed for many years. Leaders of fraternal insurance groups have for some time called their organizations "fraternal benefit societies." The designation of "fraternal secret societies" was chosen in order to distinguish the more traditional fraternal groups without insurance from the fraternal life in- surance structures. In adopting these labels, it needs to be said that the fraternal benefit societies are not in all instances without secrets. Quite a number of the insurance fraternals still consider their ritual and passwords to be secret. The primary distinction to be kept in mind is that while both types of groups may have some secrets, both do not sell insurance to their members.

To many people the presence of a ritual and secrecy are key characteristics of a fraternal organization. Thus some fraternal benefit societies that have removed all rituals and secrecy may no longer appear to be fraternal groups. Such a conclusion would also seem to follow from the definition formulated by the National Fraternal Congress* (an association of fraternal benefit societies formed in 1886) and the National Association of Insurance Com- missioners. Their definition says that one characteristic of a fraternal benefit society consists of an organization's having "a lodge system with ritualistic form of work. . . . A lodge system is defined as

A society having a supreme or legislative or governing body and subordinate lodges or branches by whatever name known, into which members are elected, initiated or admitted in accordance with its constitution, laws, ritual and rules, which subordi- nate lodges or branches shall be required by the laws of the society to hold regular meetings at least once a month. (*Uniform Code for Organization and Supervision of Fraternal Benefit Societies*, National Association of Insurance Commissioners and National Fraternal Congress of America, 1962, p. 1.)

Yet a number of fraternal benefit societies no longer have either a ritual or secrecy, and some have never had either one. The reason that a given order without a ritual qualifies as a fraternal society is imbedded in the laws of the state in which the society receives its legal charter. Some states do not require that a society have a ritual in order to be classified as fraternal.

The National Fraternal Congress and the National Association of Insurance Commissioners also define what they mean by a fraternal benefit society. The definition reads: "Any incorporated society, order or supreme lodge, without capital stock . . . conducted solely for the benefit of its members and their beneficiaries and not for profit, operated on a lodge system with ritualistic form of work, having a representative form of government, and which makes provision for the payment of benefits. . . ." (See the *Uniform Code for Organization and Supervision of Fraternal Benefit Societies*, 1962.)

This definition has some similarities to, but also some differences with, a seventeenth-century definition formulated by Randle Holme, one of the first nonoperative Masons in the era of operative Masonry in England. Holme said a

Fraternity, or Society, or Brotherhood, or Company, are such in corporation, that are of one and the same trade, or occupation, who being joyned [sic] together by oath and covenant, do follow such orders and rules, as are made, or to be made for the good order, rule, and support of such and every of their occupations. These several Fraternities are generally governed by one or two Masters, and two Wardens, but most Companies with us by two Aldermen, and two Stewards, the latter being to receive and pay what concerns them. (Cited in Bernard E. Jones, *Freemasons' Guide and Compendium*, 1956, p. 103.)

While the United States in the eighteenth and nineteenth centuries provided a hospitable environment for hundreds of fraternal societies, the idea of forming fraternal benevolent societies did not originate in the United States. The ancient burial societies that existed in Greece before the birth of Christ, for example, apparently were quite fraternal in nature. These societies were by no means ephemeral organizations; many had regulations, officers, regular meetings, conferred degrees, paid benefits to appropriate beneficiaries, and received formal state recognition. In fact, the names of some of those ancient groups have been borrowed in part by American fraternal orders. The Greek state of Rhodes had some groups called Sons of Minerva, Sons of Bacchus, Sons of Jupiter the Savior, and the like. The Roman era had its *collegia* and also societies that spent some of their collected fees on funerals for deceased members. The medieval era had its guilds that flourished in Europe well into the sixteenth century. After the guilds began to decline, the friendly societies came to prominence in eighteenth-century England.

The fraternal benefit societies that arose in the United States by the hundreds during the late 1800s and early 1900s in many ways resembled the British friendly societies, yet there is really no evidence to suggest that the American fraternals were patterned after the societies in England. Instead, most of them imitated Freemasonry in regard to rituals and secrecy, but in their insurance programs they simply operated on a trial-and-error basis. They could have learned about insurance from the English friendly societies, but for some reason did not.

Instrumental-Expressive Organizations

Sociological research literature has provided empirical evidence that in the realm of voluntary associations there are organizations that range from the instrumental to the expressive end of the continuum. (See C. Wayne Gordon and Nicholas Babchuk, "A Typology of Voluntary Associations," *American Sociological Review*, 1959; Arthur P. Jacoby and Nicholas Babchuk, "Instrumental and Expressive Voluntary Associations," *Sociology and Social Research*, 1963.)

Instrumental groups are organizations that exist as a means to accomplish specific ends or goals; their activities are externally oriented, and their members receive delayed gratification in that the organization's goals are not attained immediately. Expressive associations function as an end in themselves; their activities are internally oriented, and their members receive immediate gratification in that the group's goals are realized rather immediately. An example of an instrumental group is the Democratic party. An expressive association would be a recreational organization such as the YMCA or a garden club.

In applying the instrumental-expressive typology to fraternal organizations, one notes that most fraternal secret orders in America are largely expressive in nature. Their instrumental qualities, if any, are usually incidental to the organizations' primary objective, which is to enable their members to come together in a context of fraternal fellowship. Freemasonry, the Shrine, the Order of the Eastern Star, the Elks, the Pythian Sisters, and other similar groups all are strongly expressive in their orientation.

In discussing the instrumental-expressive typology, it is appropriate to note that Freemasonry in North America, and in England as well, is significantly different from Freemasonry on the continent of Europe. Masons in France, Italy, and Germany have usually been very politically oriented, hence instrumental in their basic posture. Continental Masons have commonly been opposed to the Roman Catholic Church and to royalty as well. In 1877 the Grand Orient (French Masonry) changed its constitution, eliminating reference to any deity in its ritual. It also removed the requirement that its members believe in a supreme being. Such action is unacceptable and unthinkable to English-speaking Masons in North America or the

British Commonwealth. In fact, soon after the Grand Orient of France made its constitutional changes in 1877, the Grand Lodge of England (Masons) in protest refused to allow French Masons to visit British lodges. As a result, British Masonry and most American grand lodges have not recognized French Masonry.

Whereas the fraternal secret societies are primarily expressive, the fraternal benefit organizations are somewhat less expressive. Many of the benefit societies, through the National Fraternal Congress, keep very close watch on what laws are being proposed in the state legislatures and in the United States Congress. Proposed legislation that has the potential of affecting fraternal benefit societies is keenly analyzed, with appropriate responses. Other than concern about legislation that could affect fraternal benefit societies, there is little or no concern with affecting social or political change in the state or country. For the most part, the fraternal benefit societies have adapted themselves to the conditions of a given time rather than to producing social change. For example, in the late 1800s, when most people had virtually no social and economic security, the fraternal benefit groups did not lobby or seek ways of persuading the government to create change that would relieve the economic plight of their members. Instead, they established insurance programs to cope with the exigencies of their time.

The most instrumentally oriented fraternal order in American society is the Patrons of Husbandry* (the Grange). This group, since its origin, has sought specific social changes to benefit the farmer and, more recently, rural residents as well. Although the Grange is highly instrumental, it is not without expressive qualities; its rituals, degrees, and social events are quite expressive in nature.

Secrecy

Every fraternal secret society attempts to keep certain organizational practices secret, as do some fraternal benefit groups. Secrecy in certain organizations has been around for hundreds of years. Long before the medieval guilds or Freemasonry came into being, given groups such as the Egyptian mystery schools (which functioned at least 1500 years before the birth of Christ), the Gnostics, and the orders of knighthood during the Crusades practiced secrecy.

Some interesting things can be noted regarding secrecy. Many fraternal orders, especially Freemasonry, will assert that they are not a secret society, but rather a society with secrets. Because secrecy is practiced by so many fraternal groups it has led some of those outside the fraternities to become suspicious of them. This posture has frequently been detrimental to many societies. The anti-Masonic era that occurred in the United States from 1826 to about 1845 is a case in point. Thousands of Masons, Odd Fellows, and other fraternal society members were hurt by the contagious prejudice that spread across many states, especially in the northeastern section of the country.

. Another characteristic that one finds with respect to secrecy is the seriousness that fraternal members have regarding it. Many—probably most—believe that their organization's ritual, for example, really is secret, despite the well-established fact that anyone who really desires to see a ritual can do so. For example, most rituals that are copyrighted can be found and read in the Library of Congress, and sometimes in other libraries as well. One leading Freemason once put it this way: "A large part of the ritualistic work is printed in Monitors; the Book of Constitutions [see Freemasonry in present volume for a discussion of this document], in which is contained the basic laws of the Fraternity, has been openly published since 1723, and copies are on the shelves of many public libraries." Yet, the myth persists, even among many leaders of fraternal societies, that their order's ritual is really secret. One more realistic officer, who is well acquainted with the mentality of many fraternal society officers, recently summed it up well by saying that "asking them [fraternal society leaders] for facts concerning their rituals is like enquiring if they are virgins." Some leaders, however, are becoming more realistic regarding the so-called secrecy of their rituals. Quite a number of societies sent the author a ritual.

Rituals and Degrees

If secrecy is important to most fraternal groups, so are rituals and degrees. Some societies, for example, Freemasonry, see the ritual as the essence of their organization's being. To the fraternal secret societies, rituals are the vehicle for teaching members high principles, virtues, brotherhood, morals, and even religious values. Most of the rituals are somber, almost austere. There are exceptions, of course. For instance, the Shrine ritual contains a great deal of levity. Degrees that are conferred on individual members are part of the ritual format. When a society has several degrees, it seeks to teach specific truths with each degree.

In recent years some organizations have abbreviated their rituals in order to accommodate individuals who feel their society's ritual is too long and antiquated. Others have reduced the number of degrees to one. The Elks, for instance, once had three degrees, but now have only one. On the other hand, some groups have strenuously resisted changing their rituals or reducing the number of degrees. Freemasonry on occasion receives overtures from its members to modernize its ritual, but it has consistently thwarted any and all such attempts. Of all fraternal organizations, Freemasonry will surely be the last order to alter its rituals and degrees.

Fraternal Fantasy

As already noted, at the height of their popularity fraternal orders attracted millions of American residents. There were several reasons (some are discussed later) for the phenomenal fraternal growth and prosperity of seventy-five to a hundred years ago. One reason was the feeling of importance or worth that fraternal participation gave to the common man. Where else could John Doe experience and be part of a group or subculture that employed exotic names and titles and provided a touch of fantasy?

When the member attended his society's local meetings, he did not go to a hall, but to a "court," "nest," "tent," "homestead," "grange," "circle," "lodge," "encampment," "pond," "forest," "caravan," "conclave," "council," "hive," "clan," "aerie," or "grotto." The principal officer was not called president, but "Worshipful Grand Master," "Supreme Potentate," "Grand Illuminator," "Exalted Grand Master," "Sachem," "Supreme Chancellor," "Grand Chief Orient," "The Most Puissant Grand Master," or "Grand Eminent Commander." (One critic said it was surprising that none called their head officer "Supreme Being.") Rank and file members referred to themselves as "knights," "veiled prophets," "sojourners," "shriners," "foresters," "red men," and so on. If an individual belonged to one of the so-called animal lodges, he took pride in being called an "eagle," "owl," "moose," "elk," "oriole," "beaver," or "buffalo."

Although the exotic names and titles seem to have lost much of their appeal, as evidenced by declining memberships, their use has declined only slightly, and then only in the fraternal benefit societies. The fraternal secret orders still seem to be enamored by exotic labels and fantasy. For instance, the Improved Order of Red Men is not an organization of American Indians. In fact, until several years ago, only white men were allowed to join this order. The groups that use the word "ancient" in their organization name are really not ancient at all, as most of them were founded within the last hundred years. Similarly, when claims are made that Martin Luther and Isaac Newton were Freemasons (long before speculative or nonoperative Masons existed), the informed individual can best explain such claims in terms of the fantasy that has characterized American fraternal secret societies since their inception.

Organizational Structure

Virtually every fraternal organization conducts its activities on three levels: the national, the regional, and the local. The local units, as indicated, are called by various names, of which the most common is the name "lodge." It is on the local level that members usually are initiated and learn about fraternal affairs. Regional structures frequently follow state lines in the United States, just as in Canada they tend to follow provincial boundaries. Many societies refer to their regional organizations as "grand lodges." In most fraternal societies the local units and the regional structures are subordinate to the national organization, which commonly is called the "supreme lodge." The supreme lodge meets in convention and establishes basic policies through adopted resolutions. Most supreme lodges maintain national headquarters that house a permanent clerical staff. The fraternal benefit groups usually have an elected board of directors that makes key decisions between conventions.

The one major fraternal organization that does not have a national or supreme lodge structure is Freemasonry. American Freemasons have forty-nine grand lodges. Each is an autonomous entity that commonly meets in convention ("Grand Lodge Communication") annually.

Organizational Change

For the most part, it would be difficult to accuse most fraternal societies of engaging in too much organizational change. In the entire American fraternal context, the fraternal benefit societies have been more active in introducing change than the fraternal secret orders, even if often with great reluctance.

Achieving Actuarial Soundness. The first method of collecting fees to pay for the life insurance of fraternal members was the flat-rate assessment plan, frequently dubbed the "assessment-as-needed" plan. Another term for it was post-mortem plan. This plan charged every member, young or old, the same dues. As long as the organization had mostly young members with few deaths everything went fine, but as the membership grew older and the death rates increased, financial trouble began to plague many fraternal benevolent groups. In order to avoid some of the shortcomings of the flat-rate plan, some fraternal groups adopted the graded-assessment plan, which required older members to pay more than younger members paid. Although the graded plan was an improvement over the flat-rate method, it still had basic actuarial weaknesses. It did not use the data of mortality tables, and the reserve funds were too small or nonexistent. Eventually, societies on the graded plan also began encountering financial difficulties.

Although financial bankruptcy threatened the survival of many fraternal insurance groups, change to more scientific methods was frequently resisted. The Modern Woodmen of America,* to cite one example, had some delegates at one of its national conventions propose the adoption of a reserve fund. The first time this plan was suggested (in 1897), it was defeated by a vote of four to one. In fact, the society kept defeating a similar resolution for more than twenty years. Many fraternal societies felt that reserve funds were necessary only for commercial insurance firms. Apparently, most felt that the fraternal spirit would compensate for actuarial weaknesses.

Given the inadequacy of the assessment plans, as well as other difficulties, nineteen fraternal benefit societies—with the prompting of the Ancient Order of United Workmen*—banded together in 1886 and formed the National Fraternal Congress (NFC), already mentioned. This new association soon served as a powerful impetus for organizational change in numerous fraternal societies. In fact, without an association like the NFC the entire fraternal benefit system would probably have collapsed.

The NFC introduced a number of changes. In 1887, at its first convention, the association clearly stated what constituted a fraternal benefit society. In 1892 it began drafting a "Uniform Bill" that would provide uniform practices in collecting fees, distributing benefits, and the like. The following year (1893) the NFC adopted its Uniform Bill. It was also in 1893 that the association began urging states to enact legislation consistent with the Uniform Bill. Another significant change occurred when the NFC in 1897 authorized the compilation of a morality table. Two years later it approved such a table.

In 1901, in Mobile, Alabama, a meeting took place with the National Convention of Insurance Commissioners and representatives of the NFC, as well as representatives from the Associated Fraternities of America.* The last association was a rival group to the NFC. In 1913, however, the Associated Fraternities of America merged with the NFC. These three groups adopted the so-called Mobile Bill, which asked fraternal societies to adopt sound actuarial methods and establish a reserve fund system. The bill required that fraternal benefit societies also be valuated and that valuations be publicized. Moreover, each society was to improve its solvency by 5 percent every three years. Although the bill recognized the NFC mortality table, it did not require that societies use only this table. The following year (1911), the Mobile Bill was passed without substantive changes by thirteen state legislatures.

In 1912 the Mobile Bill was refined in New York City. Again the National Convention of Insurance Commissioners, the National Fraternal Congress, and the Associated Fraternities of America met, but this time there was one additional group, the Federated Fraternities.* This last group was unhappy with some of the stipulations in the Mobile Bill. After various sections of the bill were changed, it became known as the New York Conference Bill, approved in 1912. This bill soon became the fraternal law of the land, especially after the thirteen states that passed the Mobile Bill made the necessary amendments. By 1919 the New York Conference Bill became law in thirty-five states. Some of the items covered in the bill pertained to exemptions from state insurance laws, the nature of benefits, beneficiaries, establishing adequate reserve funds, the method of organizing a benefit society, mergers, licensing, requiring a supreme lodge authority, annual reports, valuation, liquidation requirements, taxation exemption, penalties, and membership requirements.

George Santayana once said that those who do not learn from the lessons of history are destined to repeat the same mistakes. In a way this was true of the American fraternal benefit societies, for had they made some effort to study and learn from the errors of the friendly societies in England, which fumbled through some of the same trials and errors to achieve actuarial soundness and financial solvency at least fifty years before the American fraternals appeared on the scene, many organizational and personal pains could have been avoided. Many societies might even have avoided going out of existence. But as the friendly societies and their experiences in England were either not known or ignored, the American fraternal benefit societies had to struggle for about forty years to attain financial solvency, something that the English friendly societies had largely accomplished by the time the first American fraternal insurance society, the Ancient Order of United Workmen, was founded in 1868.

The Status of Women. One of the relatively persistent demands for organizational change was to admit women to the all-male fraternal societies. This change, when it occurred, primarily took place in the fraternal benefit societies. Organizations that accommodated females did so in different ways. Some counted women in the total membership statistics, but still had them serve in auxiliary roles. Others enrolled women in the formerly all-male organization, but had them receive female degrees. Still others, however, accepted females as regular members with no qualifications whatsoever.

Although most fraternal benefit groups changed their rules so that ladies could become members, the fraternal secret societies have resisted taking women into their fraternal folds. For example, the Freemasons, Odd Fellows, Elks, Shriners, Grottoes,* and Eagles* have never seriously considered the question of whether women may join their ranks as equal members. Most strongly opposed to having women join its fraternal sanctity is Freemasonry. Old Masonic authority says that "for a woman to become a Freemason is as impossible as for a man to become a mother, a leopard to change his spots." Some of the fraternal secret orders even decline to recognize or approve ladies' auxiliary groups. For instance, the Elks have never officially recognized the Supreme Emblem Club* as an auxiliary, even though it has been organized since 1926.

Although women may not become Masons, Odd Fellows, or Shriners, the men not only may join the ladies' organizations, but frequently hold some office in their orders. For example, the rules of the Order of the Eastern Star require a Master Mason (third-degree member) to hold the position of Grand Worthy Patron. For the most part, men are required to hold some office in a ladies' group, apparently because the men wrote the founding constitution. Their purpose was, evidently, that the ladies should do no harm to the cause of fraternalism, as seen by a particular male group. Yet, one detects no signs of discontent on the part of the ladies, even in a day and age when the consciousness of women has been raised as never before.

Changes in Rituals. As already alluded to, most fraternal secret societies have had to face the question of whether or not to change some aspects of their ritual and its accouterments. While some have changed, abbreviated, or disbanded certain practices, generally most orders have strongly adhered to lengthy, antiquated ritualistic formulas. Modern man, however, seems to prefer rituals and ceremonies that are relatively brief. After all, he lives in an age where the culture of instantaneousness is dominant everywhere. To expect him to come regularly to lodge meetings where a lengthy and ancient-sounding ritual is rehearsed is to expect the improbable. The use of lengthy, outdated rituals is one significant reason for declining memberships and low attendance at most fraternal secret societies. Some reports show that the average Masonic lodge meeting, for instance, draws about 5 to 8 percent of its membership. Some, like the Elks, that have made significant changes in modifying their ritual, as well as other changes, have in recent years prospered and grown numerically. It is difficult not to see such changes as contributing substantially to the prosperity of the Elks, especially when Freemasonry since the late 1950s has lost about 25 percent of its members. The Odd Fellows have had even greater losses, and the Knights of Pythias are barely surviving.

Racial Integration. Another call for change has been the call to accept nonwhite applicants into the fellowship of fraternalism. Here again the fraternal benefit societies have made the greatest strides. Virtually all of them have removed all-white membership clauses from their constitutions. The fraternal secret societies, however, have been extremely reluctant to do so. Recently (in the early 1970s), the federal courts in several instances exerted pressure on some fraternal groups to admit nonwhites. Federal pressure, however, has been only moderately effective with those fraternal orders that operate clublike facilities requiring liquor permits. However, some groups that do not have clublike setups, for instance, the Odd Fellows and the Improved Order of Red Men, have voluntarily removed their all-white membership qualifications. On the other hand, Freemasonry, the Shrine, the Order of Eastern Star, the Knights Templar,* the De Molay,* the International Order of Rainbow Girls,* and numerous others have thus far made no official attempts to admit nonwhites to their fraternal membership rosters. Whether these groups will admit nonwhites in the future remains to be seen. In any event, the oldest or most tradition-oriented orders will resist the longest.

There is a touch of irony relative to the racism that exists in many of the mainline fraternal secret societies. Liberally minded elected officials (e.g., Senators George McGovern, Mark Hatfield, Hubert Humphrey, Birch Bayh, Harold Hughes, Stuart Symington, Hugh Scott, and others), who voted for the federal civil-rights laws enacted in the 1960s, continued to hold membership in fraternal orders that barred nonwhites. Either these elected officials did not notice their inconsistency, or they were not bothered by it. (For a more extended discussion on racism in fraternal orders, the reader is asked to see Alvin J. Schmidt and Nicholas Babchuk, "The Un-brotherly Brotherhood: Discrimination in Fraternal Orders," *Phylon* 34 [Fall, 1973], pp. 275–82.)

Political Posture

Almost all American fraternal groups are intent on formally keeping politics out of their meetings and discussions. In fact, they are proud to be nonpolitical. Although the fraternal societies have adopted a nonpolitical posture, one notes, however, that most are quite conservative relative to nonpartisan political issues. Their long-standing opposition to racial integration, refusal to admit women, and other attempts to preserve the status quo indicate that most fraternal secret societies are quite conservative politically. In brief, fraternal secret societies are no harbingers of social change. The one notable exception is the Grange, which has been politically active in a nonpartisan manner, effecting a number of legislative changes during its 113 years of existence.

Ethnocentrism

The concept of ethnocentrism was once defined by William Graham Sumner as a way of viewing "things in which one's own group is the center of everything, and all others are scaled and rated with reference to it." Since Sumner, sociologists have extended the concept to include the process by which groups and individuals are unable to examine their own beliefs, values, and actions.

Even though ethnocentrism is present with all individuals and organizations in varying degrees, it is difficult for a student of fraternal societies not to see the rather high degree of ethnocentrism present in so many fraternal orders, especially in the fraternal secret societies. Ethnocentrism often prevents such associations from seeing, much less understanding, the problems confronting them as organizations. Time and again, fraternal secret societies appear to be blind to the future as they revere the past. For instance, the appeal that attracts new members and retains existing ones is rapidly declining, as evidenced by huge membership decreases in recent years. Yet organization upon organization has not only failed to consider changing its methods and practices but has instead proudly recalled (even in writing) some past event to support its position (e.g., emphasizing that a president of the United States conferred some honor on the order or was a member of its fraternity). Such instances, which are very common, indicate that the myopia of ethnocentrism is firmly entrenched in numerous fraternal secret societies. This condition, unless changed, may contribute to the demise and extinction of once well-known, highly respected fraternal orders.

Nonfraternal Behavior

The word fraternal means brotherhood. Yet fraternal societies, like Christian churches, do not always practice the principles that they espouse. The practice of barring nonwhites from joining the fraternal secret societies is a prime example of the failure of many fraternal orders always to be true to their basic purpose, brotherhood.

Another type of nonfraternalism is the schisms that have occurred in some fraternal organizations. The Ancient Order of Foresters,* a transplanted British society, had several groups splinter off from its structure. The Modern Woodmen of America,* the Knights of the Red Cross of Constantine,* the Odd Fellows in England, the Pythian Sisters, and numerous others were involved in schisms and conflict. Freemasonry in England was rent in two when in 1738 the "Ancients" split with the "Moderns." This schism was eventually resolved in 1813, when a union between the two groups was effected.

Still other illustrations of nonfraternal behavior are the legal suits that fraternal orders have brought against each other. Quite a number of court cases can be found in law libraries showing that white fraternal orders filed legal suits against black orders (often called "Ape Lodges" by some white lodge members because the blacks imitated the white societies), frequently for using the same symbols, emblems, rituals, and names as the white groups. For instance, in 1912 in New York the Benevolent and Protective Order of Elks* (a white group) brought a legal complaint against the Improved Benevolent and Protective Order of Elks of the World* (a black group). In 1915 the Freemasons in the State of Texas (a white order) contended in court with the black Masons. Other cases of white lodges filing suit against black lodges could be cited. Not only did whites sue blacks, but blacks sued blacks, and whites sued whites. The instances are too numerous to mention here.

Oligarchy

Most fraternal groups pride themselves on their representative or democratic form of government. In fact, one component of the "lodge system" is having a representative form of government, as defined in 1912 by the National Convention of Insurance Commissioners. Freemasonry, as an illustration, is proud of the contributions it has made to democracy by encouraging free thought, as opposed to dogma and authoritarianism. It also likes to take credit for having provided some influence in the formation of the American system of government, with its checks and balances.

Democracy (the rule of the people), whether operative in a country or in an organization, differs substantially from oligarchy (the rule of an entrenched few). Specifically, oligarchy exists when organizational leaders repeatedly succeed themselves in one or more executive or committee positions over a number of years.

In one empirical study of fraternal secret societies that focused on sixteen statewide (grand) lodges, it was found that fraternal organizations were oligarchic in spite of their claims to be democratic. The study also revealed that fraternal orders were significantly more oligarchic during their most recent ten years of existence than they were during their first ten years. (For more details on the study, see Alvin J. Schmidt, *Oligarchy in Fraternal Organizations: A Study in Organizational Leadership*, Detroit, 1973.)

The presence of oligarchy in fraternal organizations does not single them out as unique or even as different, but rather indicates that they are quite similar to other voluntary associations that also develop into oligarchic structures in time. This phenomenon is known as confirming Robert Michels' "Iron Law of Oligarchy," as discussed in his book, *Political Parties: A Sociological Study of the Oligarchical Tendencies of Modern Democracy*, 1959. (This book was originally published in 1911 in the German language.)

THE FUNCTION OF FRATERNAL ORGANIZATIONS

Why did such a multiplicity of fraternal societies arise in the United States during the late 1800s and early 1900s? This is a question that the student of fraternal organizations inevitably will ask upon becoming familiar with the American fraternal context.

Social Integration

One reason that fraternal societies became so prolific at the end of the nineteenth century and the beginning of the twentieth century was the role they played in socially integrating millions of immigrants. From 1880 to 1920 droves of people—over 40 million—left their native country to enter a strange land, a new culture, and a different political system. Fraternal orders offered them fellowship in a socially isolated environment. At their places of work the immigrants were forced to learn a new language, but in the fraternal lodges they could interact with their own in their native tongues. Even the formal lodge proceedings and rituals were frequently in the language of the immigrant's "old country." Lodge meetings made the newcomers feel at home. But there was more! As the members participated in their lodge sessions, they slowly learned some of the democratic processes of their newly adopted country by seeing them practiced in their fraternal society's meetings. They soon learned and appreciated the value of free speech and the expression of opinions without fear of reprisal. They also learned how to conduct meetings and the importance of voting. Having learned and internalized these American values, the immigrant became a better-integrated citizen, and much credit belonged to the fraternal societies.

Economic Security

In addition to serving as an instrument of social integration, fraternal societies also provided economic security in an era that was largely laissez-faire, economically. Seventy-five or a hundred years ago there were no governmental social security programs, nor were there labor unions that helped workers obtain fringe-benefit contracts with accident, sickness, and life insurance clauses. Often when a husband died, his wife and children were left destitute. A leading member of a Jewish fraternal group apparently expressed the sentiments of countless others when around 1900 he said: "In no other civilized land in the world is the fight for survival so menaced by the unexpected and the terrible as in the United States, and in no country is there the feeling of so much insecurity, loneliness, and fear of tomorrow." (Cited in Judah J. Shapiro, *The Friendly Society: A History of the Workmen's Circle*, 1975).

Indeed, for many the fraternal benefit society, through the device of the assessment plan, provided at least some economic security. When a member died his burial expenses were covered; in addition, some extra funds were provided to help his widow and children, at least for a while. The amounts that beneficiaries received varied from one fraternal benefit group to another. A common sum paid to the beneficiaries in the latter part of the nineteenth century was $1,000. Some paid more.

The economic security offered by fraternal benefit societies was especially attractive to millions of people because they were able to obtain insurance certificates at relatively low rates. One analyst of fraternal societies, Charles Moreau Harger, said in 1906 that lodge members were able to obtain fraternal insurance "at a cost not one twentieth of that in the management of old-line companies." To be sure, as has already been noted, the low rates were based on shaky actuarial methods. This fact, however, was not accepted by the members, nor was it even very disturbing to the leaders of the fraternal benefit societies.

The economic security that individuals received by belonging to fraternal groups was not limited to fraternal benefit societies. The fraternal secret orders also provided benevolence in the form of charity and mutual aid and by establishing homes for orphans and the aged. These services made the fraternal secret orders attractive to thousands of individuals.

Social Prestige

A couple of decades before and after 1900, when there were no automobiles, radios, television sets, or movie theaters, the fraternal organization often was the only place in which individuals could experience social prestige or feel important. Numerous lodge groups enabled their members to adorn themselves in colorful regalia and then participate in public events. Such participation was especially important in small, rural towns. Fraternal members could impress their fellow townsmen, particularly nonmembers, in that by belonging to certain fraternal orders they were different and distinctive. Moreover, they and their "brothers" knew signs, passwords, and secrets that the "profane" (nonmembers) did not possess. In short, the lodge often gave members a sense of feeling privileged. After all, what transpired among the "brethren" was not known to the general public, not even their family members.

That secret societies once conferred social prestige or status upon their members by virtue of their secret rituals has been noted by social scientists for some time. Georg Simmel and Camilla H. Wedgewood, to name two, theorized in this manner (see "The Sociology of Secrecy and of Secret Societies," *American Journal of Sociology*, 1906, and "The Nature and Functions of Secret Societies," *Oceania*, 1930, respectively). A German sociologist, Max Weber, while visiting the United States in 1904 saw fraternal organizations as "typical vehicles of social ascent into the circle of entrepreneurial middle class." (See his *From Max Weber*, 1966.) Similarly, an American social scientist, Lloyd W. Warner, in studying a midwestern United States small town, referred to the relatively high social status that lodges once enjoyed in the early twentieth century (see his *Democracy in Jonesville*, 1949).

But as American society increasingly became urbanized, the social advantage of belonging to a fraternal order lost much of its appeal in the context of anonymity. When someone is unknown among large numbers of people, who is there to impress? Thus, the present decline in membership of most fraternal societies is caused not only by the lack of organizational change, such as modifying rituals (as discussed earlier), but also by the inability of fraternal orders to provide social prestige for their members as they once did.

Religion and Morality

Especially in the past, fraternal organizations provided for many Americans, a religious function through rituals, prayers, hymns, and moral teachings. One observer, Albert Blumenthal, noted in his book, *Small Town Stuff* (1932), that for some Masons "the ritual is virtually a religious practice. . . . Some of the Masons openly state that Masonry is their substitute for going to church." A Masonic writer, R. V. Denslow, made similar observations, saying that for many new settlers in the past Masonry rather than the church had furnished religious solace (see his *Territorial Masonry*, 1925).

In the sketches of individual fraternal organizations provided in the present volume, the reader will note that numerous fraternal rituals contain prayers, hymns, and moral lessons. An altar with a Bible is usually a required lodge-room furnishing. Well-known fraternal authorities often assert that their respective orders are religious. "Every Masonic lodge is a temple of religion," said Albert Pike, a onetime renowned member of Freemasonry and other fraternal groups. The Eagles, to cite another example, maintain that they teach their members about the "universal Fatherhood of God." And as recently as in the 1960s, the Odd Fellows issued a statement saying: "Free and extensive use of the Holy Scriptures is made in much of the secret work [ritual] of the Order and in the lectures." Moreover, virtually every fraternal society requires prospective candidates to profess belief in a supreme deity. Freemasonry, for instance, asserts that belief in a supreme being is one of its "landmarks" (unchangeable laws). The Elks say— "No person shall be accepted as a member of this Order unless he be . . . a believer in God." Finally, it should be noted that the Scottish Rite Masons* and some other fraternal secret orders refer to their lodge halls as "Temples," indicating the religious character of many fraternal secret societies.

The religious qualities of many fraternal societies are also apparent by their rituals. In fact, one might say that the average lodge ritual is very similar to a church's worship agenda in that it commonly includes prayers, pledges, and hymns.

CONCLUSION

It needs to be said, in concluding this discussion of the fraternal context in America, that fraternal societies have made great contributions to the American society. They have helped people learn and appreciate the American democratic way of life either by introducing countless members to democratic values or by reinforcing such values in the conduct of their organizational meetings and activities. They also provided economic security at a time when millions would have become wards of society or simply suffered extreme poverty. Had the latter been permitted to occur, it would have indeed left blight on American society. But, with the benevolent concern manifested by hundreds of fraternal societies, a dimension of the American character came to the fore that has enabled the United States to prosper and flourish. That quality was American persistence, so evidenced by fraternal orders that seemingly always came to the rescue of thousands of needy individuals. Even after some fraternal benefit societies collapsed because of inadequate actuarial methods, new groups continued to appear. Often a given fraternal group had hardly gone out of existence when many of its deserted members turned right around and organized new societies. Apparently a strong belief existed that fraternalism could and would conquer financial exigencies.

SKETCHES
OF FRATERNAL
ORGANIZATIONS

_A_

AEGIS, ORDER OF. Founded in 1892 in Baltimore, Maryland, by individuals who were members of well-known fraternal orders, including the Knights of Pythias* and the Independent Order of Odd Fellows.* The society was a fraternal benefit society, whose motto was "Fraternity, Protection, Equality, and Security." REFERENCES: _Cyc. Frat._; _DSOS_.

AHVAS ISRAEL. A fraternal benefit society that was founded in the city of New York in 1890. Its founders were members of the Masons,* Odd Fellows,* Independent Order of B'rith Abraham,* and the Sons of Benjamin. REFERENCE: _Cyc. Frat._

AHEPA, THE ORDER OF. The name of the organization is an acrostic derived from: The American Hellenic Educational Progressive Association. World War I and the Turkish invasion of 1922 forced many Greeks to emigrate to the United States. Eight concerned men met in Atlanta, Georgia, in 1922 to help their fellow Greeks learn the English language and become acquainted with the American way of life. Thus the eight men founded the Order of Ahepa in 1922. These eight also comprised the first supreme lodge. Present-day headquarters are in Washington, D.C.

The Ahepa patterned its organization after lodge groups like Masonry, Odd Fellows, and others in that it has a ritual, a vow of secrecy, signs, the blackball method of rejecting undesirable candidates for membership, and regalia. When the order dons its regalia, the members wear white trousers and fezzes that resemble the fezzes commonly worn by Shriners on parade. Its emblem consists of a double circle with eight stars, four on each side. On the inner portion of the circle lie olive branches, a cross set on top of the rising sun, and an eagle with outstretched wings perched on the cross.

At the time of its origin, the Ahepa adopted the following objectives:

a) To advance and promote pure and undefiled Americanism among the Greeks of the United States. . . . b) To educate the Greeks in the matter of democracy, and in the matter of the government of the United States. c) To instill the deepest loyalty to the United States. d) To promote fraternal sociability. e) To practice benevolent aid among this nationality.

From its inception Ahepa forced its foreign-born members to learn the English language, as it conducted its meetings in English. For many members during the 1920s it was a high achievement to have gained fluency in English. At first only Greeks were eligible for membership, but soon (at the order's third meeting or five days after its first meeting) men of non-Greek descent were welcome to join. Most members during the 1920s came from the ranks of business.

Ahepa has attracted some prominent individuals to its membership roster. In 1931 Franklin Delano Roosevelt, then governor of New York, joined the society. A number of years later (in 1946) President Harry Truman became an Ahepean. At least two vice-presidents, Spiro Agnew and Hubert Humphrey, have been members. The organization also has been proud to have some of its supreme lodge officers photographed with Presidents Coolidge, Hoover, Roosevelt, Truman, Eisenhower, Johnson, and Nixon.

Although Ahepa purports to be a nonsectarian and nonpolitical society, it has on occasion spoken out on political issues. In 1955 it formed the Justice for Cyprus Committee, which endorsed the Cypriot struggle for independence. In 1965 it issued still another statement concerning the difficulties in Cyprus.

In terms of lending its resources to altruistic ends, Ahepa has come to the aid of flood and hurricane victims; brought Greek orphans to the United States; acquired a sanatorium in New Mexico; participated in war bond drives during World War II; established a grammar school (St. Basil's Academy) for orphans in Garrison, New York; supported cancer research; established the Ahepa Hospital in Salonika, Greece; built the Ahepan Health Center in Thebes, Greece; and provided hundreds of scholarships.

The Order of Ahepa is quite civic-minded. One of its proud activities is to present statues or busts of famous individuals. In presenting statues, the order sees itself continuing an honorable and ancient tradition of its Greek forebears in fashioning sculptures of famous individuals. In 1928 the Order of Ahepa unveiled the statue of Gen. Demetrius Ypsilanti (a famous Greek general) in Ypsilanti, Michigan. A statue of the "American Doughboy" was placed in Mason City, Iowa, in 1932. A bronze bust of the "War President" (Franklin D. Roosevelt) has been set in Hyde Park, New York. In 1963 the Ahepan Truman Memorial (a twelve-foot statue of Harry Truman) was dedicated in Athens, Greece. The Ahepeans presented this memorial out of gratitude for Truman's rushing aid to Greece and saving the ancient country from communism.

In 1929 the organization held its first Ahepa National Banquet in Washington, D.C., honoring the Congress of the United States. In recent years the banquet has been held every two years. It is at these banquets that the order also bestows the Ahepa Socratic Award. Some of the recipients have been President Lyndon B. Johnson, Senator Everett Dirksen, Henry R. Luce (former publisher of *Time* and *Life*), Vice President Spiro Agnew, and His Holiness Patriarch Athenagoras I. The award consists of a small bust of Socrates, accompanied by a scroll.

Organizationally, the Ahepa operates on three levels: chapter (local), district (state or territory), and supreme lodge (national). All officers on the district and chapter level are under the jurisdiction of the supreme lodge. Chapter charters can be granted only by the supreme lodge. The district organizations originally were called "Superior Lodges," and chapters were known as "Subordinate Lodges." The principal officers of the supreme lodge leadership are the Supreme President, Supreme Vice President, Supreme Secretary, Supreme Counselor, Supreme Treasurer, Executive Treasurer, Executive Secretary, Supreme Athletic Director, Supreme Vice President of Canada, six Supreme Governors, who serve on the Supreme Board, and a Supreme Board of Trustees.

Ahepa is an all-male society. However, it has two auxiliary organizations, the Daughters of Penelope* and The Maids of Athena.* The latter is a junior auxiliary order of the former. A junior order of males, The Sons of Pericles,* is also in existence. The four groups are sometimes referred to as the "Ahepan family."

The current (1978) membership of the Ahepa order is over 25,000. The society has over 400 chapters in the United States and Canada. It also operates in Australia.

Literature sources on the Order of Ahepa are scarce. George J. Leber's *The History of the Order of Ahepa* (1972) gives a detailed account of the order's history from 1922 to 1972. *The Ahepa*, a magazine published by the order since 1929, provides reliable "in-house" accounts of the organization's fraternal history.

AID ASSOCIATION FOR LUTHERANS (AAL). Three Lutheran laymen in Appleton, Wisconsin, in 1899 gave $13 each to begin setting up a fund for family protection. They found several hundred others who also made contributions of $5 per person. These early founders of AAL were motivated not only by the need to have some financial protection for their families, but also by their reluctance to join existing fraternal benefit societies, largely because the latter usually required members to take secret oaths in the initiation rites. As members of the conservative Lutheran Church of Missouri, Ohio, and Other States (now known as The Lutheran Church—Missouri Synod), they were forbidden to join such societies.

The AAL received its charter from the state of Wisconsin on November 24, 1902. Its original name was Aid Association for Lutherans in Wisconsin and Other States. AAL closely patterned its structure on that of the Equitable Fraternal Union of Neenah, Wisconsin. Most of the early business was conducted in German, a practice not discontinued until 1927. It is also interesting to note that the AAL avoided using the words "life insurance" or the German "*Lebensversicherung*." In those days to take out life insurance was not to trust in God, or to be engaged in a form of usury, an act that Luther had condemned.

AAL, like most fraternal societies of the day, operated on the assessment plan, which was actuarially unsound. Being warned by the state in 1905 about the assessment plan's inadequacy, the society began to move to a legal reserve system. By 1911 it had accomplished the changeover.

The society prospered. It developed new insurance plans, and in the mid-1960s it opened its doors to Lutherans of all synods. At one time it had permitted only Lutherans who were in fellowship (i.e., in theological agreement) with Missouri Synod Lutherans to join its ranks. By the mid-1960s the society had branches in every state of the Union. In fact, currently (1979) the association is the largest fraternal benefit society holding membership in the National Fraternal Congress of America.* AAL also stands high when compared to nonfraternal insurance firms. In 1979 it ranked 13th among the 1,800 life insurance firms in the United States.

Philanthropically, the association expended $13 million in 1977 for fraternal and benevolent purposes: scholarships, support for educational institutions, and funds for training church workers. Grants are also given to agencies, boards, and homes for the aged and handicapped and to minorities. Blood-donor clinics, family health activities, and workshops for families are conducted regularly. Recently the society has joined the National Center for Voluntary Action, a nonprofit, nonpartisan institution that is dedicated to expanding and improving voluntarism in the United States.

In recent years AAL has directed considerable attention to what it calls its "three major thrusts of the fraternal operations department." The first thrust is to provide stronger and more effective branch structures. A second major objective is to achieve "more fulfilling benevolences." The third goal is to help establish "healthier Lutheran families." In order to accomplish the third thrust the head office in Appleton, Wisconsin, has formed a family health program that attempts to provide assistance to families through a variety of modern methods and programs. The society has also become quite research conscious in the last years.

The association has no ritual or initiation ceremonies. Members join by taking out an insurance certificate, just as one would in a mutual or stock insurance firm. The state of Wisconsin does not require fraternal benefit societies to have a ritual. Although AAL has no ritual or initiation rites, it does operate on the "lodge system."

Males and females hold equal membership rights and privileges. The association has no auxiliaries or youth department. Total membership in

1978 was about 1,200,000 in 5,019 branches. This represents an increase of 25 percent over the past decade, for in the late 1960s the society had 792,000 members. Every local branch is affiliated with some Lutheran congregation. AAL does not call its local units "lodges" because the word has always had a negative connotation to conservative Lutherans in that it reminds them of oath-bound, ritual-laden groups such as Freemasonry, Odd Fellowship, and other fraternal secret societies.

Organizationally, AAL has two levels of government, national and local. There are no statewide administrative structures. It has no national conventions or a supreme lodgelike assembly. Instead, its board of directors meets four times each year. This group makes the key policy decisions. Headquarters are in Appleton, Wisconsin.

For further information the reader may consult the association's quarterly periodical, *Correspondent*, which provides news about the society. In the summer of 1969 this publication carried a brief article, "Our Pioneers Are Gone, But What A Legacy They Left," on the association's history. The AAL also publishes a bimonthly periodical known as *Yes*.

ALHAMBRA, INTERNATIONAL ORDER OF (IOA). If the Knights of Columbus* are the Catholic answer to Freemasonry, then the Order of Alhambra is the Catholic answer to the Nobles of the Mystic Shrine (Shriners).* This order, which admits only third- and fourth-degree members of the Knights of Columbus, was founded in 1904. It was organized to promote sociability and to preserve Roman Catholic historical sites. The name "Alhambra" comes from the Spanish fortress in Granada, Spain, where the Moors surrendered to Ferdinand and Isabella in 1492, after having occupied Spain for 900 years.

The ritual of the IOA tries to recapture some of the ancient past. For instance, the initiation ceremony, according to William J. Whalen, *Handbook of Secret Organizations* (1966), "depicts the deliverance of Christian Spain from the Moors. Since the ceremony demands elaborate equipment and costumes most neophytes go to a central location where one of the larger Caravans conducts the rite." The regalia worn by the IOA members resembles the garb worn by the Shriners. The order's emblem has the red tower of Castile surmounting the Arabian crescent with the word "Alhambra" beneath these two symbols. "Alhambra (Kelta-al-hamrah, the red castle) was the citadel of Granada and the home of the Moorish king when the city was one of the principal seats of the empire of the Moors in Spain," according to an IOA publication.

The IOA not only wears fezzes and colorful costumes, resembling those of the Shriners, but also engages in city parades as do the Shriners. A typical IOA parade has its members dressed in colorful Moorish garb led by live camels. Frequently some of the parade participants form a musical band.

The degree work for the initiation of a new member revolves about the theme of Spain being delivered from the Moors by Christians. Once each year the Grand Divan is responsible for arranging a religious ceremony, which includes holy Mass. All members of the order are required to participate in this ceremony.

The IOA has never officially been recognized by the Knights of Columbus. Some believe that this lack of recognition has kept the order from growing. Nevertheless, it has attracted archbishops, cardinals, and priests to its membership roster. Its current (1978) membership is 11,000, a drop from the 1960s, when its membership was above 13,000. The members refer to themselves as "Sir Nobles." Only Catholic men over eighteen years of age may join, by being invited by a Sir Noble. The order counts Pope Paul VI as one of its former members.

On the charity front, the IOA has contributed to programs for mentally retarded children. It has also helped underwrite scholarships for teacher training in the work of mental retardation. These efforts have not been confined to the United States but have also been extended to Japan, the West Indies, and Canada. Since 1958, the order has given five million dollars to aid mentally retarded children. Because of its emphasis on charity the order calls itself "a fraternal order of Catholic men dedicated to assisting retarded children."

Structurally, the IOA refers to its national organization as the "Supreme Caravan." The regional structures are called "Grand Caravans," and the local chapters are referred to as "Caravans." The officers on the national level are the "Supreme Divan." This group makes the order's rules and regulations. On the regional level, the officers are part of the "Grand Divan." A local meeting place is called "Alcazar." The national headquarters are in Baltimore, Maryland.

Reading material on the IOA is scarce. The order has some published brochures, but no detailed historical accounts in article or book form. Secondary accounts occasionally appear in newspapers across the country. Its bimonthly periodical is known as *The Alhambran*, a magazine that prints news and a great number of pictures in every issue.

ALLIANCE OF POLES, THE (AOP). Not long after thousands of Poles left their native land to come to the United States in the latter part of the nineteenth century, some of them decided to form a fraternal organization. Thus on September 22, 1895, the Alliance of Poles was born in Ohio. The society began as a fraternal benefit organization. Less than two months after it was founded the order paid its first death benefit of $300 for the death of a female member. In 1914 the society adopted its present name, The Alliance of Poles of America.

The AOP has always tried to keep alive a strong fondness for Poland. This emphasis, however, has never interfered with the members' loyalty to the United States. For instance, when the United States was at war during

World War I and World War II, the society not only sent its sons to combat but also aided the American war effort in other ways.

To become a member of the AOP, either sex is eligible. Each individual applying for membership takes an oath that he or she will obey the order's constitution and bylaws. In terms of age the prospective member must be between fifteen and sixty-five years of age. Other requirements for membership call for "good moral character, physically and mentally healthy, Polish, Lithuanian by birth or consequinity [sic]." Presently (1979) the AOP has 20,000 members in seventy-two local units. This membership total represents an increase from 16,000 in the late 1960s.

The strong accent on keeping the Polish spirit alive manifests itself in the society's newspaper, The Alliancer, or in Polish, Zwiazkowiec. In a recent issue (February 22, 1979) the newspaper tried to boost Polish pride by speaking about the new Catholic Pope being Polish. Another article entitled "Do Something Polish in 1979," among other things, advised its readers about how to cope with Polish jokes. First, the paper said: "Whatever you do, do not tell or politely listen to a single Polish joke." Second, the paper counseled individuals to counterattack Polish jokes by replying: "Why are Polish jokes short? So the morons who tell them can remember them." Another column in the same issue was captioned: ". . . if I were Polish, I'd be proud. In fact, I'd be proud to be Polish." The newspaper always carries some selection in the Polish language.

The AOP has no ritual, but like other fraternal groups it has an insignia, which on its face has an eagle pursuer and St. Michael mounted with a crown. Two inscriptions appear on the emblem: Alliance of Poles of America and the year of the order's organization, 1895.

Local units are known as "Groups," and regional groups are called "Circles." The national structure, referred to as the "Central Body," meets quadrennially. Officers are president, vice president, lady vice president, secretary, treasurer, directors, and so on. Headquarters are in Cleveland, Ohio.

For further information the reader will have to content himself with the society's biweekly paper, The Alliancer, for the most part. The constitution and bylaws provide about the only other source available on the AOP.

ALLIANCE OF TRANSYLVANIAN SAXONS (ATS). This ethnic fraternal group was founded in 1902 in Cleveland, Ohio, by a number of Saxons. When they first met on July 5, 1902, they called their new society the Siebenbuerger Bund. On August 31, 1902, at the group's first convention, the name was changed to Central Verband der Siebenbuerger Sachsen; and in 1965 the name was changed to The Alliance of Transylvanian Saxons. The society, as a fraternal benefit insurance organization, seeks to keep its 800 years of Saxon heritage alive.

From the beginning, the ATS established an "informal dues and death benefit system." The first death benefits were set at $200. By 1908 these benefits were raised to $300, and by 1912 the benefits were raised again, this time to $400. At its twelfth convention, in 1913, the society established three classes of membership. Those joining between eighteen and thirty-five years of age paid $6 per year and were "first class" members. "Second class" members were those who joined between thirty-five and forty-five years of age and paid $9 per year. "Third class" members were between forty-five and fifty years old and paid $15 per year. The practice of three levels of assessment according to age was quite common in a number of fraternal benefit societies in the early 1900s. Known as the graded assessment plan, this method differed from the flat assessment plan, which assessed every individual the same amount.

By 1923-24 the former methods of assessment were eliminated, and the society adopted the sound actuarial methods that were being urged by new insurance codes and laws. Today the ATS is a highly solvent fraternal benefit group operating on the legal reserve system.

The ATS has no formal ritual pledge or initiation ceremony. Individual branches commonly have their own brief and simple installation procedures whereby the new members promise to uphold the constitution of the local branch and the national organization.

Membership requirements call for applicants to be "of Transylvanian Saxon birth or descendant thereof, or married to a Saxon or descendant thereof, or of German birth or a descendant thereof." Only those between sixteen and sixty years of age may join, if they are healthy enough to pass the insurance requirements. Every applicant is also to have a sound mind and exemplary habits and to be of high moral caliber. In 1922 the ATS established a juvenile department that enabled youth to be insured. The membership count in 1976 stood at 8,629, compared to 9,871 in 1967. Thus the ATS endured a loss of about 12 percent over a period of ten years.

Work of philanthropy in the ATS is largely done through its National Committee. This committee has donated funds to the American Museum of Immigration in New York City. It contributed financial aid of $22,000 in 1970 and 1971 to Romania for flood losses. Previously, the society had helped repatriate Saxon prisoners of war by bringing them out of Siberia back to Saxony in 1918. In 1920 the order sent $33,000 to help the Saxon National School in Hermannstadt, Germany, primarily a school for orphans. The society has a regular orphan fund.

At home the ATS has sponsored various youth programs. In 1927 it organized the Saxon Basketball League. In 1931 the Transylvanian Saxon Juniors Association was formed. This group conducts a number of sports programs: track and field, swimming meets, golf, softball, and bowling tournaments. In 1925 the society began Saturday German-study classes for its youth.

The highest authority in the ATS is the national convention, which meets annually. There are regional or statewide structures. Local groups are called "Branches," of which there were forty-three in 1978. The national headquarters are in Cleveland, Ohio.

For further information on the society see the *Saxon Year Book, 1902-1977*, published in 1977 in commemoration of its 75th anniversary. Every Monday the *Saxon News* (*Volksblatt*) is published, the official newspaper of the society. The paper prints news of the ATS as well as news of the day, including national and international news.

ALLIED MASONIC DEGREES OF THE UNITED STATES, THE GRAND COUNCIL OF (AMDGC). In Salisbury, North Carolina, representatives of three councils met on April 16, 1932, to organize the Grand Council of Allied Masonic Degrees of the United Staes of America. This grand council was created to control the allied degrees of Masonically related groups.

The order works fourteen degrees: Royal Ark Mariner, Secret Monitor, Knight of Constantinople, Saint Lawrence of the Martyr, Architect, Grand Superintendent, Grand Tyler of Solomon, Superintendent, Master of Tyre, Excellent Master, Installed Sovereign Master, Installed Commander Noah, Red Branch of Eri, and Ye Ancient Order of Corks.

Membership is attained only by invitation, and only Royal Arch Masons (seventh-degree holders in the York Rite*) are eligible to join. The writer was unable to acquire current membership statistics.

Subordinate units are named "Councils." The governing body, known as the "Grand Council," meets in convention annually. Headquarters are located in Charlotte, North Carolina.

Additional information may be acquired by consulting the council's annual proceedings, *Annuals and Miscellanea*. The Masonic Service Association's "Allied Masonic Groups and Rites" (mimeographed, 1978) also provides some background on the AMDGC.

AMARANTH, THE ORDER OF (TOA). When this order was first organized in June of 1873 in New York, New York, it was intended to be a higher degree in the Order of the Eastern Star.* The Amaranth degree was to be the third degree, and the Eastern Star and the Queen of the South were to be the first and second degrees, respectively. This plan was developed by James B. Taylor. However, the plan did not meet with the approval of the Order of the Eastern Star (OES). After the OES rejected Taylor's proposal, the Order of Amaranth became an independent order in 1895 in Brooklyn, New York.

The order's name was derived from the Swedish organization, Order of Amaranta, which was formed by Sweden's Queen Christina in 1653. The Swedish order was a strictly social group for the queen's friends. Its membership consisted of fifteen knights, fifteen ladies, and the queen. It had no Masonic features. The TOA has no historical ties to the Swedish group, even though some have made this claim.

Membership in the TOA is drawn exclusively from Masons and their relatives. Many also come from the Order of the Eastern Star. One Masonic publication once said that TOA membership had "the cream of the Order of the Eastern Star and the Masonic Fraternity. . . ." Since the order's members only come from Freemasonry and the OES, the order does not initiate nonwhite candidates. Its members can come only from the wives, mothers, daughters, legally adopted daughters, widows, sisters, half sisters, and granddaughters of Master Masons. All are required to believe in the existence of a supreme being. In 1975 the TOA had over 83,000 members.

The TOA, in the tradition of Masonically related groups, has a secret ritual, which was first prepared by James B. Taylor and later revised by Robert Macoy, an influential Masonic figure. In the preface to the ritual, its purposes are stated: "The ceremonies are intended to impress upon us our duty to God; to our country; to one another, and to be a means of doing good. . . ." The one-degree ritual of the TOA has a number of religious qualities. In the initiation ceremony the candidate is asked: "Do you believe in the existence of a Supreme Being?" Another portion of the initiation rite requires the candidate to wash her hands in a font of pure water while the Conductress (one of the ritual officials) reads: "Who shall ascend the hill of the Lord? And who shall stand in his holy place? He who has clean hands and a pure heart. . . ." (Psalm 24:3-4). After taking the "Obligation," vowing to keep the ritual secret, the candidate is requested to seal the bond of the order by eating, from an altar, the bread and salt of friendship. At the initiation at least one Master Mason must be present.

Through the years the order has undergone very little organizational change. Soon after the TOA was founded, attempts were made to introduce a mutual assessment beneficiary plan for its members. This was discontinued almost as soon as it was implemented. Today the order is only a fraternal society.

Structurally, the TOA has its "Supreme Council" on the national level. The regional organizations are referred to as "Grand Courts." Locally the groups are known as "Subordinate Courts." The supreme council meets in convention annually. Headquarters are located in Westfield, New Jersey.

For additional reading the reader may consult John R. Pettis, *What Is the Order of Amaranth?* The annual proceedings volumes also are a good, informative source to consult.

AMERICAN BENEFIT SOCIETY. A fraternal benefit society that was incorporated in 1893, the American Benefit Society enrolled men and women between fifteen and forty-five years of age, provided they were white, believed in a supreme being and were able to earn a livelihood. The society once had over 6,000 members, attracting lawyers, physicians, bankers, editors, and other high-status individuals. However, by the early 1920s the order had less than 1,500 members, and by 1931 the society disbanded. Its headquarters were located in Boston, Massachusetts. REFERENCES: *Cyc. Frat.*; *DSOS*.

AMERICAN BROTHERHOOD. Founded in 1844 in the city of New York, the brotherhood was a fraternal secret society with ritual and other fraternal practices. The society's name later was changed to Order of United Americans. REFERENCE: *DSOS*.

AMERICAN BROTHERHOOD, U.S.A. This group came into being in 1915 as a fraternal benefit society with a strong interest in furthering patriotism by enlightening its members relative to the American Constitution and the country's institutions. Only American citizens were permitted to join. The order's ritual conferred three degrees: Unity, Service, and Attainment. Members were given grips and passwords. Chicago was the site of its headquarters. REFERENCE: *DSOS*.

AMERICAN FRATERNAL CONGRESS (AFC). Founded in Omaha, Nebraska, in 1898, this association of fraternal benefit organizations was formed by eighteen societies to help attain actuarial stability. Although the purposes of the AFC were quite similar to those of the National Fraternal Congress,* the AFC came into being because a number of fraternal beneficiary groups differed with the National Fraternal Congress, especially with regard to the reserve system.

In order for fraternal benefit groups to qualify for membership in the AFC they had to adopt the reserve system. At the time the AFC was organized the reserve system was not yet an obligatory criterion for membership in the National Fraternal Congress, even though some of the leaders in that association pointed to the necessity of adopting a reserve system.

The organization is no longer in existence.

AMERICAN FRATERNAL UNION (AFU). This group, organized in 1898 as the South Slavonic Catholic Union, is primarily involved in selling fraternal insurance designed for family protection. In 1941 the society assumed the name of American Fraternal Union. The AFU provides orphan benefits, old-age assistance, disaster relief, and dread-disease benefits. Socially the AFU sponsors baseball teams, bowling and golf tournaments, and other sports. Along the line of charity, the society contributes to the abolition and abatement of disease, hunger, and illiteracy in the United States. Contributions also are made to civic projects and to the sick, disabled, and needy.

The AFU has a simple ritual and initiates its new members. Membership, because the organization is largely a life insurance entity, is open to members from birth to seventy years of age. In 1979 there were 24,000 members on the AFU roster, as compared to 28,000 in 1968.

Every four years a national convention is held. Local chapters are called "Lodges." Headquarters are located in Ely, Minnesota.

Information on the AFU is sparse. It has no published history. Its newspaper, *New Era*, is published biweekly by the national office. The paper provides about the only source of information on the AFU. See also the society's *Constitution and Bylaws* (1972).

AMERICAN HOME WATCHMEN (AHW). The founder of this fraternal benefit society was a Presbyterian clergyman, Moore Sanborn. The order was incorporated in Pennsylvania in 1909. The AHW sought to improve its members socially, morally, and intellectually; to offer relief and aid to sick and distressed members; to help provide homes for aged and invalid members and their orphans and helpless beneficiaries; and to aid its members in maintaining and defending the dignity and honor of the home and womanhood.

To join the AHW it was necessary to believe in a supreme being and to be white and at least sixteen years of age. Creed, politics, or ethnicity were unimportant in attaining membership. Its membership never grew very large. The members all resided in Pennsylvania.

The ritual of the AHW accented the "Triple H." These were "Honor, Hope, and Help." Two degrees conferred were the Watchmen and Scout degrees. The ritual, as in most fraternal groups, was secret.

Local units were called "Forts." The highest authority structure was known as the "Supreme Fort." Pittsburgh served as the society's headquarters.

For further information, see back issues of the AHW's periodical, *The Scout*. Also see Arthur Preuss, *A Dictionary of Secret and Other Societies* (1924). The present discussion used the latter source quite extensively.

AMERICAN HUNGARIAN CATHOLIC SOCIETY (AHCS). This organization, a fraternal benefit society, was founded in 1894 to provide fraternal insurance protection for Hungarian Catholics, most of them immigrants. The society is dwindling in membership. In 1965 it had 2,430 members, whereas in 1977 it had only about 1,200 members.

The group provides the usual types of fraternal activities practiced by fraternal benefit societies: assists aged members, visits the sick and bereaved, and provides service to local parishes. A weekly publication used to be issued, but the author has not been able to determine whether the publication still is being printed. In fact, all attempts to contact the organization bore no results. The society headquarters are located in Cleveland, Ohio.

AMERICAN INSURANCE UNION. Founded in Columbus, Ohio, in 1884, by disgruntled members of the Fraternal Mystic Circle.* The Knights of Pythias,* Odd Fellows,* Masons,* and the National Union also helped form the new organization. Membership was confined to men and women between the ages of fifteen and forty-nine years, who lived in the more "healthful" sections of the United States. The society paid the usual fraternal benefits to its members. The ritual was secret, and its motto was "All for one and one for all." Its membership grew quite rapidly, and by 1922 the roster contained 110,370 members. Home offices were located in Columbus, Ohio. In 1931 the society reincorporated as American Insurance Union, Inc. REFERENCES: *Cyc. Frat.*; *DSOS*.

AMERICAN KNIGHTS OF PROTECTION (AKP). This fraternal beneficiary group, which had a strong patriotic bent, was founded in 1894 in Baltimore, Maryland. Some of its organizers held membership in other fraternal societies: Knights of Pythias,* Knights of the Golden Chain,* Junior Order of United American Mechanics,* and others. The society sought to protect the public school system, provide benevolence for its members, and strengthen American patriotism. Unlike many groups, beneficiary membership was optional. Even more unusual, the AKP admitted both black and white races. The ritual was reputed to be *sui generis*. The emblem of the order was an eagle standing on a pedestal, symbolizing protection, patriotism, and prosperity. Headquarters were housed in Baltimore, Maryland. REFERENCES: *Cyc. Frat.*; *DSOS*.

AMERICAN KRUSADERS. Founded in 1923, this order was started by members of the Ku Klux Klan. The society was incorporated in the state of Arkansas. Membership requirements called for applicants to be "male white persons of good health and morals." REFERENCE: *DSOS*.

AMERICAN LEGION OF HONOR. During the prime years (1870-1910) of fraternal benefit societies, this society was reportedly one of the best known among the larger fraternal assessment organizations. It was formed in 1878 in Boston, Massachusetts, by Darius Wilson, who once belonged to the Ancient Order of United Workmen.* Wilson, a physician, also founded the Royal Arcanum* and the Knights of Honor.* Only white men and women between eighteen and fifty years of age were enrolled as members. Initially, the upper age limit was sixty-four. Local groups were known as

"Subordinate Councils," and regional structures were called "Grand Councils." The national body was referred to as the "Supreme Council." The society went into receivership in 1904. REFERENCES: *Cyc. Frat.*; *DSOS*.

AMERICAN ORDER OF CLANSMEN. See Clansmen, American Order of.

AMERICAN ORDER OF DRUIDS. See Druids, American Order of.

AMERICAN ORDER OF UNITED CATHOLICS (AOUC). In January of 1896 this group came into being to resist the American Protective Association, known as the "A.P.A. Movement." It was founded by Catholics in the city of New York. The society sought to overcome and fight the discrimination against Roman Catholics that was prominent for a number of decades from the 1840s on. The AOUC was a secret society but did not require its members to be "oath bound," as that was prohibited by the Roman Catholic Church as the result of the opposition of the Catholic Church to Freemasonry,* Odd Fellows,* and the like.

AMERICAN POSTAL WORKERS ACCIDENT BENEFIT ASSOCIATION (APWABA). This group first was organized by five men, who named the society the National Association of Railway Postal Clerks, in 1898 in Portsmouth, New Hampshire. The new association had several objectives, namely, to operate as a fraternal benefit society,

to promote closer social relationships among Railway Postal Clerks; to better enable them to perfect any movement that may be for their benefit as a class or for the benefit of the Railway Mail Service; to provide relief for its members and their beneficiaries and make provision for the payment of benefits to them, in case of death, sickness, temporary or permanent physical disability, either as a result of disease, accident or old age.

In 1904 the name of the society was changed to Railway Mail Association. After the national convention in Omaha, Nebraska, in November, 1949, the society again changed its name. This time the change read: National Postal Transport Association. Twelve years later (1961), the name was changed again, now to United Federation of Postal Clerks Benefit Association. In 1972 still another change was made in the society's name, to American Postal Workers Accident Benefit Association, its present name. The society is a member of the National Fraternal Congress of America.

Membership is open to all members of the American Postal Workers Union, AFL-CIO, who are employed as postal workers. No medical examination is required to become a certificate holder in the society. In 1979 the society had 23,000 members in 604 local units, called "Branches."

In terms of programs and projects, the APWABA sponsors blood banks, conducts drives for community funds, assists its members when stricken by disasters that are "acts of God," supports various medical research funds, and visits and contributes to the sick and disabled members. Youth projects are supported, especially the Boy Scouts.

The society has a brief ritual, which is exercised at the initiation of new members and when elected officers are installed. The vow taken by the new member calls for upholding the laws of the society and the American Constitution. It also asks the candidate "to be considerate to the widow and the orphan; the weak and the defenseless; to defend freedom of thought and expression; and to promote the spirit of fraternity." Another request of the candidate is to have him become acquainted with the history and objects of the association and to defend its principles. The ritual, unlike most rituals employed by fraternal societies, has no religious elements in its entire format. It should be noted, however, that the regular order of business has provision for an invocation on its agenda.

The emblem of the APWABA is a shield depicting the red and white stripes of the American flag. The upper fourth portion has the inscription AMERICAN POSTAL. Just below this wording is a semicircular band bearing the words WORKERS ACCIDENT, and below this band is a mail bag, lying on its side, portraying the letters ABA. Under the mail bag symbol is a horizontal bar carrying the inscription BENEFIT ASSOCIATION. The colors of the emblem are red, white, and blue.

Local units, as already noted, are referred to as "Branches." All branches are required by the constitution to meet at least once per month. Branch meetings are held concurrently with the meetings of the American Postal Workers Union, AFL-CIO. The highest authority is called the national convention. It meets biennially. Head offices are in Portsmouth, New Hampshire.

The interested researcher is confined to brochures, the constitution, and other miscellaneous information such as the *National American Postal Workers Union* magazine. This publication includes the society's financial reports. The ritual is appended to the society's constitution. The organization does not publish a periodical.

AMERICAN PROTECTIVE ASSOCIATION (APA). Clinton, Iowa, was the birthplace of this fraternal group that primarily directed its energies toward "patriotism." Founded in 1887, the APA very much resembled the Know-Nothing Party, except that it admitted any American citizen as a member, whereas the Know-Nothing Party only admitted native-born Americans. The APA reportedly had over 2,000,000 members by 1900. One reason the society attained such a large membership was that it absorbed "thousands of members of older patriotic orders," according to Albert C. Stevens, *Cyclopedia of Fraternities* (1907).

The society opposed Roman Catholicism. It also favored segregating "the subjects of the Pope" in nearly all larger cities. Being so strongly "patriotic," the society played a prominent role in American politics, especially during the first seven years of its existence. Its political clout began to wane after 1894. By World War I the society seems to have become inactive.

The ritual of the APA, of course, was considered highly secret. The secret nature of the ritual, however, was greatly diminished when it was published in the *Congressional Record* (October 31, 1893). REFERENCES: *Cyc. Frat.*; *DSOS*.

AMERICAN PROTESTANT ASSOCIATION (APA). The exact date of this fraternal, patriotic group's origin is not known. However, it was founded in Pittsburgh, Pennsylvania. Some of the society's literature placed the order's founding date to be December 19, 1849. Other reports set the date as early as 1844. The APA was strongly anti-Roman Catholic. Albert C. Stevens in his *Cyclopedia of Fraternities* (1907) says this order was "The oldest American, exclusively anti-Roman Catholic secret society, a prototype of the original 'A.P.A.' or American Protective Association."*

The society endured a number of schisms. One of the primary reasons for the first schism was the leadership's decision to reduce the society's five degrees to three. The first secession resulted in the formation of the Order of American Freemen in 1884.

Although it was a secret society with ritual and degrees, its emphasis was less fraternal than "patriotic." Its membership, at its high point, stood at 200,000. With the turn of the century, the society began to decline, although Arthur Preuss, *A Dictionary of Secret and Other Societies* (1924), said the society still existed in the early 1920s. As far as can be determined, the society no longer exists. REFERENCE: *Cyc. Frat.*

AMERICAN SLOVENIAN CATHOLIC UNION (KSKJ). Organized in 1894, this fraternal benefit society has always served Slovaks adhering to the Catholic religion. As a Catholic fraternal benefit group, the society maintains close relationships with the Catholic Church on the local and national level.

Relative to fraternal and social activities, the KSKJ sponsors award and recognition dinners, annual regional and state outdoor activities, athletic contests for children, picnics, and Christmas parties. These events are usually conducted by the local lodges. Charities of various kinds are supported by the local units, as well as by the national organization. The society also awards scholarships for college and for vocational education.

Membership presently stands at 42,000 in 130 lodges in nineteen states. All Catholic Slovaks are eligible for membership. Both males and females may join. The headquarters of the society are located in Joliet, Illinois.

For further information, see the society's history and archives in the University of Minnesota library, Minneapolis, Minnesota. The KSKJ publishes no magazine for its members.

AMERICAN STARS OF EQUITY. This fraternal beneficiary society was formed in 1903 in Illinois. The society admitted men and women to its membership roster. It furnished accident, partial disability, and total disability insurance benefits. The membership count in 1905 numbered 1,295 benefit members. Apparently the organization disbanded between 1910 and 1915. Headquarters were situated in Freeport, Illinois.

AMERICAN UNION, ORDER OF THE. Organized in the city of New York in 1873 by members of the Order of the American Shield, this society, like many other "patriotic" groups, sought to preserve the American Constitution and oppose "the Roman hierarchy." The society had no beneficiary features. Its activities were "very secret." The order began to decline rather quickly after an expose of it was published in 1878 or 1879. However, it reorganized itself in 1881 and boasted 1,500,000 members in 1890. Eventually the society was absorbed by the American Protective Association.* REFERENCE: *Cyc. Frat.*

AMERICAN WOODMEN, THE SUPREME CAMP OF THE (AWSC). Incorporated in the state of Colorado on April 4, 1901, this organization was formed by white men. In August, 1910, the society was taken over by black men. Cassius M. White and Granville W. Norman, both of Austin, Texas, were the key black men in the organizational transition. Soon after the organization's new management in 1910, it prospered and grew. By the 1950s the society had some 50,000 members.

In 1966 the delegates of the Supreme Camp of the American Woodmen voted to accept the recommendation of a consulting firm to form the American Woodmen Life Insurance Company, a stock life insurance company. This vote meant giving away $10,000,000 in assets and additional millions in revenue that would have been realized as income. A couple of years later the AWSC lost control of the American Woodmen Life Insurance Company when it merged with the Crusaders Life Insurance Company. Between 1972 and 1974 the AWSC was trying to overcome law suits that tried to wrest additional assets from its domain. On May 19, 1978, however, the AWSC and the American Woodmen Life Insurance Company signed an agreement to work in fraternal harmony.

Although the American Woodmen Life Insurance Company has changed some of the AWSC's functions as a fraternal benefit society, the AWSC is still permitted to write insurance certificates in California, Texas, and Colorado. In twenty-one other states the AWSC no longer issues insurance certificates. Fraternal members from the sixteen states (Alabama, Arkansas, Delaware, District of Columbia, Kentucky, Louisiana, Maryland, Michigan, Missouri, New Jersey, North Carolina, Ohio, Oklahoma, Pennsylvania, South Carolina, and Tennessee), however, participate in the activities of the Supreme Camp.

Membership of the AWSC is composed entirely of black citizens. In typical Woodmen fashion, like the white organizations (e.g., Modern Woodmen of America* and Woodmen of the World Life Insurance Society*), the AWSC employs some of the same terminology. Members are called "Neighbors," a local unit is a "Campus," and most officers bear the same titles as in the older Woodmen societies.

The AWSC has a ritual that also conforms quite closely to the other Woodmen societies. Although the ritual is intended to be kept secret, the AWSC takes the secrecy somewhat less seriously than many other fraternal groups. The emblem of the organization consists of two rings. The smaller or inner circle displays the words "Brotherhood of Man, 1901," over a view of the rising sun. Below the rising sun stands the inscription, "Protection of the Home." Between the inner and outer circles is the name of the society: Supreme Camp of the American Woodmen.

Administratively, the AWSC has its local units, called "Subordinate Camps." On the national level, the society refers to its structure as the "Supreme Camp." This entity meets in convention quadrennially. In the time interval between conventions a board of directors expedites given business matters. Headquarters of the AWSC are in Denver, Colorado.

Sources on the AWSC are meager. The society's official periodical, *The American Woodmen Informer*, has not been published since 1970. A brief history of the society is available in mimeographed form. The interested reader may also consult the *Constitution and Laws* for additional background.

AMERICAN WORKMEN. This fraternal benefit society was incorporated in 1908 in Washington, D.C. The society paid benefits to men and women, covering death, old-age, sickness, and accident benefits. Its members lived in the southeastern states. The order worked six degrees. *The American Workmen* was the official periodical of the organization. REFERENCE: *Cyc. Frat.*

ANCIENT AND ACCEPTED SCOTTISH RITE OF FREEMASONRY FOR THE NORTHERN MASONIC JURISDICTION OF THE UNITED STATES OF AMERICA (SRNJ). The Northern Jurisdiction of the Scottish Rite was founded August 5, 1813, in New York City. The founder was a Sovereign Grand Inspector General of the Southern Jurisdiction. Unlike the Supreme Council of the Southern Jurisdiction, the Supreme Council of the SRNJ limits its membership to sixty-six active thirty-third-degree Masons. The purpose of the SRNJ is to oversee and regulate the conferring of the twenty-nine degrees that come under its domain.

The charitable activities of the SRNJ since 1934 have largely been directed toward research on schizophrenia. To date (1978) more than $6,000,000 has been donated toward this project. The Leon M. Abbott Scholarship Fund, in operation since 1952, grants scholarships to a number of state universities. Some aid is also given to homes operated by the grand lodges of Blue Lodge Masonry. On April 20, 1975, the SRNJ opened its Museum of Our National Heritage in Lexington, Massachusetts. The building houses within its 82,000 square feet a library, a museum, and an auditorium.

Administratively, the SRNJ calls its statewide jurisdictions "Councils of Deliberation." These meet annually in convention, as does the Supreme Council. The head of the Supreme Council is the Sovereign Grand Inspector General. The headquarters for the SRNJ is Boston, Massachusetts.

For further discussion and information on the Scottish Rite the reader is asked to see Freemasonry* and the Ancient and Accepted Scottish Rite of Freemasonry for the Southern Jurisdiction of the United States of America, The Supreme Council 33°, Mother Supreme Council of the World,* as both are discussed in the present volume. Other helpful sources are: Henry Ridgely Evans, "The Ancient and Accepted Scottish Rite of Freemasonry," *Little Masonic Library*, Book III (1946); S. H. Baynard, *History of the Supreme Council, 33 Degree, Ancient and Accepted Scottish Rite of Freemasonry* (1938); Albert Pike, *Morals and Dogma* (1881). The SRNJ publishes its own periodical, *The Northern Light*.

ANCIENT AND ACCEPTED SCOTTISH RITE OF FREEMASONRY FOR THE SOUTHERN JURISDICTION OF THE UNITED STATES OF AMERICA, THE SUPREME COUNCIL 33°, MOTHER SUPREME COUNCIL OF THE WORLD (SCSJ). The Masonic *Grand Constitutions of 1786*, which are disputed relative to origin and authenticity, were nevertheless used as the basis for founding the first Supreme Council on May 31, 1801, in Charleston, South Carolina. The following year, on December 4, 1802, the council issued a manifesto announcing its establishment. The name in the manifesto appeared as "Supreme Council of the 33rd Degree for the United States of America." The word "Scottish" was not part of the group's name even though the French word *Ecossais* appeared in some of the twenty-nine degrees of the Mother Supreme Council. The word Scottish in the United States came to be commonly used with the renowned Freemason Albert Pike, who in 1859 became Grand Commander of the Southern Jurisdiction.

The fact that the word "Scottish" appears in the Scottish Rite does not mean that the rite originated in Scotland. Rather, the name was chosen in honor of Scottish Masons who fled to France after the Jacobite Rebellion failed in 1715. Thus Scottish Rite Masonry really has its roots in France. It should be noted, however, that this position, although widely accepted, also has some points of uncertainty.

The Southern Jurisdiction has made a number of scholarship contributions to individual colleges and universities. It sponsors two hospitals for crippled children, one in Decatur, Georgia, and one in Dallas, Texas. In 1958 the California Scottish Rite Foundation established a program to train children with severe language difficulties. This program operates at Stanford University's School of Medicine. A related program is in operation in Denver, Colorado.

The Supreme Council of the Southern Jurisdiction has under its authority and supervision the administration and conferring of twenty-nine degrees. (The reader is asked to see a brief account of each degree under the discussion of Freemasonry in the present volume.) The Council "elects its own members and is self-perpetuating. It charters subordinate bodies in cities and States [sic], which are called Valleys and Orients respectively." The chief officer of the Council is called the Sovereign Grand Inspector General. The Supreme Council consists of thirty-third-degree Masons only. From the Council, forty-five men are selected for "active" status to function as a board of directors. On the state level there is the Council of Deliberation. Both the Supreme Council and the Council of Deliberation meet separately in annual conventions. Headquarters for the Supreme Council of the Southern Jurisdiction is Washington, D.C.

For additional information on the Supreme Council of the Southern Jurisdiction the reader may see a variety of booklets and brochures published by the order. For a scholarly account of the entire Scottish Rite see Henry Ridgely Evans, "The Ancient and Accepted Scottish Rite of Freemasonry," *Little Masonic Library*, Book III (1946). Another good reference is S. H. Baynard, *History of the Supreme Council, 33rd Degree, Ancient and Accepted Scottish Rite of Freemasonry* (1938). Finally, Albert Pike's *Morals and Dogma* (1881) is an excellent source on the Scottish Rite. Pike is often credited for having established the rite in the United States on a solid basis. The SCSJ also published a monthly periodical, *The New Age*.

ANCIENT AND ILLUSTRIOUS ORDER KNIGHTS OF MALTA. See Knights of Malta, Ancient and Illustrious Order.

ANCIENT AND ILLUSTRIOUS STAR OF BETHLEHEM. See Star of Bethlehem, Ancient and Illustrious.

ANCIENT ARABIC ORDER OF THE NOBLES OF THE MYSTIC SHRINE. See Shrine, Ancient Arabic Order of the Nobles of the Mystic.

ANCIENT EGYPTIAN ARABIC ORDER OF NOBLES OF THE SHRINE.
See Shrine, Egyptian Arabic Order of Nobles of the.

ANCIENT MYSTIC ORDER OF SAMARITANS. See Samaritans, Ancient
Mystic Order of.

ANCIENT OAKS, ORDER OF. When the local nest of the Order of Owls
in Grand Rapids, Michigan, ceased to exist, the members of that lodge
formed the Ancient Order of Oaks in 1912. The secession of the Owls in
Grand Rapids was voluntarily decided in protest of the unethical way that
John W. Talbot and his associates managed the affairs of the national Owls.
REFERENCE: *Cyc. Frat.*

ANCIENT ORDER OF FORESTERS. See Foresters, Ancient Order of.

ANCIENT ORDER OF FREESMITHS. See Freesmiths, Ancient Order of.

ANCIENT ORDER OF HIBERNIANS IN AMERICA. See Hibernians,
Ancient Order of.

ANCIENT ORDER OF KNIGHTS OF THE MYSTIC CHAIN. See Knights
of the Mystic Chain, Ancient Order of.

ANCIENT ORDER OF PYRAMIDS. See Pyramids, Ancient Order of.

ANCIENT ORDER OF SANHEDRIMS. See Sanhedrims, Ancient Order of.

ANCIENT ORDER OF UNITED WORKMEN. See Workmen, Ancient
Order of United.

ANONA, DEGREE OF (DOA). This organization is the junior group of
the Degree of Pocahontas,* the ladies auxiliary of the Improved Order of
Red Men.* The DOA was founded in 1952.

Some of the reservations (state groups) of the Red Men readily responded
to the idea of encouraging the formation of the Degree of Anona. Other
reservations appeared to be indifferent to the new junior ladies order.

Presently the DOA is best represented in the New England states. In all,
the society has ninety local units, called "Councils." The current (1979)
membership stands at less than 5,000.

Additional information may be acquired by consulting the *Record*, a
proceedings publication of the Improved Order of Red Men. The Red Men
society also issues publicity brochures and pamphlets.

ANTI-POKE-NOSES, ORDER OF. Founded in Searcy County, Arkansas, in 1923, this society's goal was to oppose the Ku Klux Klan. In the order's preamble to the constitution, there was the statement saying that the members were "opposed to any organization that attends to everyone's business but their own." The society functioned as a fraternal secret organization. REFERENCE: *Cyc. Frat.*

ANTLERS, THE. Since a number of fraternal groups had junior orders, it seemed proper for the Benevolent and Protective Order of Elks* (BPOE) to have one too. Thus in February of 1922 the San Francisco Lodge No. 3 organized a junior order for young males. The society was named The Antlers. In 1927 the national organization (Grand Lodge) officially approved the junior order. The grand lodge session also approved the drafting of a ritual for the new organization. The 1927 grand lodge also stated: "The Grand Exalted Ruler shall have power to grant permits to subordinate lodges to institute organizations of young men under 21 years of age in the manner prescribed by statute."

The junior society grew. By 1933 it had 3,594 members in forty-five local units. During World War II, however, the order all but disbanded as so many young men joined the armed services. After the war the order had difficulty reestablishing itself, even though there were eighty-three local lodges in 1946. That same year (1946) the adult grand lodge session repealed all references to The Antlers in the BPOE *Constitution and Statutes.* Today only a handful of lodges reportedly can be found, according to one Elk official.

For additional information, see "The Antlers" in James R. Nicholson and Lee A. Donaldson, *History of the Order of Elks*, 1969.

ARCTIC BROTHERHOOD. Very little is known about this organization, which was founded as a secret society in 1899 on board the streamliner Seattle. Apparently gold prospectors formed the fraternity on their way to Alaska. President Warren Harding joined the order on his visit to Alaska in July of 1923. The ritual of the society reportedly required kindness to horses and dogs. The author has not been able to determine whether the order still exists. Most likely, however, the society is now extinct. REFERENCE: *Cyc. Frat.*

ARTISANS ORDER OF MUTUAL PROTECTION (AOMP). While Dr. James M. Bunn was involved in helping establish the Ancient Order of United Workmen,* he also was deeply involved in organizing the Artisans Order of Mutual Protection. In the summer of 1867 the physician and a few like-minded individuals met in Erie, Pennsylvania, to discuss the formation of a new fraternal society, one that would have improvements over existing societies in terms of benevolencies. In 1872 the founding group met again, this time in St. Louis, where Bunn appeared with a ritual. In order to safe-guard the ritual's secrets, he administered the obligation (vow) to the other men at the meeting. The following year (1873), at another meeting in Washington, D.C., Bunn was authorized to institute assemblies of the order, Artisans Order of Mutual Protection. Bunn was made leader and given the illustrious title of Most Excellent Master Artisan.

The AOMP strongly resembled Freemasonry,* especially in its ritual. Originally, a member had to obtain three degrees, just as in Masonry. These degrees were Endentured Apprentice, Fellow Workman, and Perfect Artisan. Early in the order's existence some, most of whom were Masons, were unhappy with the ritual, primarily because it was too Masonic and also because it was too lengthy. This sentiment led to the ritual being short-ened. The shortened version is essentially what the AOMP employed in the 1970s.

The order flourished, and by 1930 it had more than 30,000 members. The economic depression of the 1930s, which took its heavy toll of most fraternal groups, hardly affected the AOMP. In fact, in 1933 a junior department was created; its membership consisted of young males from thirty days to eighteen years old. The junior department was almost exclusively insurance-oriented. During the 1950s the combined senior and junior membership reached a high of 36,000. The membership had dropped to 32,000 by 1967, however. Today (1978) the society has less than 26,000 members, a decrease of 23 percent over a period of about ten years.

The order has experienced some organizational change. Its benevolencies have become more life-insurance oriented over the years. In 1955 the AOMP established a female department with its own assemblies. A stronger com-munity and civic-mindedness has also shown itself in the order in recent years.

Every adult member (sixteen or older) who joins the AOMP is initiated "in a dignified and impressive ceremony," according to the society's litera-ture. Part of the initiation requires the candidate to take an obligation. The order still resembles Masonry in some ways. For instance, some of the regalia, like the wearing of a white apron, reminds the viewer of the apron worn by the Masons.

The emblem of the society displays a triangle encircled by a ring. On the triangle is the screw and pulley, symbolizing the artisan heritage. The emblem also depicts the words "Peace, Power, and Protection." Around the ring that encircles the triangle is a diamond-shaped square. Each corner of the square portrays one letter of the order's initials, AOMP.

Local gatherings are known as "Assemblies." In 1978 the order had sixty-four assemblies. The national organization, called "Most Excellent Assembly," meets annually. This group elects a Most Excellent Master Artisan (head officer) each year. The national office is located in Philadel-phia, Pennsylvania.

For additional information see the article, "History of the Artisans

Order of Mutual Protection," *The Artisan* (May, 1948). The centennial publication by Elias H. Borden, *A Century of Fraternalism: 1873-1973*, provides an illustrated historical account. Finally, the AOMP publishes a periodical, *The Artisan*, which appears in January, March, April-May, June-July, September, and November.

ASSOCIATED FRATERNITIES OF AMERICA (AFA). This association of fraternal benefit societies was organized on March 21, 1901, in Chicago, Illinois, as a protest movement against the National Fraternal Congress of America. Many of the early leaders of the AFA came from fraternal benefit societies in Iowa. In 1913 the association merged with its former enemy, the National Fraternal Congress. The merger adopted the new name of National Fraternal Congress of America.*

ASSOCIATION CANADO-AMERICAINE (ACA). This fraternal benefit society was organized in Manchester, New Hampshire, in 1896. The society's objective is to work toward "the union of Catholics of French ancestry or affinity in America and the promotion of their religious, civic, cultural, social and economic progress." In order to achieve its objective, the ACA assures the economic well-being of its members by offering them a variety of life insurance programs, awards scholarships to worthy members, and sponsors fraternal and social activities.

Three classes of membership are available: beneficiary, social, and honorary. The beneficiary consists of adult and infant members. The latter become adult members upon reaching the age of eighteen years. Social members carry no insurance. They may vote, except on issues dealing with insurance. Honorary members are those who have been selected on account of their "unusual services to the Catholic faith, social or economic science, to the arts, to education, to the French culture generally or to any other ideal of the Association." In 1939 the ACA absorbed the Foresters Franco Americains. The 1979 membership has 26,000 members, compared to the count of 30,424 in 1967.

Like many other fraternal benefit societies, the ACA still has a ritual that has initiation, installation, and other ceremonial rites. The ritual truly reflects the religious values of the society, whose patron saint is St. John the Baptist.

The motto of the association is "Religion, Patriotism, and Fraternity." These elements are also embodied in the society's official emblem. The emblem consists of the American and Canadian coat of arms which

symbolize the two countries where the Association is operating; the cross and the fleur-de-lis represent the Catholic faith and the French culture; the hammer is for the City of Manchester and the fasces of the lictor the State of New Hampshire where the Home-Office is located; the handclasp designates the mutual benefit, and the numeral 1896, the year of foundation.

Structurally, the ACA operates "Courts" on the local level. Regional groupings are known as "Districts." The national authority is the "Supreme Court," which is composed of delegates from the local courts and members of the "High Court." The high court has the power to designate the boundary lines of the society's districts. It also is "vested with all the executive, administrative and disciplinary powers of the Association." The supreme court meets quadrennially. National headquarters are located in Manchester, New Hampshire.

The writer knows of no scholarly history that has been written on the ACA. If the reader is able to read French, he may consult the society's bimonthly publication, *Le Canado-Americain*. The *Charter-Constitution and By-Laws* (1976) provides a good perspective on how the association governs its affairs.

ASSOCIATION OF LITHUANIAN WORKERS. See Lithuanian Workers, Association of.

ASSOCIATION OF THE SONS OF POLAND. See Sons of Poland, Association of.

_B

BAGMEN OF BAGDAD, ANCIENT MYSTIC ORDER OF (AMOBB). This society might be called the "inner circle" of the Order of United Commercial Travelers of America* (OUCTA). The AMOBB was incorporated in Ohio in 1895. Frequently this order is seen as the shrine or Shriners of the OUCTA.

In the past the society had a secret ritual. Now, according to the Imperial Clerk of Records and Revenue of the AMOBB, there is "no set ritual." However, the order still in most instances appears to be using a ritual. On festive occasions the members wear uniforms resembling those of Turkish soldiers.

In order to join the AMOBB one must first hold membership in the OUCTA. Presently (1979) the organization has 6,600 members, calling themselves "Bagmen of Bagdad." The name "Bagmen" has reference to the days when the society was composed only of commerical travelers and salesmen. In comparison to the OUCTA, the membership of the AMOBB is quite small. Apparently the idea of having a "playground" or "fun" organization does not appeal to most OUCTA members. The present membership represents an increase from the mid-1960s, when the society had about 4,000 members.

The head office of the society is located with the national secretary, who is named Imperial Clerk of Records and Revenue. The Imperial Ruler is located in another town or city. Local groups are called "Subordinate Guilds." The national convention structure, known as "Imperial Guild," meets annually.

The AMOBB publishes no periodical. It does have a constitution that provides a good understanding of its organizational structure. Occasional information on the society is published in the periodicals of the OUCTA.

BAPTIST LIFE ASSOCIATION (BLA). This organization was founded in the state of New York in 1883 by a group of German Baptists, who felt a need to provide protection for widows and orphans. This perceived need led the founders to establish life insurance benefits, whose financial base rested upon the funds obtained on the basis of the assessment plan. Today the objectives of the society are to protect its members "against financial loss upon disability or death through insurance and by providing security in old age through annuities. . . ." A second major objective is to promote the "spiritual, physical and cultural welfare of its members" through fraternal activities. Until 1934 the society was known as German Baptist Life Association.

The society's motto is "Honoring God While Serving Mankind." This motto, says the BLA, is also the way the society endeavors to conduct its business affairs. In keeping with the motto, the association expedites its business by means of two departments: the insurance benefit department and the Christian service and fraternal affairs department. It is through the latter department that the society offers home-study Bible courses prepared by the Moody Bible Institute of Chicago, Illinois. Local churches are assisted through the Branch Match Program, which offers a given branch (local unit) up to $100 for some parish program, provided the local branch contributes at least 50 percent of the cost. A world relief program is also an ongoing endeavor of the BLA.

In addition to the benevolent insurance programs that are part of the BLA, the society also serves its members by a number of other projects. Art and photo contests are annually held for insured members. Family camping and Bible conferences are regular summertime activities that the members of the association enjoy. Like most fraternal benefit groups, the BLA also awards scholarships in amounts ranging from $800 to $2,000. These scholarships are available to members who are high school seniors.

Presumably membership is open only to Baptists. The bylaws of the society, however, make no mention of having to be a Baptist to join the BLA. Two categories of memberships are available: insured and associate. The latter is ineligible for insurance benefits and has no voice or vote in the management of the association. Currently (1979) the BLA has approximately 13,000 members. This figure is slightly higher than the one of 1965, when the society had 12,335 members.

The BLA has forty-nine branches in twenty-six states. In geographical areas, where the society has no organized branches, it operates "at-large" branches. The highest authority is the national convention, which meets quadrennially. Headquarters are in Buffalo, New York.

Further information may be acquired by reading the back issues of the *Baptist Life Association News*, a quarterly publication. There is no published history on the BLA.

BAVARIAN NATIONAL ASSOCIATION OF NORTH AMERICA. Organized in 1884 by immigrants from Bavaria, the order was a fraternal benefit group seeking to protect the whole family. The society had about 3,500 members in fifty-six lodges during the early 1920s. In 1934 the society merged with Unity Life and Accident Insurance Association. The headquarters were maintained in Buffalo, New York. REFERENCE: *DSOS.*

BEAUCEANT, SOCIAL ORDER OF THE (SOOB). One of the brochures of the SOOB reads: "The Social Order of the Beauceant is an organization of Christian women whose membership is limited to the wives and widows of Knights Templar." The order was founded in Denver, Colorado, on February, 1890, after the thought of forming a women's group was first suggested by several members of the Knights Templar* in 1889. Initially, the order was known by the name "S.O.O.B. Society." The letters stood for "Some Of Our Business." By 1913 the letters were changed to stand for "Social Order of the Beauceant," the latter name being derived from the banner of the historic Knights Templars of the Crusades. In 1920 the society organized itself on the national level by forming its "Supreme Assembly."

The SOOB essentially is an auxiliary of the Knights Templar. The society sees its basic objective as promoting "loyal friendships among the wives and widows of the Knights Templar and to aid Commanderies [local units of the Knights Templar] when requested to do so." The order also supports the Knights Templar by contributing to the Knights Templar Eye Foundation. Since 1957 the SOOB has donated over $500,000 to the eye project. Like its male counterpart, the Knights Templar, the SOOB has a ritual which it deems "beautiful, impressive, and helpful in every day life. . . ." The theme of the ritual is "Faith, Loyalty, and Love for God, the Order of Knights Templar, and each other." The ritual, which is kept secret from nonmembers, has been revised several times in the history of the order. Since 1913, the Knights Templar have granted SOOB power to confer the degree interpreting the legend of the society.

As has already been stated, the society has a national structure known as the "Supreme Assembly." Its chief leader is the Supreme Worthy President. Local units are called "Assemblies," of which there currently (1970) are 201 in the United States. An assembly may be organized only "where there is a regular, active Commandery of Knights Templar of sufficient membership to warrant it." The present total membership is 18,183. The head office resides with the national secretary, the Supreme Recorder, who lives in Calimesa, California.

The present writer knows of no scholarly treatment concerning the order. If the reader wants additional information, he is compelled to confine his efforts to a brochure, "The Social Order of the Beauceant of the World: Its Origin and Mission." The order does not publish a periodical.

BEAVERS, FRATERNAL ORDER OF (FOB). This fraternal benefit society, which resembled the Eagles,* Moose,* and Red Men* in its day, was founded in 1911 and reorganized in 1919. According to an advertisement placed by the order in the *Fraternal Monitor* (1923), the ritual:

stacks up with any Order in existence—brief snappy opening ceremony, including beautiful Patriotic Flag [sic] exercises; is especially appropriate for an Order that is 100 per cent American; dignified and impressive oral initiation; special dramatic degree exemplifying the Beavers in the Valley of the Turquemenau and their conflict with the Iroquois tribe of Indians, the candidates (Algonquin captives) being borne through the rapids in a canoe to Ahmeek, King of all Beavers.

The FOB did not concern itself with the religious, political, or national background of prospective members. However, only white applicants were admitted. Belief in a supreme being was also a requirement. The eligible age range for membership was from sixteen to fifty-five. The order had about 12,000 members in the early 1920s.

Local units were called "Lodges." The national headquarters were in Philadelphia, Pennsylvania.

For additional information, see Arthur Preuss, *A Dictionary of Secret and Other Societies* (1924). The present account drew extensively from Preuss' work.

BEAVERS NATIONAL MUTUAL BENEFIT, THE (BNMB). A fraternal benefit society that in 1916 absorbed the Supreme Assembly of the Defenders and the Fraternal Order of Rangers shortly after its own origin. In 1919 the Beavers also absorbed the National Fraternal League. The society arose out of the Beavers Reserve Fund Fraternity.* By 1923 it had more than 9,000 members in 244 lodges in Illinois, Minnesota, and Wisconsin. The order had a ritual, which it discarded when in 1931 it adopted the name National Mutual Benefit. The former organization made Madison, Wisconsin, its headquarters. The present society is also located in Madison.

BEAVERS RESERVE FUND FRATERNITY. This order, a fraternal benefit society founded in 1902, operated only in Wisconsin, with headquarters in the state capitol of Madison. Initially, headquarters were in Stoughton, Wisconsin. In 1923 the society had approximately 17,000 members. REFERENCE: *DSOS*.

BENEVOLENT ORDER OF BEREANS. See Bereans, Benevolent Order of.

BENEVOLENT ORDER OF BUFFALOES. See Buffaloes, Benevolent Order of.

BENEVOLENT AND PROTECTIVE ORDER OF ELKS. See Elks, Benevolent and Protective Order of.

BEN HUR LIFE ASSOCIATION (BHLA). When this society was first formed in 1894 in Crawfordsville, Indiana, it was known as the Supreme Tribe of Ben Hur. One of the founders was General Lew Wallace, the author of the book *Ben Hur*. The society was founded in Wallace's home in Crawfordsville, Indiana. The popularity of the book made the fraternal order popular. Initially, some of the cofounders of the society wanted to name the organization "Knights of Ben Hur," but Wallace dissented. He said that in the days of early Christendom there were no knights, but only tribes. Thus the name of Tribe of Ben Hur was selected.

The ritual was drawn from *Ben Hur*. As was true of most fraternal rituals in the 1890s, the ritual had a secret oath, degrees, and other ceremonies. The orientation of the ritual was moral, religious, and patriotic. In 1920 the society added its "New Temple Degree." This degree was given only during the meetings of the Supreme Tribe of Ben Hur.

From the time of its inception, the society was a fraternal beneficiary order. The society began with the graded assessment plan and also had a reserve fund in its early years, at a time when the idea of a reserve fund was not popular with many fraternal benefit societies. The BHLA also was a leader in establishing free scholarships for eligible members. By 1920 a successful applicant was able to obtain a free scholarship of $500 per year of college education. The society still awards scholarships today; however, the nature of the awards has changed. Presently the society also operates a monthly allowance program for eligible orphans, from birth to eighteen years of age.

At one time (in the 1920s) the society operated in thirty states. Today

(1979) it is licensed to sell fraternal insurance in only sixteen states and in the District of Columbia. Membership in 1910 stood at 106,216 in 1,309 local lodges. Presently (1979) the organization has about 31,000 members in 217 local units. Ever since its origin, the society has been admitting women to its membership on an equal basis with men.

The BHLA has been quite responsive to organizational change. It, like other fraternal benefit groups, had two classes of membership: beneficial and social. However, the society also adopted a stance of not being rigid in terms of requiring its oath for all members in all instances. In 1930 the society changed its name to Ben Hur Life Association.

Local groups are called "Courts." The number of courts currently are about one-fifth of the number in existence during the 1920s. The national organization meets in convention every four years. The main offices are in Crawfordsville, Indiana, where the society was born.

For further information, see the society's periodical, *The Chariot.* Reading Lew Wallace's novel, *Ben Hur*, will also provide a better understanding of the BHLA.

BEREANS, BENEVOLENT ORDER OF. According to Albert C. Stevens, *Cyclopedia of Fraternities* (1907), this was an anti-Roman Catholic society that functioned as a fraternal benefit group. It was founded between 1847 and 1850 as the result of a nativistic outgrowth that led to the formation of the Order of United American Mechanics,* the Know-Nothing Party, and other chauvinistic organizations. The headquarters were in Philadelphia, Pennsylvania. REFERENCE: *Cyc. Frat.*

B'NAI B'RITH INTERNATIONAL (BBI). B'nai B'rith in Hebrew means sons or brotherhood of the covenant. The organization was formed by German Jews to foster education and to improve the Jewish image in America. Twelve Hebrew men met on October 13, 1843, in the city of New York, to form the Independent Order of B'nai B'rith, as it was known then. Some of the twelve founders were members of Freemasonry* and of the Odd Fellows.* The early structure of the B'nai B'rith borrowed a number of features from Masonry and Odd Fellows. It adopted a secret ritual (six degrees), its members had secret recognition signs, and it used the blackball method of rejecting undesirable applicants for membership. During the first few years some of the lodges in the order conducted their business in the German language.

The BBI from its very first meeting was a fraternal and benevolent society. Each lodge was obligated to collect dues from all its male-only members so that a fund for widows and orphans could be operated. Dues were paid according to member's ages during the early years of the organization's life. Those between twenty-one and thirty paid $10 a year; between thirty and forty, $15; between forty and forty-five, $25. No one over forty-five years of age was accepted as a member because he was seen as a poor insurance risk.

Countless fraternal orders in the United States once served to integrate their immigrant members into the mainstream of American life. The BBI was no exception. Two years after its inception, some members participated (in lodge regalia) in the funeral procession of President Andrew Jackson in June 1845. The concern to become American soon made itself felt in other ways. One lodge (Emmanuel Lodge of Baltimore) petitioned the Constitutional Grand Lodge in New York to permit the initiation of "non-Israelites." When Emmanuel Lodge's request was denied, it voted in 1851 to surrender its charter.

Virtually from its beginning the BBI has been concerned with overcoming anti-Semitism. In 1851 the order sent letters of protest to the American Secretary of State, Daniel Webster, and others regarding anti-Semitism practiced in Switzerland, which in a treaty at that time with the United States prevented Jews from living in given Swiss cantons.

The B'nai B'rith has undergone a fair amount of internal change over the years. In the 1860s it changed the titles of its officers from the Hebrew to standard English. By 1863 the order's preamble to its constitution was amended with reference to the group's mission. It no longer used the words, "the highest interests of Judaism," but referred only to "the highest interest of humanity." In 1913 it organized the Anti-Defamation League as a program to fight prejudice against Jews. By 1920 it officially recognized the role of women by authorizing ladies auxiliaries. In the 1920s secrecy was dropped as part of the group's posture. After 1910 it slowly abandoned the blackball method of voting, although the practice was not completely abolished in all lodges until 1948. The order began with the German language, but soon changed to conducting its business in English.

The BBI has supported a wide variety of programs: community volunteer services, health drug-abuse education, helping the disabled, prisoner rehabilitation, disaster relief, world hunger relief, assisting new immigrants and refugees, helping older adults, and other programs. In order to become a member of the BBI today the individual must be male, at least twenty-one years of age, of good moral character, and of the Jewish faith. Women and young people must join their own separate organizations. The youth group is known as B'nai B'rith Youth Organization. In 1978 the B'nai B'rith had about 500,000 members (about the number that the society had in the late 1960s) in seventy-five regional grand lodges. This membership figure includes the B'nai B'rith Women, Anti-Defamation League, Hillel, and the B'nai B'rith Youth Organization. The number of local lodges stood at 3,500.

The B'nai B'rith is truly an international group in that it has lodges in a number of countries. It founded a lodge in 1882 in Germany, and by 1888 it had also established a lodge in Jerusalem. After 1948 it reopened lodges in eastern European areas.

Structurally, the BBI is organized on three levels: international, regional, and local. The international operation has since 1935 been known as the "Supreme Lodge." Prior to that time, it was the "Constitutional Grand Lodge." The international headquarters have been in Washington, D.C., since 1938. Regional groups are called "District Grand Lodges," and local entities are referred to as "Lodges." International officers use the titles of president, vice-president, secretary, and the like. However, on the district or regional level the old lodge nomenclature prevails: Grand Nasi Abh, Grand Aleph, and so on.

Published materials available for further reading on the BBI may be found by reading the order's *B'nai B'rith Magazine*, as it was called prior to 1934. From 1934 to 1939 this magazine was known as *B'nai B'rith National Jewish Monthly*, and in 1939 it was changed to *The National Jewish Monthly*, its present name. A good scholarly source on the BBI is Edward E. Grusd, *B'nai B'rith: The Story of a Covenant* (1966). A short treatment in booklet form (*This is B'nai B'rith: A Story of Service* [n.d.]) is available in a publication produced by BBI.

BNAI ZION (BZ). The Bnai Zion is the oldest Zionist fraternal organization in the United States. The society was formed in 1908 and named Order of Sons of Zion by Jodah Magnes, Rabbi Stephen S. Wise, and Joseph Barondess. The society retained the name Order of Sons of Zion until 1945. The BZ sees itself as a nonpolitical fraternal Zionist organization, even though its periodical, *Bnai Zion Voice*, carries numerous politically oriented articles in support of Zionism. The society says it embraces Americanism, fraternalism, and Zionism. Although the society has a multifaceted program, its primary objective on the American scene is the promotion of United States-Israel friendship.

Through the society's Bnai Zion Foundation, a large number of projects are being conducted. In Israel the BZ has established the artists' colony near Haifa, as well as a school of applied arts and a new hostel for students who come from all over the world to learn art. An agricultural settlement, Kfar Bnai Zion, of over 500 residents was created a few years ago. A home for retarded children also has been built in Israel. Other Israel projects could be cited. In the United States the society sponsors the United Jewish Appeal, which helps resettle Jewish immigrants, especially those from Russia. Israel bonds are sold in order to help create jobs for citizens in Israel. One of the outstanding events for the BZ is the annual award dinner when they present an award to someone who has promoted the ideals of Americanism and Zionism. Some recent honorees have been President Gerald Ford, Senator Robert F. Kennedy, Senator Hugh Scott, Vice-President Hubert Humphrey, and Senator Frank Church. The BZ also operates the American-Israel Friendship League, a nonsectarian organization to promote deeper understanding between Americans and Israelites. This league distributes books and periodicals to more than 2,000 university libraries, funding seminars, and discussion groups.

As a fraternal benefit society, the BZ offers its members a variety of life insurance certificates, including hospitalization and medical policies. The insurance program also offers individual retirement plans. The society is licensed to sell insurance in eleven states.

Although the society is a Jewish group, its membership does not come only from the Jewish community. Non-Jews also are eligible. The current (1979) membership is approximately 40,000. In the late 1960s the society had about 24,000 members.

The official insignia consists of the Star of David placed on a blue circular background that bears the words Bnai Zion in English and in Hebrew. On the face of the star is a candelabra, displaying seven candles.

The BZ calls its local gatherings "Chapters," of which there are about 115. The national convention, as in most fraternal benefit groups, is the highest authority. This group meets annually. The national headquarters are situated in New York, New York.

For information see the society's bimonthly periodical, *Bnai Zion Voice*. The February 1977 issue contains a brief history of the organization.

B'RITH ABRAHAM, INDEPENDENT ORDER OF (IOBA). While the Order of B'rith Abraham* (founded in 1859) was assembled at its national convention in 1887, a group of dissatisfied members broke from their order. The malcontents formed the Independent Order of B'rith Abraham because they felt the administration of B'rith Abraham was incompetent. The new society retained the old order's objectives, which were to aid and assist German and Hungarian Jews, most of whom were immigrants. Later the order also added Russian and Polish Jews.

The order grew and prospered. By 1917 it had a membership high of 206,000, making it the largest Jewish fraternal order of that time. In 1924 the IOBA introduced a noninsurance class of membership. The society's prosperity, however, did not last, for by 1940 its membership had dwindled to 58,000. The writer was unable to obtain the membership count for 1979.

In 1968 the IOBA changed its name to B'rith Abraham, omitting the words "Independent Order of." Its objectives since 1968 are threefold: (1) Foster fraternity in the context of Jewish ideals, tradition, and welfare. (2) Provide fraternal benefits to the members. (3) Support programs for underprivileged children and senior citizens. The order also espouses Zionist values.

Local or subordinate units are known as "Lodges." The national structure is called "Grand Lodge." It meets annually in convention. Headquarters are maintained in the city of New York.

For additional background on the IOBA, consult the society's monthly magazine, *Beacon*. This magazine provides good coverage of the order's activities and events.

B'RITH ABRAHAM, ORDER OF (OBA). Two Jewish men, Oscar Wilner and Leonard Leisersohn, founded this order in the city of New York on June 12, 1859. The order was in part fashioned along the lines of other fraternal organizations, especially the Independent Order of Free Sons of Israel.* The OBA sought to provide insurance benefits to its members and to assist them in becoming good citizens. The latter goal was quite pertinent, as most of the members were German and Hungarian Jews, recent immigrants. Later the order also appealed to Russian and Polish Jews.

In 1887 the OBA suffered a schism. A sizeable contingent of delegates at the order's convention felt the administration was incompetent, and so they formed the Independent Order of B'rith Abraham.* The new, independent order grew and prospered. In fact, the OBA soon fell behind in a number of ways.

The objectives of the OBA were fivefold: (1) Aid members in financial need. (2) Give medical assistance to sick members. (3) Bury the deceased members in conformity with Jewish religious laws. (4) Provide for families of deceased members. (5) Assist members in becoming good American citizens. These objectives were faithfully pursued until 1927, when the order had to dissolve because of financial insolvency, as it could no longer meet its financial benefit obligations.

While the OBA existed, it called its local units "Lodges." The national structure was known as the "Grand Lodge." Its main offices were headquartered in the city of New York.

BRITH SHOLOM (BS). In 1905 when the fraternity was organized it was known as the Independent Order of Brith Sholom. The group was founded largely to help Jewish immigrants find themselves in their newly adopted country, the United States. Brith Sholom (covenant of peace) provided the new Jewish immigrants with some elementary needs, such as learning the English language; discovering how the American system of economic, political, and social life operated; and at times obtaining financial aid when employment could not be found. The society also provided death and burial benefits to the survivors of deceased members.

The BS changed when it no longer had immigrants coming to the United States. It began focusing on Jewish rights, but this emphasis later changed to the concern about human and civil rights. After World War II the society opened its membership to non-Jews. In fact, membership was no longer premised on religious background. These and other changes reflect a belief quite prevalent in the BS, namely, the saying of a Jewish hero, Hillel: "separate not thyself from the community."

Officially, the BS has a ritual and an initiation ceremony for its members. In the words of one official, the rituals are used "only by a few lodges." This individual also recently said: "The rites are secret, although their nature is so universal, I wonder why." The emblem of the BS is a blue, oval-shaped background, displaying a white dove carrying the olive branch of peace in its beak.

Membership, as already noted above, is open to non-Jews as well as to Jews. Women have their own group (Brith Sholom Women) within the Brith Sholom. Anyone sixteen years old or older is eligible to join. The current (1979) total membership—men and women—is about 20,000, essentially the same number that belonged ten years ago.

In the area of philanthropic activities the BS maintains a senior citizens home, housing some 500 elderly persons, in Philadelphia. Presently the order is in the process of establishing a multimillion-dollar rehabilitation center for Israel's permanently disabled war veterans. This center will be located in Haifa, Israel. The society rescued fifty children, ages five to fourteen, from being executed by the Nazis during World War II. These children were housed, fed, clothed, and educated in Camp Sholom. At the Albert Einstein College of Medicine at Yeshiva University, New York, the society established a laboratory for cancer research. It also contributed a sixty-five-acre tract of land for the establishment of Eagleville Sanitorium. Scholarships are offered to deserving students.

The BS is also involved in athletic and civic activities. It claims to have the "largest fraternal sports program in America." Public speaking leadership programs are regularly sponsored by the fraternity, as well as vacation outings, tours, dances, and art exhibits. The latter activities are primarily conducted by local lodges.

Administratively, the national business of the society is conducted from the head office in Philadelphia, Pennsylvania. On the state level the BS has only three statewide organizations. Locally it has about 130 lodges. The national convention takes place annually.

For additional information the reader may consult the national headquarters, as no known scholarly work has been published on the society. The BS, however, does print a weekly periodical known as *Brith Sholom News*. A *Community Relations Digest* is published irregularly.

BROTHERHOOD OF AMERICA. This fraternal benefit group was formed in 1890 in Philadelphia. It admitted men and women on an equal basis. In the early 1920s the order had a little more than 3,000 benefit members. The social membership was about 11,000. In 1935 the organization merged into

The Maccabees.* Headquarters were maintained in Philadelphia, Pennsylvania. REFERENCE: *Cyc. Frat.*

BROTHERHOOD OF AMERICAN YEOMEN. See Yeomen, Brotherhood of American.

BROTHERHOOD OF THE UNION (BOU). This society came into being in Philadelphia, Pennsylvania, in 1850, along with a variety of similar other groups that appeared in the 1840s and 1850s. These organizations were primarily superpatriotic, following the spirit of the Know-Nothing Party.

The ritual accented "The Gospel of Nazareth and the Declaration of Independence." The society's chief officers were called, "Supreme Washington," "Supreme Jefferson," and "Supreme Franklin," respectively.

Administratively, the society called its local groups "Circles." Regional units were known as "State Councils," and the national structure was referred to as "Supreme Circle." The female auxiliary was named "Home Communion." Headquarters were housed in Philadelphia, Pennsylvania. REFERENCE: *DSOS.*

BUFFALOES, BENEVOLENT ORDER OF. This fraternal benefit society was founded in the city of New York in 1881. The society had a secret ritual. Insurance benefits were paid with regard to sickness and death of its members. The group apparently became extinct in the eary 1900s. REFERENCE: *DSOS.*

BUFFALOES, LOYAL ORDER OF. Established in New Jersey in 1911, the society did not offer insurance, although it had death, sickness, accident, and disability benefits. It also provided free family physician services, all for a $6.00 initiation fee, plus 75 cents dues per month. The governing body was known as the "Home Range." Head offices were in Newark, New Jersey. REFERENCE: *DSOS.*

BUGS, ORDER OF. This society was founded around 1912, apparently in Massachusetts. Local units were called "Bughouses." The head of the society was known as "Supreme Exalted Bugaboo." REFERENCE: *DSOS.*

BUILDERS, ORDER OF THE (OOB). In a sense this order is very similar to the Order of De Molay* in that its objective is to train boys who, it is hoped, will become good, active Freemasons. It was organized on March 2, 1921, in Chicago, Illinois. The primary organizer was Arthur M. Millard.

Membership is open to young men ranging from ages thirteen to twenty-one. The order soon after its formation attracted a substantial membership so that by the end of 1921 it had over 4,500 boys on its roster in forty-five chapters. Today's membership figures were not available to the writer.

The ritual teaches the members spiritual values and the American way of life, and as is typical of Masonically related organizations, the OOB ritual is kept secret from nonmembers. Meetings are supervised by an advisory council of Master Masons of the Blue Lodge.*

Local units are called "Chapters." A regional or state group is known as "Grand Chapter," and the national authority system is named the "Central Council." The chief officer is the Supreme Master Builder. Headquarters presently are in New Castle, Pennsylvania.

For further information, see the Masonic Service Association's "Allied Masonic Groups and Rites" (mimeographed, 1978).

C

CAMELS, ORDER OF. Founded in 1920 in response to the American prohibition laws that were ushered in by the Eighteenth Amendment of 1919 and the Volstead Act of 1920. The order was strongly opposed to prohibition. The camel was selected as the order's emblem because it could withstand long dry periods. Members took but one oath, namely, to oppose prohibition. Any male over twenty-two was eligible to join the society. Local lodges were called "Caravans." The society was founded in Milwaukee, Wisconsin. REFERENCE: *DSOS*.

CANADIAN FORESTERS LIFE INSURANCE SOCIETY (CFLIS). Back in November of 1879 a number of individuals (about twenty-nine) who were members of the Independent Order of Foresters decided to secede from the American order to form a Canadian organization. Thus on November 26, 1879, the Canadian Order of Foresters was born in London, Ontario. The new society began with 390 members. The first High Chief Ranger was the Reverend G. G. McRobbie, who later also served as chaplain of the order. In 1969 the order's name, by special act of the Parliament of Canada, was changed to Canadian Foresters Life Insurance Society.

The latest (1976) constitution states the society's objective as uniting "fraternally into the Society all male and female persons of sound health, physically and mentally, and of good moral character, for the purposes of mutual fraternal benefit in accordance with the principles of Liberty, Benevolence and Concord. . . ." These latter three words are the watchwords of the order.

The order prospered and grew. By 1896 it had 23,000 members, and by 1907 the roster had grown to 64,000. The prosperity of the society, however, did not last. Like so many other fraternal benefit societies whose memberships declined after the 1920s, the Canadian Order of Foresters experienced a similar trend. Today (1979) the society has 30,000 members in 221 local courts. In 1967 it still had 41,000 foresters.

Like many other fraternal benefit orders, the CFLIS still has a ritual that has religious and Masonic overtones. The religious qualities reveal themselves in the hymns that are played, references to God, a funeral ceremony making use of Psalm 23, and an altar in the lodge (court) room. The Masonic features show themselves in the signs, grips, and passwords and especially in the expression "So mote it be." The ritual has an initiation ceremony that revolves around the theme of Robin Hood and his merry men of Sherwood Forest. One initiation ceremony is available for men and another for women. Some of the principal officers in charge of the ritual are the Conductor, Warden, Special Guard, Inner and Outer Guards, Chaplain, and the Chief Ranger. The basic objective of the ritual is to teach the principles of fraternity, service, and benevolence.

A number of fraternal activities are sponsored by the society such as mother-and-daughter meetings, father-and-son gatherings, annual banquets, family nights, evening and dinner dances, birthday and Christmas parties, lectures, card parties, amateur talent nights, food sales, and carnivals. The society also promotes softball, golfing, bowling, basketball, baseball, swim meets, rifle and trapshooting competition, hockey, cycling, and other sports.

Philanthropically, the CFLIS directs much of its attention to fighting cancer. For 1979 it had set a goal of collecting $100,000 to be given to cancer research. This amount has been referred to as the "Centennial Goal" of the organization. The society also supports mentally retarded children's programs and homes for senior citizens. Youth movements, the Red Cross, Cerebral Palsy, and other charities have also received assistance from the CFLIS.

Membership since 1952 has been open to females. Prior to 1952 the society was an all-male fraternal group. In 1969 the constitution was changed to admit social members, whom the society calls "associate" members, who carry no insurance with the society. The CFLIS prides itself in being the first order in Canada "to confine its efforts and membership to this Dominion."

On the local level the society calls its organizational units "Local Courts." Conforming to provincial boundaries, the society has "Provincial Assemblies," and subordinate to the provincial assemblies are "District Councils." The national authority is known as the "High Court." Its headquarters are in Brantford, Ontario. The high court meets in convention every two years.

Further information may be gained by consulting an unpublished mimeographed document, "Historical Facts," issued by the Public Relations Department of the CFLIS. Other documents such as the society's ritual and its constitution are also helpful in understanding the order. The bimonthly periodical *The Canadian Forester* provides good coverage of the society's affairs.

CANADIAN FRATERNAL ASSOCIATION, THE (CFA). This fraternal association is the Canadian counterpart to the National Fraternal Congress* in the United States. Canadian fraternal benefit societies, like those in the United States, grew rather rapidly in the 1870s and 1880s, largely because of the appeal of the assessment plan, which provided low rates for insurance protection for fraternal members. The rapid growth of benefit groups prompted the formation of the Canadian Fraternal Association in 1891. The association enabled member organizations to strive for stable, uniform practices at a time when about 25 percent of all Canadian life insurance was sold by fraternal benefit societies. Today (1979) only about 2 percent of all life insurance is provided by the fraternal societies in Canada.

From the beginning the CFA was concerned about financial solvency of its member organizations. This objective was given added impetus during the first decade of the 1900s as federal and provincial laws were passed requiring fraternal benefit groups to adopt sounder actuarial methods, replacing inadequate assessment plans. Like its American counterpart, the CFA seeks to promote favorable legislation relative to the fraternal insurance enterprise. Presently (1979) there are eighteen fraternal benefit societies holding membership in the CFA. These eighteen organizations represent about 90 percent of the members of all Canadian fraternal benefit groups.

The CFA meets annually in convention. It has its elected officers, who come from its member organizations. Headquarters are in Toronto, Ontario. Its current president is a member of the Grand Orange Lodge of British America Benefit Fund.

For additional information the reader may wish to obtain publicity items from the CFA. This report is based in part on a paper that briefly described the CFA to the Ontario Select Committee on Company Law (September 26, 1979) and was authorized by David A. Griffin, president of the CFA.

CANADIAN ORDER OF CHOSEN FRIENDS (COCF). This society was essentially an offshoot of the Order of Chosen Friends* founded in Indianapolis, Indiana, in 1879. The Canadian order was incorporated in 1887 in the province of Ontario. The society in Canada began because a number of Canadian members were dissatisfied with their membership in the American group.

For a number of years there was considerable litigation between the Canadian and American orders. Some court cases involved the use of the name "Chosen Friends," and others pertained to financial interests.

The society had the usual fraternal benefits. In 1890 it established a sick-benefit department, and in 1917 it also began a child insurance department licensed under the Ontario Insurance Act of 1916. In 1915 the society made some very necessary actuarial adjustments in its rates, which led to a significant decrease in the membership. However, by the early 1920s the society prospered again with about 32,000 members.

In 1943 the COCF changed its name to Reliable Life Insurance Society. In 1964 the latter group became a stock-owned life insurance company. Headquarters of the COCF were maintained in Hamilton, Ontario.

CATHOLIC AID ASSOCIATION, THE (CAA). In 1878 German Catholics, who frontiered in Minnesota, formed the Catholic Aid Association in order to provide life insurance and fraternal bonds for the members. The order began with 464 members from ten parishes. As was common during the latter 1800s, the society collected its insurance dues by the assessment method. When the association was first founded, it was known as the *Deutsche Roemish Katholisch Unterstuetzunds Gesellschaft von Minnesota*. In 1923 the name was changed to the present one.

Similar to most fraternal benefit groups, the CAA has a number of activities serving its members and the Catholic community. The Matching Grants Program provides financial assistance to Catholic elementary schools or religious education programs. Another financial activity of the society is the College-Tuition Scholarship Program, which has thus far helped 800 young members of the CAA receive college degrees. Other contributions regularly assist local parishes, mission projects, Catholic colleges, and the Holy Father. Socially and recreationally, the CAA sponsors banquets, family outings, dances, and youth activities. These programs are supplemental to the insurance protection that the members enjoy.

Membership is open only to Roman Catholics who are sixteen or older, with age sixty-five the upper limit. The current constitution has one limitation on membership that is somewhat different, namely, "any person who is a member of any secret society positively forbidden by the Roman Catholic Church . . ." may not join the CAA. Membership of the society currently (1979) stands at approximately 78,000, an increase of about 20,000 from 1965, when there were 58,722 members. The society says that it has "consistently been among the nation's top fraternal life insurance societies in membership percentage growth."

Like so many other fraternal benefit societies, the CAA has a ritual that attempts to exemplify the principles of the organization. The ritual contains ceremonies for the initiation of members, installation of officers, and other rites. The emblem of the association is a circle with cross superimposed upon it. On the border of the circle are the letters C.A.A. and the year (1878) of the society's origin. The upper (vertical) arm of the cross portrays the communion chalice, and the lower arm displays an anchor.

Local units are referred to as "Subordinate Councils," of which there are 240. The national or supreme body, called the "Grand Council," meets annually in convention. The association's headquarters are housed in St. Paul, Minnesota.

For additional background, see the society's constitution. The official publication, *Catholic Aid News*, issued monthly is quite helpful for obtaining greater familiarity with the association. Brochures and pamphlets issued by the head office in St. Paul provide brief information on the society.

CATHOLIC ASSOCIATION OF FORESTERS (CAOF). Founded on the principles of fraternity, unity, and Christian charity, the CAOF was incorporated July 30, 1879, in the state of Massachusetts. Its name was Massachusetts Catholic Order of Foresters. The society was formed by a small group of Catholic men, who were dedicated to providing financial protection for their families, as Catholics in the latter 1800s were unable to obtain protection. In 1961 the society assumed its present name.

The current objectives of the CAOF are still the same ones the society had when it was formed: fraternity, charity, and unity. The society seeks to accomplish fraternity by assisting its members by "every honorable means." Mutual aid is the means to achieve unity, and charity by "doing good unto others as we wish that others should do unto us."

In terms of benevolences, the CAOF awards scholarship amounts of $500.00 each to eligible members of the society. With respect to entertainment, an annual St. Patrick's Day Show is held in Fall River, Massachusetts. In support of religion, the society holds an annual communion breakfast each spring.

Only Roman Catholic members are eligible to join the CAOF. Two categories of membership are available, benefit and social. As in other fraternal benefit groups, a social member is uninsured. The 1979 membership roster had about 30,000 members, a decline from 50,000 in 1966.

As the society calls itself "Foresters," it follows the terminology that other forester orders employ. The principal officer of the CAOF is known as the High Chief Ranger. Local units are referred to as "Subordinate Courts." The ritual also is flavored with forestry language.

In addition to subordinate courts, the society has its national (supreme) convention, which meets every year between May 1 and June 30. Head offices are situated in Boston, Massachusetts.

No history has been published on the CAOF; however, brochures and pamphlets may be consulted for further information. A bimonthly periodical, *The Forester*, is also helpful in providing background about the CAOF.

CATHOLIC DAUGHTERS OF AMERICA (CDA). The Catholic Daughters of America is the largest organization of Catholic women in the world. The society was founded in 1903 by members of the Knights of Columbus.

Today the CDA accents four basic goals: personal renewal, apostolacy, community participation, and youth work. Personal renewal stresses prayer, spiritual reflection, and cultivating fraternal friendship. Apostolacy is achieved by showing one's concerns for the elderly, the sick, the homeless, and others in need. Community participation focuses on activities ranging from religious education to community action programs. Concern for youth encompasses working with young people, understanding the needs of youth, and instilling in them the desire to serve. The society's concern for youth showed itself relatively early in the organization's existence, when in 1925 it formed the Junior Catholic Daughters of America.*

The emblem of the CDA is a purple circle portraying a white cross and gold-colored crown. The cross displays the letters C.D. of A. To become a member of the CDA one must be a female member of the Catholic Church and at least eighteen years of age. The current (1979) membership roster lists 174,103 members, a decline from 215,000 that the society enjoyed in the late 1960s.

Local units are called "Courts." The society has 1,579 such courts in 38 states, the Dominican Republic, Mexico, Guam, and the Virgin Islands. When at least five local courts exist in a given state, a state court is organized. Local and state courts are governed by a national board. The CDA meets every two years in a national convention. New York City serves as the society's headquarters.

For additional information, see the society's quarterly periodical, *Share*. The summer 1978 issue had four special sections (A, B, C, D) discussing the organization's diamond jubilee. These sections provide helpful historical background data on the CDA.

CATHOLIC FAMILY LIFE INSURANCE (CFLI). On August 16, 1868, a Catholic priest, the Rev. Dr. Joseph Salzmann, Procurator of St. Francis Seminary, Milwaukee, Wisconsin, and a group of like-minded men formed the Catholic Family Protective Association. Father Salzmann was appointed by Bishop Henni to organize a Catholic benevolent society. The organization later (1950) was renamed Catholic Family Life Insurance.

The basic objectives of the society are "to foster friendship and true charity among its members through help and relief to them and their families, and enable them through membership in this fraternal benefit society to assist themselves and others . . ." through a variety of programs and activities in the local branches.

The society is proud of a number of "firsts." It was the first Catholic life insurance society in the United States. Moreover, it was the first to insure women and children. According to the society, it was the first insurance group "of its kind" to adopt the legal reserve system. It was the first insurance organization to offer holy Masses for its living and deceased members. Finally, it was the first to pay dividends to its members as a fraternal life insurance society.

The CFLI has a number of philanthropic programs. It sponsors a home missions emphasis as well as a foreign missions outreach. Considerable energy is directed to the pro-life (anti-abortion) movement. The society refers to the latter as the "Respect For Life" program. This program also includes concern for the aged and handicapped. Another project is the "Catholic Rural Life" movement that promotes the welfare of the family farm. The society's public charities support the Cancer Fund, the Heart Fund, the Red Cross, and the Community Chest. Finally, through its local branches a number of worthy community projects are supported on the local scene.

Membership may be acquired only by members of the Catholic faith eighteen years of age and older. For those not wishing to carry any insurance the society has associate memberships. The insurance holders are "benefit members." Currently (1979) the society has 47,000 members in fifty-four branches. This enrollment represents an increase of 10,000 since 1967. The order does not have a ritual.

In the fraternal activities context, the society sponsors summer camps, social dances, athletic events, family camp-outs, picnics, and teen parties. These events are particularly directed toward the youth. Spiritual services such as daily and weekly Masses are also held to further the bonds of fraternity among the members.

As a fraternal insurance society, CFLI invests many of its funds in Catholic churches, schools, hospitals, and other religious institutions. The society feels that these are exceptionally safe places to invest the members' money. The organization, however, not only invests but also loans money to Catholic parishes for building churches and schools.

Like all fraternal benefit societies, the CFLI has a representative form of government. It operates on the local level, where its units are called "Branches." The national structure is known as the "Supreme Governing Body." National conventions occur every four years, and the society also has intermediate conventions that resemble the regional or state gatherings that many other fraternals hold. The national headquarters are in Milwaukee, Wisconsin.

For further information the reader may consult the society's quarterly publication, *The Family Friend*. This periodical carries articles on rural life, family farms, family camp-outs, and most of the activities that the CFLI attempts to promote as a fraternal benefit organization.

CATHOLIC FRATERNAL LEAGUE. See Union Fraternal League.

CATHOLIC KNIGHTS AND LADIES OF ILLINOIS (CKLI). Founded in 1884 as a fraternal benefit society, this Catholic fraternal group is closely tied to the Catholic Church. For instance, every month Mass is offered to the members on the local level. The society makes annual contributions to the Catholic Communication Foundation. Assistance is also given to the "Teens Encounter Christ" retreat program for high school youth. In addition to these efforts, the CKLI operates a "Continuing Education Fund" for priests.

In terms of insurance, the society offers the usual array of fraternal life insurance certificates to its members. In 1977 the organization had $42,000,000 of insurance in force. The society also is active in promoting Fraternal Week each year.

Membership in 1978 stood at about 13,000, a significant increase from the 8,500 members of 1965. Both males and females are eligible to join the society, provided they are Roman Catholic.

The number of local units currently totals forty-five. Illinois is the only state in which the society is licensed to sell insurance. The supreme legislative body meets quadrennially. The main offices are located in Belleville, Illinois.

As the society never responded to the author's request for specific information concerning its organization, the present account of the CKLI is largely based on the society's report published in *Statistics, Fraternal Benefit Societies* (1978). The writer does not know of a scholarly published history.

CATHOLIC KNIGHTS INSURANCE SOCIETY (CKIS). This fraternal insurance organization originally was known as the Catholic Knights of Wisconsin when it was organized in Green Bay, Wisconsin, in 1885. The Catholic Knights of Wisconsin was a branch or extension of the Catholic Knights of America* that began in 1877 in Nashville, Tennessee. Except for a few regional or state differences the Wisconsin group was the same as the society founded in Nashville. For additional information the reader is asked to see the Catholic Knights of America discussion in the present volume.

The CKIS today (1979) is a prosperous fraternal insurance group, the largest Catholic fraternal insurance society in Wisconsin. Its headquarters are in Milwaukee, Wisconsin.

CATHOLIC KNIGHTS OF AMERICA (CKA). This Catholic fraternal benevolent order was founded, like many others, in response to keeping Catholics from joining the many other fraternal groups in the United States. As the Catholic Church during the nineteenth century forbid its members to join orders like the Odd Fellows,* Knights of Pythias,* and Sons of Temperance,* it was compelled to provide an alternative, and it did. Thus in 1877 James J. McLoughlin, a member of the Knights of Honor, a non-Catholic fraternal society, was moved by his priest's sermon warning Catholics against belonging to secular fraternal orders. McLoughlin soon met with his friends in his hometown of Nashville, Tennessee, to form the Catholic Knights of America on April 23, 1877. At first the founders had difficulty selecting a name, but by June 19, the name Catholic Knights of America won out over the Order of United Catholics and the Catholic Knights of Honor. From its inception the order was a benevolent fraternity.

Following the course of all American fraternal groups of the nineteenth century, the CKA had an oath, which read in part: "I further solemnly promise . . . that I shall aid a member of this Order when in need or distress . . . shall favor a member of the Catholic Knights of America. . . ." The CKA, in keeping with fraternal ritual and regalia, has a uniformed contingent that was established in 1893. The female members have a uniformed rank of their own.

Like other fraternal orders, the CKA practiced some discrimination against women, although with less intensity than most. By 1895 a women's auxiliary was formed. The auxiliaries were permitted to have their own sessions and "meet jointly with the Branch [local group] on occasions of a social nature." In 1916 women were placed in the same category as men relative to insurance certificates, and in 1952 the first woman was elected to the Supreme Board of the CKA at its national convention. That same year a woman also became national secretary. A juvenile department for youth was created in 1929. The 1979 membership of the CKA had 25,000 knights, which represents an increase of about 4,000 during the last decade.

Virtually all of the fraternal charity of the CKA is extended to Catholic needs. It supports orphans of its members, provides high school scholarships as well as aid for seminarians, promotes pro-life efforts, and endorses a law enforcement recognition program.

The CKA emblem is in the form of a knight's shield. On the shield the Latin cross is held by the iron-clad hands of a knight. The CKA is placed under the patronage of St. Joseph, the foster father of Jesus.

The CKA operates on the national, regional, and local level. The national structure used to be called the Supreme Council. Now it is known as the national convention. Local groups are known as branches. Headquarters are in St. Louis, Missouri.

For additional information the reader may consult the book by Vincent L. Naes, *Rounding Out a Century: The Catholic Knights of America* (1974). A special periodical publication by the CKA that briefly surveys the one hundred years of its existence is *100th Anniversary: Yesterday, Today, Tomorrow* (April 1977). This document is a special issue of *The C.K.A. Journal*.

CATHOLIC KNIGHTS OF OHIO, THE (CKO). On September 20, 1891, a number of Catholic men met in Hamilton, Ohio, eager to establish a Catholic fraternal insurance society. The founders, like the founders of many other fraternal benefit groups, were in part motivated by the idea of low-cost fraternal insurance. As the CKO got underway, the twenty-seven founders joined by paying an initiation fee of $1.00. By March 20, 1892, the society had 1,018 members who paid the $1.00 initiation fee during a special six-month offer.

The CKO was one of the early adopters of the resrve system in fraternal insurance. In 1894 it made the reserve system more secure by placing it in the hands of five reserve-fund commissioners. Initially, the reserve funds were kept in the local branches. Today the CKO has a reserve fund of over $6,500,000. In 1918 the society entered the field of juvenile insurance, enrolling individuals under sixteen years of age. In 1920 the organization voted to admit women to full membership. The first women's branch was established at St. Vitus Church, Cleveland, Ohio.

During the Great Depression in the 1930s the society's membership and its insurance in force dropped rather sharply, yet not one claim went unpaid. The society remained relatively firm and stable during a time when many fraternal benefit groups met their Waterloo. In 1946 the society undertook a number of changes, offering a new portfolio of insurance certificates with a number of new features. The changes caused new growth and vitality.

The society supports the Catholic school system; presents fifty-year gold rosaries to qualified members; underwrites a church vocations program, which includes burses for the education of priests; and supports the Bishop's Catholic Communications Foundation. Scholarships for Catholic schools are regularly awarded. On the local branch level, activities aid the disabled, sick, and handicapped. Local branch members visit the sick and bereaved. Recreationally, the branches conduct athletic events, ranging from bowling to baseball.

Membership is open to Catholics who are sixteen or older. Each new member goes through an initiation ceremony, receiving a fraternal degree in the process. The society also has a ritualistic secondary degree ceremony, designed to motivate members to greater commitment. Complementary to the society's ritual is the slogan or motto: "Morality, Manliness and Manners." The society's symbol is the Holy Family of Nazareth. Its emblem is a circle with the wording CATHOLIC KNIGHTS OF OHIO inscribed along the border. In the center is a white shield with a Latin cross.

Currently (1979) the CKO, which has branches in Ohio and Kentucky, has 18,000 members in fifty local units. Each branch is affiliated with a Catholic parish.

In addition to the local branches the society has its supreme conventions, known as "State Councils." Headquarters are located in Lakewood, Ohio.

For further information, see the society's periodical, *Messenger*. It is published monthly. In commemoration of the order's eighty-fifth anniversary, it published *The Fullness of Fraternalism: A History of The Catholic Knights of Ohio* (1976). This document is available from the head office.

CATHOLIC KNIGHTS OF ST. GEORGE (CKSG). After the war of 1870-71 between France and Prussia (Germany), many Catholics were troubled by the *Kulturkampf* in Germany, which compelled Catholics to compromise some of their religious principles. Unhappy with what was happening in Germany, many Catholics placed faith above fatherland and emigrated to America. A good number of these German Catholics settled in the state of Pennsylvania. The individuals who in 1881 founded the "German Roman Catholic Knights of St. George" settled in the Pittsburgh area.

From its beginning, the Knights of St. George have been close to Catholic parishes. In fact, the order really grew out of the parish context. When the order was formed, it presented the constitution to the Rt. Rev. Bishop for his approval. Before the society was founded, it had received permission from the Bishop of Pittsburgh in 1880. Close ties with the church persist to the present day.

The CKSG began as a fraternal benefit society, and like other societies offering benevolence to their members, the order operated on the actuarially unsound assessment plan to collect monies that eventually were earmarked for beneficiary payments. By 1894 some future-oriented individuals in the society realized that the assessment plan was inadequate and that a better system of dues and rates had to be adopted. The new method, among other things, required members to pay according to age. The literature of the society does not clearly say, but the new system apparently was the graded assessment plan. By 1915 the society abandoned the assessment plan and adopted the "Mortuary Fund," which "placed it on a par with the life insurance companies of the day," according to the words of the CKSG.

The society has been active in a number of areas. It has helped organize the American Federation of Catholic Societies (now defunct). When the National Catholic Welfare Council was formed in Chicago, the CKSG gave a helping hand. Another group, the Catholic Central Verein, has always received generous support from the knights. The CKSG is busily engaged in other philanthropic activities. One notable project involves collecting medical supplies from local physicians and shipping them to various missions in the world. In 1923 the society opened a home (Knights of St. George) for the aged and the infirm, located on 505 acres forty miles from Pittsburgh in Wellsburg, West Virginia. Each year scholarships are awarded to high school seniors who have been beneficial members of the CKSG for at least two years. To encourage parish participation on the part of young boys the society conducts an altar boy recognition project. In 1978 the society extended the altar recognition award to include girls too. More recently the organization has enthusiastically supported the "Respect for Life" campaign by trying to inform and educate individuals not to opt for abortion. The society calls this program a "campaign of love." As a national fraternal project, the CKSG has since 1969 been operating Camp Rolling Hills for boys and girls between the ages of nine and fourteen. The purpose of this camp is to "provide outdoor camping experience for needy boys and girls in a Catholic atmosphere." Non-Catholics are eligible. The camp is located in Wellsburg, West Virginia.

In 1939 the order organized the first branch of a ladies' auxiliary. Soon other branches of the auxiliary were formed. The women support a number of projects and programs. They have a deep interest in the Knights of St. George Home, and on a regular basis they help finance the education of young men studying for the priesthood.

Currently (1979) the CKSG has 70,000 members in 300 local branches located in thirteen states. Illinois is the farthest state west for the society. As in 1967 the society had only 16,000 members in eight states, the order has experienced a phenomenal growth during the past twelve years.

Local units are known as branches, and each branch is affiliated with a Catholic parish. Regional groups are referred to as "Districts." The highest authority is the "Supreme Assembly," which meets biennially. The national headquarters are in Pittsburgh, Pennsylvania.

The reader may consult society's official monthly periodical, *Knight of St. George*, for further information. It has been published for seventy-three years. A wide variety of brochures also is available for additional information.

CATHOLIC ORDER OF FORESTERS. See Foresters, Catholic Order of.

CATHOLIC WOMEN'S FRATERNAL OF TEXAS K.J.Z.T. (KJZT). This fraternal benefit society for Slovak women was founded in 1894 and incorporated in 1927. Ever since its inception, the society has been very supportive of maintaining Czech culture and traditions, as well as giving much assistance to the Catholic Church. The latter is supported through contributions given to: the Newman Clubs at the University of Texas and Texas A & M University; the KJZT Clerical Endowment Fund for the education of priests; the Czech Christian Academy in Rome, Italy; the Texas Conference for Right to Life; parishes in Texas; and newly graduated priests. The society also helps support Radio Free Europe.

Socially and fraternally the KJZT is quite active in its monthly meetings of local lodges. The local units conduct a variety of programs, ranging from fund-raising to Christmas caroling. Youth days are held to spread fraternalism to the young members of the organization. One of the youth attractions is the annual coronation of the state KJZT queen. Still another fraternal activity is the visitation program that encourages visiting sick and disabled members.

Membership in the KJZT has increased slightly in recent years. In 1972 the society had about 24,000 members. Today (1977) it has approximately 25,000. Virtually all the members reside in Texas, the only state in which the society is licensed to sell fraternal insurance certificates.

The society has 130 local units, plus a number of "Districts." Headquarters are maintained in Austin, Texas.

This account is largely based on the report published in the *Statistics, Fraternal Benefit Societies* (1977).

CATHOLIC WORKMAN (CW). Founded in 1891 by a group of Czechs, this fraternal benefit society is one of many Catholic fraternal insurance orders operating in the United States. Since its formation, the society has absorbed two fraternal benefit groups. In 1930 the Western Bohemian Catholic Union joined hands with its fellow Czechs in the CW, and in 1937 the Daughters of Columbus also merged with the society.

The society offers the usual fraternal insurance plans available in most fraternal benefit organizations. A number of programs are regularly sponsored on the local level in order to involve junior and senior members, as well as the entire families of members. The society also supports various community projects such as the Girl Scouts, Boy Scouts, Red Cross, and other worthy community endeavors.

As a Catholic organization, the CW consistently supports a variety of parish functions, takes part in church retreats, encourages its members to visit the sick, assists needy families in the community, offers daily religious Masses for the members, and helps support students studying theology. Contributions are regularly made to Catholic educational institutions.

Membership is open only to practicing Catholics. Present (1979) membership is just over 18,000 members. This figure is down slightly from the roster of 1965, when the society had approximately 19,000 members.

Three levels of organizational functions operate in the CW, the local, regional, and national. Presently (1978) the society has 124 local units and twelve state groups. The national convention meets every four years. New Prague, Minnesota, serves as the site of the society's headquarters.

For further background information, see the society's monthly publication, *Catholic Workman*. In addition to the monthly periodical, the reader may consult the society's constitution and publicity brochures. The author knows of no published history on the CW.

CHALDEANS, MODERN ORDER OF (MOC). This fraternal benefit organization was founded in Brownsburg, Indiana, in 1888. The society was almost exclusively comprised of the working class. The order appears to have gone out of existence in the early 1900s. Headquarters were located in Brownsburg, Indiana. REFERENCE: *DSOS*.

CHOSEN FRIENDS, INDEPENDENT ORDER OF. When a schism occurred in the Order of Chosen Friends in 1897, this group was organized in California. The California-based society was one of several schisms that the Order of Chosen Friends* suffered throughout its twenty-one-year history. The new society functioned for only a few years. REFERENCE: *DSOS*.

CHOSEN FRIENDS, ORDER OF (OCF). On May 28, 1879, at Indianapolis, Indiana, this fraternal benefit saw the light of day. The OCF provided benefit payments for the members' sickness, death, and accident. In addition to providing financial benefits, the order also sought to unite its members fraternally, socially, and morally.

The origin of the OCF was prompted by some individuals believing that an organization ought to exist that would pay disability or old-age benefits. The OCF was the first fraternal society to give full membership to women. A good number of the founders were members of the Odd Fellows* and Freemasons.*

True to fraternal custom, the OCF had a ritual shrouded in secrecy. T. G. Beharrell (a Methodist clergyman, an Odd Fellow, and a Freemason) was a key figure in formulating the order's ritual. The society's emblem consisted of a chain of seven links, fraternal hands clasped, and a representation of the Good Samaritan.

As noted in the introduction to the present volume, fraternal societies were not immune to conflict and schisms. In this regard the OCF was a schism-stricken group. Five fraternal orders split off from the OCF. In 1881 in the state of New York, the Order of United Friends arose because of conflict over the insurance practices of the OCF. The next year in 1882 the Chosen Friends in California became an independent jurisdiction. In 1889 the third offshoot occurred when the United Friends of Michigan was created. Two years later (1891) the Canadian Order of Chosen Friends was born in Ontario, Canada. Finally, in order to accommodate German members, the United League of America was established in Chicago, Illinois, in 1895.

The OCF had more than 12,000 members before its schisms occurred. In spite of its conflicts, however, the order more than recovered its membership loss by 1899, when it had 32,255 members. After 1899 trouble of a different kind struck the OCF. Newspapers reported that the society was in financial difficulty, and this news set the order back so that it never recovered. It has been extinct since the early 1900s.

While the order existed, it called its local units "Councils." State groups were referred to as "Grand Councils," and the national structure was known as the "Supreme Council."

For further informaton, see Albert C. Stevens, *Cyclopedia of Fraternities* (1907). This account was drawn in part from Stevens' volume.

CLANSMEN, AMERICAN ORDER OF. Founded in 1923, this group was organized in 1915 as a "nationwide, patriotic, social, and benevolent secret society." One of its primary purposes was to unite all loyal white Americans. In 1919 it was reorganized as a fraternal benefit society. The reorganized group also took only white English-speaking candidates into its membership. The society used to participate in public and patriotic events, complementing its emphasis on Americanism. The headquarters were in San Francisco, California. REFERENCE: *Cyc. Frat.*

CLOVER LEAVES, FRATERNAL ORDER OF. This society was founded and incorporated in Missouri in 1911 as a fraternal beneficiary order. The society sort of limped along for many years. In fact, by 1923 it still had only 600 members and three local lodges. Apparently the order did not survive beyond the 1920s. REFERENCE: *DSOS*.

COLUMBIAN LEAGUE. This was another of the many fraternal benefit societies formed as the result of an organizational secession. Some members of the Ancient Order of United Workmen were convinced that given changes were required to keep the order prosperous. When their suggestions were not heeded, a number of the members founded the Columbian League in 1896 in Detroit, Michigan. The society's name was chosen in honor of Christopher Columbus, and every year on October 12 a celebration was held by the members. Only white men were eligible for membership. The step-rate assessment system was used to collect insurance funds. The society apparently disbanded in the early 1900s. Home offices were in Detroit, Michigan. REFERENCE: *DSOS*.

COLUMBIAN SQUIRES (CS). The Knights of Columbus (KC)* convention in 1922 went on record as saying it needed to enter the field of boys' work. A committee was formed to report to the 1923 convention in Montreal, Quebec. At the 1925 convention of the Knights of Columbus, held at Duluth, Minnesota, the Columbian Squires fraternity was officially launched when the KC initiated thirty-seven boys, handpicked by the Reverend Barnabas, chief architect of the Columbian Squires. The Duluth group became known as "Circle #1."

Over the fifty-four years of the Squires' history, the society has grown and prospered. It has developed spiritual, civic-cultural, social, athletic, and welfare service programs. In its spiritual program the order has fostered increased devotion to the rosary by publicizing the slogan: "Pray the rosary every day." It has also campaigned to "Keep the Christ in Christmas." On the civic-cultural level the CS conducts tours to historic or governmental sites and sponsors career nights. For its social program the CS takes trips to amusement or state parks and sponsors community parties and dances. Athletically, the society promotes physical fitness and organized team sports. Its service projects focus on fighting abortion, assisting the elderly, aiding parish priests, helping the mentally retarded, promoting motorcycle safety, and giving Red Cross first aid courses.

Regarding membership eligibility, the constitution requires the applicant to be a "practical Catholic who has passed his twelfth birthday but not his eighteenth. . . ." Membership is not limited to any racial or ethnic group. As of 1979 the society had 18,000 members in 900 local circles in Canada, Mexico, Puerto Rico, the Philippines, and the United States. In 1967 the order had about 22,000 Squires. Thus a decrease of 18 percent has occurred in the membership roster over the last twelve years.

The society has a ritual containing an initiation ceremony that every new member must go through. An initiation fee is also assessed of each new member. Along with the ritual, the society values the symbolism of its emblem, which is in the shape of a circle. On the face of the circle is an eight-cornered Maltese cross. The left arm of the cross displays the letter "I," which stands for intellectual development. The letter "C" on the right arm symbolized civic development. The "S" on the upper arm represents spiritual development, and the "P" on the lower arm indicates physical development. From the upper to the lower arm of the cross, the emblem portrays a large "S," which stands for squiredom and service. The upper half of the large "S" forms the letter "C," which is to remind every member that it stands for Christ, the Squires' model. At the very center of the cross is the letter "K," which is intended to remind every Squire that the Knights of Columbus founded their order. On the upper portion of the emblem's circle is the word *Esto*, and on the bottom portion appears the word *Dignus*.

Administratively, the order is under the supervision of the Knights of Columbus. Local units are known as "Circles." Any subordinate council or fourth degree assembly of the Knights of Columbus may organize a circle for the CS. Every circle must have the following officers: Father Prior, Chief Squire, Deputy Chief Squire, Notary, Bursar, Marshall, Sentry, and three auditors. Regional groups in the United States are called "State Circles." The highest authority is the Supreme Council, whose headquarters are in New Haven, Connecticut.

For additional information the reader may wish to consult the *Squires Newsletter*, published monthly. It provides detailed information about the society's activities. An informative historical article, "Columbian Squires . . . 50 Years of Building Leadership," appeared in a special golden anniversary booklet.

CONCORDIA MUTUAL LIFE ASSOCIATION (CMLA). This fraternal benefit group was formed in 1908 to provide life insurance for Lutherans. Presently (1979) the society is licensed to sell insurance in eleven states. Its membership stands at about 25,000 members. Headquarters are housed in Chicago, Illinois.

CONTINENTAL FRATERNAL UNION, ORDER OF THE. Like so many other fraternal organizatons founded by members of the Ancient Order of United Workmen,* Odd Fellows,* Knights of Honor,* and Freemasonry,* the Order of the Continental Fraternal Union was also organized by members of these societies. The date of origin was 1890 in Richmond, Indiana. The society paid sick and death benefits. Its emblem was a shield portraying the fraternal-clasped hands, surrounded by a wreath of oak leaves. The emblem also displayed the word Union above the letters U.H.F. The society apparently dissolved sometime between 1900 and 1910. Home offices were in Richmond, Indiana. REFERENCES: *Cyc. Frat.*; *DSOS*.

CORKS, YE ANCIENT ORDER OF (YAOC). The order claims some connection with the Jolly Corks, an order founded on February 16, 1868, and today known as the Benevolent Protective Order of Elks.* The connection to the forerunners of the Elks, however, is difficult to confirm. The YAOC was really founded in 1933 when it became the fourteenth and final degree of the Allied Masonic Degrees of the United States.* The society draws its members exclusively from the Royal Arch Masons (seventh degree in the York Rite*). In conformity with the order's name, the order meets in "Cellars" instead of lodges. REFERENCE: *Cyc. Frat.*

COURT OF HONOR (COH). Organized in Springfield, Illinois, in 1895, this fraternal benefit society levied its first assessment on March 1, 1896. The COH grew quickly. By 1898 it had more than 24,000 members, and by 1920 it had over 75,000 benefit members and 2,300 social members. During its prosperous days the society had a rather elaborate ritual, complete with prayers and other religious elements. In the early 1920s the order changed its name to Court of Honor Life Association, and in 1924 it incorporated as Springfield Life Insurance. In 1934 it merged with Abraham Lincoln Life, and in 1935 it was reinsured with Illinois Bankers Life. Headquarters were housed in Springfield, Illinois.

COWBOY RANGERS, NATIONAL ORDER OF. Incorporated in Wyoming in 1914, this fraternal benefit organization paid sick, accident, and funeral benefits. In addition to paying fraternal benefits, the society sought to emulate the true characteristics of the "Great West" by exemplifying the spirit of the men who pioneered the western United States. The society admitted cowboys, ranchmen, businessmen, laborers, professional men, and men from all honorable walks of life. A ritual was part of the society's organizational makeup. The national structure was called "Supreme Ranch" and was located in Denver, Colorado. REFERENCE: *DSOS*.

CROATIAN CATHOLIC UNION OF THE UNITED STATES OF AMERICA (CCU). Founded in 1921 by a small group of Croatians, the society exists to provide fraternal insurance to its members. As a Catholic organization, the society is a devout supporter of the Catholic Church's mission. Every year the society contributes financial assistance to Catholic institutions, theological students, and charities operated by the church.

Other activities sponsored by the CCU range from sports events to patriotic projects. Scholarships are awarded annually to juvenile members upon their graduation from grade school. Works of mercy are extended to fellow members who are ailing or hospitalized. Financial aid is extended to disaster victims in need.

Membership can be attained only by being a Croatian or married to someone of Croatian descent. Prospective members are also required to be a member of the Roman or Greek Catholic Church. The membership since 1965 has remained relatively stable. In 1965 there were 13,772 members, and in 1978 there were still about the same amount with about 13,500 members.

The CCU has 119 local units, with members in sixteen states and Canada. The national convention meets quadrennially. Headquarters are located in Hobart, Indiana.

To gain further understanding concerning the CCU, see the society's weekly publication, *Nasa Nasa*.

CROATIAN FRATERNAL UNION OF AMERICA (CFUA). When this society was first founded in 1894, it was known as the National Croatian Society of the United States of America. In 1924 the name was changed to Croatian Fraternal Union of America, its present name. The society was organized to help Croatian immigrants become socialized to the American way of life and to maintain a fund for the infirm and aid the families of deceased members. In 1925 the CFUA absorbed the Croatian League of Illinois, and in 1939 the Slovanic Croatian Union was absorbed.

The CFUA, as a fraternal benefit insurance group, sponsors educational, cultural, and athletic programs by directly providing subsidies to the local lodges. The society operates what it calls the "Junior Tamburitza Groups." These groups engage in cultural, ethnic dances. Once each year the children of the Croatian members gather for a tamburitza festival in some large city of the United States. The festivals feature Croatian songs and Croatian folk dances.

Benevolence, other than the society's insurance, is directed toward maintaining aid for the aged and providing scholarships for members who seek higher education. Hospitals and nursing homes in the areas of some local lodges have on occasion received assistance from the CFUA to purchase medical equipment.

Membership is open to males and females who are of Croatian descent. Non-Croatians married to Croatian spouses also may join. As with most fraternal benefit societies, juvenile memberships are also part of the society's roster. The CFUA had about 100,000 members in 1979, compared to 110,000 in the late 1960s. This is a loss of 9 percent in about ten years' time.

The society still has a fair amount of fraternal lodgelike terminology in its organizational makeup. Male members are referred to as "brothers" and female members as "sisters."

The insignia of the CFUA is a ring with an inner circle forming a black circular border, which bears the words Croatian Fraternal Union of America. In the center of the ring is a shield with a checkered design. Upon the shield stands an eagle with outstretched wings.

The society has over 1,000 local lodges in twenty-six states and several Canadian provinces. National headquarters are located in Pittsburgh, Pennsylvania.

A weekly newspaper, *Zajednicar*, is published as the official organ of the society. No published history exists. A small booklet, *Charter of the Croatian Fraternal Union*, provides a few historical gleanings from 1894 to 1957.

CROATIAN LEAGUE OF ILLINOIS. See Croatian Fraternal Union of America.

CZECH CATHOLIC UNION (CCU). The roots of this society go back to 1867, when St. Ann Society No. 1 was formed as an altar and rosary society. Later in 1871 St. Ludnila Society No. 2 was organized. Both groups were formed in St. Wenceslaus Parish in Cleveland, Ohio. In 1879 these two groups "merged" to form the Czech Roman Catholic Central Union of Women. Like many other benevolent groups of that time, the new order provided death benefits to the spouse and children of the deceased. Upon the death of a member 25 cents was contributed by each member of the society, providing a benefit of $100.00, initially. In 1938 the society's name was changed to Czech Catholic Union. Today (1979) the CCU is a legal reserve fraternal benefit society.

Although the CCU seeks to foster love and honor for the traditions of the old country, it strives to instill in its members a strong sense of patriotism for the United States. The society prides itself on teaching its members to respect established authority and advancing democratic values. The order also sees itself as a strong supporter of the Catholic Church.

During World War II the CCU purchased a bomber; and its local groups in Cleveland, Ohio, bought an ambulance, which was donated to the Red Cross. Many of the members assisted the Red Cross during World War II. Donations have been made to Catholic colleges and seminaries. Other charitable contributions are continuing to be made, for example, to combat cancer, cerebral palsy, kidney ailments, and heart problems.

The headquarters are in Cleveland, Ohio, where the order is incorporated. In 1979 there were 9,800 members in eight states, most of them in the Midwest. This membership count represents a 3,000-member increase since 1967, when the society had 6,600 members. The CCU meets in convention every four years.

For further information see the society's quarterly publication, *Posel*. It provides news, for the most part, but occasionally historical information about the CCU also appears. No other publications seem to be available.

CZECHOSLOVAK SOCIETY OF AMERICA (CSA). This fraternal benefit society is virtually the oldest ethnic fraternal group in existence in the United States. It was founded in 1854 in St. Louis as the Bohemian Slavonian Union to provide financial assistance and fraternal fellowship for Czech Americans. Today the society, under the present name, is a prosperous fraternal life insurance entity, operating on the legal reserve system rather than on the old assessment method that once was employed by almost every fraternal benefit group.

The CSA is more ritual-minded than are many other fraternal benefit societies. The organization not only requires an initiation ceremony but also still operates ritual or degree teams. The latter put on "meaningful and inspiring exhibitions" at lodge meetings and public functions. The ritual also accents the society's motto: "Equality - Harmony - Fraternity." As is true in most fraternal groups that have a ritual, the CSA furnishes each lodge room with an altar, upon which lie the constitution and bylaws of the order. A member who wishes to enter a lodge meeting in session must give "three light knocks upon the door. These are symbolic of the motto of our Society 'Equality - Harmony - Fraternity.' " Following the three knocks, the sentry asks for the annual password, and then checks with the vice-president before the tardy member is admitted.

The official emblem of the CSA is a white five-pointed star superimposed on a blue circular background. Next to the blue background is a red circular band, which bears the words A Fraternal Benefit Society, Founded 1854. In the center of the star are the letters CSA in blue.

Membership is open to those from eighteen to sixty-five years of age. Each new member must be initiated by either the short or the full initiatory ritual. The 1979 constitution no longer states that members have to be of Czech ancestry. In 1967 the CSA had about 52,000 members, and in 1979 it had about 50,000. In 1977 the society absorbed the Unity of Czech Ladies and Men. Previously the Society of Taborites had been absorbed in 1933.

The CSA helps support the Bohemian Home for the Aged, a school for retarded children, the Chicago Lung Association, the St. Jude's Children's Research Hospital, the American Red Cross, the Heart Research Foundation, the Cancer Research Foundation, the Muscular Dystrophy Association, firemen's and policemen's benevolent associations, and a number of other humanitarian projects. Local lodges sponsor fraternal and social programs for members.

Three organizational divisions make up the CSA. Local groups are called "Lodges," regional structures are referred to as "District Councils," and the national and highest authority is the quadrennial convention. Between conventions, business on the national level is executed by a board of directors and an executive staff. National headquarters are situated in Berwyn, Illinois.

Additional information can be gained by reading the *CSA Journal*, which is published monthly. The February 1979 issue printed the new constitution. *A Story of Growth*, a small booklet, gives a good outline of the development of the CSA.

__ *D* __

DAMES OF MALTA (DOM). In terms of legend this order likes to trace its origin back to the eleventh century, when in Jerusalem there existed the Hospitalers of St. John, dedicated to charity, hospitality, and devotion. When the order was first founded in the United States, in 1896, it went by the name of the Ladies of Malta. In 1902, however, a merger took place with the Daughters of Malta, and a new name was chosen for the consolidated group, Dames of Malta. A brochure issued by the DOM says that the order is an auxiliary to the Ancient and Illustrious Order Knights of Malta.

In order to join the DOM the individuals "must be white female Protestants, over sixteen years of age, competent to pursue some useful occupation; a believer in the doctrines of the Holy Trinity as expressed in the Apostles' Creed." The membership requirements also state that a prospective member must be "A true Protestant, not married to a Roman Catholic, physically able to give the unwritten work [password and ritual] correctly, able to read, write and speak the English language." A male may be admitted only if he is "a Red Cross Knight in good standing in the Commandery to which he belongs." The membership in 1978 was slightly over 5,000 members. In the 1920s the society once had 28,000 members.

Because of the society's relatively small membership, it does not have an extensive program directed toward charity. It does, however, select one charity project each year. In 1978 it chose to contribute about $3,000 to the National Heart Fund.

Of its ritual, which is held to be highly secret, the society says it is based on the marvelous history of the order's "glorious past, the deep religious significance of its institution and the fact that it is the only Knightly Order having one Universal Passwork [*sic*] that admits to all Council Chambers around the Globe. . . ." The order, given its unqualified belief in its ritual, once said that "It is destined to play an important part in the history of America's progress. . . ." This statement is still found in a brochure that was sent to the author in August of 1978.

The insignia of the order consists of two circles, a smaller ring inside a larger one. Inside the smaller circle is a Maltese cross, which has superimposed on it a shield bearing the Latin cross. Below the cross and shield are the letters K.H.S.J.J. These stand for Knights Hospitalers of St. John of Jerusalem. Above the cross and shield appears the word ZENODACIA, which is a chief governing body of the order. Between the smaller and larger circles appears the inscription: DAMES OF MALTA—JERUSALEM 1099—AMERICA 1896.

Organizationally, the DOM calls its local units "Commanderies." The chief governing structure is the Zenodacia, which in turn is under the jurisdiction of the Supreme Commandery of the Ancient and Illustrious Order Knights of Malta, the male group. The Zenodacia meets annually. Headquarters are situated in Pittsburgh, Pennsylvania.

For further information the reader has to rely on brochures issued by the DOM. He may also consult the society's periodical, *Malta Chat*, which appears three times per year. The annual proceedings provide another source for additional background.

DANISH BROTHERHOOD IN AMERICA, THE (DBA). The 1870s brought thousands of Danish immigrants to the United States. Living in various parts of their new country, the Danish immigrants soon found it necessary to come together to refresh their memories of their previous homeland. Various groups were formed. One Mark Hansen, a former Danish soldier, in 1881 organized the Danish Arms Brothers and in the same year the Omaha branch, named Lodge No. 1. Soon other Danish lodges were organized in Iowa, Illinois, and Wisconsin. In January of 1882 these midwestern lodges met in convention in Omaha, Nebraska. It was at this convention that the name The Danish Brotherhood in America was chosen to unite the several lodges in existence. At the convention a constitution was formulated, along with the selection of a new board of directors.

Virtually from its inception, the DBA assumed the posture of a fraternal benefit society. By 1889 the organization had established an assurance capital of $1,100, with a membership of 883 members. In the typical fashion of fraternal benefit functions, the DBA paid sick and death benefits to the survivors of deceased members. The society operated on the assessment plan in its early years of existence. The order also took a strong interest in perpetuating memories and traditions from Denmark for the benefit of future generations. Unlike many other fraternal benefit societies, the DBA makes no claims to being a secret society.

Over the years the DBA grew and increased its programs. Today it offers camp grants that provide aid to the physical and mental growth of Danish-American young people. Scholarships are awarded to eligible members on a four-year basis. This program began in 1960. Of course, the society provides a variety of fraternal insurance benefits.

Membership in the DBA is open to individuals who are of Danish descent or married to someone of Danish background. There are approximately

10,000 members in the society today. The society's membership has fluctuated from time to time. In the mid-1960s it had a slightly larger membership than it has currently in 1979.

The DBA, like most fraternal benefit organizations, has a juvenile membership department, the Young Vikings. In addition to obtaining insurance benefits, the Young Vikings have available to them a number of activities, one being a trip to a summer jamboree, attained by competition and contests.

The emblem of the DBA is a shield portraying an anchor. Below the anchor appears the inscription, "Since 1882."

Local units are called "Lodges" by the society. As of 1979 there were 150 lodges in the DBA. Regional groups are known as "Districts." The national convention acts as the supreme or highest authority. It meets every four years. The head offices of the society are headquartered in Omaha, Nebraska.

For further information, see the society's monthly periodical, *American Dane*. In addition to the monthly magazine, the reader may gather further information by consulting the society's constitution and its brochures and pamphlets.

DANISH SISTERHOOD, THE (TDS). Two years after the Danish Brotherhood was organized in 1881, Mrs. Christine Hemmingsen formed the Danish Sisterhood on December 15, 1883, in Negaunce, Michigan. When the Danish Brotherhood came into being, women were permitted to join the men as social members. Apparently this arrangement was not good enough for the women, who created their own fraternal group. The order paid funeral benefits to the dependents (usually to the spouse) from the time of its inception.

The TDS grew. By 1887 the sisterhood formed a supreme lodge, and by 1910 all officers of the supreme (national) lodge were women. Men no longer were represented as officers. By 1922 the order had attained 8,000 members. During the economic depression of the 1930s the membership, as it did in virtually all fraternal societies, declined. Thus by 1934 the TDS membership dropped to 7,000. Present (1979) membership is down to 4,500.

The TDS is a fraternal group providing funeral benefits not to exceed $1,000. Under certain circumstances additional benefits may be obtained by special application. No more than two beneficiaries may be designated. The order does not sell life insurance.

The order's objectives are to promote friendship and the Danish heritage, to support their ["our"] countries, to aid fellow members, and to enable each active member to receive a funeral benefit.

Membership is open to any Danish woman by "birth, descent or heritage." If a woman is married to a man of Danish descent, she may also join the sisterhood. Admission is determined by members casting ball ballots. One black ball is enough to deny an applicant membership entry. The president of the local lodge, however, always orders a second ballot to ascertain whether the first ballot was accurate. If a black ball is present in the second vote, a selected secret committee seeks to determine the cause. All applicants for membership must be at least sixteen years of age, and upon being accepted the candidate must go through an initiation rite.

As a fraternal group the Danish Sisterhood still takes its ritual quite seriously. Every lodge meeting must follow the prescribed ritual. One or two marshalls are elected in each lodge, to be in charge of ritual ceremonies. The guard makes sure that no uninitiated members have access to the secret meetings of the lodge.

The TDS lent its services to the United States government in the 1940s by purchasing defense bonds. Also during World War II the society lent considerable assistance to the American Red Cross War Fund. The sisterhood also was quite active in making preparations for the American Bicentennial.

The emblem of the society consists of a shield displaying a heart, with the letters TDS above the heart on the upper portion of the shield. The shield is cradled in the arms of a laurel wreath.

Three divisional structures are operated by the TDS. The national organization is known as the supreme lodge. It meets in convention every four years. Regional divisions are known as "Districts." On the local level, gatherings are referred to as "Lodges." Each lodge is expected to meet twelve times per year. The Supreme Lodge headquarters are in Chicago, Illinois.

Additional information may be obtained by reading the official publication of the order, *Danish Sisterhood News*. This periodical is issued monthly. See also *Constitution and Bylaws of the Supreme Lodge of the Danish Sisterhood of America* (1976). The constitution booklet has a brief history in the appendix.

DAUGHTERS OF AMERICA (DOA). This organization cannot be understood unless one is also acquainted with the Order of United American Mechanics.* The latter is sometimes referred to as the senior order because a junior order was formed as the result of a schism.

The Order of United American Mechanics has had a ladies' auxiliary since 1870, known as the Daughters of Liberty. When, in 1891, the Junior Order of United American Mechanics also desired a Daughters of Liberty organization, it met with rejection by the senior order. This rejection led to the formation of the Daughters of America in 1891. Its first charter, granted by Allegheny County, Pennsylvania, named the new order "The National Council Daughters of America." Although the order from its inception was to be an auxiliary of the Junior Order of United American Mechanics, it did not receive official recognition from the male order until 1926.

The DOA lists eight objectives. These pertain to (1) Promoting and maintaining American interests by shielding the country from unrestricted immigration. (2) Helping Americans find employment. (3) Encouraging American businesses. (4) Providing support for the American public school system and to uphold Bible reading in the schools. (5) Opposing sectarian influences in state and national affairs. (6) Promoting and advancing the Junior Order of United American Mechanics. (7) Establishing funds to support orphans of deceased members of the order. (8) Establishing funds to provide for the aged and infirm members of the order.

Membership is only open to "PATRIOTIC, WHITE MALE AND FEMALE CITIZENS OF GOOD MORAL CHARACTER, WHO BELIEVE IN A SUPREME BEING AS THE CREATOR AND PRESERVER [sic] of the Universe and who favor upholding the American Public School System and the reading of the Holy Bible in the schools thereof, must be opposed to the union of the Church and State; must be literate and capable of giving all the secret signs and words of the Order, or of explaining them if unable to give them by reason of some physical misfortune or defect" (from a recent pamphlet of the order). When the order was founded, it required its members to be at least sixteen years of age. Today (1979) it accepts members who are fourteen or older. Its present (1979) membership stands at approximately 19,000 members. In 1930 the DOA had over 160,000 members in thirty-three states. Today it is found only in twenty-eight states, with less than one-fifth of its 1930 membership.

As is partially indicated by the official membership qualification statement, the order is still very serious concerning its secret ritual. Like most fraternal groups, the DOA sees its ritual as beautiful and morally meaningful. To guard its secret sessions the order has a sentinel who guards the door so that nonmembers do not enter. The order also is firm about not discussing its business outside its council rooms, as its local chapters are known.

The emblem of the DOA consists of the American eagle, which upholds a blue flaglike banner decorated with white stars. Beneath the eagle and the banner is a shield bearing the inscription D of A above vertical red and white stripes. In the center of the shield is the open Bible, with two clasped hands of friendship directly beneath it.

The DOA operates a home for the elderly in Tiffin, Ohio. Members of the order desiring to live in this home may do so under one of two plans. The donating plan requires the individual to turn over all income and properties to the home. The contributing plan requires a monthly fee of $275. Any member may enter the home if she has been a member for at least fifteen years and is sixty-two or older. The order also provides financial aid toward the education of orphans under eighteen in the event of the member's death. The DOA calls this its "Helping Hand System."

Organizationally, the DOA has three levels of government: the national, state, and local. On the national level the structure is called the "National Council"; on the state it is the "State Council;" and on the local scene the order usually refers to its gatherings as "Councils." National headquarters are located in Harrisburg, Ohio.

Very little has been published on the DOA. A booklet, *A Brief History of the Daughters of America and Suggestions for Council Entertainment* (n.d.), published by the order is helpful for obtaining a quick view of the DOA. *The Proceedings of the National Council* are a good source for gaining further understanding of the DOA.

DAUGHTERS OF THE EASTERN STAR. See Eastern Star, Daughters of.

DAUGHTERS OF ISABELLA (DOI). The first origins of the society go back to May 1897 in New Haven, Connecticut, when the Reverend John Russell formed a ladies auxiliary to the Knights of Columbus.* Russell's group was the first "Circle" of the society. Its purpose at that time was "to unite all Catholic women into a fraternal order both for spiritual benefits and for the preservation and promulgation of higher ideals within society."

The DOI differs somewhat from most fraternal benefit societies in that it does not sell life insurance to its members. Instead it offers a mortuary benefit. This benefit fund is commonly maintained through the subordinate circles (local units). When a member dies, the beneficiary receives not less than $25 and not more than $100.

To become a member of the society, named in honor of the lady who was crowned Queen of Castile at twenty-three, one must be a Catholic woman between the ages of sixteen and fifty-nine. Two classes of membership are available: regular and social. The regular membership provides mortuary benefits; the social category does not. The social member, however, has all other "rights and privileges of members of the Order," according to the constitution. Women sixty or over may become social members. Girls between the years of eight and sixteen may join the society's junior circles. The current (1979) membership roster in Canada and the United States shows 113,000 members. This is a decline of about 6 percent from the membership of 1968, when the society had about 120,000 members.

The society also operates a Queen Isabella Foundation Scholarship Program. This program "grants complete graduate scholarships for the Master's Degree in Social Service [*sic*] at Catholic University of America." Eligibility for the scholarships is confined to members and their children and grandchildren.

In recent years the DOI has become quite active in supporting its Right to Life project, which it supports in conjunction with the Knights of Columbus. The DOI conducts this project by giving donors a small artificial rose to which a small American flag is attached, carrying the right-to-life message: "One rose . . . One Life." The donator is asked to append his signature to the flag and then send it on to his or her senator or representative in

Washington, D.C. Another project that occupies the Daughters is working to convince governmental officials to proclaim April 22, the birthday of Queen Isabella, a national holiday. The daughters also have lent their energies to serving and supporting civil defense centers, the Red Cross, blood banks, and so on.

The society is quite serious concerning its rituals and secrets. The ritual is intended for members only. Passwords are issued at quarterly meetings by the regent of the circle. Every candidate must undergo an initiation exercise, for which a fee is assessed. In keeping with the society's accent on secrecy, it has officers who serve as inner and outer guards of the circle meetings.

For its insignia the DOI has a crown looped over the Latin cross. The front part of the crown bears the inscription D of I.

The DOI executes its activities on three levels: local, regional, and international. Local units are known as "Subordinate Circles." The regional groups are known as "Provincial Circles" in Canada and as "State Circles" in the United States. The highest level of authority is the "International Circle." This circle is "vested with full rights to make, alter or repeal all laws, rules, or regulations for its control and management, and for the subsidiary bodies affiliated therewith, and to prescribe the forms, ceremonies and secret work of the Order." The international circle meets biennially. The headquarters are situated in New Haven, Connecticut.

Sources on the DOI are meager. The order does not publish a periodical. About the only information available to the reader are the various brochures and the *Constitution and By-Laws* (1977).

DAUGHTERS OF ISIS (DOI). This fraternal secret society is the female auxiliary to the black Shrine, formally known as the Ancient Egyptian Arabic Order of Nobles of the Shrine.* The DOI was founded on August 24, 1910.

The society has a secret initiation rite that confers the Creation degree, the only degree available. At lodge meetings the members wear white uniforms that are also worn on public parades, usually at the national conventions.

The ritual is primarily based on the legend of Isis, an Egyptian goddess. Part of the initiation oath has the candidate

promise and swear that I will not give or communicate the secrets of the order of the Daughters of Isis to any person in the known world except it be to a lawful and true Daughter of Isis. . . . I further promise and vow, with a firm and steady purpose to perform and keep the same under no less penalty than having my body severed in fourteen pieces and thrown into the river, if I violate any part of this obligation.

In order for the obligation to be complete the candidate is required to kiss the Bible three times, the Koran once, and the red stone once.

The DOI helps support a number of philanthropic projects: research in mental retardation, hypertension, and sickle-cell anemia. Selected college students who have a "C" grade-point average receive scholarships. Those with a higher average are ineligible. The society also gives financial donations to the Special Olympics.

Membership is open to black women who are related to members of Prince Hall Freemasonry.* Currently (1979) the society has 12,000 members in 184 courts. Most of the courts are located in the United States; however, the order has three courts in West Germany and one in Okinawa.

Organizationally, the DOI operates on two levels: national and local. The national structure is known as the "Imperial Court." It meets in convention annually, each year at a different site. The local unit is called "Constituent Court." The national leader is referred to as the Imperial Commanderess. "Headquarters" are usually located with the national secretary. Presently (1979) the secretary resides in Fort Wayne, Indiana.

This information was obtained by means of a personal interview with the national secretary. There appears to be no scholarly material on the order.

DAUGHTERS OF MOKANNA (DOM). Rock Island, Illinois, is where this ladies auxiliary of the Mystic Order of Veiled Prophets of the Enchanted Realm* was organized in 1919. The primary organizer of the society was Mrs. Joseph Mace. Ever since its formation, the order has seen its basic purpose as assisting the Prophets of Grotto. To this end, the order also seeks to promote a closer fellowship bond with the Grotto members.

The DOM has one degree in its ritual, the Admission degree. This degree is conferred upon the applicant, who is the wife, daughter, legally adopted daughter, granddaughter, sister, or mother of a Grotto member. Only white applicants are accepted. In the latter part of the 1960s the society had about 8,000 members.

In addition to assisting the Grottoes, the DOM also sponsors a humanitarian project, the National Humanitarian Project for the Spastic Child.

The DOM, unlike some fraternal auxiliaries, has the authority to organize and control its own affairs. Local units are called "Caldrons." The national organization is referred to as the "Supreme Caldron." It meets annually as the supreme or highest authority. The chief national officer is known as the "Supreme Mighty Chosen One." Headquarters are located wherever the national secretary, the "Supreme Rodeval," resides. Currently (1979) the supreme rodeval resides in Rochester, New York.

The present discussion was in part based on the mimeographed copy, "Allied Masonic Groups and Rites (1978)," issued by the Masonic Service Association. Another helpful source for further information is the annual convention report.

DAUGHTERS OF THE NILE, SUPREME TEMPLE (DON). The thought leading to the formation of the Daughters of the Nile originated in the home of Mrs. Mable R. Krows, Seattle, Washington. She and a number of other Shriners' wives on February 20, 1913, formed the Ladies of the Nile Club. The first local unit (temple) was named "Hatosu" in honor of an Egyptian queen. Although the order was formed in 1913, it did not become incorporated until 1949.

Men have typically played a vital role in structuring and organizing women's fraternal orders. The Daughters of the Nile is no exception. For instance, the ritual for the DON was written by Charles Faustis Whaley.

The purpose of the order is to pursue "a philosophy of living which will enable them [the members], when shadows lengthen, to look back on a life well spent." The order also assists the Shriners in their work pertaining to crippled children. The emblem of the order is a white rose.

Membership is open to wives, mothers, daughters, sisters, and widows of Shriners. Currently (1978) the order has 78,000 members, compared to the 69,000 members it had in 1966. Only white candidates are accepted into membership.

As has already been noted, local units are known as "Temples." On the national level the society refers to itself as the "Supreme Temple." It meets in convention annually.

Additional information may be obtained by consulting Harold V. B. Voorhis, *Masonic Organizations and Allied Orders and Degrees* (1952). The present discussion is indebted to this source for some of the information.

DAUGHTERS OF NORWAY. See Sons of Norway.

DAUGHTERS OF PENELOPE. See Penelope, Daughters of.

DAUGHTERS OF SCOTIA, THE ORDER OF THE (DOS). New Haven, Connecticut, is where this society was formed in 1895. The following year (1896) the order became incorporated under the laws of Connecticut. In 1899 the Grand Lodge was organized. When the DOS was first founded it had two men, along with twenty-three women, who were instrumental in fashioning the order. The men were members of the Order of Scottish Clans.* After the DOS was firmly established, the male members withdrew. The society has always been an auxiliary of the Order of Scottish Clans.

The society strongly accents Scottish culture, history, traditions, and ideals. Along with the accent on Scottish values, the order draws its members only from those who are wives, mothers, daughters, sisters, and widows of members of the Order of Scottish Clans. Also eligible for membership are women who are of Scottish descent or adopted by members of DOS or the Order of Scottish Clans. Two types of memberships are available, donation and social. The former requires women to be between sixteen and forty-five years of age and in good health. Social applicants must be over forty-five and not physically qualified to become a donation member. Social members are entitled to all privileges, except participation in the donation fund benefits.

The donation fund provides death benefits to beneficiaries of the departed member. The fund is maintained by assessing each member a nominal fee. The donation fund is not to be equated with the typical fraternal insurance certificate of most fraternal benefit societies.

The DOS has a ritual, including an initiation ceremony for new members. Every initiate is required to pay an initiation fee. Presently (1979) the society has about 17,000 members in Canada and the United States. Canadian members are "social" members only.

Local groups are known as "Clans." The national structure is called the "Grand Lodge." It meets annually in convention. Secretarial offices are maintained in Troy, Michigan.

Information about the DOS is difficult to obtain. The present discussion on the DOS was developed on the basis of brochures and leaflets.

DAUGHTERS OF SCOTLAND (DOS). This fraternal group is not to be confused with the Daughters of Scotia.* The DOS was founded in Ohio and incorporated on October 3, 1899. The society was formed to receive into membership only those of "Scottish blood."

The DOS ritual resembled that of most traditional fraternal societies. It had formulations pertaining to signs, oaths, and prayers. In fact, the society prided itself on its religious posture. The author was unable to ascertain whether the society still exists today.

DEER, IMPROVED ORDER OF. This order was formed in 1913. It had more than 500,000 members in 522 lodges in 1920, according to *Statistics, Fraternal Societies* (1921). Headquarters were located in Seattle, Washington. REFERENCE: *DSOS*.

DEGREE OF ANONA. See Anona, Degree of.

DEGREE OF HIAWATHA. See Hiawatha, Degree of.

DEGREE OF HONOR PROTECTIVE ASSOCIATION (DOHPA). The origin of this group goes back to 1873, when it had become the ladies' auxiliary of the Ancient Order of United Workmen (AOUW)* at the national convention of the AOUW, held in Cincinnati, Ohio. This convention approved an appropriate degree for daughters, mothers, and sisters of AOUW members, to be called Degree of Honor. Insurance was not a part of the Degree of Honor until 1882. In 1896 the ladies formed its Superior Lodge, and in 1910 the Degree of Honor became a separate organization, independent of the AOUW. It also placed its insurance on a legal reserve basis in 1910. In 1926 it opened a junior membership department, and soon men were also admitted as members. Its national officers, however, are all women.

The order's 1977 *Articles of Incorporation and Bylaws* state six objectives: (1) aid members and their families; (2) conduct meetings and ritualistic work; (3) receive, approve, or reject membership applications for fraternal benefits; (4) suspend members and social members for nonpayment of dues or misconduct; (5) use lodge dues to support the lodge and its members; (6) acquire, own, sell, mortgage, lease, and manage personal property to the benefit of the lodge.

Along with its insurance, the DOHPA takes its ritual quite seriously. The constitution specifies that "the Board of Directors shall supervise adherence to the prescribed ritualistic work. . . ." To inspire its members, the motto *Talitha Cumi* is used in the ritual. Both words are Aramaic, meaning "maid arise." The expression appears in the New Testament in Mark 5:41 where Jesus said: "Talitha Cumi" to a dead girl (twelve years old), and she arose and walked. One member—the grand president—once said: "By this motto we try to live our lives, doing charitable work for the needy, and extend our care and sympathy outside our own membership." The ritual also accents the watchwords of the DOHPA: constancy, honor, and purity. The ritual employs a fair amount of religious trappings. There are prayers, a hymn (Blest Be The Tie That Binds), and an altar in the center of the lodge room. A burial service also is printed in the ritual.

According to its constitution, the DOHPA no longer bars nonwhites from joining its ranks. Its membership statement reads: "Any person of good moral character and a believer in the existence of a Supreme Being, who is between the ages of sixteen (16) and sixty-five (65) years, . . ." may join. There are two classes of membership, insured and social. The latter carries no insurance. Balloting for the admission of new members is done by ball ballot. Three black balls reject the applicant. In 1979 there were 86,000 members in 390 lodges, compared to 120,000 members in 1967. This membership decline represents a loss of 28 percent over the last decade or so.

Boasting that its organization is a "family affair," the DOHPA promotes a wide variety of activities: patriotism, friendship, civic projects, social activities, adult and junior meetings, and financial security through life insurance. Yearly scholarships are provided to eligible graduating high school students.

The DOHPA insignia is a shield with a heart in the center. Diagonally across the heart are the words *Talitha Cumi*, and beneath the heart are the letters D of H. The heart is surrounded by a laurel wreath.

Structurally, the DOPHA has its national organization, which meets in convention annually. The delegates to the national convention are elected by the state convention. The local lodges select delegates for the state convention. The national headquarters are in St. Paul, Minnesota.

Reading material on the Degree of Honor Protective Association is not very abundant. Myron W. Sackett, *Early History of Fraternal Beneficiary Societies* (1914), gives some helpful information. Keith L. Yates, *A Brief History of the A.O.U.W.* (1966) also is good to read in order to gain a better understanding of the AOUW and its ladies' auxiliary, the DOHPA. The *Proceedings* furnish a good perspective of the growth and changes of the order. The *Articles of Incorporation, Bylaws* (1977) are helpful in understanding the order's structure. See also *The Degree of Honor Review*, the official bimonthly publication of the society. The society's *Ritual and Rules of Procedure* (1951) is helpful in understanding the ceremonial aspects of the DOHPA.

DEGREE OF POCAHONTAS. See Pocahontas, Degree of.

DE MOLAY, THE ORDER OF. The origin of this Masonically sponsored male youth group goes back to the time of World War I, when some astute Masons perceived the coming decline of Freemasonry that became a marked reality in the 1950s and 1960s. The name of the order was chosen in honor of Jacques de Molay, the fourteenth-century leader of the Knights Templars, who was executed (burned at the stake) in A.D. 1314 by King Philip IV of France with the help of Pope Clement V. The De Molay fraternity was organized in Kansas City, Missouri, in 1919 by Frank S. Land, a prominent Freemason. The order's objective is "the encouragement and development of good citizenship and sound character among youth."

The De Molay, the "farm club" of Masonry, has a two-degree ritual. The first ritual is the Initiatory degree, and the second is known as the De Molay degree. As part of the Initiatory degree, the candidate is blindfolded (hoodwinked) and asked a series of questions. After he has taken the obligation (vow), the hoodwink is removed before he kisses the Bible. In the first-degree ceremony the candidate witnesses seven preceptors each placing a "jewel" in the "Crown of Youth." These seven "jewels" are filial love, reverence for sacred things, courtesy, comradeship, fidelity, cleanliness, and patriotism. Each of these is explained in terms of its meaning. The De Molay degree dramatizes the trial and execution of Jacques de Molay. Near the end of the ceremony for the second degree, the candidate(s) is told: "Before . . . we will receive you into the fellowship of lasting fraternity, you must kneel at the Altar and bind yourselves to us by a final vow, taken in the light of experiences unknown to you when you first entered our Chapter Room."

The order places considerable emphasis on religious values. The ritual has a number of references to religious meanings. The memorial and funeral ceremonies also highlight given religious features. During these services, the chaplain reads Ecclesiastes 12:1-7 and offers a prayer, which in part says: "Our Father in heaven, we thank Thee for the comforting assurance of the faith implanted in our hearts, without which we would indeed sorrow as those without hope." An evergreen sprig is laid upon the altar during a memorial service. The sprig is "emblematic of the Everlasting Chapter into which our brother has entered through the opened door of death."

The order's emblem consists of a jeweled crown with a five-armed Maltese type of cross, which has ten stars surrounding a crescent at its center. Behind the crown are two crossed swords. The shielded head of a medieval knight is perched on top of the crown.

Membership in the order is attained by being a white male (fourteen to twenty-one years of age), who has a Masonic background or is a relative of a Freemason. Some also enter the order on the basis of petition signatures by two De Molay members. Once a member reaches the age of twenty-one he may no longer attend a De Molay meeting unless he becomes a Master Mason. This is one way in which the De Molay members are "encouraged" to become Freemasons. The De Molay claims that since its formation over 4,000,000 young men have been initiated into its order and that over 40,000 of these have become Protestant clergymen. The order's current (1978) membership is in the neighborhood of about 100,000.

In order for a local chapter to operate it must be sponsored and supervised by a regular Masonic group such as the Blue Lodge of the Scottish Rite* or York Rite* or a Shrine Temple.* Each local chapter has an advisory council of Master Masons, plus one advisor who usually is known as "Dad." Any Master Mason may attend the De Molay sessions.

The order has not experienced a notable amount of organizational change. At its inception it permitted only sons of Master Masons to join, but now if a young male has a Masonic relative or background, he may join the group. In 1964 the De Molay's whites-only membership was critically noted in the public presses of the United States after the Masons of Pajarito Lodge 66, A.F. & A.M. of Los Alamos, New Mexico, withdrew sponsorship of the local De Molay Chapter before the group could vote on accepting a black applicant. The group's charter was officially lifted by the state executive officer of the International Supreme Council of De Molay. The whites-only policy apparently has not yet been changed or canceled.

Organizational projects focus on anticommunism, blood donation, teenage safety, antidrug campaigns, vocational guidance programs, and oratorical contests.

The structure of the De Molay, in addition to its advisory council of Master Masons, has the following officers on the local chapter level: Master Councilor, Senior and Junior Councilors, Senior and Junior Deacons, Senior and Junior Stewards, Orator, Chaplain, Marshal, Scribe, Treasurer, Almoner, Standard Bearer, seven Preceptors, and a Sentinel. The order is headquartered in Kansas City, Missouri.

The best source of firsthand information on the De Molay is its official magazine, *De Molay Councilor*, published monthly. The Masonic periodical *The New Age* carries occasional articles on this youth order. Additional information can be obtained by consulting the proceedings of the Supreme Council, which meets annually.

DESOMS, ORDER OF (OOD). This order of deaf men is relatively new compared to most fraternal societies. It was formed in the state of Washington in 1946. The name Desoms is an acronym for deaf sons of Master Masons. The primary objective of the society is to further the spirit of Friendship among deaf men who are related to Freemasons.

The Masonic Service Association reports in its "Allied Masonic Groups and Rites" (mimeographed, 1978) that in 1961 the Desoms tried to change their order's name to the Most Worshipful Grand Lodge of Washington, Ancient Delta Guild Free and Accepted Masons of North America. This name change, however, was legally prevented by the Grand Lodge of Washington. The Washington Masons resisted the name change because the Desom society is not a bona fide Masonic group.

The ritual of the Desoms contains one degree, the Initiatory degree, which is given to all eligible members. In order to join the OOD one must be a deaf male of good moral character and be able to show that he is closely related to a Master Mason. Current membership statistics were not available to the writer.

Local groups within the order are known as "Lodges." The national unit is called "Grand Lodge." It meets once every year as the supreme body and authority.

Additional information on the Desoms is sparse. The reader will, however, obtain some helpful background by consulting Harold V. B. Voorhis, *Masonic Organizations and Allied Orders and Degrees* (1952). The Masonic Service Association's "Allied Masonic Groups and Rites" (mimeographed, 1978), also provides a brief account of the Desoms. The present discussion used both of these sources quite extensively.

DOES, BENEVOLENT AND PROTECTIVE ORDER OF THE (BPOD).
The complete official name is Benevolent and Protective Order of the Does of the United States of America. The writer was unable to determine the date and place of origin of this female society that has never received official recognition from its male counterpart, the Benevolent and Protective Order of Elks* (BPOE). Where the society operates it usually employs a ritual.

One version of the ritual bases the initiation rite on the liturgical Magnificat of Mary. Elsewhere the ritual makes reference to the thirteenth chapter of Saint Paul's first letter to the Corinthians, emphasizing love and charity. The candidate vows: "I, . . . before God and these witnesses . . . sincerely promise and vow: that I will never in speech, writing or otherwise, reveal any of the secrets of the Benevolent, Protective Order of Does of the United States of America." The oath also has the initiate pledge loyalty to her country's flag.

The writer was not able to find any membership statistics on the BPOD, nor was he able to find any helpful printed matter about the society. All that can be said is that the group exists in various localities, apparently with no real national or even state structure. Undoubtedly, the lack of official recognition from the BPOE has contributed to the all-but-unknown stance of the Does. The BPOE passed a resolution in 1907 that said: "There shall be no . . . adjuncts or auxiliaries. . . ." Evidently the Elks take that seventy-year-old resolution very seriously.

As best as can be determined, the BPOD has no national conventions, and its activities are all conducted on the local level.

DRUIDS, AMERICAN ORDER OF. Begun as a fraternal benefit society, this group was chartered on May 17, 1888, in the state of Massachusetts. The order admitted men and women. The society dissolved in the early 1900s. Headquarters were in Fall River, Massachusetts.

DRUIDS, UNITED ANCIENT ORDER OF (UAOD). The origin of this fraternal order goes back to London, England, in 1781. The society was transported to the United States in 1830, and in 1839 the first lodge, named George Washington Lodge No. 1, was established in New York City.

The history of the Druids is a maze of legends and myths. Some accounts trace the origin of this group to ancient Gaul, some only to England, and still others think the priestly group originated in the Orient. Most observers believe that the Druids were priests who lived in forests and caves while serving as religious teachers. Some of their teachings held to the transmigration of the soul. Reportedly it was a custom among the Druids to have an annual human sacrifice, and usually a criminal was used. But very little is known about these rites because of the high degree of secrecy that this group has always practiced. However, it is known that the mistletoe had a high standing and that oak groves were favorite retreat sites. The circle was the symbol of the supreme being. It is also known that the Druids were expert mechanics. Cromlechs and dolmens (specially fashioned stones of great size) were used in their secret rites.

The UAOD ritual was based on the history and legend of the Druids of old. Lodge rooms had altars (designed after the cromlech or dolmen), which had three stones resting upon one another or one large stone with an opening through it. The lodges in which these altars were placed were called "Groves." Some of the rites and ceremonies revealed Masonic influences. For instance, all members had to hold three degrees.

The UAOD sought to provide mutual protection, foster fraternalism, relieve the sick and destitute, and protect widows and orphans of its departed members. Only white males who were eighteen or older, in good health, and of good character were eligible for membership in the society. Ladies could become members in the auxiliaries called "Circles." These circles also had male members.

For some years the UAOD grew. For example, in 1896 it had 17,000 members. By 1923, according to *Statistics, Fraternal Societies* the membership stood at 35,000. The order began to decline, however, in the 1930s. Today it no longer appears to exist.

For further information, see various accounts of the Druids in well-known encyclopedias. See also Albert C. Stevens, *Cyclopedia of Fraternities* (1907).

_E_

EAGLES, FRATERNAL ORDER OF (FOE). Back in 1898 in Seattle, Washington, a small group of theater owners met to form a fun organization. They called it the "Seattle Order of Good Things." A few years after its inception, the order chose the eagle as its symbol, calling itself the Fraternal Order of Eagles.

In time, the fun orientation of the FOE became less pronounced, and the society shifted its emphasis to fraternal service. The order, however, still has fun too. It has drill teams and bands and in some localities participates in public parades with a motorcycle contingent. The fun spirit also manifests itself in the numerous Eagle clubs, where bowling, billiards, and beer are available.

One of the Eagles' publications expresses the change in the following words: "In line with modern needs and up-to-date procedures, the colorful regalia trappings of yesterday are no longer. Gone, too, is the secret password, the roughhouse initiation." Still another Eagle publication says: "The emphasis has shifted from solely recreation to a more balanced program of fun and fraternal activities of wide scope. The accent now is no longer on secrecy but rather on service."

The change in the Eagles' objectives from fun to more of a service posture also showed itself in the order's offering its members life insurance. In 1927, however, it was decided not to sell regular life insurance any longer, but rather to make available sick and funeral benefits for those who desired to pay somewhat higher membership fees. As a result, the FOE has two categories of memberships, beneficial and nonbeneficial.

The service orientation of the FOE has not been confined to its own members. In 1941 the order donated funds for the construction of a dormitory at Boys Town, Omaha, Nebraska. A few years after the Boys Town contribution, the society built Eagle Hall at Home on the Range for Boys, Sentinel Butte, North Dakota. High Girls Ranch near Midland, Texas, has also received a dormitory from the FOE. With the establishment of the Eagles' Memorial Foundation in 1946, the order has regularly given financial assistance to various medical research projects. In recent years the FOE has joined the environmental ecologists by lending strong support to the efforts to protect the bald eagle from extinction. It has also lent its influence to save the golden eagles as well.

Ever since Franklin D. Roosevelt's New Deal, the FOE has been actively engaged in promoting social legislation. The order has furthered the cause of workmen's compensation, mother's pensions, old-age pensions, and the Social Security system. Currently (1980) the society is contending for citizens to be able to work beyond age sixty-five. It is also trying to get the federal authorities to return the Social Security system to its original purpose, and to secure the integrity of the Old Age and Survivors Trust Fund. An article in the January 1979 issue of the order's bimonthly periodical, *Eagle*, clearly showed the Eagles' sentiments relative to senior citizens. The article was entitled: "Freedom from Want for Senior Citizens."

Late in 1959 the FOE began building a retirement home for elderly Eagle members. Located in Bradenton, Florida, the home is part of Eagle Village, where other facilities are available to the senior citizens. More recently the Eagles have embarked on their "Hometown, U.S.A." program, which seeks to make hometowns better places to live. The "Home and Family" program, also a recent undertaking, is designed to preserve and strengthen the American family.

Regarding membership eligibility, the FOE requires an applicant to believe in a supreme being, be twenty-one years of age, possess a good character, not be a Communist, and be a Caucasian. While the written requirements in recent years do not formally bar nonwhites from joining the Eagles, the society has not really welcomed them. Like most fraternal secret societies, the FOE employs the ball-ballot system. This system makes it difficult for a nonwhite applicant to gain admittance. Prejudiced members can easily cast blackballs as the voting on new membership applications takes place. Thus while in theory a fraternal group does not bar nonwhites, in practice the blackball method may keep the society all-white for a long time.

The *Milwaukee Journal* recently (May 26, 1979) reported that the Eagles in Milwaukee were attempting to have a federal lawsuit dismissed that alleged the FOE was violating the 1964 Civil Rights Act by not allowing blacks to use the athletic facilities of the order. The newspaper article noted that an Eagle official could cite only Joe Louis as a black who held membership in the FOE.

Although the FOE membership is predominantly composed of blue-collar men, it has attracted some high-status individuals. Presidents Theodore Roosevelt, Warren Harding, Franklin D. Roosevelt, Harry S. Truman, and John F. Kennedy were members of the FOE. Other renowned individuals like Earl Warren, J. Edgar Hoover, Father Flanagan, Stan Musial, and Jack Dempsey have also brought honor to the order by their membership in the fraternity. More recently, the FOE has been proud to claim President Jimmy Carter and Vice-President Walter Mondale as members. The present membership roster has about 800,000 members. This figure has remained relatively constant over the past decade.

All members are required to go through an initiation rite. Part of the ritual has the candidate say: "Before God, and on my honor, I promise that I will never make known to anyone the rituals of this Order, except to Eagles in good standing, and then only if I am authorized to do so." Willful violation of the candidate's pledge is reason for expulsion from the organization. The ritual is interspersed with religious phrases. Prayers, for example, are usually spoken by the aerie chaplain. The lodge room is furnished with an altar and Bible.

The structure of the FOE is similar to that of most fraternal orders. Local units are known as "Aeries." The order has fifty state groups. The national structure is known as the "Grand Aerie." It meets in annual conventions. Columbus, Ohio, serves as the order's headquarters.

For information, see the society's monthly publication, *Eagle*. The *Eagle Digest*, a weekly, is also helpful. If the reader desires, he may also consult the annual proceedings. Another brief but interesting source is an article praising the FOE that appeared in the *Congressional Record*, February 3, 1977. The article is entitled "Word Portrait." An older source is Conrad H.

EASTERN STAR, ORDER OF / 97

Mann, *Much About the Fraternal Order of Eagles* (1921). This work provides a good historical background.

EASTERN STAR, DAUGHTERS OF THE (DOES). This order for young women (ages fourteen to twenty) whose fathers and mothers were members of the Order of the Eastern Star* was organized in October 15, 1925, in the state of New York. The society was sponsored by the grand Chapter of the Eastern Star in New York. As far as can be determined, the DOES never had any chapters outside of New York. It appears that the order no longer exists. The objective of the DOES was to influence young girls to become ideal American women. Although not specifically stated, the Eastern Star members also hoped to see many of the "daughters" join the Eastern Star when they reached adulthood.

The DOES had three degrees: Initiatory, Honorary Majority, and Public. The Honorary degree was automatically given to members when they reached age twenty-one. The ritual pertaining to the degrees was secret.

Local groups were called "Triangles." Each triangle had an advisory council that met once each year. There was no national or supreme body, as commonly found among fraternal groups.

For additional information, see Harold V. B. Voorhis, *Masonic Organizations and Allied Orders and Degrees* (1952).

EASTERN STAR, ORDER OF (OES). Although Masonically linked, this female group is not Freemasonry.* It is commonly known as belonging to Freemasonry's "Rite of Adoption." There is some ambiguity regarding the origin of the OES. Some believe that the order was in existence as early as 1793 and that it was engaged in benevolent work during the War of 1812. While there seems to have been an organization known as the Ancient and Honorable Order of the Eastern Star at least as early as 1793, the present OES really has a more recent date of origin.

The individual responsible for founding the OES was Robert Morris, a schoolteacher and a poet. His first attempt to create a Masonic order for women failed. Fellow Masons accused him of betraying Masonic secrets in his effort to write a degree ritual for women. Determined, however, to share the teachings of Masonry with the entire family and not leave them to the men only, Morris, while confined to bed in 1850, again undertook the task of writing a ritual that he hoped would become an Adoptive Rite of Freemasonry.

During the late 1850s and early 1860s, Morris was active in communicating degrees and appointing cooperative Master Masons to confer degrees on others, particularly on female relatives of Masons. Around 1857 Morris organized groups he called Families of the Eastern Star. By 1866 Morris's work was taken over by Robert Macoy, a Mason who managed his own publishing house. Macoy revised Morris's ritual, adding some degrees in the process: Queen of the South, Past Matron's Degree, and the Amaranth Degree. In 1876 the General Grand Chapter of the Eastern Star was organized in Indianapolis, Indiana. The latter date is the one officially recognized by the OES today.

Unlike the Masonic initiation rites, the OES ritual does not require the candidate to be hoodwinked, cable-towed, or disrobed. Instead she is asked to remove her gloves, hat, and wrap. After this a thin veil is placed over her head and face. Then she is led to the chapter room, where she is instructed and asked to take the "obligation" (vow), which pertains to secrecy, loyalty, and other behavior. In comparison to the Masonic oaths, the obligations taken by the OES candidate are mild. No reference is made to corporeal punishment in the event a violation should occur. The candidate agrees to ". . . maintain with vigilance the absolute secrecy to which I now assent, promising never to reveal unlawfully any of the ceremonies, signs, or passes of the Order of the Eastern Star." The vow is taken by the candidate holding an open Bible against her breast, as she kneels before an altar. The obligation is administered by the Worthy Patron, a Master Mason.

The OES ritual consists of five degrees, based on the stories of five women in the Bible. The five degrees are symbolically derived from the order's five-pointed star. The first degree (or the star's first point) symbolizes obedience to the vows made in the initiation rite. Adah, Jephthah's daughter, is used to illustrate the quality of obedience. The second degree signifies devotion to religious values, and Ruth of the Old Testament serves as the model to be emulated. Fidelity is the third degree's meaning, exemplified by Esther. Faith in the power and merits of a Redeemer underlies the fourth degree, and Martha, whose brother Lazarus was raised from the dead by Jesus, personifies this degree's qualities. The fifth degree, tied to the star's fifth point, teaches charity, whose feminine model is Electa. The latter name is derived from the opening statement, "The elder to the elect lady . . ." in the Apostle John's second New Testament epistle. To underscore the importance of the family and its roles, Adah reminds the OES members of the daughter role: Ruth, the widow; Esther, the wife; Martha, the sister; Electa, the mother. All five degrees are worked in one ceremony.

Like so many other fraternal orders, the OES has a funeral ceremony for its departed "sisters." The ceremony includes religious music, Bible readings, and a eulogy. Part of the funeral rite reads: "To you my sisters and my Brothers . . . our dear Sister . . . has just stepped through the heavenly portals into that larger and more beautiful life that awaits us in that city not made with hands. . . . We have but to keep the faith and, 'beyond the smiling and weeping' we, too, shall join the loved ones gone before."

The emblem of the OES is the five-pointed star with a pentagon in the star's center. The pentagon in turn has an altar with an open Bible in its center. Within the borders of the pentagon are the letters F.A.T.A.L. These letters stand for a Cabalistic message: "Fairest Among Thousands, Altogether Lovely." Moreover, juxtaposing these five letters spells FATAL, which is intended to remind each initiate that "it would be fatal to the character of any lady" were she to divulge OES secrets (see F. A. Bell, *Order of the Eastern Star*, 1956). The slogan of the order is "We have seen His star in the East, and are come to worship Him."

From its beginning, the OES has been an organization directed by Freemasonry. Not only were its rituals written and revised by Masons, but Masonry has always kept a watchful eye on the order by having one of its members serve as a patron in each OES subordinate chapter. The sisters are reminded of the influence and rules of Masonry by hearing the Worthy Matron read the following words at the conclusion of the five-degree instructions: "We are not a part of the Masonic institution. . . . Women cannot be made Masons. This is a rule that has been handed down with other rules of Masonry for thousands of years. . . . Therefore, Masons cannot invite us to visit their lodges."

Membership in the OES is open to Master Masons, their wives, daughters, legally adopted daughters, mothers, widows, sisters, half-sisters, granddaughters, stepmothers, and stepsisters. All members are Caucasian. The order has primarily attracted Protestants to its ranks, although Jews and non-Christians are eligible for membership. Its present (1978) membership stands at about 3,000,000.

In the realm of philanthropy, the OES operates a number of homes for its members, as well as orphanages and hospitals. Most of these charitable institutions serve the order and its relatives.

Structurally, the OES has three governing bodies. The General Grand Chapter operates on the national and international level and includes chapters in every American state except two, plus Germany, Japan, the Netherlands, Cuba, Mexico, the West Indies, and the Philippines. The two states not under the General Grand Chapter are governed jointly by the Independent Grand Chapter of New York and New Jersey. The OES also exists in Scotland, England, South Africa, South Wales, Canada, New Zealand, and Australia. On the state level, the structure is known as the Grand Chapter. Locally, it is the Subordinate Chapter. Five subordinate chapters may unite to form a grand chapter, if none exists in a given state. Each subordinate chapter has the following officers: Worthy Matron, Worthy Patron, Associate Matron, Secretary, Treasurer, Conductress, and Associate Conductress. These are usually elected. Appointed officers are Chaplain, Marshall, Organist, Adah, Ruth, Esther, Martha, Electa, Warden, and Sentinel. They are appointed by the Worthy Matron. On the general grand level essentially the same array of officers exists. Their titles, however, have a more honorific sound: The Most Worthy Grand Matron, Right Worthy

Associate Grand Matron, Most Worthy Grand Patron, and the like. The General Grand Chapter's head offices are located in Washington, D.C.

Helpful literature on the OES may be found in F. A. Bell, *Order of the Eastern Star* (1956); Robert Morris, *Light and Shadows of Freemasonry* (1852); and Sarah H. Terry, *Brief History of the Order of the Eastern Star* (1976). The proceedings of the society also provide useful information for the interested reader.

EASTERN STAR, PRINCE HALL GRAND CHAPTER OF THE (PHES). Black men who are desirous of belonging to a Masonic lodge may join Prince Hall Masonry.* This society in many ways resembles white Free-masonry* in terms of rituals and symbols. Black women, who are relatives of black Masons, may join the female group known as the Prince Hall Grand Chapter of the Order of the Eastern Star, an organization that is quite similar to the white Order of the Eastern Star (OES).*

While the white OES has a national structure in addition to the state (grand) groups, the PHES is only organized on the state level. The national structure that exists consists exclusively of past grand matrons. This latter group held its thirty-third annual convention in 1979.

Similar to the white OES, the PHES has a ritual that encompasses the symbolism of the five points (degrees) of the order's symbol, the star, into one initiation ceremony. The ritual, as in the white OES, is permeated with religious references and meanings. The five-pointed star, for example, portrays an altar with the open Bible on its top.

Like the white OES, the PHES has male members. In fact, each local lodge is required to have a worthy patron as a male officer, along with the several female officers. However, unlike the white OES, the PHES has a racially mixed membership. Whites may join if they are married to black PHES members. Consequently, it should be noted that the number of white members is quite small. Presently (1980) the total PHES membership stands at about 175,000.

Each grand (state) organization has fraternal projects. The jurisdiction of Indiana, for instance, operates a home for its infirm members. Prince Hall Masons also are served by this facility. In recent years the PHES has given nurses scholarships. The order also sponsors the "Queen" of the grand chapter and the "Miss Prince Hall" contests.

Additional information can be obtained by consulting the annual proceedings of the various grand (state) lodges. Some helpful references can also be found in some of the literature pertaining to Prince Hall Masonry.

ELKS, BENEVOLENT AND PROTECTIVE ORDER OF (BPOE) [U.S.A.]. The Elks began as a fellowship of fun-loving, merrymaking singers and actors, who first met in an alehouse in New York City on November 15,

1867. These merrymakers called themselves "Jolly Corks," a name derived from the "cork trick" that Charles Algernon Sidney Vivian, a recent immigrant from London, England, introduced to his fellow entertainers. The cork trick consisted of the Jolly Corks (usually a small group sitting at a table in the ale house) asking a newcomer to join them. If he agreed, he would pay a fee of 50 cents. Then everyone would produce a cork and place it on the table. The newcomer (or victim) of the trick also was given a cork. He was told that when the Imperial Cork counted to three, the last man to lift his cork had to buy the drinks. At the count of three all members would shoot out their hands and slap their palms down over the cork. The newcomer would, however, triumphantly raise his cork on high. The others laughed and then would explain that they do not raise their corks. Since their corks were never raised, the newcomer's action was not only the first but also the last. Embarrassed, the victim had to pay for all the drinks. However, his embarrassment soon subsided among his newly found friends. Moreover, he looked forward to playing the cork trick on some other unsuspecting victim. Every Jolly Cork had to carry a cork with him at all times. Failure to do so meant having to buy a round of drinks.

Charles Vivian soon became the official leader of the loosely organized, fun-loving Corks. The group grew. The members enjoyed themselves. Yet, there was one major obstacle, namely, New York's newly (1866) enacted law outlawing drinking in saloons on Sundays. Strict enforcement of the law by the city police superintendent led Vivian to organize a genuine social club that required every member to pay for refreshments. These were purchased and stored on Saturdays and consumed on Sundays in a private location.

On February 16, 1868, the Corks resolved to become a benevolent order. A committee was appointed to select a name and draft a constitution. Vivian, who was a member of the British Antediluvian Order of Buffaloes, preferred the name "Buffaloes." Other suggestions included "Bears," "Beavers," and "Foxes." The name "Elks" was finally chosen after the committee toured Barnum's Museum on Broadway. Aside from its grace and beauty, the elk was appealing because it attacked no other species but would fight when attacked. (Some evidence exists that the Corks had erroneously identified a moose head as that of an elk.)

The first constitution, adopted in March 1868, contained fifteen articles and bylaws. The preamble stated that the order was formed to "promote, protect and enhance the welfare and happiness" of its members. The preamble to the 1977 constitution reflects somewhat broader objectives: "To inculcate the principles of Charity, Justice, Brotherly Love, and Fidelity; to promote the welfare and enhance the happiness of its members; to quicken the spirit of American patriotism; to cultivate good fellowship; to perpetuate itself as a fraternal organization and to provide for its government. . . ." The Elks' constitution has been revised from time to time. For instance, from 1868 to 1890 two degrees were required for regular membership, but since 1890 only one degree has been required. Some stipulations have not changed, however. For example, since 1868 negative votes (blackballs) continue to bar a candidate from membership.

The years 1868 to 1905 were filled with many organizational changes, as the Elks broadened their appeal and membership beyond the entertainment world. The ritual, which at first revealed strong Masonic influences, was considerably modified and simplified. To quote Fehrenbach, an Elks historian: "The apron went in 1895. The 'secret password' expired in 1899. The badge and grip died natural deaths in 1902 and 1904 respectively. The test oath and a few other extraneous things disappeared and the Elks began to be themselves and look less like a cross between the Masons and a college fraternity." Some say that the Elks' success in continuing to attract new members while other fraternal groups are declining is due in part to their modification of the ritual and other organizational changes that other fraternal orders have been reluctant to undertake.

Like other fraternal groups, the Elks consistently have supported traditional American values, conducting national bond drives, promoting civil defense programs, and assisting in Flag Day observances. During World War II, they helped recruit personnel for the Army Air Corps and designated the week of March 15, 1942, as "Win the War Week." Later (1949-1950) an Elks National Service Commission was established, and in 1961 the grand lodge convention in Miami issued "A Declaration of American Principles."

The Elks sometimes speak about the order's "spreading antlers of protection" with reference to its charity contributions. Like most fraternal societies, the Elks have their own benefit programs, primarily to aid those who are members. In Bedford, Virginia, the BPOE supports its Elks National Home for elderly members. But the order does not confine its charity budget to taking care of its own. Ever since 1871 (three years after its origin) the Elks have provided assistance to needy and unfortunate individuals. It has helped victims of the Chicago fire, given to flood relief, contributed to the work of the Red Cross, aided Scout work, supported hospitalized veterans, and provided scholarships. According to the Elks' own records, over $8,000,000 was given in 1966-1967 for charitable expenses. The Elks no longer sell insurance to members. The order discontinued this type of benevolence in 1907.

Beginning in the late 1960s, however, the Elks found themselves in conflict with one prominent American value, civil rights. From its inception, the order, like most others, barred nonwhites from membership. Black American males had to join a black Elks society, the Improved Benevolent Protective Order of Elks* (IBPOE). During the early 1970s, state and federal courts ruled that the BPOE was illegally barring nonwhites from its club and leisure activities; this conflict was aired repeatedly in the public press.

Bowing to pressure, the 1976 grand lodge convention lifted the restriction against blacks, nevertheless, a proviso was adopted to reinstate the white requirement if again permitted by law. The whites-only clause was officially and reluctantly removed at the grand lodge session of 1976. A number of litigations also preceded the change. In nearly all instances the exclusion of nonwhites was made public after given individuals sought entrance to some Elks' club that usually offered dining and beverage facilities. Many clubs are located on beautiful estates where golfing also is available, but only members of the Elks (and an occasional guest) may use the premises.

In the formal debates preceding the removal of the all-white membership requirement, one member on the floor of the grand lodge session said in 1972: "It cannot be said, I think, that there is any Lodge in the country where there are not at least three members who would blackball any non-white put up. . . ." If this statement is an accurate assessment of all Elks' lodges, then the removal of the all-white clause may have little or no effect, and the Elks may have de facto racial discrimination.

A prospective Elk must be male, twenty-one years of age, and of sound body and mind. He must believe in God, be a citizen of the United States, and not be a member of the Communist Party.

The Elks also have been involved in interorganizational conflict with at least one other fraternal group. In 1912 the Benevolent and Protective Order of Elks (BPOE) brought legal suit against the organization of black Elks, The Improved Benevolent and Protective Order of Elks of the World (IBPOE). The suit sought to have the black Elks drop the use of the name "Benevolent and Protective Order of Elks."

Women are not able to become Elks, nor does the BPOE have an official organization for women. However, several unofficial women's groups have tried to append themselves to the BPOE. One such organization was The Lady Elks. Others are The Benevolent and Protective Order of Does* and the Supreme Emblem Club of the United States of America.*

The BPOE has grown more than any other fraternal group, increasing annually in recent years while most fraternal groups in North America have been declining. Between 1966 and 1976, for example, membership increased by 225,000 to 1,611,139. Currently (1978) there are over 2,200 subordinate lodges in fifty states. This growth compares very favorably, for example, with American Freemasonry, which lost over 400,000 members during the same period.

While the Elks ritual purports not to be secret, its contents are not made public indiscriminately. Religious principles permeate the ritual. Each meeting of the subordinate lodge takes place in the presence of an altar. The Esquire places a Bible on the altar as part of the opening ceremony, and a chaplain leads the "brethren" in prayers and psalms. The funeral ritual also consists of prayers. Belief in God is a membership prerequisite that dates back to 1892 when the words "belief in a Supreme Being" were inserted into the Elks' constitution; in 1946 the word "God" was substituted for "Supreme Being."

The initiation rite and oath are couched in moralistic and religious terminology. The candidate vows "in the presence of God" to accept a "solemn and binding obligation" never to "reveal any of the confidential matters of this Order which have been, or may hereafter be, committed to my charge and keeping." He promises also to uphold the Constitution of the United States, to protect brother Elks and their families, to support only worthy candidates for BPOE membership, and never to introduce political or sectarian elements into the order. Should the oath be broken, the candidate calls upon himself the pain of wandering "through the world forsaken . . . pointed out as bereft of decency and manhood, unfit to hold communion with true and upright men." No one becomes a legitimate member without going through the initiation rite. So-called social memberships are not permitted by the order's constitution. The initiation fee ordinarily is $25.00.

Fraternity is sought by Elks in addressing one another as "brother." It also is expressed symbolically in the order's emblem, an elk head superimposed on the face of a clock with its hands pointing to eleven o'clock. This is a visible reminder of the "Eleven O'Clock Toast," which reads in part: "Wherever an Elk may roam, whatever his lot in life may be, when this hour falls upon the dial of night the great heart of Elkdom swells and throbs. . . . Living or dead, an Elk is never forgotten, never forsaken." The society also has a funeral ritual for burying its dead members, a rite known as the "Lodge of Sorrow."

The BPOE operates on national (grand), state, and local (lodge) levels. National headquarters are located in Chicago, near Lake Michigan, housed in a large, beautiful building dedicated in July 1926. The rotunda displays murals and statues symbolizing the "four cardinal virtues" of the Elks: charity, justice, brotherly love, and fidelity. Its frieze depicts the "Triumphs of War" on one side and the "Triumphs of Peace" on the other. Large bronze elks flank the entrance.

Most of the titles of the national or grand Elks officers are high-sounding and exotic, as is true of many fraternal groups. These are the Grand Exalted Ruler (the chief officer), the Grand Esteemed Leading Knight, the Grand Esteemed Loyal Knight, the Grand Esteemed Lecturing Knight, the Grand Secretary, the Grand Treasurer, the Grand Tiler, the Grand Inner Guard, and the Grand Trustees. All are elected by the grand lodge at its annual national convention. The three Knights assist the Grand Exalted Ruler and officiate in his absence. The Esteemed Loyal Knight also acts as prosecutor in cases where an Elk is accused of an offense contrary to the order. The Grand Secretary, though elected annually like other officers, is usually reelected repeatedly and thus provides organizational continuity between the annual grand lodge sessions (conventions). The Grand Treasurer administers financial transactions. The Grand Tiler is in charge of regalia and jewels; he also sees that no one attends sessions without an admission card. The Grand Esquire (appointed by the Grand Exalted Ruler) organizes the grand lodge sessions by requiring officers to assume their proper stations and serves as marshall of Elk parades often held at convention time. The Grand Inner Guard is essentially a doorkeeper, allowing no "eavesdroppers" to enter. The Grand Chaplain (an appointed position) is in charge of devotional exercises. The Grand Trustees have general authority over funds and property owned by the grand lodge. The grand lodge, which meets annually, utilizes a number of standing committees; prominent among them are those concerned with Americanism, elections, credentials, judiciary, publications, youth activities, and ritual.

On the state level, the order calls its organizational structures "State Associations." State officers consist of president, vice-president, secretary, and treasurer. On the local scene, the BPOE refers to its assembly as the "Subordinate Lodge." Most local officers bear the same titles as those of the grand lodge, except that the designation "Grand" is omitted. Likewise, the committee structure closely resembles that of the grand lodge. Subordinate lodges may establish leisure clubs (offering dining and recreational opportunities) for members bearing the name or emblem of the order.

Notable national individuals have held (and still hold) membership in the BPOE. The order is proud to list Franklin D. Roosevelt, Harry S. Truman, John F. Kennedy, Barry Goldwater, Richard Daley, and others too numerous to mention here.

Primary sources on the BPOE are less difficult to obtain than for some other fraternal groups. The reader may consult the *Constitution and Statutes, 1977-1978*, published by the Benevolent and Protective Order of Elks. Earlier constitutions are also helpful. The annual *Proceedings* of the grand lodge sessions provide excellent information on the changes that have occurred in Elkdom. See also T. R. Fehrenbach, *Elkdom U.S.A.* (BPOE, 1967), and James R. Nicholson and Lee A. Donaldson, *History of the Order of Elks, 1867-1967* (BPOE, 1969). *The Ritual of the Subordinate Lodges, Benevolent and Protective Order of Elks* (1963) is not readily available. The order also publishes *The Elks Magazine*, which is largely devoted to publishing news within the fraternity.

ELKS, THE BENEVOLENT AND PROTECTIVE ORDER OF, OF CANADA (BPOEC).

This fraternal secret society arose largely as a result of the "excellent reputation enjoyed by the American Order. . . ." Thus on September 12, 1912, the BPOEC was founded in Vancouver, British Columbia. The first local unit (lodge) was called Vancouver Lodge No. 1.

One of the organizers of the Canadian Elks hailed from Seattle, Wash-

ington. The greatest tribute, however, for really making the early days of
the BPOEC a success goes to Charles Edward Redeker, a former resident of
Philadelphia, Pennsylvania, who made his home in Vancouver. Redeker
became the first Grand Exalted Ruler of the BPOEC when it formed its
grand lodge structure. In 1913 Redeker was successful in obtaining a federal
charter for the order by a special Act of Parliament. The charter stated that
the BPOEC was organized for "Benevolent, provident, moral and charitable
purposes." It further said that the Canadian Elks would pursue "social
intercourse, mutual helpfulness and mental and moral improvement, and
rational recreations, but such purposes shall not include sickness, funeral,
accident or disability benefits, or any other form of insurance."

The BPOEC requires every member to "swear that he will honor and
respect the flag under which he lives." As part of the initiation ceremony,
the candidate for membership is told: "you are now to learn the sublime
mysteries of the Order. Charity, Justice, Brotherly Love and Fidelity are
the cardinal principles of Elkdom." The blindfolded candidate pledges
himself to secrecy and that he will live up to the teachings of the society.
Among other things, he vows never to "violate the chastity of the mother,
sister, wife or daughter of a Brother Elk, and this vow shall keep them as
sacred to me as my own mother." As a final promise, he pledges to follow
the oath "without any mental reservation. . . ." After the vow is completed
the lodge chaplain offers a prayer. The paraphernalia found in a lodge
room commonly are an altar, Bible, flag, clock, ballot boxes, emblems of
officers, a replica of the elk's head, hoodwinks, rituals, and skull.

Many of the customs and practices of the BPOEC are similar to those of
the BPOE* in the United States. The Canadian Elks, however, appear to
be somewhat more elaborate with their ritual, especially during initiation
rites. The names of officers in most instances are the same as those of the
American Elks. One notable exception exists when one compares the
Canadian Elks with the American counterpart. The BPOEC officially
recognizes a ladies' auxiliary, the Order of the Royal Purple.* The American
Elks do not recognize any of the several women's organizations that seek
to function as auxiliaries to the BPOE.

Membership is open to "Any male person who has been a resident of
Canada for at least six months immediately preceding the date of his application; of sound mind and body; of good reputation; a believer in the
Supreme Being. . . ." He must also be twenty-one years of age. In special
instances a candidate may join at age eighteen. Apparently the BPOEC has
never concerned itself with limiting its membership to whites only, as has
the BPOE in the United States. Currently (1979) the BPOEC has about
300,000 members.

Local units are known as "Subordinate Lodges." Provincial structures
are called "Districts." The national organization is referred to as the "Grand

Lodge." The grand lodge headquarters are housed in Regina, Saskatchewan.

Additional information may be found by consulting the *Constitution and Bylaws of the Benevolent and Protective Order of Elks of Canada.* The society's ritual also is helpful in gaining a more comprehensive view of the BPOEC. The proceedings of the grand lodge provide a glimpse of the order's business and activities on the national level. See also *How "The Elks" Began in Canada* (1960). The latter is a small pamphlet-like booklet issued by the BPOEC.

ELKS, DAUGHTERS OF INDEPENDENT, BENEVOLENT, PROTEC-TIVE ORDER OF, OF THE WORLD (DIBPE). For a number of years prior to the order's founding in 1902 in Norfolk, Virginia, Emma V. Kelley saw the need to form a black female fraternity. Mrs. Kelley felt a fraternal society would help alleviate the suffering of black people. The first public meeting of the DIBPE occurred in July 1903 in St. John African Methodist Episcopal Church, with forty women participating.

On September 9, 1903, the Improved Benevolent and Protective Order of Elks* helped organize the "Grand Temple" of the DIBPE. The grand temple functions as the national structure. At this meeting the order received its first constitution and bylaws, as well as its ritual. In 1907 a juvenile department was formed.

The DIBPE is officially recognized by its male counterpart, the Improved Benevolent and Protective Order of Elks. The white women's groups that seek to function as auxiliaries to the Benevolent and Protective Order of Elks (white) operate without any official male recognition. The DIBPE espouses the principles of charity, justice, and sisterly and brotherly love. The spirit of patriotism is also supported strongly. These principles, according to the order, are based on I Corinthians 13. The society is best known for its Department of Education, which for fifty years has contributed more than two million dollars in scholarships to youth of all races. In addition to its educational efforts, the DIBPE has striven for racial justice and in the last two decades greatly aided the civil rights movement in the United States.

The membership, together with that of the IBPOE, currently (1979) stands at 450,000. "Temples" (local units) are established in the United States, Canada, Mexico, Cuba, the West Indies, the Virgin Islands, and Panama. The supreme structure is known as the "Grand Temple." Headquarters are located in Winton, North Carolina.

ELKS, IMPROVED BENEVOLENT AND PROTECTIVE ORDER OF (IBPOEW). Officially, the society is known as the Improved Benevolent and Protective Order of Elks of the World. This fraternal secret organization of black Americans prides itself on being "built on the shoulders of the first formal black society, The Free African Society," which was founded by Absolom Jones and Richard Allen in Philadelphia, Pennsylvania, in 1787.

As a separate organization, the IBPOEW came into being in Cincinnati, Ohio, in February of 1897. The founders were Arthur J. Riggs (a Pullman porter) and B. F. Howard. The former resided in Covington, Kentucky, and the latter in Cincinnati, Ohio. The order began with the objectives of "the expression of ideals, services and leadership in the black struggle for freedom and opportunity." In September of 1898 the order's ritual was copyrighted by the Register of Copyrights of the Library of Congress, Washington, D.C.

The society is proud to recall that at its 1926 national convention it formed its Civil Liberties Department. Eleven years later one of the Civil Liberties Department reported to the grand lodge session: "The Civil Liberties Department is spearheading in many instances movements which would give to the negroes of America rights which had been denied them. . . ." In 1927 the Civil Liberties Department, through its representative members, fought against the racial segregation of high schools in Gary, Indiana.

In 1912 the IBPOEW was taken to court by the white Elks (the Benevolent and Protective Order of Elks*) in the state of New York. The white Elks sought to prevent their black counterpart from using the name Elks. The judge ruled in favor of the white Elks. He said: "If its members desire the name of an animal, there is a long list of beasts, birds, and fishes which have not yet been appropriated for such a purpose" (see *Northeastern Reporter*, 1912). Apparently the ruling of the judge in New York had very little effect because the black Elks are still known today by the same name as in 1912.

As noted, the IBPOEW has had a ritual since 1898. Along with employing a ritual, the society has its members clad in full, colorful regalia on certain occasions. As best as can be determined, the black Elks have not abbreviated their ritual over the years, while the white Elks did.

Membership in the IBPOEW stands at approximately 450,000. Officers bear names similar to those of the white Elks. For instance, the head officer of the national ("Grand Lodge") structure is known as the Grand Exalted Ruler, the same title given to the head of the Benevolent and Protective Order of Elks.

The society meets annually in its grand lodge session. Headquarters currently are in Winton, North Carolina.

Most of the present report was drawn from mimeographed materials that the writer obtained from officials of the order. The writer is unaware of any scholarly publication in existence pertaining to the IBPOEW.

ELKS MUTUAL BENEFIT ASSOCIATION (EMBA). Most members of the Benevolent and Protective Order of Elks (BPOE) probably have never heard that their society once sponsored an insurance operation. Records seem to indicate that the EMBA was founded in 1878. By the 1885 grand lodge session (national convention) it was noted that the insurance branch was prospering. However, it was also at this session that a committee reported that the EMBA conducted its financial affairs in a careless manner. After this report several more grand lodge sessions reviewed the advisability of having an insurance entity as part of the BPOE. Thus by 1907 the grand lodge convention ruled: "There shall be no branches or degrees of membership in the Order, nor any insurance or mutual features, nor shall there be other adjuncts or auxiliaries. . . ." This, of course, ended the existence of the EMBA.

Additional information may be found by consulting back issues of the Elks' proceedings. A brief account of the EMBA may also be found in James R. Nicholson and Lee A. Donaldson, *History of the Order of Elks* (1969).

EMBLEM CLUB OF THE UNITED STATES OF AMERICA, SUPREME (SEC). Back in 1917, while the United States was fighting World War I, a small group of women who were wives of men belonging to the Benevolent Protective Order of Elks* (BPOE) met regularly to wrap bandages to be sent to wounded soldiers in the war. These meetings not only provided the women an opportunity to help their country, but also served as a convenient vehicle of social fellowship. In time these women in Rhode Island called their group the Emblem Club, and by April 26, 1926, they had their organization incorporated in the state of Rhode Island.

In its articles of incorporation the Emblem Club stated that one of its primary objectives "was to unite under one head, all existing and future Clubs commonly known as Elks' Ladies Clubs, Committees or groups." The order also seeks to "promote sociability among the members of Elks' families, share community welfare work . . . assist with social affairs . . . promote better understanding and further the ideals and purposes for which each organization was established." Questions of politics or religion are not permitted for discussion in the society's club meetings.

The SEC is engaged in a number of activities embracing patriotism and community service. Similar to its male counterpart (the BPOE), the SEC has adopted a formal program promoting Americanism. Each year one week in June is set aside as "Americanism Week." There are other projects as well. Scholarships are granted to sons and daughters of the society's members. Since 1964, a national disaster fund has been set up. This fund was prompted by the Alaskan earthquake in 1964. In a number of localities the club members are quite active in community services. Together with the Elks, the ladies help support the Elks National Home in Bedford, Virginia.

Although the SEC is not an auxiliary of the Elks, their influence has not been lacking. For instance, the SEC ritual was written by officers of the grand lodge of the BPOE. Briefly, the ritual "consists of a non-denominational prayer, a salute to the Flag of the U.S. of A., and recitation of the officers' duties. It is a short, and beautiful effective part of the Regular and Special meetings." As is true of most rituals, the SEC ritual contains the initiation pledge that the candidate is required to give. The ritual is not considered to be secret; however, it is not really public either.

The insignia of the Emblem Club consists of two circles, a smaller and a larger one. In the confines of the smaller circle is the head of an elk, surrounded by laurellike leaves. Between the larger and smaller rings appears the name of the society: SUPREME EMBLEM CLUB of the UNITED STATES of AMERICA. Below the elk's head are the three watchwords of the SEC: Justice, Truth, Charity. The official colors are purple and gold.

Membership can be attained only by wives, mothers, sisters, daughters, stepdaughters, and widows of an Elk member. The minimum age is eighteen. The 1979 membership roster had 40,000 members in 500 affiliated clubs. This membership count was approximately the same as a decade ago. Thus while the Elks have been growing in membership, their lady counterparts have basically been only holding their own.

Local units are known as "Emblem Clubs." In eleven states the clubs have formed "State Associations." This is the same name that the BPOE gives its state groups. The national structure is the "Supreme Emblem Club." It presently (1979) operates through the Supreme Executive Secretary in Rutherford, New Jersey.

The interested reader will not find much published material on the SEC. A few brochures are available, plus the society's periodical, *Emblem Topics*, which is issued ten times annually.

EQUITABLE AID UNION OF AMERICA. Formed in Columbus, Pennsylvania, in 1879, this fraternal benefit group was primarily founded by Freemasons. As a secret fraternal group, it provided insurance up to $3,000. The assessment plan was employed. Membership requirements permitted both men and women to join its "Unions" (local lodges). The society had 30,000 members in 1896, but the next year it went into receivership. REFERENCE: *Cyc. Frat.*

EQUITABLE FRATERNAL UNION. See Equitable Reserve Association.

EQUITABLE RESERVE ASSOCIATION (ERA). In August of 1897 in Neenah, Wisconsin, nine men formed the Equitable Fraternal Union. A few years later in 1902 another group of men founded the Fraternal Reserve Association in Oshkosh, Wisconsin. In 1930 these two organizations merged to form the present Equitable Reserve Association. Following this merger, two other fraternal benefit societies joined the ERA. In 1949 the Germania Mutual Life Assurance of Wisconsin merged with the ERA, and in 1970 the Royal League* of Berwyn, Illinois, was absorbed by the ERA.

The society has two types of memberships, social and beneficiary. Only the latter carries insurance. Individuals must be sixteen or older to join the ERA. Both men and women are eligible. The 1979 membership count for the society stood at approximately 45,000.

The society offers the usual array of fraternal insurance certificates to its members that most fraternal benefit groups provide. It also awards scholarships to eligible members attending college. Socially, the society sponsors softball, junior league baseball, and children's Christmas parties. These activities are usually conducted through the local units of the society.

The society still has a ritual, which is printed in what is called "Official Guide Book." The ritual specifies that ballotting for new members is done by ball ballot. Black balls reject, and white ones elect. Each year in October members are given a new password. During a ritual ceremony there is an Inner and Outer Guard on duty. The emblem of the society is a ring with a triangle inside. Encircling the triangle are the words Equitable Reserve Association, and on each side of the triangle is one of the letters E.R.A., respectively. The society's motto is "Not For Self But For Each Other."

Local units are known as "Assemblies." The national or supreme structure is called "General Assembly." It meets in convention quadrennially. Main offices are located in Neenah, Wisconsin.

Additional information may be found by consulting the society's monthly periodical, *Equitable Reserve Guide*. The reader may also see the society's *Laws of the Equitable Reserve Association* (1978). The ritual is also a helpful information piece.

EQUITY, ORDER OF. Founded in Indianapolis, Indiana, the order began in 1889 as a fraternal benefit society. The ritual of the order revolved about the parable of the Good Samaritan and the healing of th lepers by Jesus. In 1897 the order went into receivership. REFERENCE: *Cyc. Frat.*

F

FEDERATION LIFE INSURANCE OF AMERICA (FLIA). When this fraternal order was first formed in 1911 in Milwaukee, Wisconsin, it was known as the Federation of Polish Catholic Laymen. The group began in 1911 as a strong laymen's movement, expressing loyal Polish sentiments. Some of the lay concerns were that Poles should have the right to have Polish bishops, the right to have better schools, and the right to elect Catholic laymen to manage and control parish funds and that the wealth of rich and poor parishes should be shared. Fraternal insurance did not really become part of the society until 1913, when the federation was legally incorporated in Wisconsin.

Soon after its incorporation the society changed its name slightly to Federation of Poles in America. Then in 1924 the society by a special referendum changed its name again, this time to Federation Life Insurance of America, the society's present name. In 1940 the federation established a women's division.

Like most fraternal benefit societies, the FLIA promotes community and civic projects as well as its own internal programs. During World War II the society sent food and clothing to Poland and to Polish refugees in other countries. Since the war the society has been providing aid to the Ochronka Orphanage in Poland. The Red Cross has also received assistance from the FLIA. Along the cultural line, the organization has been supporting the International Folk Fair, an annual attraction in the city of Milwaukee.

The emblem of the FLIA is a shield that portrays the Polish white eagle. The shield is flanked by the American flag on the left and the Polish flag on the right. The letters F.L.I.A. are mounted on the shield's top.

Membership in the FLIA has remained quite stable. In 1960 the society had 5,500 members, and in 1979 the count stood at 5,543. Poles or Polish descendants are eligible to join the federation.

Local units are called "Lodges." There are twenty-eight lodges in seven states. The national convention meets every four years. Headquarters are maintained in Milwaukee, Wisconsin.

Additional information may be obtained by reading the society's *A Brief History of Federation Life Insurance of America, 1913-1976*. The organization also publishes a quarterly newsletter, *The Voice.*

FEDERATION OF MASONS OF THE WORLD (FMW). The preamble of this federation reads: "We the members of the Federation of Masons of the World, Inc. of differing jurisdictions in order to promote a more perfect unity, to foster our domestic welfare, to establish justice, to provide for common defense, do for ourselves, our lodges and our jurisdictions establish this Federation of Masons of the World, Inc." The federation was formed in 1957 in Detroit, Michigan. The FMW has four basic objectives: (1) To recognize all established jurisdictions of Freemasonry,* regardless of how the jurisdictions originated. (2) To promote charity within and without Masonry. (3) To "cement bonds of brotherly love and friendship" of all Freemasons. (4) To help Masons "present a common united front."

According to O. H. Elliott, the executive secretary of the FMW, the current (1979) membership is about 300,000, plus 103 grand lodges, representing the United States and thirty-two foreign countries. The emblem of the FMW consists of an outer and an inner circle. Between these circles are the words: Federation of Masons of the World, 1957. In the center of the inner ring is the all-seeing eye, with an open book (presumably the Bible) directly beneath it. On the face of the open book is the Masonic square and compass. Two hands clasped in fellowship are immediately below the book. The words "stability, union, strength" partly surround the open book symbol.

The federation meets in convention annually in different countries. It elects officers such as president, vice-president, and secretary. Presently the head office is situated in Austin, Texas.

There are no known publications on the FMW. The present report is based on contacts made with the FMW office.

FIRST CATHOLIC SLOVAK LADIES ASSOCIATION (FCSLA). The writer has not been able to obtain much by the way of up-to-date information about this society that was organized in 1892 as a fraternal benefit group. Previously the society was named First Catholic Slovak Ladies Union. In 1969 it absorbed the Catholic Slovak Brotherhood, whose membership was about 1,500.

Presently (1978) the society has 95,000 members in 800 local lodges. This membership roster represents a loss since 1965, when the society boasted 102,000 members.

The society helps support a theological seminary in Rome, Italy. A priest scholarship is underwritten by the Cleveland Diocese. In addition to these support efforts, the society also gives financial aid to convents and monasteries through Catholic and Slovak agencies. Supplementing the religious donations, the society also awards nursing and college scholarships of about $10,000 annually. A home for the aged is maintained in Beachwood, Ohio.

Socially and fraternally, the FCSLA conducts a biannual youth congress for members from sixteen to twenty years of age. This event emphasizes the fraternal benefit system. The society recognizes adults who have been members for twenty-five years with an award of pins, given through the local branches. Fifty-year members receive a cash award. All of these efforts are to live up to the society's objectives, namely, to promote the spiritual and material welfare of all its members.

Local units are known as "Branches." The organization has branches in twelve states and two Canadian provinces. The national convention assembles every four years. Head offices are located in Beachwood, Ohio.

For further information, see the monthly publication, *Fraternally Yours*. The constitution also is a helpful document.

FIRST CATHOLIC SLOVAK UNION OF THE UNITED STATES OF AMERICA AND CANADA (FCSU). On May 5, 1889, the Reverend Stephen Furdek organized St. Joseph's Society for Slovak Catholics in Cleveland, Ohio. This society soon (April 13, 1890) voted to work toward the union of all Slovak Catholic societies in the United States. This resolution led to a union convention on September 4, 1890, in Cleveland, Ohio, where seven Catholic Slovak groups united to form the First Catholic Slovak Union. The FCSU stated that its objectives were to preserve the Catholic faith, to retain and extend the use of the Slovak language, and to provide benevolent assistance to widows and orphans.

Membership in the FCSU had some rather strenuous requirements: a faithful Catholic who lives his faith, sends his children to a Catholic school, supports the parish and the parochial school, never ridicules the church's religious ceremonies, and never writes anything against the church and clergy. Today the requirements for membership are somewhat less comprehensive. The 1977 constitution states:

Each member, male or female, shall be Slovak by birth or descent, or in the family by marriage with a person of Slovak birth or descent, sound in body and mind, of exemplary habits, of good moral character and a practical Roman Catholic of the Latin or Byzantine Rite, residing in the United States of America or Canada, and shall be approved by a priest recognized by the Roman Catholic Church authorities and shall observe the laws of the Roman Catholic Church and his country.

If an individual lives in unlawful wedlock, he is ineligible to join. Currently (1979) the membership of the FCSU stands at 105,000. This roster is essentially the same in number as ten years ago.

The society has been a helpful arm of the Catholic Church. For instance, it has taken an active part in organizing Slovak Catholic parishes in Canada and the United States. When these new parishes reached a given membership, the society would also form a local lodge.

In terms of sponsoring programs, the FCSU awards scholarships to worthy students. The society conducts a summer camp, bowling, golfing, and other activities that appeal to youth. On the public service scene, the order promotes civic and cultural events and donates aid in response to natural disasters.

The society conducts initiations for new members. The candidate takes an oath to be loyal to the society. The ritual requires that each local meeting be opened and closed with prayer. Like most fraternal rituals, the FCSU ritual has various officiants participate, for example, a guard, a sergeant-at-arms, the secretary, and the local president.

The emblem of the society is an ornate cross that has a circle encompassing each of the four arms. The center of the cross has two circles forming a border, which portrays the society's name in English and in the Slovak language. At the center of the inner circle is another cross and the date (1890) of the society's origin.

Organizationally, the society calls its local gatherings "Branches." Each branch is affiliated with a Slovak Catholic parish. There are over 600 branches in Canada and the United States. Regional structures are called "Districts." The national assembly is referred to as the "Supreme Convention." It convenes every three years. Between conventions a board of directors expedites decisions. Head offices are in Cleveland, Ohio.

The FCSU or *Jednota*, as the members frequently call their organization, publishes a weekly newspaper consisting of a dozen pages that provide a wide variety of news items affecting the society. This is a good source for additional information about the society. Another good source is the *Jednota Annual*. Published annually, it reports a number of present and past events concerning the FCSU. The *By-Laws of the First Catholic Slovak Union* (1977), of course, are also available.

FORESTERS, ANCIENT ORDER OF (AOF). As far as the present writer can determine, this society is the lineal descendant of the British order formed in England in 1813. Some less reliable accounts cite the founding date of the British society as early as 1790. The British order, the Royal Order of Foresters, began as a convivial club that modeled itself after the English Odd Fellows providing relief for the sick and needy members. The first American "Court" (local lodge) was established in Philadelphia in 1832. The present society officially calls itself the Ancient Order of Foresters of California.

The society grew in the United States, but in 1874 a major schism erupted over the issue of local self-government of the order. The first notable result of the schism was the formation of the Independent Order of Foresters* in 1874. After the schism the name Ancient Order of Foresters was assumed more formally by the group from which the secession occurred.

The AOF has always been a fraternal benefit society. Initially, it operated on the graded assessment plan, exacting assessments based on a member's age at entry and upon experience tables. The order's ritual was largely based on the lore of Robin Hood and his merry men. Masonic influences have also been present since the origin of the society.

Because of the numerous schisms that occurred among the Foresters, there is a wide variety of fraternal groups bearing the name Foresters in Canada and the United States. Some societies, of course, also bear the name Foresters even though they do not stem from the Ancient Order of Foresters. The AOF presently (1979) has only 336 members, an all-time low. Even after the 1874 schism the AOF grew, for it had 119,000 members in 1896.

Local groups are called "Courts." The supreme structure is known as the "High Court." The latter meets in convention biennially. Headquarters are maintained in San Francisco, California.

For additional background, see the society's quarterly publication, *Ancient Order of Foresters* (Friendly Society). The reader may also wish to consult the book by Warren Potter and Robert Oliver, *Fraternally Yours* (1967), a history of the Independent Order of Foresters.

FORESTERS, CATHOLIC ORDER OF (COF). In 1883 seven men from a Roman Catholic parish in Chicago received a charter from the Secretary of State of Illinois to call their organization the Illinois Catholic Order of Foresters. John F. Scanlan, the chief organizer, became the order's High Chief Ranger. In 1887 the group changed its name to Catholic Order of Foresters.

The COF was brought into being with the objective of providing a death benefit of $1,000, which would help a widow overcome the financial costs incurred by her husband's death. During the first two decades the order grew and prospered. By 1894 the COF organized itself on the state and provincial levels, the latter term being applicable to Quebec, where the order gained a foothold in 1888. At its 1929 convention in Quebec the COF formed a juvenile branch that admitted Catholic boys from birth to age sixteen. In 1965 the order absorbed the Catholic Central Union, a Czech-oriented fraternal society organized in 1877.

Currently the COF has two divisions for its youth. From birth to age six, boys and girls may enter the Rangers. From seven to fifteen-and-a-half, they join the Forest Rangers.

Members are drawn exclusively from the Catholic Church. Individuals who are sixteen years of age may join the COF. Women may become regular members since the order changed its constitution in 1952. The society does not discriminate against blacks. If they are members of the Catholic Church, they are eligible for membership. The total number of members in 1979 was 171,000, which represents a decline from 192,000 in 1967.

Relative to charity, COF awards college scholarships to high school graduates. It contributes to radio and television programs for Catholic programs and also supports Catholic charities. Catholic seminarians also receive assistance. Many of the COF members visit the sick, help the handicapped, and assist individuals in times of natural disasters.

The COF, as a fraternal and benevolent group, has a three-degree ritual: the Degree of Protection, the Exalted Degree, and the Legion of Honor Degree. The constitution requires that every applicant for membership be initiated and also take (sign) the obligation of the society. Similar to other Forester bodies in the fraternal realm, the COF employs legends in its ritual pertaining to Robin Hood.

Administratively the COF has its "High Court" on the national level. Its officers are High Chief Ranger, Vice High Chief Ranger, High Secretary, High Treasurer, and ten High Court Trustees. The state or provincial groups are known as "State Courts" or "Provincial Courts." Local groups follow parish boundaries and are called "Subordinate Courts." Headquarters are in Chicago, Illinois.

Additional information on the COF may be found by reading its bimonthly periodical, *Catholic Forester*. It prints news about the order and its activities. A short history was published by the fraternity in 1973, known as *90 Years of History*. The *Constitution and By-Laws of the Catholic Order of Foresters* (1977) provides firsthand insight concerning the order's structure and policies.

FORESTERS, INDEPENDENT ORDER OF (IOF). This Canadian-based fraternal benevolent society was born in 1874 as a result of a schism in the Ancient Order of Foresters.* The schism arose when the Ancient Order of Foresters, headquartered in England, refused to grant the American Foresters a subsidiary high court for more self-rule. The result was the formation of the first independent "Court" (the society's term for chapter) in 1874 in Newark, New Jersey. On June 16, 1874, a national convention was held in Newark creating the Independent Order of Foresters.

By 1878 the IOF had more than 10,000 members, and by this time it was prepared to pay $1,000 to a deceased member's beneficiaries. In 1926 the IOF merged with the Ancient Order of United Workmen from the province of Ontario. This merger increased the IOF membership more than 8,000 bringing it to a total of 152,000 Foresters. In 1931 the Royal Templars of Temperance and the Modern Brotherhood of America merged with the IOF. The Catholic Mutual Benefit Association came into the IOF in 1952, and in 1972 the Order of Scottish Clans was absorbed. Today (1979) the IOF, as a fraternal insurance group, operates its affairs out of its own modern twenty-one-story building in Toronto, Ontario.

The Foresters trace their legendary origin to the era of the medieval crusades when guilds of foresters guarded the king's forests. These organizations formed fraternal bonds similar to the brotherhood attributed to Robin Hood and his men. They banded together to protect their families and rights, assisting each other in a fraternal manner. In the early 1800s the practices of the Foresters were incorporated by the Ancient Order of Foresters, a group in the British Isles. Although the modern Foresters no longer guard the king's forests, they do, however, retain the values of brotherhood, liberty, and mutual aid and protection.

The fraternity uses terms and titles that were the language of the foresters in the day of Robin Hood. Thus "forest homes" are meeting houses; officers are known as Chief Ranger, Vice Chief Ranger, Senior Woodward, Senior Beadle; the ritual draws from the legends of Robin Hood and his forest environment.

According to recent publicity furnished by the IOF every candidate for membership takes the "Forestric Pledge" upon being initiated into the order. The official view holds that the ritual is "a solemn and beautiful ceremony." As part of the initiation rite, the candidate is asked whether he believes "in God, the Creator and Ruler of the universe." After the initiation the candidate receives a lapel pin that bears the order's insignia. The emblem is an eight-cornered cross portraying the all-seeing eye on its top arm, a human figure on the left and right arms, and the letters L.B.C. on the lower arm. The abbreviation L.B.C. stands for liberty, benevolence, concord, the watchwords of the order, which were taken from the Ancient Order of Foresters. In the center of the cross are the letters IOF, and perched on top of the cross is the royal crown. The cross and crown are cradled in the arms of a circular wreath of leaves. The colors of the order (red, white, and blue) are displayed on the insignia. Red represents God's faithfulness and the members' unalterable fidelity and benevolence. White stands for the purity of heart that is supposed to adorn the life of every forester, and blue signifies the forester's obligation to God.

Membership is open to men and women without distinction pertaining to race or color. Women, however, may not serve on the Executive Council or the order's Supreme Court. For juvenile boys the IOF has what it calls the Robin Hood Band. This group is dressed in garb resembling the attire of Robin Hood and his men. For adult men there is a uniformed rank or degree that has been existence since 1875. In 1978 the IOF had over 1,500,000 members in Canada, the United Kingdom, and the United States.

The IOF has three levels of organization: the "Supreme Court" as the international jurisdiction, the "High Court" in the regional sphere, and the "Local Court." The Supreme Court meets every four years, and the High Courts meet every two years. Between conventions the Supreme Court administers its business out of the headquarters in Toronto, Ontario.

Additional information may be found by obtaining the book by Warren Potter and Robert Oliver, *Fraternally Yours* (1967). This volume gives a comprehensive history of the IOF. A small publication (pamphlet) known as *What Does It Mean?*, printed by the IOF, provides a nutshell view of the order. The order also publishes its own periodical, *The Independent Forester.*

FRATERNAL AID UNION (FAU). In Lawrence, Kansas, on October 14, 1890, a number of members from the Ancient Order of United Workmen,* Modern Woodmen of America,* Knights of the Maccabees,* and others founded this fraternal benefit organization. The society enrolled white men and women between eighteen and fifty-five, provided they were not engaged in hazardous occupations. When the society was first organized, it was called Fraternal Aid Association. In 1917 the society merged with the Improved Order of Heptasophs.* According to *Statistics, Fraternal Societies* (1920), the new society had 94,000 members in 1920, but by 1930 its membership was down to 67,385 benefit members. The society later (1933) changed its name to Standard Life Association. Home offices were maintained in Lawrence, Kansas.

FRATERNAL LEGION. Organized as a fraternal benefit society in Baltimore, Maryland, in 1881, the order levied its first assessment in May 1883.

The order apparently did not survive very long, for no record of it exists in the 1898 *Statistics, Fraternal Societies*. Headquarters were maintained in Baltimore, Maryland.

FRATERNAL MYSTIC CIRCLE. Organized in 1885, this group was a fraternal benefit society. It was founded to provide safe indemnity for professional and business people. Local units were called "Subordinate Rulings." Regional groups were known as "Grand Rulings," and the national structure was referred to as the "Supreme Ruling." The ritual of the society was secret and religiously flavored, similar to countless other fraternal rites and ceremonies. The order was honored to have had President McKinley as one of its members. By 1910 the society had more than 22,000 members, but by 1915 the order's membership dropped to 17,458. The home office was located in Philadelphia, Pennsylvania.

FRATERNAL ORDER OF BEAVERS. See Beavers, Fraternal Order of.

FRATERNAL ORDER OF CLOVER LEAVES. See Clover Leaves, Fraternal Order of.

FRATERNAL ORDER OF EAGLES. See Eagles, Fraternal Order of.

FRATERNAL ORDER OF POLICE. See Police, Fraternal Order of.

FRATERNAL ORDER OF REINDEER. See Reindeer, Fraternal Order of.

FRATERNAL TRIBUNES. A fraternal beneficiary order founded in 1897 in Rock Island, Illinois, the society had 9,084 benefit and social members in in 1908. Its insurance certificates were backed by a loan and indemnity firm. This was touted as a unique feature. Apparently the order only existed for a couple of decades, as no record of its existence can be found in *Statistics, Fraternal Societies* of 1915. The home office was in Rock Island, Illinois.

FREE AND REGENERATED PALLADIUM. This Masonically linked society reportedly was instituted in 1730 and established in Charleston, South Carolina. It remained dormant until 1884. After this date it was reformed to "impart new force to the traditions of high grade Masonry." The society admitted men and women, the former to the grades of Adelphos and Companion of Ulysses and the latter to the grade of Penelope. The society held all of its "Councils" in strict secrecy. It never printed any proceedings and very much restricted its membership. REFERENCE: *Cyc. Frat.*

FREEMASONRY, ANCIENT FREE AND ACCEPTED MASONS (A.F.A.M. or F. and A.M.). No other organization in the fraternal world is so prominent and so large as Freemasonry. Hundreds of books and articles have been written about this fraternal order during its more than 250 years of existence. Much of what has come from the pens of its own members, who often embellish the order's origin, legends, and symbolism, lacks objectivity and accuracy. On the other hand, some of the finest scholarly discussions on Freemasonry have also come from its own ranks. Masons such as Albert G. Mackey, Robert F. Gould, George W. Speth, William J. Hughan, Delmar D. Darrah, Bernard E. Jones, Douglas Knoop, H. W. Coil, and others have separated myth and imagination from historical facts.

Not all Masonic orders are alike. For instance, Freemasonry in Continental Europe is quite different from Masonry in the British Isles and North America. Continental Masonry has generally been politically revolutionary and strongly opposed to ecclesiastical and regal authority. In fact, the Grand Orient (French Masonry) officially is atheistic. On the other hand, Freemasonry in England, Canada, and the United States has deliberately divorced itself from politics and has been very supportive of churches and religion. Most of its members belong to some church, and church parades are sponsored by many Masonic lodges.

In spite of what one may read about Freemasonry's origin going back to King Solomon's day, or even to Adam, who was the first to wear an "apron" (an example of Masonic myth and imagination), the established fact is that the order's real origin began in A.D. 1717 in London, England. It was in London's Goose and Gridiron Tavern that modern Freemasonry was born.

During the latter 1600s and early 1700s, the guildlike social institution of operative masonry (comprised of stonemasons) in the British Isles began to decline. (Although operative masonry resembled the medieval guilds, it never really was a guild.) The decline prompted operative groups to enroll nonmasons as honorary members, who were called "Accepted Masons."

The name "Freemason," which the nonoperative or accepted members retained, had been used by the operatives apparently for several centuries. Its exact meaning, however, is unknown. One possibility indicates that the operative mason was *free* from feudal serfdom, another points to his having been a worker who fashioned *free*stone, and still another possibility is that the "freemason" was not an operative mason. These are only some of the possibilities. Others could be cited.

In 1717 some members of four London lodges met at the Goose and Gridiron Tavern to form a centralized structure, which they called the "Grand Lodge." Details of that meeting are lacking. In fact, the earliest minutes of the Grand Lodge go back only to 1723. By 1723 the order had accepted James Anderson's *Constitutions*, which he had been requested to prepare as a revision of the Old Charges of operative masonry. Anderson (a Presbyterian clergyman) called the Old Charges the "Gothic Constitutions." He preferred to call his revised work "The Charges of a Freemason." The Old Charges had been used by operative masonry since about the fourteenth century. Although the Old Charges were lengthy in that they consisted of a number of manuscripts, for the most part they dealt with: (1) God and religion; (2) the craft of masonry, including geometry; and (3) regal duty.

Anderson's *Constitutions* took on the flavor of deism, whereas the Old Charges had had a Christian tone. For instance, the 1723 document omitted the Trinitarian invocation and spoke of a "religion in which all men agree." In 1738 Anderson produced yet another revision, which he called "The Old Charges of the Free and Accepted Masons." Thus by 1738 operative masonry had evolved into accepted Freemasonry, and by the second half of the eighteenth century the organization had further evolved into speculative Freemasonry.

The term "speculative" means that Freemasonry interprets the symbols and artifacts of operative masonry in an allegorical, religious manner. These interpretations speculate about the character of God and the universe. Operative masons built stone edifices; speculative masons are engaged symbolically in the building of spiritual edifices. Although one can frequently see the letters A.F.A.M., or A.F. and M., adorning a Masonic lodge hall, the order really is not so much ancient, free, and accepted as it is speculative.

In the literature concerning the three degrees that Freemasonry requires for someone to become a Master Mason, it is believed by most scholars that in operative masonry there were grades, not degrees. Among operative masons it was the individual's skill and work that identified his grade, not word or ceremony, as it is now with speculative Freemasonry. The origin of the three degrees appear to have arisen in the 1720s. The fraternity, as a nonoperative group of Masons, grew rapidly from four lodges in 1717 to 126 in 1733.

Although Freemasonry was born in the British Isles, it soon came to the United States. The first duly constituted lodge was established in the United States on April 13, 1733. It was granted a dispensation (that is, a charter) by the Grand Lodge of England. Once in the United States, Freemasonry flourished, with few exceptions, for over two centuries. It became an influential institution in the United States in a number of ways.

There is considerable evidence indicating that the American Revolution was inspired by American Freemasons (see Bernard Fay, *Revolution and Freemasonry, 1680 to 1800*, 1935; James David Carter, "Freemasonry in Texas: Background, History, and Influence to 1846" (Ph.D. diss., University of Texas, 1954).

There also is ample evidence showing Freemasonry to have been influential in the formation of the American Constitution, even in the design of the Great Seal of the United States. James David Carter believes that the Great Seal contains a number of Masonic symbols. For example, the obverse side displays the American Eagle with thirty-two feathers in his right wing and thirty-three in his left. To a Freemason the thirty-two feathers represent the thirty-two degrees of the Scottish Rite. The thirty-three feathers also signify the Scottish Rite* with its additional degree bestowed for honorary purposes. The eagle has nine tail feathers, which correspond to the nine degrees of the York Rite.* The thirteen stars above the eagle's head form the Star of David, which reminds a Mason of King David's dream of building a temple, which his son King Solomon finally realized. Considerable masonic legend traces the origin of Freemasonry to the building of Solomon's temple. The glory above the eagle's head, which contains the thirteen stars, is divided into twenty-four equal parts. These remind a Mason of the Masonic gauge, which also is divided into twenty-four parts that signify obligated service. The Latin inscription, *E Pluribus Unum*, indicates brotherhood to Masonry. The seal's reverse side with its All-Seeing Eye set within a triangle, surrounded by a golden glory, is so obviously Masonic that anyone with only a rudimentary acquaintance with speculative Masonry recognizes the Masonic symbolism here. The unfinished pyramid below the All-Seeing Eye reminds a Mason of the soul's immortality, which he will complete in eternity. It also recalls the unfinished temple of Solomon (a familiar story to every informed Mason) that resulted because the master architect was killed.

Many students of Masonry also contend that the public school system largely stems from Masonic impetus and philosophy. To this very day one can find innumerable references in Mason literature that venerate the public school system.

Finally, Freemasonry made its mark on American society by serving as a model for hundreds of other fraternal orders that sprouted throughout the entire North American continent. Charles Merz, writing in 1927, estimated that there were over 800 different fraternal orders in the 1920s. Nearly all of these adopted given Masonic features by employing secrecy, signs, passwords, rituals, regalia, oaths or obligations, and degrees.

BLUE LODGE

All third-degree Masonic members (Master Masons) are initiated into the craft in the Blue Lodge, sometimes also referred to as Symbolic Masonry. The word "lodge" goes back at least to A.D. 1278, to operative masonry. At that time, "lodge" referred to a temporary shed or hut erected near the new construction site, where it served as a storehouse for the master's tools. It also was used as a place to eat, meet, and on occasion sleep. As to the meaning of the term "blue lodge," there are different explanations. One belief is that the word blue in Masonry comes from the operative era when the color symbolized perfection, derived from the Hebrew *tekelet*. Another position holds that blue was adopted in imitating the nobility and knighthood, who employed blue colors. Still another explanation says that the ancient craft met under the blue canopy of heaven. Today blue reminds

Freemasons of universal brotherhood and friendship and that Masonic virtues should be as extensive as the blue arch of heaven.

The emblem of Blue Lodge Masonry is the interlaced square and compasses with the letter "G" commonly in the center. Some authorities say the "G" stands for Grand Architect of the Universe (G.A.O.T.U.). Others believe it represents geometry. The letter "G" or its equivalent is not found in non-English Masonic lodges.

The three degrees that each regular member possesses are the Entered Apprentice, Fellow Craft, and Master Mason. However, before a candidate is accepted a committee investigates him and reports at a regular meeting. Each applicant is voted on by the lodge members. If one blackball appears, the vote is "foul," and a second vote is ordered by the Worshipful Master (head of the local lodge) because a negative vote could have occurred by mistake. If the second ballot again has a blackball present, the candidate is rejected for membership. This method is justified by Masons in that they believe a unanimous ballot helps keep their order harmonious and unified.

Once the applicant is accepted, he is required to submit himself to the three-degree ritual. In addition to taking the long unconventional oaths, being hoodwinked, and engaging in esoteric exercises, he is stripped of his clothing, except for his shirt and drawers. For the Entered Apprentice degree his *left* breast, shoulder, and arm are bared. He is hoodwinked and a cable-tow (rope) is placed around his neck. For the Fellow Craft degree he is again divested of his apparel; however, this time his *right* shoulder, arm, and breast are exposed. The cable-tow is tied around his upper right arm. The third or Master Mason degree once more requires the candidate to disrobe. He is blindfolded for the third time, and the cable-tow is wound around his body three times. In all three instances the candidate goes through this procedure before he takes an obligation (oath) for each degree. The Master Mason obligation, according to one edition (different editions may vary slightly), in part reads:

. . . I promise and swear, that I will not write, print, stamp, stain, hew, cut, carve, indent, paint, or engrave it [Masonic secrets] on anything moveable or immovable . . . *binding myself under no less penalty than to have my throat cut across, my tongue torn out by the roots, and my body buried in the rough sands of the sea at low water mark* [emphases not in the original], where the tide ebbs and flows twice in twenty-four hours; so help me God, and keep me steadfast in the due performance of the same.

Most Masonic writers fail to discuss the nature of obligations (vows) that call for mutilation of the member's body should he violate the promise. However, one experienced and highly respected Mason, Bernard E. Jones, in Britain has taken note of the "severe penalties" called for in the obligations. Says Jones:

Whether the medieval penalty clauses of a masonic obligation are in keeping with the days we now live in, and, if not, whether they should continue to be included as an essential element in the Obligation, is a question arising now and then. Brethren have asked whether, inasmuch as some penalty clauses reflect the cruelty and mental darkness of other days, Obligations including them as essentials may properly be sworn on the V.S.L., and have ventured to wonder whether any reasonable modification would leave the Craft any the poorer or constitute an "innovation" affecting any true landmark of the Order? (See his *Freemasons Guide and Compendium*, 1956.)

More recently (1974), Allen Roberts, a long-time Mason, briefly alluded to the strange penalty provisions of the Masonic oaths. He said: "The Penalty for the violation of [the] obligation appeared strange. It was. It is symbolic only. It has never been enforced. It never will be." (See his *The Craft and Its Symbols*, 1974.)

Some Masons on occasion will dispute the accuracy or reliability of "nonauthorized" published rituals that contain the obligations. However, former Masons and some authorities in Masonry have attested to the accuracy of "unofficial" renditions. In spite of the great emphasis that Masonry places upon secrecy, numerous books have been published on lodge rituals. Very little, if anything, really is secret if someone desires to study the rituals as a nonmember. Noel P. Gist (a former Mason) underscores this by saying: "While it is true that chapters on ritualism contain materials which the members attempt to conceal from outsiders, the data are available to anyone who will take the time and trouble to inquire into the problem." (See his "Secret Societies: A Cultural Study of Fraternalism in the United States," *The University of Missouri Studies*, 1940.) There is also a difference between British and American Freemasonry in that the British Masons permit their rituals to be considerably more public.

Freemasonry asserts that it does not solicit members. "One of the fundamental concepts of Freemasonry is that application for membership must be wholly a voluntary act." So says the Masonic Service Association. Masonry also frowns upon anyone desiring to join the order for pecuniary or business advantages. In the United States an applicant for membership must be twenty-one or older, male, white, and believe in a supreme being. The last requirement goes back to Anderson's first article in his *Constitutions* of 1723, which contained the following statement: "A Mason is oblig'd, by his Tenure, to obey the moral Law, and if he rightly understands the Art, he will never be a stupid Atheist, nor an irreligious Libertine."

Since only whites may join American Masonry, blacks have their own Masonic lodges, known as Prince Hall Masonry.* White Masonry in the United States, however, has not officially recognized black Masonry. One renowned Masonic authority, Delmar Duane Darrah, expressed the sentiment of Freemasonry in the following words: "Regardless of the way and manner that Negro Freemasonry arose in America it is today regarded as spurious and illegitimate." (See his *History and Evolution of Freemasonry, 1967*.) Masonry has frequently referred to Prince Hall Masonry as "clandestine" or "illegitimate."

A key rationalization commonly cited by American Masonry for not recognizing black Masonry is what Masons refer to as "territorial jurisdiction." By territorial jurisdiction, American Masons mean there can be but one grand lodge in a given state; no grand lodge outside a given state may create a lodge within the jurisdiction of an existing lodge in that state. Since Prince Hall Masonry was authorized in Boston in 1784 by the Grand Lodge of England, when a white grand lodge was already in existence in Massachusetts, it is held to be "illegitimate" by most American Masons. This reasoning has been employed by grand lodges in virtually every state. This argument, however, breaks down when it is noted that American Masonry recognizes the York Grand Lodge of Mexico, even though the Mexican Grand Lodge has concurrent territorial jurisdiction.

To justify and rationalize the exclusion of nonwhites, as individuals, from American Freemasonry, the society has pointed to one of its "landmarks," which states only *"free-born"* males are eligible. Operative masonry in the medieval era rejected a bondman for membership because he was bound to the feudal lord or to a guild. What American Freemasonry did was to translate and interpret *bondman* as *free-born* or *free and well-born*, meaning that if an applicant had slave status at one time, he was ineligible for lodge membership. Thus the term *free-born* was applied to blacks in the United States in a way never originally intended. Indeed, the Grand Lodge of England (Freemasonry) struck the word *free-born* (which the English Masons never understood as applying to blacks) from the list of candidates' qualifications by substituting the word "free." It made the change in 1838.

The firm antiblack stance on the part of white Masons in the United States appears to be slowly "softening." For instance, Harold V. B. Voorhis, a renowned American Mason and scholar of the order, in 1971 referred to black (Prince Hall) Masons as "brethren." In fact, he titled the book *Our Colored Brethren*. There appear to be other portents. Black Masonic officials (in personal communication) have told the writer that while open fellowship and transfer of members does not yet exist between Prince Hall Masonry and white Masonry, there is a growing receptiveness on the part of many white Masons. Black Masons feel that they are no longer seen as "clandestine" but rather as Prince Hall Masons who are a part of the ancient fraternity.

The number of landmarks cited by different Masonic authorities vary. Mackey lists twenty-five. Darrah cites Roscoe Pound, a distinguished Masonic organizational jurist, who lists seven: "(1) belief in God; (2) belief in the persistence of personality; (3) a 'Book of the Law' as an indispensable part of the furniture of every lodge; (4) the legend of the third degree; (5) secrecy; (6) the symbolism of the operative art; and (7) that a Mason must be a man, free born, and of age.'' Although landmarks may vary in number and kind, some are unequivocally accepted by all masons. One of these is that no woman can every become a Freemason. Even if a woman were initiated into the Blue Lodge by some "misguided" lodge, or by clandestine methods, she would not be regarded as a Mason. One Masonic publication asserts: "For a woman to become a Freemason is as impossible as for a man to become a mother, a leopard to change his spots."

The Blue Lodge, as the core of speculative Freemasonry, abounds with allegory and symbolism. In American lodges there are the "three great lights:" Bible, Square, and Compasses. (Freemasons commonly use "compasses" as a singular noun.) The Bible signifies truth, faith, and hope; the square is a symbol of morality; and the compasses symbolizes spirituality. During the initiation the compasses is symbolically hidden by hoodwinking the candidate. This teaches the candidate that his human senses can only grope slowly from darkness to spiritual light. It also reminds Masons to circumscribe their passions and evil desires.

Masonry also has "three lesser lights." These are commonly placed about the altar in the form of a triangle. One light represents the sun, another the moon, and the third signifies the Worshipful Master (head of the local lodge). The lodge's altar symbolizes sacrifice of a Mason's self-interest. The covering of a lodge is a clouded canopy with Jacob's ladder reaching to the star-decked heaven, which is visible through an opening in the canopy. This pictures signifies to every good Mason that his desire is to get to the starry heaven by climbing the visionary ladder of perfection.

Freemasonry lays great importance on its "immovable jewels," the square, the level, and the plumb, which are worn by three lodge officers. The Worshipful Master wears the emblem of the square; the level is worn by the Senior Warden; and the plumb is worn by the Junior Warden. Without these jewels or three officers no lodge may legally be in session. That is an immovable rule, and hence the term, "immovable jewels."

Some of the other significant symbols of the Masonic craft are the white lambskin apron, the cable-tow, the hoodwink, the level, the plumb, the trowel, the all-seeing eye, and the acacia sprig. The apron, which must be made of lambskin, stands for purity, innocence, honor, and distinction. It is worn at official functions; deceased members are buried with it. The cable-tow, tied around the neck for the Entered Apprentice degree, around the right shoulder for the Fellow Craft degree, and around the waist for the Master Mason degree, signifies outward submission and fidelity. It also symbolizes the promise to assist another "brother," even at the risk of his life. Often it is referred to as the "mystic tie" that binds the craft together. The hoodwink or blindfold calls to mind the darkness and ignorance that the candidate lived in before coming to the "light" of Masonry. The operative masonic tool, the level, represents equality among members of Freemasonry. The plumb signifies righteousness, an upright life before God and fellow man. Another symbol of the craft is the trowel. It reminds Masons to spread brotherly love. The ancient all-seeing eye (discussed briefly earlier) indicates that the Grand Architect (the Masonic term for God) is omnisciently and providentially watching man. It is thought to be a relic of primitive sun-worship. Because of its never-fading quality, the acacia stands for immortality of the soul. Some Masonic works, apparently influenced by Christianity, also depict the acacia as a symbol of the resurrection. "No symbol is more important to the masonic student than the acacia." So says Albert G. Mackey, *Symbolism of Freemasonry* (1975).

Freemasonry prides itself on its "antiquity." That is one reason that it calls its order Ancient Free and Accepted Masons. Some Masonic publications even use the old spelling of Antient when talking about the craft. The love of antiquity is also seen in some of the expressions heard among Masons. *Hele* is often used, meaning "cover" in the expression, "I will always *hele*, conceal, and never reveal." An even more common expression is the optative exclamation: "So Mote It Be!" This phrase goes back to the fourteenth century to operative masonry.

Is Freemasonry with its Blue Lodge rituals and symbolism a religion? This question is often asked. Some Masonic authorities say yes and some say no. Those who say no prefer to argue that the order is religious but not a religion. Most of the Masonic writers seem to take this position.

Another message that many Masonic authors seek to convey is that their fraternity is not a secret society but rather an organization that has secrets. By this is meant that the public knows of Masonry's existence and thus it is not secret.

In its three centuries of existence, and already during the latter decades of the operative era, Freemasonry attracted not only artisans and intellectuals but also royalty. King George VI was a Mason, and in 1952 Prince Philip (Duke of Edinburgh) also was "raised," a common expression among Masons for those who have become Master Masons. The United Grand Lodge Constitution of Freemasonry in England stipulates that its Grand Master (head of the national lodge) must be of the nobility. This makes for a triple alliance: crown, church, and lodge.

Although Masonry officially makes much of the concept of brotherhood and equality with respect to intralodge activities and status, the British Masons typically enroll the "best" people in the community's oldest lodge. Some lodges enroll only special occupational groups. The Mendelsohn Lodge in London initiates only musicians, and Guildhall Lodge enrolls only aldermen. No such pattern seems to exist in North America.

American Masonry has also attracted many individuals of high social status to its altars. Of the United States' thirty-nine presidents, Masonry's Blue Lodge has had fourteen of them: Washington, Monroe, Jackson, Polk,

Buchanan, Andrew Johnson, Garfield, McKinley, Theodore Roosevelt, Taft, Harding, Franklin Roosevelt, Truman, and Ford. On occasion one may read that about half of the presidents in the United States were Masons. Such statements are definitely false. Some very scant evidence points to Jefferson and Pierce having been Masons, but the best scholarly publications by Masons and non-Masons do not include Jefferson and Pierce. See, for example, J. Fairburn Smith, *Masonic Presidents of the United States* (1946); William L. Boyden, *Masonic Presidents, Vice-Presidents and Signers* (1927). In addition to presidential members in the Masonic craft, numerous governors, U.S. senators, and representatives have also sought the Masonic arcana. In 1978, thirty-six senators and one hundred representatives were Masons. Of the fifty governors, fourteen belonged to the Masonic lodge. During the last three to four decades, Freemasonry has primarily been attracting its new members from the blue-collar (upper-lower) and white-collar (lower-middle) classes. Proportionately fewer now come to Masonry's ranks from the professional and higher-status occupational groups than did one to two generations ago.

Masons in the Blue Lodge operate a number of homes for aged and infirm members. There is a Masonic home in virtually every state. In addition to taking care of their own, Masons on occasion make contributions to various public charities and civic or educational endeavors. In the past Masons participated in numerous public cornerstone-laying ceremonies. In recent years there has been a decline in these activities.

The ancient fraternity has had its share of conflict during its existence of more than 250 years. In England a schism occurred in the ranks of the order in 1751 when the "Antients" broke from the "Moderns." The Antients formed their own grand lodge in opposition to the Moderns largely because the Antients felt the Moderns violated a number of ancient Masonic practices. Some of the alleged violations were transposing the modes of recognition for the first and second degrees, de-Christianizing the craft, abbreviating the ritual, and omitting prayers in lodge sessions. The schism endured until 1813, when the two groups reunited. The schism had very little effect on American Masonry.

Only thirteen years after British Masonry resolved its internal conflict in 1813, American Masonry was confronted by an external conflict in 1826. This was the year the anti-Masonic fever began spreading across large sections of the United States. Hatred, fear, and suspicion was directed toward the entire Masonic fraternity as a result of what became known as the "Morgan Affair."

William Morgan of Batavia, New York, reportedly a Freemason, said he was in the process of publishing a book containing Masonic rituals. On September 11, 1826, he was arrested on a charge of petty larceny. On

September 12 he was released on bail after bail money had been paid to the jailer's wife because the jailer was absent. According to one Masonic member and scholar,

several misguided members of the lodges at Batavia and Canandaigua, later assisted by some as far away as Rochester and Niagara Falls, abducted Morgan, escorted him by horse-drawn carriage across western New York, imprisoned him some days in the old powder magazine at Ft. Niagara, and finally took him across the international boundary and assertedly released him into the custody of Canadian Masons. Since he was never afterwards heard of (though there were unconfirmed sightings of him) the Masons were accused of having cast him into the Niagara rapids. (See Henry Wilson Coil, *A Comprehensive View of Freemasonry*, 1954.)

Morgan's disappearance set off a strong anti-Masonic sentiment that even led to the formation of a political party, the Anti-Mason Party, in 1827. Although Masonry repudiated the acts of the abductors and cooperated with authorities to bring the guilty to justice (none, however, were convicted), it suffered severely from the public outcry. The Anti-Masonic Party asserted that Masons were subversive of good government. Churches barred Masons from the pulpit. Many Masons had to renounce their fraternity in order to live in the community. Some burned their aprons, and numerous lodges surrendered their warrants. Masonic memberships dwindled.

While Masonry suffered and declined during the anti-Masonic era from 1826 to about 1845, American fraternalism was far from dead. Ironically, a number of new orders sprang up in the 1830s, for example, the Improved Order of Red Men* was founded in 1834, the Ancient Order of Hibernians* in 1836, and the Order of United American Mechanics* in 1845. A number of secret college fraternities were also organized in the 1830s.

After 1845 Freemasonry began to revive, and by the time of the Civil War it had virtually recovered from the twenty-year onslaught of prejudice and discrimination. A number of observers have contended that Freemasonry grew because it was attractive to many soldiers in the Confederate and Union armies. When captured, a Mason reportedly received better treatment at the hands of a Masonic captor.

Freemasonry also has had to contend with opposition from the Roman Catholic Church. Only twenty-one years after Freemasonry formed its first grand lodge in England in 1717, the first papal bull against Masonry was issued by Pope Clement XII in 1738. This bull, as well as the seventeen others that followed up to 1917, often were really more applicable to Freemasonry on the Continent than to English or American Freemasonry. For instance, the bull of 1821, issued by Pope Pius VII, was really directed against the Carbonari in Italy. There were, however, in all eighteen papal bulls some common condemnations that did apply to Freemasonry outside the Continent. These condemnations referred to Masonry's natural religion, its medieval oaths, and its deistic posture. All papal bulls had the effect of barring Catholics from joining Masonry.

"If you cannot beat them, join them." So goes a common saying, and that is in effect what the Roman Catholic Church did in 1976 when the Pope opened the door for Catholics to become Freemasons by taking Masonry off the condemnation list. The Masons of the Grand Lodge of New York were quick to capitalize on the Pope's new posture by inviting Cardinal Cooke to address their grand lodge in 1976. In February, 1977, *Religious News Service* carried a report that a Catholic priest in Mankato, Minnesota, had joined the Masonic lodge. (Officially, however, the Catholic Church has not approved Masonry for its clergy.) Freemasonry that survived the anti-Masonic era of the nineteenth century had now survived an even more powerful foe, the Roman Catholic Church. Moreover, Masonry did not have to compromise or change its teachings one iota, either as a result of the anti-Masonic era (1826 to 1845) or as a result of Catholic opposition (1731 to 1976).

Opposition to Freemasonry also has come from churches in the Protestant sector. As early as 1757 the "Original Secession" of the Presbyterian Church in Scotland repudiated Freemasonry. In 1927 the Free Presbyterian Church of Scotland did not permit its members to join Masonry. The Orthodox Presbyterian Church of America had a committee at its General Assembly in Rochester, New York, in 1942 condemn Freemasonry on the grounds of religious indifference. Some other Protestant churches that have opposed Masonry include the Dutch Reformed Church of South Africa, the Salvation Army, the Wesleyan Methodist Church, the Mennonite General Conference, Seventh-Day Adventists, the Church of the Nazarene, Assemblies of God, the American Lutheran Church, the Luthern Church-Missouri Synod, and the Wisconsin Evangelical Lutheran Synod. They have all taken positions against the naturalistic and deistic religious teachings of Freemasonry. For the most part, Masonry has not publicly or officially reacted to the anti-Masonic stances taken by the various Protestant denominations, perhaps because a number of denominations in time have become tolerant of the fraternity by permitting church members to join Freemasonry.

Although Masonry may have weathered the anti-Masonic era of the early nineteenth century and opposition from the Catholic and Protestant churches, it seems to be succumbing to another obstacle. During the last twenty-five years or so the membership rolls in almost all grand (statewide) lodges have been declining year after year. The American Blue Lodge once had a high of 4,103,161 Master Masons, in 1959; but now (in 1979) it has dropped to 3,200,000 members, a decline of 22 percent in twenty years.

Various grand lodges have shown great concern over the decline in memberships that seems to reflect a decreasing interest in the ancient craft. One

Masonic observer recently noted: "It is no secret that we—as a fraternity—are hurting. . . . Our membership is sagging, our attendance is dismal, our impact on today's society is at a low ebb. . . ." (See Gilbert K. Bovard, "Will There Be Another Hundred?" *Grand Lodge Bulletin* [Iowa], 1969.) Another member is more critical: "Masonry is pretty well defeated! Our spark and spirit are lost. We grope in the dark chasing philosophical phantoms." (See Charles Van Cott, *Freemasonry, A Sleeping Giant*, 1959.) Change has been advocated, but thus far it has been strongly resisted. Note, for instance, the following remark:

. . . there is nothing wrong with Freemasonry; there may be something wrong with its members and I am rather sick and tired of listening to these individuals, and some of them highly placed in our Order, who tell me or make remarks to the effect that our Institution has lost popularity, that it has lost its punch, that we should find new ways to go out into the highways and byways for members, or we should turn our Institution into service clubs. . . . (See J. H. N. Morgan, "To Be A Freemason," *Grand Lodge Bulletin* [Iowa], 1967.)

The resistance to organizational change seems to stem largely from the fact that the order is so intimately tied to tradition and antiquity. The posture of resisting change is reinforced by the craft's unalterable landmarks, "To which nothing can be added, and from which nothing can be taken away," according to one high-ranking Mason. It is to comments like these that some other Masons, also of high rank, have reacted. Says H. W. Coil: "It is difficult to understand why so many have deemed fixation a Masonic virtue, for nothing could be more dreary than a society, private or general, which, like a stagnant pool, receives no freshening stimulus but remains the same year after year." (See his *A Comprehensive View of Freemasonry*, 1954.) Another Mason asserts: "In the English-speaking world, the original philosophical or speculative Masonry has been changed over the years, and it is now in the nature of a dogmatic, pseudo-religious cult." (Harvey Newton Brown, *Freemasonry Among Negroes and Whites in America*, 1965.)

In addition to the preceding remarks, a number of Masons desire to have the order place less emphasis on its esoteric—often mystical—teachings embodied in the degree rituals. Others would prefer to see the craft become less austere and more socially oriented, involving the entire family—not just the men—in its lodge sessions. Here is what a Mason says in Michigan: "We changed from Operative Masonry to Speculative Masonry and now why not Realistic Masonry? Our Masonic Laws are archaic. . . . Why don't we get in tune with the times." (Wells Chapin, "What's Wrong With Masonry?" *Grand Lodge Bulletin* [Iowa], February, 1979.)

Whether Masonry in the future will adopt any significant changes or remain on its well-trodden path, it clearly faces a dilemma. For if it introduces noteworthy changes affecting its rituals and "landmarks," many will say that the order has lost its Masonic identity and in effect gone out of existence. If the craft clings to its old, established rites and symbolism—confined to older men—it will retain its Masonic character but at the price of continuing membership decline until one day it may cease to exist as a viable organization. Which course the ancient fraternity will choose remains to be seen.

The structure of the American Blue Lodge differs from that of British Masonry. In England the grand lodge is a national, centralized administration. Whereas in the United States each grand lodge (a jurisdiction, as Masonry calls it) most commonly is a statewide structure. There is no national grand lodge structure for Blue Lodge Masonry in the United States. There are rather forty-nine grand lodges, each an independent authority. A similar pattern obtains in Canada, where there are nine grand lodges, following provincial boundaries for the most part. Each grand lodge meets annually in convention or "communication," as Masonry calls it. The principal officer on the grand lodge level is the Grand Master. His term of office is for a one-year period, not to be succeeded by the incumbent.

The local lodge is headed by the Master, commonly called the "Worshipful Master." He is elected for a one-year term only, and he may not succeed himself. The senior Warden, Junior Warden, Secretary, and Treasurer are usually elected positions. The Senior Deacon, Junior Deacon, Chaplain, Marshall, Stewards, and the Tiler (doorkeeper) are appointed by the Master. The wardens and deacons assist the master in the initiation rites. The chaplain offers the prayers. Processions in and outside the lodge room are the responsibility of the marshall. The stewards prepare and introduce candidates for initiation. The tyler, as doorkeeper, is charged with making certain that no "profane" (uninitiated) individual enters the lodge in session. According to the ritual, the tyler is armed with a flaming sword to fend off the intruder(s). He is generally chosen for his ability to remember names and faces. Since his is a lonely position, sitting outside the door of every lodge meeting, he is frequently paid a wage. In many lodges he also serves as custodian and janitor.

Published sources on the Blue Lodge or Symbolic Masonry are abundant. Only a few selected publications are cited here. An excellent one-volume treatment of Freemasonry is that by Delmar Duane Darrah, *History and Evolution of Freemasonry* (1967). A more lengthy one-volume scholarly discussion is Bernard E. Jones, *Freemasons' Guide and Compendium* (1956). Duncan's *Masonic Ritual and Monitor* (1968) illustrates the three degrees of the Blue Lodge and also provides ritual information for the fourth, fifth, sixth, and seventh degrees of the York Rite. For a good understanding of Masonic rules and regulations, consult Albert G. Mackey's *Jurisprudence of Freemasonry* (1947). The book by Douglas Knoop and

G. P. Jones, *The Genesis of Freemasonry* (1949), is an excellent source that surveys operative and speculative Masonry. Another volume by Knoop and Jones is *A Handlist of Masonic Documents* (1942). This work contains brief summaries of the Masonic documents and manuscripts, going back to the *Regius Poem* of A.D. 1390. To read the two earliest manuscripts of operative Freemasonry, one should consult Douglas Knoop, G. P. Jones, and Douglas Hamer, eds., *The Two Earliest Masonic MSS* (1938). The reader who wants a more lengthy treatment on Masonry may wish to read R. F. Gould, *History of Freemasonry* (1885), a four-volume work. Larger public libraries often carry a number of books on Freemasonry. *The Revised Ritual of Craft Freemasonry* (1962) is a good British source with reference to the Masonic rituals. See also Harold B. Voorhis, *Facts for Masons* (1979).

THE SCOTTISH RITE

Once a man has become a member of the Blue Lodge with the degree of Master Mason, he may obtain additional degrees by opting to go the route of the Scottish Rite, where he may acquire another twenty-nine degrees. Some publications, especially non-Masonic ones, speak of "higher" degrees. Most Masons do not favor this designation because they argue there are only additional, not higher, degrees.

The reader is asked to consult the present volume's discussions of the following two organizations: Ancient Accepted Scottish Rite of Freemasonry for the Northern Masonic Jurisdiction of the United States of America and the Ancient and Accepted Scottish Rite of Freemasonry for the Southern Jurisdiction of the United States of America, The Supreme Council 33°, Mother Supreme Council of the World.

The following discussion of the twenty-nine degrees is largely indebted to Harold B. Voorhis, *Facts for Masons* (1979). The reader may wish to consult it for greater detail.

Secret Master (fourth degree). This degree currently costs about $150, as does each of the Scottish Rite degrees from the fourth through the thirty-second. Since most Masons who join the Ancient Arabic Order of Nobles of the Mystic Shrine get there by way of the Scottish Rite, it is relatively easy to see why no Shriner is poor. The Secret Master degree symbolically refers to King Solomon's Temple and the appointment of expert master masons who served as special guardians of the Sanctum Sanctorum (Holy of Holies). The degree teaches the recipients secrecy, silence, and fidelity.

Perfect Master (fifth degree). The ritual of this degree teaches that due respect is to be given to a deceased "worthy brother," since the degree commemorates the mythological slaying of Hiram Abiff (the principal architect sent by King Hiram to King Solomon to supervise the construction of Solomon's Temple).

Intimate Secretary (Sixth degree). Sometimes this degree also is known as the Confidential Secretary. The mythology of the degree refers to King Solomon saving the life of a supposed eavesdropper. That one should never pry into a brother's secrets is one of the key lessons taught by the degree.

Provost and Judge (seventh degree). The legend of this degree revolves around King Solomon's appointing judges to administer justice among the workmen building the temple. The lessons taught are justice, equity, and impartiality.

Intendant of the Building (eighth degree). As the temple's construction was delayed by Hiram Abiff's death, according to masonic legend, King Solomon had to appoint five architects—one for each department of architecture—so that construction on the temple would continue. The degree teaches that charity and benevolence are to be propagated.

Elu or *Master Elect of Nine* (ninth degree). The degree's mythology says Solomon elected nine men to investigate the slaying of Hiram. The Lesson taught is that one's zeal should not be permitted to lead one astray, even for a good cause.

Elu or *Master Elect of Fifteen* (tenth degree). This degree work recounts the arrest and punishment of Hiram's slayers. It teaches that ambition and fanaticism are conquered by the sword of justice and freedom.

Elu of the Twelve or *Sublime Master Elected* (eleventh degree). According to the ritual of this degree, twelve Masters Elect, out of the fifteen, were instrumental in bringing the murderers of Hiram to justice. For their efforts Solomon rewards them by making them heads of the twelve tribes of Israel. The moral taught by the eleventh degree is that a true and faithful "brother" will eventually receive his just reward. It also accents sincerity, honesty, and earnestness.

Grand Master Architect (twelfth degree). As is true of the twelfth degree in the Scottish Rite, this rite symbolizes a training school for workers working on the Temple of Solomon. The principles of architecture and their relationship to the liberal arts and sciences also are elaborated upon. Virtue and talent are the teachings of this degree.

Royal Arch of Solomon or *Master of the Ninth Arch* (thirteenth degree). This degree is the keystone of the arch in that it has discovered what is revealed in the succeeding degree of Perfection.

Perfect Elu or *Grand, Elect, Perfect and Sublime Mason* (fourteenth degree). Here the assertion is made that the secret vault under the "Santum Sanctorum" has been found in which the "Pillar of Beauty" rests with the Tetragrammaton (the holy four-letter name in Hebrew meaning *Yahweh*). The degree's lesson is that if one has properly prepared and consecrated his life, he will be rewarded on the "completion of the Temple."

Knight of the East or *Sword* (fifteenth degree). This degree symbolizes the Babylonian captivity and the return of the Hebrews to Jerusalem, where the rebuilding of the Temple of Solomon occurred. The moral taught is "Fidelity to conviction."

Prince of Jerusalem (sixteenth degree). This degree speaks about the trick the workers endured in rebuilding the Temple of Solomon, and how they succeeded with the aid of King Darius. The moral accent is on the majesty of truth.

Knight of the East and West (seventeenth degree). The ritual of this degree shows that the "Word" is lost again and that the third or spiritual temple (in man's heart) is to be erected and dedicated to God.

Knight of the Rose Croix (eighteenth degree). The "lost Word" is being sought by the novice, who in his searching discovers three virtues: faith, hope, and charity. The degree teaches the meaning of the "New Law."

Pontiff or *Grand Pontiff* (nineteenth degree). The conflict between good and evil is dramatized by this degree. It teaches patience and work.

Master of the Symbolic Lodge or Master Ad Vitam (twentieth degree). This ritual portrays the roles of a Masonic Master and how he obtains the right to govern, namely, by patient work and intelligence. Three prerequisites (justice, truth, and toleration) are necessary for becoming a good Master.

Noachite or *Prussian Knight* (twenty-first degree). Here the story of the medieval Crusaders is told: how they protected the innocent and fought for justice. The degree teaches that all are innocent until proven guilty.

Knight of the Royal Axe or *Prince of Libanus* (twenty-second degree). This degree rite relates how cedars on Mount Libanus were cut for Noah's Ark. That work is honorable is the lesson taught here.

Chief of the Tabernacle (twenty-third degree). The Old Testament ceremonies pertaining to the tabernacle are recalled in this degree. Only those with pure hearts are permitted to participate in the holy rituals.

Prince of the Tabernacle (twenty-fourth degree). The duties of the prince in the tabernacle are spelled out in this degree. Instead of sacrifices of flesh and blood, prayers are to be offered to God.

Knight of the Brazen Serpent (twenty-fifth degree). This ritual recalls the Old Testament account of the brazen serpent that Moses made for the Israelites to look upon for a cure from serpent bites.

Prince of Mercy (twenty-sixth degree). This degree imparts the legend of Christian Masons meeting in the catacombs of early Christendom to celebrate given mysteries. It also tells the candidate that Masonry belongs to all ages and is not a partisan religion.

Knight Commander of the Temple or *Commander of the Temple* (twenty-seventh degree). This ritual relates how the Teutonic Knights of the House of St. Mary of Jerusalem fought Saladin, the infidel, and nursed the sick by night, as well as having guarded the city of Jerusalem so that it would be safe for Christians. The five qualities (humility, temperance, chastity, generosity, and honor) of the Teutonic Knights are extolled.

Knight of the Sun or *Prince Adept* (twenty-eighth degree). In this degree nature is said to be the primary and certain revelation of God. It also talks about science, reason, and faith.

Knight of St. Andrew (twenty-ninth degree). The candidate (now Knight of St. Andrew) is told about how he is now an exponent of truth. The degree seeks to teach equality and toleration.

Knight of Kadosh (thirtieth degree). This degree instructs the recipient in the virtues of the Scottish Rite and how he is to portray qualities of steel outwardly and faith and love inwardly.

Grand Inspector Inquisitor Commander (thirty-first degree). The recipient of this degree is taught to be impartial in justice and also to remember the human weaknesses.

Sublime Prince of the Royal Secret (thirty-second degree). This is the final degree that a candidate may receive by means of petition. It teaches the candidate to be diligent in war against the age-old enemies of mankind. He is to love wisdom and be a messenger of fraternity, liberty, and equality. Having attained this degree in the Scottish Rite, the individual may proceed to the Shrine.

Sovereign Grand Inspector General (thirty-third degree). This is an honorary degree conferred at the annual sessions of the Supreme Council. A Scottish Rite pamphlet says this degree "is conferred upon those members who have been outstanding in their contributions to Freemasonry, the Scottish Rite, or who have shown in their community the leadership which marks them as men who exemplify in their lives the true meaning of the Brotherhood of man under the Fatherhood of God."

The twenty-nine degrees from the fourth through the thirty-second are grouped by the Scottish Rite into the following categories:

Lodge of Perfection = 4° through 14°
Chapter Rose Croix = 15° through 18°
Council of Kadosh = 19° through 30°
Consistory = 31° and 32°

Once an individual has traveled the entire route of the Scottish Rite, he has not only paid hundreds of dollars by paying at least $150 (1978 fees) per degree, but he has also taken a bucketful of oaths. The oaths sound quite similar to those taken in the Blue Lodge. For instance, the tenth degree (Elu or Master Elect of the Fifteen) requires the candidate to vow, in part:

I, . . . , do promise and swear upon the Holy Bible, never to reveal where I have received this degree. . . . To keep exactly in my heart all the secrets that shall be revealed to me. And in failure of this, my obligation, I consent to have my body opened perpendicularly, and to be exposed for eight hours in the open air, that the venomous flies may eat my entrails, my head to be cut off and put on the highest pinnacle of the world, and I will always be ready to inflict the same punishment on those who shall disclose this degree and break this obligation. So may God help and maintain me. Amen.

The Northern Jurisdiction (founded in 1813) includes fifteen states, north of the Ohio and east of the Mississippi rivers. Its headquarters in Boston,

Massachusetts. The Southern Jurisdiction (founded in 1801) encompasses the remaining states. It is located in Washington, D.C.

For further information on the Scottish Rite, see Henry Ridgely Evans, "The Ancient and Accepted Scottish Rite of Freemasonry," *Little Masonic Library*, Book III (1946). Another reference to consult is S. H. Baynard, *History of the Supreme Council, 33rd Degree, Ancient and Accepted Scottish Rite of Freemasonry* (1938), 2 vols. J. Blanchard, *Scottish Rite Masonry Illustrated* (1953), presents the degree rituals of the Scottish Rite. The reader may also refer to R. F. Gould's *History of Freemasonry* (1885), a 4-volume work. Finally, the reader may also see Harold V. B. Voorhis, *Facts for Masons* (1979), which, among other things, provides helpful information on the degrees of the Scottish Rite.

THE YORK RITE

As was stated earlier, a Master Mason may obtain additional degrees by going the way of the Scottish Rite, or he may take the other fork on the Masonic road by "traveling" along the York Rite (also known as the American Rite). At the end of either rite he may enter the Shrine. A few Masons go through both rites. The York Rite has nine degrees. If one counts the Knights Templar degree, it can be considered to have ten degrees. The Knights Templar degree, however, does not carry a numeral identification.

The name of the York Rite, of Anglo-American origin, is considered by some to be a misnomer in that it reminds Masons of the Ancient York Masons, an organization that came into being in 1756 in England as a result of the schism in Masonry. It ceased to exist in 1813. Critics believe the name American Rite is more appropriate.

The York Rite consists of three distinct and separate bodies: the Royal Arch Chapter,* the Council of Royal and Select Masters,* and the Commandery of Knights Templar.* In this respect the York Rite is substantially different from the Scottish Rite, which is a continuous entity, organizationally.

Mark Master (fourth degree). Again, after one has become a Master Mason by obtaining three degrees in the Blue Lodge, he may petition for the fourth degree in the York Rite. The mythology of this degree revolves about a young Fellow Craft Mason, who in the quarries of Tyre, found a stone of peculiar form and beauty that was marked with a double circle, as well as other mysterious characters. The young craftsman presented the stone as his own workmanship. It was rejected and thrown among the rubbish. Later when one of the arches of Solomon's Temple was nearly completed it was found that one keystone was missing. After searching the correct stone was found. It was the one thrown away on the rubbish. Moreover, its marks were those of Hiram Abiff. The lessons taught by this ritual are to be on the level and correct one's irregularities.

Past Master (fifth degree). This degree ritual is less elaborate than others and essentially devoid of mythology. Its basic lesson seeks to teach the candidate that one must be qualified to govern in a position of leadership and that a lack of competence leads to chaos.

Most Excellent Master (sixth degree). Here the ceremony revolves about the completion of King Solomon's Temple. The candidate has become a Most Excellent Master by virtue of having completed the temple with the capstone. The moral points to covering another's faults and imperfections with the mantle of brotherly love.

Royal Arch Mason (seventh degree). The legend of this degree relates how three Most Excellent Masters were taken into captivity by Nebuchadnezzar and how they returned to rebuild Solomon's Temple. In clearing away rubble from the temple's ruins, the three Most Excellent Masters discover secrets valuable to the craft.

Royal Master (eighth degree). This degree's legend refers to the conference that took place between Adonhiram (Hiram Abiff's successor) and the two kings. The conference is prompted by Hiram Abiff's death.

Select Master (ninth degree). Chronologically the legend of this degree precedes Hiram's death, even though it follows the Royal Master degree. In the ritual Hiram deposits his secret pertaining to the construction of Solomon's Temple. From this degree the candidate may enter the Commandery, which consists of the Order of the Red Cross, the Order of the Knights of Malta, and the Knights Templar. From the Knights Templar access to the Shrine (AAONMS)* is permissible.

Super Excellent Master (unnumbered degree). This degree is an honorary degree and thus not necessary to complete the York Rite. According to Masonic authorities, this degree is the most dramatic in its ritual.

Order of the Red Cross (unnumbered degree). Once the seventh degree (Royal Arch Mason) has been acquired, an individual may go the route of the Royal Master (eighth degree) or join the Order of the Red Cross. Its legend pertains to rebuilding the Temple of Solomon.

Order of the Knights of Malta (unnumbered degree). From the Order of the Red Cross the candidate goes to this degree, whose ritual legend tells the candidate that he has now received the pass degree to the Order of the Knights of Malta, a once-hostile group. Masons often refer to this degree as a "Christian degree."

Order of Knights Templar (unnumbered degree). Having obtained the Order of the Red Cross and the Order of the Knights of Malta, the individual may proceed to the Order of the Knights Templar. This degree in its mythology goes back to the Knights Templar, who participated in the medieval Crusades. As stated above, once the individual has become a Knight Templar, he may join the Shrine (AAONMS).*

The York Rite degrees, like the Scottish Rite degrees, are categorized in three groups:

Chapter or Capitular Degrees = 4° through 7°
Council or Cryptic Degrees = 8° and 9°
Commandery Degrees = Order of the Red Cross, Order of the Knights of Malta, and Knights Templar.

Each of the York Rite degrees requires an oath of obligation. The Select Master or ninth degree, for instance, has the candidate swear:

. . . binding myself under no less penalty, besides all my former penalties, to have my hands chopped off at the stumps, my eyes plucked out from the sockets, my body quartered, and then thrown among the rubbish of the Temple. . . . So help me God, and keep me steadfast in the same. (See Jabez Richardson, *Monitor of Freemasonry*, n.d.)

The York Rite is not an unbroken and continuous whole, unlike the Scottish Rite. It has no programs of charity. Such activities are directed individually by the three groups: the Royal Arch Masons, the Council of Royal and Select Masters, and the Commandery of Knights Templar.

Separately published books or articles pertaining to the York Rite, as such, do not exist. To read about the York Rite, the reader is advised to read about the three separate bodies that make up the York Rite. The *Royal Arch Mason*, a quarterly publication, is helpful in understanding the several groups comprising the York Rite.

FREEMEN'S PROTECTIVE SILVER FEDERATION. Founded in Spokane, Washington, in 1894, this secret, oath-bound society sought "to unite the friends of silver under one banner to battle for the white metal and to wage war against the gold monopoly." Reportedly the society was an outgrowth of the National Order of Videttes. Bankers and lawyers were ineligible for membership. The society went out of existence soon after the turn of the century.

FREESMITHS, ANCIENT ORDER OF (AOF). This fraternal society, which kept its activities very secret, was organized in Baltimore, Maryland, in 1865. The order traced its roots back to *Der Alte Orden der Freischmiede* of Germany. Some accounts traced the order back to the eighth century during Charlemagne's reign. The society's objectives were directed toward "intellectual development, the extension of wisdom and toleration, sick benefits and life insurance."

Unlike most fraternal societies in the United States, the AOF ritual did not have any religious features. The order worked six degrees. Colorful regalia usually accompanied the degrees. "Truth, Fidelity, and Secrecy" was the society's motto.

The order did not limit its membership to those of German background; however, Germans were the dominant ethnic group. All members, by their oaths, obligated themselves to help the unfortunate and distressed brethren.

Local units or lodges were known as "Smithies." According to Albert C. Stevens, the society had lodges in virtually every state by 1896. Headquarters were located in Baltimore, Maryland. REFERENCE: *Cyc. Frat.*

FREE SONS OF ISRAEL, THE (FSOI). Founded in 1849, the FSOI is the oldest national Jewish fraternal order in the United States. The first lodge was started on January 10, 1849, in the city of New York. Three months later the organization formed its Constitutional Grand Lodge. The grand lodge met three times during the month of March in 1849. At its third meeting it adopted rules for the establishment and government of subordinate lodges as well as regulations pertaining to ritual, regalia, and other fraternal elements.

The Independent Order of Free Sons of Israel, as it was first known, apparently borrowed certain forms and nomenclature from Freemasonry* and Odd Fellowship.* Its motto, "Friendship, Love, Truth," is the same as that of the Odd Fellows. It has a secret ritual, initiation ceremony, and accompanying passwords.

Some of the FSOI's objectives are:

to assist its members in translating into practice our [Jewish] heritage and freedom; to help Jews to freedom both here and abroad; to advance the principles of human equality on a worldwide basis; to join experience in human understanding with the advances in social science and communications and the influence of laws to achieve these ends; to protect Jews from oppression and, as practicing Free Sons, to render fraternal aid and assistance to its members.

Any Jewish male or female eighteen or older is eligible for membership in this Jewish fraternal society. Presently (1979) the order has 10,000 members in forty-two lodges. The membership has changed very little during the past decade. In the late 1960s the order also had about 10,000 members in forty-six lodges.

Altruistically, the FSOI conducts blood banks, directs bond drives for the United Jewish Appeal, and distributes toys to handicapped girls and boys. It also helps support homes for senior citizens, convalescent homes, and summer camps for elderly citizens and for needy children, which projects are supported by means of foundation funds. The FSOI also operates The Free Sons Athletic Association, which teaches youngsters various sports such as baseball, track and field, golf, softball, basketball, year-round bowling, and ping-pong. A scholarship program for elementary and high school students benefits a number of Jewish students who show high performance in Hebrew.

The religious and cultural heritage of the Jewish people is underscored by

Chanukah and Purim parties held by The Free Sons. These activities are largely directed to the young so that they may value their Jewish roots.

Two separate divisions characterize the FSOI: the fraternal and the insurance divisions. The insurance department offers its members the usual life insurance found in most fraternal benefit societies. A Free Sons Credit Union enables members to borrow money at conveniently low rates of interest.

The emblem of the FSOI consists of three rings superimposed on a rose-like design. The outer ring portrays the words Free Sons of Israel; the inner circle displays the society's motto, Friendship, Love, Truth; at the center of the emblem is a picture of two persons, one of them seated and one standing. The standing one, with arm outstretched, conveys the sign of blessing or anointment upon the one in the seated position.

The national convention of the society meets triennially. The head officer of the grand lodge is referred to as "Grand Master." All other grand lodge (national) officers also carry the prefix title of "Grand." There are no statewide or regional organizations. Local gatherings are known as subordinate lodges. National headquarters are in New York, New York.

Each quarter the society publishes a newspaper called the *Reporter*. The reader may consult this periodical for further information on the order. No known scholarly publication has been produced on the FSOI.

_ *G* _

GALILEAN FISHERMEN, GRAND UNITED ORDER OF. The date of origin for this black fraternal benefit order was 1856. It was founded in Washington, D.C. This early date of origin made it one of the first organized fraternal societies in the United States. The Society claimed to be of Masonic origin. It paid sick and death benefits. The society's emblem displayed a fish, a cross, a rose, and the letters I.N.R.I. of the eighteenth degree of Scottish Rite Freemasonry.* Both men and women were eligible for membership. REFERENCES: *Cyc. Frat.*; *DSOS*.

GEORGE WASHINGTON MASONIC NATIONAL MEMORIAL ASSOCIATION (GWMNMA). This association was organized in 1911 to provide greater security for the mementos pertaining to George Washington, the first president of the United States and also a highly honored Mason. The GWMNMA is incorporated in the state of Virginia, and the association's affairs are managed by a board of directors. Membership consists of grand lodges as well as individual Masons. Since its organization, the order has built and maintained a Masonic memorial temple dedicated to George Washington. The order offers no degrees and has no subordinate units. Its "headquarters" are situated in Alexandria, Virginia, where the executive secretary resides.

GERMAN ORDER OF HARUGARI. See Harugari, German Order of.

GLEANER LIFE INSURANCE SOCIETY, THE (GLIS). Cairo, Michigan, in 1894 served as the site for this fraternal society, which upon its founding was named the Ancient Order of Gleaners. When the order was first organized, it admitted only persons who were actively engaged in farming, gardening, and related occupations or small-town (up to 3,000 people) residents. These restrictons no longer apply. Today (1979) any "person who is of good moral character, not under the age of sixteen (16) years . . . who furnishes satisfactory evidence of insurability, shall be eligible to [*sic*] benefit membership. . . ." Membership voting is done by ball balloting. Two or more black balls means the candidate is rejected for membership.

The GLIS has two additional membership categories, cooperative and junior. The cooperative membership is similar to what most fraternal benefit societies call a social membership in that such members have no insurance rights vis-à-vis the society. Junior membership includes those who are insured with the GLIS from birth to fifteen years of age. When the junior member reaches twenty-one; benefit membership is attained automatically. It is through these three kinds of memberships that the society seeks to "unite all persons—regardless of sex, nationality, political preference or denominational distinctions—into one fraternal brotherhood, the members of which recognize and believe in the existence of a Supreme Being, the Creator and Preserver of the Universe." Presently (1979) the society has 47,000 members in ninety-eight active arbors (lodges). This represents a decline from about ten years ago, when there were about 55,000 members.

The society not only operates with the lodge system, but it still has a ritual that focuses on four degrees: Introductory, Adoption, Ruth, and Dramatic degrees. The Introduction degree is required of all new members. After a brief instruction the candidate takes an obligation promising to obey the society, be faithful to the society's principles, and not bring harm to any members. The Adoption degree consists of lectures pertaining to the society's basic principles. A good portion of this degree's moral instruction is drawn from the Biblical story of Naomi, Ruth, and Boaz. (The reader probably recalls that Ruth and her mother-in-law, Naomi, are gleaners mentioned in the Old Testament.) Symbols of the initiatory degree are the sheaf, sickle, and hourglass. The second degree (Ruth) appears to be a rite for women. It too draws from the Book of Ruth in the Old Testament. The Dramatic degree ritual requires the candidate to be hoodwinked. In part, this degree also points to Ruth, Naomi, and Boaz; however, other items are also included.

The ritual employs a fair amount of religious symbolism. For instance, the room where the Gleaners meet has an altar in its center; prayers are spoken and hymns are sung. And as is true of most fraternal rituals, the prayers and hymns are designed to be nonsectarian by omitting any reference to Christianity or its founder, Jesus Christ. The ritual also contains an installation format and a funeral ceremony.

The GLIS provides scholarship assistance for college students, and through its insurance programs it gives benefits to its members' orphans. The Gleaners' Fraternal Blood Group Program operates "a living blood bank as a health guard to Gleaner members." This program operates on a volunteer basis at the local arbor (lodge) level.

In terms of fraternal functions, the society sponsors various recreational activities such as bowling, baseball, and square dancing. As a family-oriented fraternal group, the GLIS conducts its "great Gleaner picnics" for the entire family. These picnics are held by state and regional Gleaner associations.

The emblem of the society portrays a family of four—father, mother, daughter, and son—on a circular design. In the hands of the parents lie stalks of grain, symbolizing the role of gleaners. Across the grain stalks are the Latin words *Prudens Futuri* (thought for the future). Encircling the family portrait is the inscription: The Gleaner Life Insurance Society. The society's watchwords are benevolence, protection, and fraternity.

As has already been noted above, the local units in the GLIS are known as "Arbors." It is on the arbor level that members are initiated into the society. Each arbor elects a Chief Gleaner, Vice-Chief Gleaner, Secretary and Treasurer, Chaplain, Conductor, Conductress, Lecturer, and Guard. The last five have ritual duties. The national level is called the "Supreme Arbor." It meets in convention every two years. Representatives are chosen from every local arbor. Birmingham, Michigan, is the site of the society's head offices.

Sources on GLIS are not abundant. One good source is the quarterly publication *The National Gleaner Forum*. The society's various brochures may be obtained from the national headquarters. Another helpful publication is the society's ritual. The latest edition was issued in 1961. The *Constitution and By-Laws* (1977) also are helpful in understanding the society.

GOLDEN CHAIN, ORDER OF (OGC). Back in 1929 a group of Master Masons and their immediate families met in Asbury Park, New Jersey, to form an organization that was to be solely dedicated to fraternalism. The OGC is one of the orders that belongs to what is commonly called Adoptive Masonry. One of the order's publicity brochures says: "Like Masonry, we strive for a better way of life, irrespective of race, color or creed. Our members are dedicated as one family in upholding the torch of understanding and promoting the finer ideals of life and living.''

Although the order was founded solely for fraternal purposes, it has now become quite involved in extrafraternal matters, namely, various forms of philanthropy. In 1950 the OGC dedicated a 138-acre summer camp in Blairstown, New Jersey. Here underprivileged and handicapped children may enjoy wholesome activities. The camp, which has a ten-acre lake, is also used by groups such as the Boy Scouts,* De Molay,* Girls of the Golden Court (a group sponsored by the OGC), and others. Each year, one Sunday in June is set aside as "Golden Chain Day" at the camp. This day allows the members of OGC to mix work with pleasure by inspecting the camp and also relaxing in its peaceful environment.

The order is also engaged in sponsoring a pragmatic educational camp with Gallaudet College in Washington, D.C. This program has grown into a project embracing the National Association for the Deaf and other handicapped youths. Scholarships are also given to students at Gallaudet College.

As a Masonically related organization, the OGC has a secret ritual that it says "could be used at any interdenominational service as a shining symbol." The language and symbolism of the ritual has a Masonic ring. For instance, it speaks of its six officers as "jewels," as does Masonry. Each officer ("jewel") exalts some ideal of womanhood. Like most traditional fraternal groups, the OGC has a standing ritual committee.

The insignia of the order has six oblong chain links forming a hexagon. Inside of the hexagonal chain-link border are six shields, each portraying a separate symbol. At the hub or center of the insignia are the letters OGC.

The OGC has "Links" (chapters) in Connecticut, Massachusetts, New Jersey, New York, Pennsylvania, Delaware, and Michigan. The national organization is known as the "Grand Link." It meets in convention annually. In 1967 the order had about 10,000 members in thirty-nine links, but in 1978 it had only 5,000 members and twenty-five links. National headquarters are in West Caldwell, New Jersey.

For further information one may consult the order's annual proceedings, its semiannual newsletter, and a number of publicity brochures.

GOLDEN CIRCLE, ORDER OF (OGC). This organization is a black female structure that serves as an auxiliary to black Masons who have attained the 32d and 33d degrees in the United Supreme Council, Ancient and Accepted Scottish Rite—Prince Hall Affiliate.

The OGC was organized in 1886. Similar to some other auxiliary orders allied with Masonry (black or white), the OGC employs some form of male supervision. The highest ranking male official is known as "Illustrious Deputy."

The OGC has a ritual part of which is a secret obligation or oath. Each female member takes the one-degree oath. Upon being elected by means of the ball-ballot method, each female member is referred to as a "Loyal Lady." The head officer bears the title of "Loyal Lady Ruler."

Organizationally, the OGC operates on the local and state level. The latter structure is known as the "State Grand Association." The grand lodge meets annually.

Philanthropically, the OGC supports national black organizations. The National Association for the Advancement of Colored People and the National Urban League are two groups that receive financial contributions from the Golden Circle fraternity.

Very little published material appears to be available on the OGC. Most of the information in the present sketch was obtained through personal interviews with some members of the OGC.

GOLDEN CROSS, UNITED ORDER OF (UOGC). This fraternal benefit society was founded in 1876 in the New England states. Its members had to be total abstainers from all alcoholic beverages. Both men and women belonged to the society. The organizers of the UOGC, according to Albert C. Stevens, *Cyclopedia of Fraternities* (1907), were primarily Freemasons.

The UOGC operated its beneficiary programs and policies on the basis of the graded assessment plan. In 1910 the society had about 18,000 members. In 1962 the society merged with Woodmen of the World Life Insurance Society. Former headquarters were in Lewiston, Maine.

GOLDEN KEY, ORDER OF (OGK). Not much current information is available on this Masonic order. The group had its origin at the University of Oklahoma, Norman, Oklahoma, in 1925. It was started by the Beta Chapter of Sigma Mu Sigma fraternity. Almost twenty years later, in 1943, a "Sovereign Preceptory" (national organization) was started at Joliet, Illinois.

According to the Masonic Service Association the objective of the OGK was "To establish and perpetuate a University to include an entire community and a Center of Learning based on Masonic philosophy. . . ." Membership is open only to those who belong to the Knights Templar. Two degrees are available: the Pledge or Chief Craftsman degree and the Initiatory or Knight of the Golden Key degree. As recently as 1978, the Masonic Service Association did not know the address of the OGK.

GOLDEN LINKS, ORDER OF. Founded in Wheeling, West Virginia, in 1905, this order was a fraternal benefit society for men and women. Its small membership of 1,000 in 1921 partially accounted for the society's merger with the American Insurance Union in 1922. The merger meant the society ceased to function as a separate fraternal organization. REFERENCE: *Cyc. Frat.*

GOLDEN ROD, ORDER OF THE. This society was founded in Detroit, Michigan, in 1894, by members of the Knights of Macabees,* Woodmen of the World,* and other fraternal orders. The society provided beneficiary insurance. Sometime during the early 1900s the order dissolved. REFERENCE: *Cyc. Frat.*

GOLDEN STAR FRATERNITY. This was a fraternal benefit society, organized in 1881 in Newark, New Jersey. Both men and women were admitted as members. Its ritual accented benevolence and charity. New York, New Jersey, and Connecticut were the only states in which the society operated. REFERENCE: *Cyc. Frat.*

GOOD FELLOWS, ROYAL SOCIETY OF. A fraternal beneficiary society that was organized in Rhode Island in 1882. As in so many other instances, this order was founded by individuals who held membership in such societies as Freemasonry,* Knights of Honor,* Royal Arcanum,* Independent Order of Odd Fellows,* and the Ancient Order of United Workmen.* The society admitted both men and women to its membership roster.

The emblem of the order consisted of a crown surmounted by a Latin cross. These two items were surrounded by a ring of twelve small tangential circles. In eleven of the circles appeared the letters spelling Good Fellows. The twelfth circle displayed a five-pointed star. The society also had a secret ritual. Headquarters were in New York City. REFERENCES: *Cyc. Frat.*; *DSOS*.

GOOD SAMARITANS AND DAUGHTERS OF SAMARIA, INDE-PENDENT ORDER OF. This fraternal benefit society, which was abstinence-oriented, was founded September 14, 1847, in the city of New York. The society was organized for black men and women. Instrumental founders of the order came from the white group known as the Grand Lodge of the Grand United Order of Good Samaritans.

The society offered fraternal benefits as well as educational programs for its members. Somewhat atypically for fraternal orders at the time, the society offered old age and annuity benefits. The watchwords of the order were "Love, Purity, and Truth." Its headquarters were housed in Washington, D.C. REFERENCE: *Cyc. Frat.*

GOOD TEMPLARS, INTERNATIONAL ORDER OF (IOGT). When this order was first founded in Utica, New York, in 1850, it was called the Knights of Jericho.* The society was a total and secret abstinence organization. Its chief organizer was Daniel Cady of Lansingburg, New York. Cady was a member of the Sons of Temperance, which was founded in 1842, a fraternal benefit organization that sought to reform drunkards and prevent others from becoming drunks.

When Cady's organization began it had only one degree, but in the year 1851 when it changed its name to the Good Templars it also added two degrees to its ritual. The first one was the degree of Heart, the second was the degree of Charity, and the third was called the degree of Royal Virtue. Now (1979) the order has only one degree in its ritual, the degree of Justice. In the initiation rite the candidate (male or female) is asked to promise to do all in his power "to promote total abstinence of intoxicating beverages both through the enforcement of laws and through your own way of life." The ritual, as is true of many lodge rituals, has a prayer. It also provides for the singing of a song. The order is not overly concerned with the secrecy of its ritual.

The Good Templars order underwent some changes over the years. In 1852 a schismatic group from within its midst formed the Independent Order of Good Templars. The split, however, did not last long, for in the same year (1852) the factions came together and formed the Grand Lodge of the Independent Order of Good Templars of the State of New York. After 1852 the order enjoyed tremendous prosperity. According to Albert Stevens, *Cyclopedia of Fraternities* (1907), the Good Templars had about 350,000 members around the year 1900. In 1868 the society spread to England. Today (1979) the membership in the United States has dwindled to less than 2,000 members, but the worldwide membership exceeds 700,000.

In order to cope with its declining memberships the IOGT has made a number of changes. Some years ago, it tried to improve its image by changing the word "Order" to "Organization." The "Chief Templar" became "President." The "use of regalia and rituals was diminished or eliminated, and other changes were made to modernize," says a recent letter from the national president. His letter also said: "I cannot account for the decline in the United States, but it is one of the sad facts of life. I know of no cause that needs the support more at this time, when the use of the drug alcohol is costing this country 42.7 billion dollars yearly. . . ."

The IOGT promotes itself as a fraternal order that builds good citizenship and democracy. It is proud that early in its existence women were admitted as regular members in the fight against the use of alcoholic beverages. One of its brochures says that the society is "dedicated to attempts to heal the hurts which man inflicts upon himself and his fellowmen, and, by education and example, try to prevent these hurts."

The emblem at first look reminds one of the back of a silver dollar. On a circular background it displays the American eagle, clutching both olive branches and arrows in its claws. The words National Council U.S.A. Inc. encircle the eagle. The founding date, 1851, and the letters I.O.G.T. appear above the eagle's head.

On the national level the society calls its structure "The National Council of the United States." The national structure is made up of regional groups. These may be called "Grand Lodges" or "District Lodges," according to the IOGT constitution. Local units are commonly called "Lodges." A few years ago, however, the society permitted lodges to call themselves "Chapters," if they so desired. The national council meets triennially.

The order publishes the *National Good Templar*, a monthly periodical except for July and January. This publication primarily pivots around one theme: don't drink alcohol! Various data and facts are marshaled to support the basic premise of the order. The articles are by no means simplistic or pious in their reasoning.

For further information see the society's historical material catalogued at the University of Michigan, Ann Arbor, Michigan. Back issues of the *National Good Templar* provide helpful insights into the order's history.

GRAND COLLEGE OF RITES OF THE UNITED STATES OF AMERICA, THE (GCR). On May 12, 1932, nine Masons got together to form this organization in Washington, D.C. The basic objectives of the GCR are to study the history of all Masonic rites, to control the present rites so uniformity may be maintained, especially in clocking the proliferation of rites not under proper jurisdiction; to collect and preserve existing rites; and "to print rituals of dormant Masonic Rites and Systems."

The GCR has no degrees that it bestows upon its members. As it confers no degrees, the order also has no ritual.

Membership is limited to one hundred active "Fellows" in the United States. An additional forty *Fellows-Honoris Causa* may be admitted from outside of the United States. All must be Master Masons. The college also admits "an unlimited number of Members, selected by invitation, from which Active Fellows are selected when vacancies occur, upon recommendation of a Committee appointed by the Grand Chancellor. Members have the same rights and privileges as Fellows except that they shall have no vote."

There are no subordinate units in the society. Headquarters are in Chesapeake, Virginia, home of the Grand Registrar.

The present report is largely based on the unpublished document, "Allied Masonic Groups and Rites" (1978), produced by the Masonic Service Association.

GRAND FRATERNITY. Incorporated in the state of Indiana, this secret benefit society came into being in 1885. In 1893 the order was reincorporated in Pennsylvania. Its organizers, as in so many other instances, held membership in Masonry,* the American Legion of Honor,* the Royal Arcanum,* and other fraternities.

The society had a rather lengthy catalogue of objectives. These were to unite acceptable white persons who were over sixteen years of age, to foster and strengthen fraternalism among the members, to aid in furnishing homes and schools, to establish benefit funds for the members, and more.

Membership in the society was open to both sexes. Every member was known by the name *Frater*. In 1923, according to *Statistics, Fraternal Societies*, the society had 15,259 members, plus a juvenile group of 1,056 members. In 1936 the society merged with Ben Hur Life Association.* Headquarters were in Philadelphia, Pennsylvania. REFERENCES: *Cyc. Frat.*; *DSOS*.

GRAND MASTERS OF MASONS IN NORTH AMERICA, CONFERENCE OF (GMMNA). The beginning of this conference apparently goes back about to 1909, when grand masters met in Philadelphia and Baltimore. According to the Masonic Service Association, the purpose of the conference is "To obtain views of brethren from different parts of the country on Masonic problems, to get an educational viewpoint on various Masonic subjects and, by personal contact, help cement the ties between Grand Jurisdictions which promote the unity and universality of Freemasonry."

Membership consists of grand masters of the grand lodges (statewide jurisdictions) of Canada and the United Staes. The group has no subordinate units or bodies. It also does not offer any degrees or have a separate ritual. Currently (1979) the "headquarters" reside with the executive secretary in Towson, Maryland.

GRAND UNITED ORDER OF GALILEAN FISHERMEN. See Galilean Fishermen, Grand United Order of.

GRAND UNITED ORDER OF ODD FELLOWS IN AMERICA. See Odd Fellows, Grand United Order of.

GRANGE, THE. See Patrons of Husbandry, Order of.

GREATER BENEFICIAL UNION OF PITTSBURGH (GBU). This society was officially incorporated on April 14, 1892, in Allegheny County in Pennsylvania. The founding name of the organization was the *Deutscher Unterstuetzungs-Bund* (German Beneficial Union). The society was formed because the German residents felt that the "German-American element was facing a state of disintegration." To prevent the perceived disintegration, many German residents of Pittsburgh felt a fraternal spirit would be the solution.

Within one month of the society's formation the organization had 243 members in six districts. By 1893 the GBU established a publication, the *Union Reporter*, to keep its members informed, who numbered about 2,000 by that time. Today the publication is known as the *GBU Reporter*. Occasionally the periodical carries German articles that are of interest to long-time members, who feel "at home" by reading some items in German.

The GBU employs a ritual that is quite simple and brief. New members are received ("initiated") by signing the membership application and hearing the president of the local lodge address the candidate about the privileges of his or her membership. The ritual also instructs the new member how to enter the lodge sessions by giving proper identification to the guard at the door. No oath or religious elements, except for an opening prayer, are contained in the ritual.

Membership is open to male and female applicants, provided they are sixteen or older. Presently (1979) the society has 37,000 members in 123 districts. In 1965 the membership roster had 50,000 members.

The structure of the GBU operates on two levels: local (known as "District") and national. The national convention meets every four years. Headquarters of the society are located in Pittsburgh, Pennsylvania.

Over the years the GBU has kept pace with the advances in modern fraternal insurance practices. Today it has $120,000,000 in insurance, making it one of the top forty fraternal benefit societies. The society sponsors fraternal activities such as outings, GBU baseball days, and other social events. Although the society began as a German ethnic group, it now welcomes individuals from all ethnic backgrounds.

Additional information may be obtained by consulting the *GBU Reporter*, published monthly. The *Ritual and Guide* (1967) also is helpful in providing a better understanding of the society. Finally, the organization's bylaws provide a good view of the society's structure.

GREEK CATHOLIC UNION OF THE UNITED STATES OF AMERICA (GCU). Originally, this organization was known as the Greek Catholic Union of Russian Brotherhoods when it was founded in 1892 in Wilkes-Barre, Pennsylvania. The society was formed by fourteen independent Greek Catholic lodges that joined themselves into one larger group. The early organizers sought unity, protection, education, and assistance as their main objectives. In spite of organizational adversity during the society's early years, the organization progressed. By 1906 a juvenile branch was created for children who could be insured from ages six through sixteen. In 1911 a gymnastic branch was formed to promote physical culture and athletic values for the members of the GCU.

As the society's name would imply, the relationship between the Greek Catholic Church and the GCU has always been quite cordial. Many of the local units have arisen out of the church's local parishes. In the organization's structure a spiritual advisor is chosen as a regular officer, and the officers' pledge is very religious in content. For instance, "I (name) swear by one God in the Holy Trinity, by the Most Pure Virgin Mary, by the Patron Saint (name) of my lodge, by Saint Nicholas, and by all the Saints of our Church. . . ."

The GCU offers the usual array of fraternal insurance programs and benefits. In addition to the insurance plans, support is given to church institutions, education, cultural programs, athletic activities, and fraternal assistance. A recreation-retirement headquarters has been built in Beaver County, Pennsylvania. The complex takes in members who are fifty-five or older. The 544-acre complex houses an eighteen-hole golf course, an Olympic-size pool, tennis courts, and other recreational facilities.

Requirements for membership specify that one must be a member of a Catholic church (Greek or Latin rite), of "Russian or other Slav origin, race or nationality, excepting those instances where a member marries and such a spouse is not of a Slav nationality. . . ." After sixty-five membership is closed to those who have never belonged to the GCU. Presently (1979) the membership roster has approximately 50,000 members. This figure has been rather constant since at least 1965.

The emblem of the GCU is an eagle perched on the American flag and the Patriarchal cross. Above the eagle is a blazing five-pointed star. The society has no ritual.

Local units are called "Subordinate Lodges." Each local lodge is required to meet monthly. The highest authority structure is the "National Lodge," which convenes as a legislating body every four years. Headquarters are located in Minhall, Pennsylvania.

Further information may be obtained by consulting the *Constitution and By-Laws of the Greek Catholic Union of the U.S.A.* Also helpful is a booklet, *Facing the Future Fraternally*, published by the GCU. In 1979 the society issued the *1979 GCU Yearbook*. This provides an update for the year of 1979.

GROTTOES OF NORTH AMERICA, SUPREME COUNCIL. This order also is commonly known as the MYSTIC ORDER OF VEILED PROPHETS OF THE ENCHANTED REALM (MOVPER). It has its roots of origin with LeRoy Fairchild, a Freemason, who in 1889 met with a few likeminded individuals in Hamilton, New York, to organize a group that would have mirth, song, and laughter for fun-loving Masons. Initially, the group was named the "Fairchild Deviltry Committee." By June 13, 1890, the group called itself the "Supreme Council of the Mystic Order of Veiled Prophets of the Enchanted Realm." Fairchild's purpose in founding the order was to have an organization of "Master Masons where gaiety should rule supreme, and thus afford ample opportunity for the development of that happy companionship which he [Fairchild] esteemed essential to the full rounding-out of the Masonic characters." "The Grotto [a meeting place] is the play-house of the craft [Freemasonry*]—the place where world-worn men can get together, forget their cares, and be, as it were, boys again, for within the portals of the Grotto the stiffness and formality which keeps men apart melts away. . . ." Charles Ferguson, in his *Fifty Million Brothers* (1937), describes the order as trying "to rival the inspired absurdities of the Shrine, but its costumes and lingo have a more fabricated and stilted quality, not unlike the top-lofty whimsies of a high school fraternity."

The MOVPER has its own ritual, which it says is founded on "a very ancient Persian manuscript, discovered in a secret vault in one of the sacred temples of Teheran, the City of Mystery. . . ." In spite of the unsupported claim for the ritual's Persian origin, the ritual was revised in 1940 by Americans. The order believes that its ritual is "Perhaps the most spectacular, colorful and elaborate ritual seen anywhere." The ritual ceremonies "are entirely different from those of any fraternal organizations. A large stage is required for properly presenting the Order, and considerable money for costumes, stage scenery and paraphernalia. . . ." By means of the ritual the order teaches "high ideals of manhood, and points unerringly to the path of duty." The "Veiled Prophet" part of the order's name indicates that in its ritual there are:

many strange and mystic rites . . . wonderful and weird. . . . Veiled to the profane [nonmembers], but, lifted often to give the inquisitive Neophyte a chance to gaze upon the "Veiled Mokanna" the well known ruler of fiction whose presence in our midst seems to stimulate and excite the magic brain of those enthusiastic Masons who, while apparently dreaming, have been awakened by the lifting of the veil and seeing the fabled visions as they tread the mystic way. . . .

The MOVPER is very careful in making it clear that it is in no way a Masonic group, offering an additional Masonic degree. It does not intend to represent itself as Masonic, even though its members can only be drawn from Freemasonry. One of the order's twelve commandments asserts: "The Grotto is a social organization for Master Masons."

Like the Shriners (another Masonically related order), the MOVPER has its members wear fezzes in public appearances. Each fez has a red tassle, and on its front appears the symbol of a turban-clad head of an Arabian prophet, who is cradled between two horns. The letters M.O.V.P.E.R. stand above the symbol. Usually when the order meets in convention it has its participants engage in a public parade, wearing colorful uniforms.

Its membership, as already mentioned, is exclusively drawn from the Masonic Blue Lodge. This means that only white males may become "veiled prophets," since Freemasonry in the United States does not admit nonwhites. The order is proud to cite well-known Americans as having joined its ranks: U.S. senators B. B. Hickenlooper and Herman Eugene Talmadge and former state governors Harold E. Stassen, Orville W. Freeman, Orville E. Faubus, Otto Kerner, and G. Mennen Williams.

MOVPER is quite active in supporting the United Cerebral Palsy Educational and Research Foundation. In order to contribute to this charitable effort the order has set up the Humanitarian Foundation of the Supreme Council M.O.V.P.E.R. Since 1970, the organization also has provided dental aid to handicapped children.

On the international level, which includes Canada and the United States, the order is known as the "Supreme Council." The supreme council meets in convention annually. Its head officer bears the title of "Grand Monarch." On the local level the order calls its lodges or chapters "Grottoes," of which there are 191. Each grotto has an Arabian name. The 1978 membership roster lists 65,000 "Veiled Prophets." This is down from the 100,000 mark that the order enjoyed a few years ago. Its ladies' auxiliary is known as the Daughters of Mokanna.* The national headquarters of MOVPER are located in Chicago, Illinois.

Reading material on the MOVPER largely consists of pamphlets and brochures published by the order. One of the most comprehensive pamphlets is *A Peep Into the Mystic Realm* (1973), published by the order.

___ *H* _____

HARUGARI, GERMAN ORDER OF (GOH). Formed in 1847 in New York as a fraternal group that would bring the German immigrants together socially and to practice their mother tongue. The order was also begun out of a concern for some group defense against the strong native-American sentiment that prevailed at that time. The name Harugari was chosen in honor of the old Teutons who were called Harugaris by virtue of their meeting in the forests. *Haruc* meant grove or forest.

The order's motto has always been "Friendship, Love, and Humanity." As a fraternal benefit society, the organization has been recognized for its altruistic demeanor. Some critics, however, have felt that the GOH has been antagonistic toward the Roman Catholic Church.

The ritual of the GOH used to have three degrees. Whether it still has three degrees the author has been unable to ascertain, as the order either moved to a new location or went out of existence during the last several years. In 1975 there were just under 1,000 members. At that time its headquarters were in South Ozone Park, New York.

For additional information, see the society's bimonthly publication, *Der Harugari*. See also Albert C. Stevens, *Cyclopedia of Fraternities* (1907).

HAYMAKERS' ASSOCIATION, NATIONAL (NHA). This fraternal society was organized back in 1879. The Haymakers' Association might be called the "fun" or "friendship" society of the Improved Order of Red Men.* No one may join unless he first holds membership in the Improved Order of Red Men. In 1980 the order had 10,000 members.

The NHA has a ritual with the typical fraternal oath and distinctive (peculiar) terminology. For instance, the secretary is known as "Collector of Straws," and the treasurer as "Keeper of Bundles." The local meeting place is called "Hayloft." The two guards or sentinels are referred to as the "Guard of Hayloft" and the "Guard of Barndoor." The initiation rite reflects vestiges of Masonic influence in that it speaks about the candidate gaining more knowledge and being enlightened by the craft.

For additional information on the Haymakers, see *Ritual of the Haymakers' Degree of the Improved Order of Red Men* (1975). See also *By-Laws of Arroas Haymaker Association*. The latter document is written for the Hayloft of New Eagle, Pennsylvania. Another helpful publication is the *Constitution, By-Laws and Constitution of Subordinate Associations of the State Haymakers' Association of Pennsylvania* (1928).

HEPTASOPHS, IMPROVED ORDER OF (IOH). Ten years after the Ancient Order of United Workmen* launched its fraternal insurance program in 1868, the Improved Order of Heptasophs was organized on August 10, 1878. Judge George V. Metzel is commonly agreed to have been the order's founder.

The IOH began as a schismatic group, separating itself from the parent order, the Order of the Heptasophs,* founded in 1852. The parent order was conservative and cautious relative to entering fraternal benevolent insurance programs. This posture made some members unhappy and so they formed an independent group, the Improved Order of Heptasophs. At first the IOH received considerable opposition from the parent order, which retarded the growth of the IOH. Eventually, however, the tension between the two societies subsided, and the IOH grew rapidly. By 1915 it had 676,887 members, about the most members the society ever had.

As other fraternal benefit societies were accustomed to doing some seventy years ago, the IOH also employed the assessment plan in collecting funds for its life insurance (death benefits). During the 1890s the order's death benefits ranged from $1,000 to $5,000. The IOH was one of the first fraternal benefit societies to place its insurance operations under state insurance departments.

Initially, the IOH operated on three levels, but after a few years of experiencing a three-level structure, it disbanded the state level and retained only the "Subordinate Conclave" and the "Supreme Conclave." The society had its head office in Baltimore, Maryland. In May of 1917 the IOH ceased to exist when it merged with the Fraternal Aid Union. The latter changed to Standard Life Association in 1933.

HEPTASOPHS, ORDER OF THE (OOH). This group was once known as the Seven Wise Men, a name derived from the Greek etymology of the word heptasophs. The society was founded in New Orleans, Louisiana on April 6, 1852. Two years later it was incorporated. Like some other fraternal orders, the OOH loved to believe that its real origin went back to the Magi of the East, mentioned in the Christmas story. Some accounts even tried to trace the society's history back to 1104 B.C., linking it with Zoroaster, who reputedly was the head of the Persian Magi. Its American founder, Alexander Leonard Saunders, reportedly was a Freemason. A considerable amount of evidence exists that the Heptasoph society was "an indirect descendant of the Mystical Seven college fraternity, founded in 1837," according to Albert Stevens, *Cyclopedia of Fraternities* (1907).

Like so many fraternal orders, the OOH required that prospective members profess belief in a supreme being. Consistent with the belief in a supreme being, the society's motto was "In God We Trust." Its emblem was a seven-pointed star, which portrayed a seven-branched candlestick, all-seeing eye, altar, and ark, plus its motto: In God We Trust. The ritual was ornate and elaborate, resembling the Masonic ritual in a number of ways.

The society, which admitted only white males in good physical and mental condition, never realized a large membership. As far as the present writer can ascertain, the order reached its highest membership count around 1906 with 4,000 members. One reason for the relatively low enrollment was due to a schism in 1878. The schism resulted in a new society, the Improved Order of Heptasophs.* The OOH was also dominated by a very conservative leadership that opposed organizational change.

Two years after the OOH had suffered the schism, it entered the insurance field in 1880 with the Improved Order of Heptasophs. In order to obtain an insurance certificate, the society added a degree, the endowment rank. Later the order also set up a fund to give aid to widows, heirs, and other beneficiaries. The insurance and mutual aid were operated on the assessment plan.

HEROES OF '76. This "fun" or side degree organization was founded in 1923 by Colonel Christopher Van Deventer. Because the group is fun-oriented, it really keeps no accurate records of memberships or activities. Unlike most fraternal groups, the Heroes of '76 does not assess a fee for the degree it confers on its members.

The Heroes of '76 is affiliated with the National Sojourners. Local groups attached to the chapters of the Sojourners are called "Camps." There were about 180 camps in 1977. The group meets in convention annually every June. Its headquarters are in Alexandria, Virginia.

The writer knows of only two brief sources that discuss the Heroes of '76. These are a one-page account in Harold V. B. Voorhis, *Masonic Organizations and Allied Orders and Degrees* (1952), and a brief chapter, "Heroes of '76," in Lavon Parker Linn, *Fifty Years of National Sojourners* (1970). Additional information may be gathered in a piecemeal manner.

HEROINES OF JERICHO (HOJ). According to some Masonic writers this society was formed in 1790 in France and introduced into the United States by David Vinton between 1815 and 1820. This female society is sometimes referred to in Masonic circles as Adoptive Rite Masonry, meaning that it is an androgynous rite that is tacitly sponsored by a legitimate Masonic order. The HOJ exists under the auspices of "Royal Arch Masonry," one of the degree orders in the York Rite* of Freemasonry. The HOJ is not to be confused with The Heroines of Jericho, a black female group, that exists under the umbrella of black Freemasonry.

The HOJ has a religiously oriented ritual requiring the services of a lodge chaplain, who has traditionally been a male member of Royal Arch Masonry. Part of the degree work calls for a symbolic purification based on Leviticus 14:48–53. Another portion of the degree initiation work has the new member take a vow, saying: "I do solemnly promise and swear with a firm and steady purpose to keep and perform the same, binding myself under no less penalty than to have my head struck off and carried to the highest mountain, so help me God. . . ." At the end of the initiation rite the candiate is "restored to light."

Members of Royal Arch Masonry may join the Heroines of Jericho as male members. Each male candidate takes an obligation (vow), promising to treat the female members as sisters by giving them protection and assistance. Current membership figures were not available to the writer.

Structurally, the HOJ consists of grand (regional) and subordinate courts. The subordinate courts are headed by an Ancient Matron, Worthy Joshua, Vice Ancient Matron, Vice Joshua, Chaplain, Treasurer, Senior Attendant, Junior Attendant, and three directors.

For additional information, see *The Book of the Scarlet Line* (1948), published by Macoy Publishing Masonic Supply Company.

HEROINES OF JERICHO (HOJ). As the present volume indicates, there are a number of black fraternal societies that not only pattern themselves after white fraternal groups, but also use the same name. The Heroines of Jericho is one of these organizations. This black female order reportedly was founded not too long after Prince Hall Masonry* was organized in 1775.

The HOJ, like its white counterpart, tries to trace its origin in terms of its ritual and symbols to the thirteenth century, when Freemasonry (operative masons) formed the Heroines of Jericho as an organization for the wives and daughters of operative masons. Today (1980) the HOJ is an auxiliary to black Royal Arch Masonry.

Like other secret fraternal societies, the HOJ has a secret ritual which in part consists of an oath that each member is required to take upon being initiated. The society has three degrees. The first degree is known as True Kinsmen; the second is Master Mason Daughter; and the third degree is Heroine of Jericho. In many instances all three degrees are worked in one night's meeting. Members are admitted by ball-ballot voting.

The HOJ supports different charitable causes. Some subordinate (local) lodges support research in sickle cell anemia; some contribute to alleviating and treating burns, and a number support still other medical or health programs.

The HOJ operates on three levels; international, state, and local. The international is primarily American in scope. The international structure meets in convention every four years. The state group, commonly known as the "Grand Court," meets annually. The local groups ("Court") usually meet monthly.

On the local (subordinate court) level the head officer is called "Most Ancient Matron." The chief male officer is known as "Most Worthy Joshua." The organization is required to have male supervision, as is also true of the black order of the Eastern Star.*

Most of the information in the present sketch was obtained by means of personal interviews. Published material appears to be difficult to locate. Some material can be found in the order's annual proceedings.

HIAWATHA, DEGREE OF (DOH). This youth organization was formed in 1952 along with the Degree of Anona.* The Degree of Hiawatha was founded by the Improved Order of Red Men* in order to interest young males in becoming members of the Red Men upon reaching adulthood. The DOH has a ritual and secrets that revolve about Indian lore and legends.

Membership in the Degree of Hiawatha has never been very large. Like its female counterpart, the Degree of Anona, most of its members reside in the New England states. Presently (1979) the society has less than 5,000 members in about 125 "Councils," local units.

Further information may be obtained by consulting the *Record*, a proceedings publication of the parent society, Improved Order of Red Men. The Red Men also issue publicity brochures and pamphlets that give thumbnail sketches of the DOH.

HIBERNIANS IN AMERICA, ANCIENT ORDER OF (AOH). The history, background, and origin of this order are somewhat difficult to ascertain, because of conflicting sources. Whalen, in his *Handbook of Secret Organizations* (1966), believes the roots of the AOH go back to 1565 when in Ireland there existed groups of Ribbonmen, who were forerunners of the Hibernians. The Ribbonmen sought to protect the persecuted Roman Catholic priests of that time. Whalen says this Irish society also tried to correct injustices practiced by English landlords.

The AOH was introduced in the United States in the city of New York in 1836, many years after it made its appearance in Ireland. The order, from its inception, had some "outward Masonic forms and pecularities," according to Albert C. Stevens, *Cyclopedia of Fraternities* (1907). During the 1860s and 1870s the secret signs and passwords of the AOH were effectively employed by Irish immigrants in the coal mines of Pennsylvania. Some of the AOH members were known as Molly Maguires, who often engaged in violence, sabotage, murder, arson, and whippings.

The association with the Molly Maguires on the part of some AOH members led the society at its 1876 national convention to condemn the Molly Maguire activities. However, the reputation of the AOH had been hurt considerably. In 1884 the AOH suffered a schism when it restructured itself so that the society could no longer be used for terrorist acts. The secessionist group called itself the Ancient Order of Hibernians Board of Erin. At the time of the schism the larger, nonsecessionist group called itself the Ancient Order of Hibernians of America to distinguish itself from the Hibernians in Ireland, with whom the schismatic group remained friendly. In 1898 the secessionist group reunited with the AOH.

As a fraternal benefit society, the AOH pays the usual array of insurance benefits to its members. The order also supports various charity endeavors. Culturally, it has provided funds for teaching the Celtic languages at Catholic University of America. Roman Catholic missions in the Orient have also been aided by the AOH.

Membership is open to those who are Irish or of Irish descent and Catholic. The present (1979) membership is more than 191,000 members. This is a gain of more than 10,000 from 1965, when the order had about 181,000. The society is proud to count former President John F. Kennedy as one of its former members. He joined the order in 1947. For the ladies the AOH has an auxiliary known as the Daughters of Erin.

Local groups within the society are named "Divisions," of which there are 736. The national structure meets in convention biennially. The main offices are located in Staten Island, New York.

Additional information may be found by consulting the society's bimonthly periodical, *National Hibernian Digest*. The proceedings are also helpful for further background.

HIGH TWELVE INTERNATIONAL (HTI). Although the constitution of this fraternal group officially calls itself "High Twelve International," it also is called the "High Twelve Club." In many ways, at least to outsiders, this group resembles the Kiwanis or Rotary club in that it meets as a noon luncheon organization. The HTO was organized by E. C. Wolcott, a Freemason and also a Congregational clergyman. Wolcott felt that members of the Masonic fraternity should have more opportunity to interact with one another socially so that Masons "might put into actual practice the great lessons and truths taught by their beloved Order." The name "High Twelve" apparently was chosen because of its symbolic significance. The term "high twelve" is found in some of the earliest Masonic rituals or catechisms, where it has reference to the noon hour. According to Masonic tradition, high twelve was the time when, in operative Freemasonry (as opposed to speculative Freemasonry), Masons were called from labor to refresh themselves.

The High Twelve Club, founded in May 17, 1921, has five basic objectives: (1) Practice the principles of Masonry by encouraging fellow Masons to be faithful in lodge activities as well as to one another. (2) Strengthen fellowship among Master Masons, i.e., third-degree Masons. (3) Support and promote the public school system. (4) Participate in constructive, noncontroversial community activities. (5) Identify with the state and international High Twelve organizational goals.

Membership is only open to Master Masons of a "recognized lodge." This requirement, of course, excludes all black (Prince Hall*) Masons, as black Masonic lodges are not recognized by white Masons in the United States. Women also are ineligible, given the Masonic "landmark" (unchangeable law) that categorically prevents any woman from becoming a Mason. In 1979, the club had 24,000 members in 324 clubs in twenty-five states and three foreign countries.

The HTI does not have a ritual of its own, nor does it initiate newcomers. It exists as a group of Master Masons, who come together for "luncheon once each week at High Twelve, where music, speaking, high class entertaining and social hour are featured."

The club's insignia consists of a burning lamp, perched on top of three triangles that give the effect of three steps. On it are the words: High Twelve International, To Reflect Upon Truth, To Talk Little, To Hear Much. It also displays a clock whose hands point to the hour of noon.

It is interesting to note that the HTI does not wish to be misunderstood as to the nature of its organization. One official pamphlet emphatically states: "*We are not a civic luncheon club*" (emphasis in the original). The pamphlet goes on to say: "We do not direct our energy in the civic direction, our interests are within the Masonic fellowship."

In 1952 the club established the Wolcott Foundation in honor of its founder. The foundation is chartered in Missouri and exists to provide one year of graduate study "for students deserving of Masonic support." This graduate program can only be taken at George Washington University's School of Government and Business Administration or its School of Public and International Affairs. The HTI also provides support to youth, especially Masonic youth such as the DeMolay,* Rainbow Girls,* and Job's Daughters.* Senior citizens in Masonic homes also receive assistance from the HTI.

Organizationally, the HTI operates on three levels. On the international (which is largely national) level, the officers consists of a president, three vice-presidents, an immediate past president, a secretary, a treasurer, and a general counselor. In its fifteen state organizations, and on the local scene, a slate of officers is elected similar to that of the international organization. The head office is in St. Louis, Missouri.

For background material the reader may consult: *Constitution and By-Laws of High Twelve International Incorporated*. The club's magazine, *The High Twelvian*, issued every two months, gives the news of its activities.

HOLY ORDER OF KNIGHTS BENEFICENT OF THE HOLY CITY (HOKBHC). According to the Masonic Service Association's portrait, this order is the oldest organization connected with Freemasonry.* It was formed in 1754 in Germany. In the United States the order was organized in 1934. The purpose of the HOKBHC is to

maintain and strengthen among its members, as well as among Masons and Masonic groups in general, the following principles: attachment to the spirit of Christianity and belief in a Supreme Power as designated under the name of Supreme Architect of the Universe; devotion to country; individual perfection by the work which every man must do within himself for subduing his passions, correcting his faults and making intellectual progress; the exercise of an enlightened charity toward all mankind without regard to nationality, political opinions, religious convictions, or social status.

Membership is attained only by means of invitation. Every prospective member must be a Master Mason. The order has a limit of eighty-one members. This membership is divided into three preceptories, each having twenty-seven members. The preceptories are the local bodies within the organization. Headquarters are in Syracuse, New York, the home of the Great Chancellor.

The present discussion on this society is largely based on the brief description provided by the mimeographed paper "Allied Masonic Groups and Rites" (1978) issued by the Masonic Service Association. The writer was unable to obtain information from the order directly.

HOMEBUILDERS, ORDER OF. Founded in 1890 as a fraternal beneficiary society in the state of Pennsylvania. The order admitted men and women between fifteen and sixty-five years of age. In addition to paying benefits, the society operated a savings department. Headquarters were in Philadelphia, Pennsylvania. REFERENCE: *Cyc. Frat.*

HOME CIRCLE, THE (THC). This fraternal benefit group was organized by members of the Royal Arcanum* in 1879 in Boston, Massachusetts. Some of the founders also belonged to the Masons,* Odd Fellows,* Knights of Honor,* and the Ancient United Order of Workmen.* Formation of the THC was motivated by men wishing they had an order in which they could enroll their wives and lady friends as beneficial and social members.

The THC ritual contained four degrees. Each degree specified a given amount of insurance, namely $500 for the first degree, $1,000 for the second, $2,000 for the third, and $3,500 for the fourth degree.

Membership was open to both sexes, provided they were between eighteen and fifty-five years of age. Individuals over fifty-five could become social members. No medical examination was required for social membership.

The society's ritual was based on the Golden Rule. It stressed morality and correct living to the members. The emblem of the THC consisted of the letter H inside a circle.

Local lodges were known as "Subordinate Councils." Regional groups in Canada and the United States were called "Grand Councils." The national body was referred to as the "Supreme Council."

This report is largely derived from Albert C. Stevens, *Cyclopedia of Fraternities* (1907). See his volume for more information.

HOME FORUM BENEFIT ORDER. This fraternal benefit society was founded in Illinois in 1892. Members of Freemasonry* and the Modern Woodmen of America* were instrumental in organizing the order. Men and women were able to join as benefit members. Social memberships were available to those who were beyond the insurable age. The society's ritual was based on Roman history, especially as it pertained to the Roman Forum, where Cicero, Anthony, Brutus, Caesar, and others met to discuss various questions and issues. Apparently the order ceased to operate in the early 1900s. Its membership was never very large, mostly confined to Missouri, Iowa, Illinois, and Michigan. REFERENCES: *Cyc. Frat.; DSOS.*

HOME PALLADIUM. This fraternal benefit society was organized in Kansas City, Missouri, in 1891. The society enrolled only acceptable white men and women. Unlike a lot of other fraternal beneficiary groups, the Home Palladium early in its existence adopted a reserve fund in order to give it a sounder financial structure. The society did not enter the southern United States because of the higher incidence of yellow fever and malaria in that part of the country. This society had no relationship to the Free and Regenerated Palladium.* REFERENCES: *Cyc. Frat.*; *DSOS*.

HOMESTEADERS, THE (TH). When John E. Paul and Clarence B. Paul were forced to resign from their offices in the Brotherhood of American Yeomen*, they put their skills to work and organized a new fraternal order: The Homesteaders. The new order was formed in 1906. The name "Homesteaders" was taken from what the Yeomen fraternity called its subordinate lodges.

The Homesteaders appealed to some of the field men from the Yeomen society to join its ranks. It also admitted women along with men, something not done by many fraternal benefit groups at that time. Some of its pamphlets and promotional literature stated that its membership was "of the highest class" and that it took extreme care "to admit none but first-class risks, physically and morally. . . ." By 1920 the society had approximately 30,000 members in twenty-three states and in Canada.

In 1923 the society changed from a fraternal benefit group to a non-fraternal insurance organization. The new name adopted in 1923 was The Homesteaders' Life Association. In 1948 the name was changed again, this time to Homesteaders Life Company. When the change was made to a nonfraternal insurance group, all fraternal titles and references were dropped too.

The society had a ritual that called for a chaplain and various religious elements. Although the organization had a ritual, which usually reveals the more serious or solemn side of a fraternal order, it also took cognizance of the lighter side of life in that local units had an officer known as the "Lady of Entertainment." Her function was to provide entertainment and sociability at society gatherings.

Local units were called "Homesteads." Regional or state groups were known as "Grand Homestead." The supreme homestead met in convention every four years during the society's latter years. Headquarters were maintained in Des Moines, Iowa. This is also where the Brotherhood of American Yeomen had its head offices.

For further information, see Arthur Preuss, *A Dictionary of Secret and Other Societies* (1924). See also the *Fraternal Monitor* (November 1923). This issue has an article on the conversion of the order to a nonfraternal insurance organization.

HOO-HOO, INTERNATIONAL ORDER OF (IOHH). This fraternal group that employs the unusual word Hoo-Hoo in its name is a lumbermen's organization. The uncommon name reportedly was coined by Bolling

Arthur Johnson, at a Kansas City lumber meeting, one month before the order received the name. Johnson whimsically dubbed the lone tuft of hair on the bald head of his friend, Charles H. McCarer, a "Hoo-Hoo." The IOHH, a fraternal order of lumbermen, was organized in Gurdon, Arkansas, on January 21, 1892. The chief architect of the order was Bolling Arthur Johnson, who was editor of the *Timberman* journal, published in Chicago. Although the IOHH is not entirely composed of lumbermen, it has had more lumbermen represented than any other occupation. The cofounders with Johnson believed that the greatest human achievement was to live a hearty, happy, and healthy life. These three characteristics also are the objectives of the IOHH. Today it accents health, happiness, and long life for its members.

The primary founder, Johnson, also was the main formulator of the order's titles, customs, and ritual. Johnson was well versed in Egyptian lore, which led him to choose the Egyptian black cat, with its curled tail, as the order's emblem. Moreover, the mythical nine lives of the cat were used for organizational purposes. The order has traditionally met at nine minutes past nine o'clock on the ninth day of the ninth month of each year for its annual convention. In recent years the annual conventions have been delayed for about nine days to enable members to bring their wives along. The society once limited its membership to 9,999, but it later changed that to 99,999. On the order's emblem, which has a black cat in the center of a circle, the words Concatenated Order of Hoo-Hoo form a border around the cat. The word "concatenated" served two purposes. It had some reference to the black "cat," and it also symbolized being "linked together, as in chain or series." The latter had significance for lumbermen.

The ritual of the IOHH has some solemn elements that compare with other fraternal groups, but it also has portions that accent the lighter side of life. The society considers the ritual to be secret.

Members are largely drawn from those engaged in the lumbering industry. The IOHH typically refers to this economic activity by speaking of "the Industry." The current (1978) membership roster has about 8,000 Hoo-Hoos in 129 "Concatenations."

The IOHH, unlike most other fraternal groups, has a code of ethics. It consists of nine ethical concerns that relate to not interfering with the rights of others; doing business by the Golden Rule; establishing "the spoken word on the basis of the written bond"; cultivating friendship among lumber people; serving society through business; holding the members' vocations as worthy pursuits; elevating humanity; promoting friendly understanding among all nations; and honoring cooperation and organization.

In terms of programs and activities, the IOHH promotes lumber and forest products at state and county fairs; it sponsors lectures and classes on the grading of lumber; it conducts workshops for boys relative to furnishing materials, tools, and building equipment; it gives awards for projects in manual arts departments for carpentry in vocational schools; it sponsors industrial arts fairs in local high schools; it cooperates with Boys' Clubs and Junior Achievement groups; it gives scholarships to forestry students; it promotes tree-planting projects; it shows a 30-minute movie, known as "The Forest Industry," which deals with forest management. The order also distributes the National Forest Products Week logo to newspapers, trade journals, and magazines throughout the world. The logo is displayed in schools and libraries during the selected week.

The officers of the Hoo-Hoo International consist of the "Supreme Nine." They are a Snark, a Senior Hoo-Hoo, a Junior Hoo-Hoo, a Bojum, a Scrivenoter, a Jabberwock, a Custocatian, an Arcanoper, and a Gurdon. On the regional level the Vice Regent Snark supervises the organization with its various concatenations (local chapters). The IOHH has its head offices in Norwood, Massachusetts.

Additional information may be obtained by reading pamphlets and brochures issued by the society. One helpful pamphlet is "Whence Came Hoo-Hoo?"

HOODED LADIES OF THE MYSTIC DEN (HLMD). A group of white women organized this society in 1923 in Baltimore, Maryland. The order was an auxiliary of the Ku Klux Klan. Objectives of the society were to unite all white Protestant women, promote the English language, and preserve the ideals of their Anglo-Saxon forebears. The HLMD also was a strong advocate of the public school. In fact, it saw the public school as the "cornerstone" of the United States. The antiblack and anti-Catholic stance motivated the order to work for stringent immigration laws. Frequently the society sought to return the Bible to the public school. The Bible was seen as an antidote to "imported evils." Headquarters were in Baltimore, Maryland.

The above report is based on Arthur Preuss, *Dictionary of Secret and Other Societies* (1923).

HOUN' DAWGS, ORDER OF. This fraternal secret group was founded in Cabool, Missouri, in 1912. The order's local units were known as "Kennels." The society apparently lasted less than a decade. REFERENCE: *Cyc. Frat.*

HUNGARIAN REFORMED FEDERATION OF AMERICA (HRFA). The society was formed in 1896 as a fraternal insurance group to assist and protect the Hungarian immigrant. The society did not respond to the several attempts made by the author to solicit up-to-date information.

As a fraternal benefit society, the HRFA sells insurance in Canada and in about twelve states, plus the District of Columbia. It supports a home for the aged in Ligonier, Pennsylvania. For students it sponsors a yearly study contest and provides student aid and loans.

Membership is open to those of Hungarian descent. In 1965 its membership roster listed 37,235. Currently it has about 28,000 members.

The society is headquartered in Washington, D.C. It meets in convention every four years. Its monthly periodical, *Fraternity*, provides news concerning the society.

I

IMPERIAL MYSTIC LEGION. Founded in 1896 in Omaha, Nebraska, as a fraternal benefit group, apparently this society had a short life span, as no record of it can found in *Statistics, Fraternal Societies* (1905).

IMPROVED ORDER OF DEER. See Deer, Improved Order of.

IMPROVED ORDER OF HEPTASOPHS. See Heptasophs, Improved Order of.

IMPROVED ORDER OF KNIGHTS OF PYTHIAS. See Knights of Pythias, Improved Order of.

IMPROVED ORDER OF RED MEN. See Red Men, Improved Order of.

INDEPENDENT ORDER OF B'RITH ABRAHAM. See B'rith Abraham, Independent Order of.

INDEPENDENT ORDER OF CHOSEN FRIENDS. See Chosen Friends, Independent Order of.

INDEPENDENT ORDER OF FORESTERS. See Foresters, Independent Order of.

INDEPENDENT ORDER OF GOOD SAMARITANS AND DAUGHTERS OF SAMARIA. See Good Samaritans and Daughters of Samaria, Independent Order of.

INDEPENDENT ORDER OF IMMACULATES OF THE UNITED STATES OF AMERICA. This society was founded in Nashville, Tennessee, in 1872, as a fraternal benefit society for black people. It admitted men and women to membership. Headquarters were located in Nashville, Tennessee. REFERENCE: *Cyc. Frat.*

INDEPENDENT ORDER OF MECHANICS. See Mechanics, Independent Order of.

INDEPENDENT ORDER OF MYSTIC BROTHERS. See Mystic Brothers, Independent Order of.

INDEPENDENT ORDER OF ODD FELLOWS. See Odd Fellows, Independent Order of.

INDEPENDENT ORDER OF PURITANS. See Puritans, Independent Order of.

INDEPENDENT ORDER OF RECHABITES. See Rechabites, Independent Order of.

INDEPENDENT ORDER OF RED MEN. See Red Men, Independent Order of.

INDEPENDENT ORDER OF SONS OF ABRAHAM. See Sons of Abraham, Independent Order of.

INDEPENDENT ORDER OF VIKINGS. See Vikings, Independent Order of.

INTERNATIONAL ASSOCIATION OF REBEKAH ASSEMBLIES. See Rebekah Assemblies, International Association of.

INTERNATIONAL GENERAL GRAND CHAPTER OF ROYAL ARCH MASONS. See Royal Arch Masons, International General Grand Chapter of.

INTERNATIONAL GENERAL GRAND COUNCIL OF ROYAL AND SELECT MASTERS. See Royal and Select Masters, International General Grand Council of.

INTERNATIONAL GENEVA ASSOCIATION. This fraternal benefit society was founded in 1904 to provide fraternal insurance benefits for workers in the hotel, restaurant, and catering trades. The author has been unable to contact the society. Its secretarial office used to be in the city of

New York. It probably still is in New York, but the specific address is not known. Membership in the organization in the mid-1970s was about 1,200. The *Geneva Newsletter* is published monthly, except during July and August.

INTERNATIONAL ORDER OF ALHAMBRA. See Alhambra, International Order of.

INTERNATIONAL ORDER OF GOOD TEMPLARS. See Good Templars, International Order of.

INTERNATIONAL ORDER OF HOO-HOO. See Hoo-Hoo, International Order of.

INTERNATIONAL ORDER OF JOB'S DAUGHTERS. See Job's Daughters, International Order of.

INTERNATIONAL ORDER OF TWELVE KNIGHTS AND DAUGHTERS OF TABOR. See Knights and Daughters of Tabor, International Order of Twelve.

INTERNATIONAL ORDER OF RAINBOW GIRLS. See Rainbow Girls, International Order of.

INTERNATIONAL SUPREME COUNCIL OF WORLD MASONS, INC. (ISCWM). Founded in 1948, this group states its purpose as organizing "consistories, social, civic and religious groups, enterprises and other organizations among its membership and associates, and to confer Masonic degrees from the 4th through the 33rd degree in accordance with the ritualistic practices which this supreme council has adopted. . . ." The council also seeks to promote "charity, brotherly love and benevolence to the sick and distressed among its members, and consideration for the welfare of the general public at all levels of civilization." The society grants scholarships, operates an employment service for members and nonmembers, and conducts classes in skilled trades, as well as in foreign languages.

Currently (1979) the council has 31,000 members in fifty groups operating in the United States and thirty-nine foreign groups. In order to join the ISCWM the individual must be a thirty-second-degree Mason in the Scottish Rite,* as the council's membership consists only of thirty-third-degree members. This degree is received by joining the council.

The ISCWM meets in convention each year. When in convention sessions, the Sovereign Grand Commander is the presiding officer. Headquarters are situated in Detroit, Michigan.

For further information, see the council's quarterly publication, *Masonic*

Round Table. Other information may be acquired by reading brochures and pamphlets pertaining to the council.

IOWA LEGION OF HONOR. Organized in Iowa in 1879 as a fraternal benefit society, the society never had a very large membership. In 1905 there were 4,300 members. Apparently the order soon went out of existence after 1910. Sales jurisdiction was confined to Iowa.

IRON HALL, ORDER OF. This fraternal benefit society was formed in 1881 in Indianapolis, Indiana. The society had a secret ritual with passwords and initiation ceremonies. At first only men were admitted. Shortly before the order went into receivership in 1892, it had also been admitting women into full membership. Its membership count in 1892 was 63,000. REFERENCES: *Cyc. Frat.*; *DSOS*.

IROQUOIS, ORDER OF. Buffalo, New York, is where this fraternal beneficiary society was born in 1898. The ritual attempted to perpetuate the fame of the Iroquois Confederation of Indiana. In August of 1922 the society was absorbed by the Fraternal Home Insurance of Philadelphia, Pennsylvania. REFERENCES: *Cyc. Frat.*; *DSOS*.

ITALO AMERICAN NATIONAL UNION (IANU). Founded in Chicago, Illinois, in 1895, the IANU has from the beginning endeavored to have Italians help Italians. By 1937 the society had restructured its former benevolent programs to accommodate fraternal life insurance. Today it is a legal reserve life insurance group.

Qualifications for membership, according to the society's constitution read: "Each applicant must be a white person of Italian origin, of sound health, of good moral character, a believer in a Supreme Being and competent to earn a livelihood for himself and family." To determine member admission to the society, the ball ballot procedure is employed. Two blackballs spell rejection for the applicant.

The society, even though it is largely a fraternal life insurance operation, nevertheless is still very much taken up by its ritual and other traditional lodgelike functions. As has just been noted, the blackball ballot is used to reject undesirable candidates for membership. The society, however, also has a ritual involving "private words, tokens, signs, grips, passwords . . . all of which are secrets to be kept inviolate. . . ." So states the IANU constitution. Any member who improperly reveals these secrets is subject to expulsion. The Supreme President is required to issue passwords quadrennially to each member of the Supreme Council. Members of the society receive semiannual passwords.

On the charity circuit the IANU provides aid to handicapped children and to the Italian Old Peoples Home. In civic matters the society annually participates in Chicago's Columbus Day parade, sponsors athletic events for the youth, and provides scholarships to deserving students.

The highest level of administrative authority is the Supreme Council, which meets every four years. The home office is maintained in Chicago, Illinois. Local assemblies are referred to as "Subordinate Lodges." The number of lodges has declined from forty in 1972 to thirty-one in 1977. Current (1979) membership is about 5,000. The society has lodges only in Illinois and Indiana.

The interested reader may obtain additional information by consulting the society's quarterly publication, *The I.A.N.U. Bulletin*. See also the society's *Constitution and Laws* (1930). The constitution, although dated, apparently is still seen as current, as the office sent this edition to the writer in January 1979.

J

JESTERS, ROYAL ORDER OF (ROJ). If a Shriner cannot have enough fun in the Shrine, the so-called playground of Masonry, he can enter the Royal Order of Jesters. One Masonic publication calls this order the "funnier of the funniest." It was founded in 1911, by Shriners on a "pilgrimage" to Alohya Temple in Hawaii. The order's slogan is "Mirth is King."

Only Shriners in good standing are eligible for membership. Members may only join by being formally invited. Applications for membership are not entertained. Presently (1979) the ROJ has 179 local units. In 1950 the order had 14,539 members. The author was unable to obtain current membership figures.

Subordinate units are referred to as "Courts" by the members. The governing body is called "Grand Court." It meets once each year. Des Moines, Iowa, serves as the headquarters city for the ROJ.

For additional information, see Harold V. B. Voorhis, *Masonic Organizations and Allied Orders and Degrees* (1952). Also see the Masonic Service Association's "Allied Masonic Groups and Rites" (mimeographed, 1978).

JOB'S DAUGHTERS, INTERNATIONAL ORDER OF (IOJD). The founder, Mrs. Ethel T. W. Mick, a member of the Eastern Star,* organized the order primarily for teenage women in 1921 in Omaha, Nebraska. The organization's name was inspired by the Old Testament passage in Job 42:15: "And in all the land there were no women so fair as the daughters of Job."

The IOJD is a sister organization to the International Order of Rainbow Girls (IORG). Both groups are junior orders for young women who are sponsored by Freemasonry* and the Eastern Star.

The ritual is secret and symbolic. A typical initiation ceremony calls for the officers to be arrayed in white Grecian robes. The initiate takes the following vow:

. . . I solemnly affirm on my honor that I will never divulge the transactions of any Bethel [a local chapter] of Job's Daughters or the ritualistic ceremony of the Order or any part of either to anyone who is not lawfully entitled thereto, that I will encourage the fidelity of all members of Job's Daughter by a faithful observance of this pledge.

The ritual also requires a chaplain to officiate at an altar, where she conducts devotions. The chaplain's duties, according to the ritual, are "piety, religion, and reverence for sacred things that are the beacon lights of life." The chaplaincy exists to help the order achieve one of its original objectives, namely, to impress its young members "with love of home and country and reverence for the teachings of the Bible."

Membership in the IOJD is made up of girls between the ages of eleven and twenty who believe in a supreme being and the Ten Commandments and the Lord's Prayer. They also must be related to Master Masons. This latter requirement bars nonwhite prospects because all Master Masons are white.

Membership in the IOJD is declining. In the late 1960s the order had 150,000 members, but by the late 1970s its membership had dropped to 100,000. The society has members in Canada, Australia, the Philippines, and the United States.

The IOJD sponsors a number of philanthropic projects. It also conducts various patriotic activities and in recent years has provided scholarships to its members.

Organizationally, the IOJD operates on three levels: national, regional, and local. On the national level, the order refers to its structure as "The Supreme Guardian Council of the World," which has jurisdiction over all its local groups. National headquarters are in Omaha, Nebraska. Local chapters are known as "Bethels." Each bethel has nineteen officers, some of which are the Honored Queen, Senior Princess, Junior Princess, Guide, Marshall, and Chaplain. It should also be noted that each bethel has an Executive Bethel Guardian Council of five adults; one of these must be a Master Mason, who is appointed by the Supreme Guardian.

To this writer's knowledge there is no separate work on the IOJD. Additional information is best gleaned from other Masonic sources. One such brief source is Harold V. B. Voorhis, *Masonic Organizations and Allied Orders and Degrees* (1952).

JUNIOR CATHOLIC DAUGHTERS OF AMERICA (JCDA). This is the junior organization of the Catholic Daughters of America.* This youth group was formed in 1925. The society conducts leadership training courses, covering spiritual, charitable, cultural, and recreational activities.

Presently (1979) the JCDA has 5,000 members in about 250 local units throughout the United States. The CDA has three age groups in its membership: Juniorettes (six to ten years), Juniors (eleven to fourteen years), and Teens (fifteen to eighteen years).

The CDA publishes a bimonthly magazine, *Counselor's Leaves*. Quarterly it publishes *Junior Highlights*.

JUNIOR LODGE. See Odd Fellows, Junior Lodge.

JUNIOR ORDER OF UNITED AMERICAN MECHANICS OF THE UNITED STATES OF NORTH AMERICA, INC., NATIONAL COUNCIL OF THE (JOUAM). This order was founded in 1853 in Philadelphia as a junior branch of the Order of United American Mechanics.* By 1885 the junior order became an independent secret society with its major emphasis directed to protecting the United States from undesirable foreigners such as the Irish, Germans, and Roman Catholics. Since 1885, the word "Junior" in the group's name has no reference to the age of its members. Similarly, the word "Mechanics" has no reference to the members' occupations. Its purposes were very similar to its parent organization, namely: "To maintain and promote the interest of Americans, and shield them from the depressing effects of foreign competition; to assist Americans in obtaining employment; to encourage Americans in business; to establish a sick and funeral fund; to maintain the public school system of the United States of America, to prevent sectarian interference therewith, and to uphold the reading of the Holy Bible therein."

Its strong support for the public school system was largely motivated by its dislike of the Roman Catholic school system. Shielding Americans from foreign competition meant that immigration was to be restricted. Many of the order's pamphlets made these concerns very clear.

Like other fraternal groups, the JOUAM devised a ritual requiring initiation and obligation procedures. Also like most fraternal groups, its ritual was quite religiously oriented. A number of Bible passages were employed.

Today the society still has a ritual that is used for initiation and other purposes such as installing elected officers.

In order to join the JOUAM one had to be white, believe in a supreme being, favor the separation of church and state, and not be engaged in any liquor business. However, in time the order changed its membership requirements so that Jews, blacks, and Roman Catholics could join. Women also were admitted as members.

Over the years the JOUAM made other changes. After it left its Nativist moorings, it concentrated on becoming a legal reserve fraternal life insurance society. By the mid-1960s it had paid more than $61,000,000 in fraternal benefits. The order also, in effect, absorbed the UAM.

At the turn of the century (1900) the JOUAM had approximately 200,000 members. But like so many other fraternal groups, the prosperity of large memberships did not endure. By 1965, for instance, the society's membership had declined to 35,172. Of this figure, 15,000 were social members holding no insurance certificates. Today (1979) the society has 8,500 members in the non-insurance segment of its order. Those carrying insurance number about one-half the number of non-insured members, according to a JOUAM official.

Local groups are called "Councils," of which the society has 400 at the moment. The national convention meets every two years. Headquarters are located in Willow Grove, Pennsylvania, a Philadelphia suburb.

Further information may be obtained by consulting the society's published convention proceedings. The society also publishes the *Junior American*, every two months.

JUNIOR STARS, ORDER OF THE CONSTELLATION OF (OCJS). If the Masons* can have junior orders (De Molay* and the Builders*) serving as a type of "farm system" that will provide future members, then why may the women of the Order of the Eastern Star* not have a junior group also? Thus in 1949 a junior order was formed. In 1952 it was incorporated in the state of New York as a "sorority for girls of Masonic families whose relationship to their sponsors qualifies them to petition for membership in the Order of the Star when they reach the age of eighteen."

The OCJS has a ritual offering six degrees: An Intuition of God; A Sense of Human Weakness and Dependence; A Belief in the Divine Government of the World; A Distinction Between Good and Evil; The Hope of a Better Life. The sixth degree is the Degree of Perfection. This degree is conferred after the Junior Star member consummates her membership in the Order of the Eastern Star.

Membership is open to young ladies who are related to Masons. Age of eligibility ranges from twelve to eighteen years. Members of the Eastern

Star and Master Masons may also attend as members of the order. Present membership statistics were not available to the writer.

Structurally, the OCJS refers to its local units as "Constellations." The national body meets annually.

For further information, see the Masonic Service Association's "Allied Masonic Groups and Rites" (mimeographed, 1978).

_ K

KAMELIA. This order, known as the Women's Ku Klux Klan, held its first convention in Oklahoma in 1923. The order furnished its members with white robes and scarlet capes. The society did not meet with KKK favor in the 1920s, and as a result the national KKK leader W. J. Simmons formed a new order known as Knights of the Kamelia. REFERENCE: *DSOS*.

KNIGHT MASONS, ORDER OF (OKM). This Masonically related society began in Ireland in 1923. An American chapter was formed in North Carolina in 1936. In 1967 the order organized its Grand Council of the United States of America. The primary objective of the society is to confer the "Green Degrees" that once were conferred by the Knights Templar in Ireland.

According to the Masonic Service Association, "Allied Masonic Groups and Rites" (mimeographed, 1952), the membership is small and restricted by invitation. Four degrees are bestowed upon its members: Knight of the Sword, Knight of the East, Knight of East and West, and Installed Excellent Chief.

Local units are called "Councils." Headquarters are located in Dover, Delaware, where the Grand Scribe (secretary) resides.

KNIGHTS AND DAUGHTERS OF TABOR, INTERNATIONAL ORDER OF TWELVE (IOTKD). Founded in 1872 in Independence, Missouri, by Moses Dickson (a clergyman of the African Methodist Episcopal Church), this black fraternal order has claimed that its real origin goes back to the Order of Twelve. The latter group had its beginning in 1846 as an antislavery group in the American South. The IOTKD was a fraternal labor and benevolent society that employed an elaborate array of titles and ceremonies. The IOTKD paid sick and death benefits to the beneficiaries of its deceased members.

The order's initiation ceremony received wide public attention in 1915, when one of the candidates for membership brought a legal suit against the Grand Temple and Tabernacle in the state of Texas. The complainant argued that the sword used during the initiation ceremony was the cause of personal injury to him. The defendant, on the other hand, contended that the ritual did not call for the use of a sword and that it was solely the lodge official's responsibility. The Texas Supreme Court ordered the society to award the complainant the amount of $12,000 that a lower court had assessed earlier.

Male members met separately from the women members. The men assembled in "Temples," and women gathered in "Tabernacles." Male and female juvenile members were called "Pages of Honor" and "Maids," respectively. Their meeting places were "Tents." In 1907 the order said it had 100,000 members in thirty states, England, Africa, and the West Indies. As far as can be determined, the order has become defunct. REFERENCE: *Cyc. Frat.*

KNIGHTS AND LADIES OF AZAR. The order was formed in Chicago, Illinois, in 1893. Four years later in 1897 the society reorganized itself, admitting women to membership on equal terms with men. The society was a fraternal benefit society with a strong interest in patriotism. REFERENCE: *Cyc. Frat.*

KNIGHTS AND LADIES OF HONOR (KLH). As happened so frequently in the context of American fraternalism, new fraternal organizations arose because of schisms and conflict. The KLH was formed when some discontented individuals in the Knights of Honor withdrew and formed their own society. The Knights of Honor, formed in 1873, created a ladies' auxiliary degree in 1875. For some reason or other the idea of a women's auxiliary did not catch on, and by 1877 the Knights of Honor had repealed its 1875 resolution creating a separate ladies' degree. The repeal prompted the formation of the KLH in 1877. Albert Stevens in his *Cyclopedia of Fraternities* (1907) says the KLH was the first "secret beneficiary society to admit women to equal social and beneficiary privileges with men. . . ."

When the KLH first was formed, it called itself the Order of Protection of Knights and Ladies of Honor. Later it was changed to the Knights and Ladies of Honor, its present name. The order, having been founded in Louisville, Kentucky, was chartered in Kentucky on December 14, 1881.

The society had three basic objectives. One was to provide benevolence and charity for its members. Another was to unite fraternally all acceptable white men and women, who had reputable occupations and were between eighteen and fifty years of age. Still another was to assist members morally and materially through education and related means. As far as membership was concerned, the KLH also had a social membership category permitting white individuals between eighteen and sixty-five to join without insurance benefits.

The KLH began as a fraternal benefit society; and as all societies at that time, it employed the assessment plan to gather its insurance funds. At first the society paid death benefits up to $1,000; a few years later (1881), however, it increased the upper limit to $5,000. The increase in benefits drew numerous individuals to the society's membership roster. By 1898 the society had more than 72,000 members. The prosperous days, however, did not last very long. As the membership grew older, the society experienced financial difficulties. In order to avoid disaster the rates kept increasing. For the first twenty-four years the society assessed each member $1.80 per month, but when the death rates began increasing the claims could not be met. This phenomenon led to a number of rate increases. By 1916 the rate was $18.40 per month for a $1,000 insurance. For some of the pioneer members the increases represented an inflation of more than 900 percent. Needless to say, the rank and file became very unhappy. Members left the society, and some even appealed to state insurance departments for assistance. The insignia of the KLH was a shield depicting a knight in armor, holding sword and shield, ready to protect widows and children, who were represented by a broken column. The shield also portrayed a triangle with the letters O.M.A. Each angle displayed one of the three letters.

Local units were termed "Subordinate Lodges," and state structures were known as "Grand Lodges." The national organization was referred to as the "Supreme Lodge." Its head offices were located in Indianapolis, Indiana.

To obtain additional information on the KLH the reader may read a summary of the order by Albert Stevens, *Cyclopedia of Fraternities* (1907), and also Arthur Preuss, *A Dictionary of Secret and Other Societies* (1924). A few insights may also gained by reading the occasional reference to the society in the periodical, *Fraternal Monitor*.

KNIGHTS AND LADIES OF SECURITY. When this fraternal benefit group was incorporated in 1892 in the state of Kansas, it was known as one of the more modern and progressive beneficiary societies in that it entered cities of 150,000 or larger. Both men and women were able to join, if they were Caucasians and physically sound. The society was one of the first to have a reserve fund. The ritual was performed in "Councils," local lodges. The society prospered during its early years. In 1910 it had more than 91,000 members. By 1919 the order changed its name to Security Benefit Association. REFERENCE: *DSOS*.

KNIGHTS AND LADIES OF THE GOLDEN RULE. In August, 1879, in Cincinnati, Ohio, this fraternal benefit society was founded by former members of the Order of Mutual Aid.* The latter succumbed because of the yellow fever epidemic that struck Memphis, Tennessee in 1878. Initially, the order was for men only and was named Knights of the Golden Rule. The society adopted the graded assessment plan in 1892. Although the society had "Castles" (local lodges) in more than a dozen states, its membership was never very large. In the latter 1890s it had about 3,000 members. Apparently the order did not survive much longer then the turn of the century. Head offices were in Louisville, Kentucky. REFERENCES: *Cyc. Frat.*; *DSOS*.

KNIGHTS AND LADIES OF THE GOLDEN STAR. This fraternal assessment society, organized in Newark, New Jersey, in 1884, was unique in its day for insuring or receiving into membership entire families. Its founders were members of the Royal Templars of Temperance. The society barred saloonkeepers and bartenders from membership. Passwords and a ritual were part of the society's ceremonial posture. The golden star in its emblem represented the Star of Bethlehem. In 1896 the membership stood at 10,000, but the order collapsed in the early 1900s. Home offices were in Newark, New Jersey.

KNIGHTS OF COLUMBUS (KC). Ever since 1738 different Popes of the Roman Catholic Church have condemned secret societies, especially Freemasonry.* These papal pronoucements made it very difficult for American Catholics who were interested in joining fraternal organizations, which prospered and flourished during the late 1800s and early 1900s almost beyond belief. A New Haven, Connecticut, parish priest by the name of Michael J. McGivney on January 9, 1882, called together a small group of trustworthy men. Father McGivney felt a fraternal order for Catholic men needed to be organized. The men agreed. The name first suggested was Sons of Columbus; however, the name Knights of Columbus was finally selected. That same year (1882), the order received its charter from the State of Connecticut. The order's objective was to render "mutual aid and assistance to its members and families."

Like most fraternal groups during the latter part of the 1800s, the KC grew rapidly, but unlike many other orders that in recent decades have declined or even become extinct, the KC has continued to prosper. Presently (1978), the order has 1,235,000 members in sixty-eight jurisdictions (districts) in Canada and the United States. As a fraternal benevolent society, it also has over two billion dollars of insurance in force, with assets over 450 million dollars.

Membership is open to Catholic males who are eighteen or older. For those under eighteen the KC sponsor the Columbian Squires.* Individuals who cannot pass the KC physical examination may become associate members. This type of membership may also be taken by those who do not desire regular memberships. In both instances, only the order's social privileges are available.

Membership is not restricted to Caucasians. In fact, William J. Whalen, *Handbook of Secret Organizations* (1966), says: "Thousands of Catholic Negroes belong to the Knights of Columbus and a few have served as Grand Knights of their councils" [local chapters]. Although nonwhite males are eligible, women are not. Moreover, the KC does not have an official ladies auxiliary, even though the Daughters of Isabella* have on occasion been considered as such.

As noted a number of times in the present volume, most fraternal orders in the United States were patterned after Freemasonry. The KC is no exception. Thus it has a degree ritual, requiring three degrees (as in Masonry) for regular membership. Each degree has signs, passwords, and hand grips. However, it does not have an oath of secrecy but merely asks the candidates to keep the ritual secret.

Some observers have described the Knights of Columbus as the Catholic answer to Freemasonry. A British scholar of Freemasonry, Walton Hannah, in his book *Light Visible*, makes bold to say that the KC is "a consolation prize for the good boys who might otherwise be tempted into Freemasonry."

The KC motto is "Charity, Unity, Fraternity, Patriotism." Its insignia is an eight-cornered (Maltese) cross decorated in blue, gold, white, and red. Superimposed on the cross is a shield displaying the inscription K of C, plus a sword crossed by an anchor behind a knight's armor and axe. The anchor has reference to Columbus sailing the seas for America, while the other symbols refer to the days of knighthood.

The order has been responsive to social change. In 1964, apparently as a result of the American civil rights movement, the KC made it considerably more difficult for prejudice to reject or blackball a new candidate for membership. It now required one-third of the members present in a given subordinate council to vote against a new applicant. Prior to 1964 only five black balls barred a new candidate. In 1900 the order introduced a fourth degree (accenting patriotism). The holders of this degree form the uniformed contingent of the KC. Some believe the fourth degree was introduced in response to anti-Catholic sentiment which saw Catholics as subversive and un-American. The society also has changed in terms of its benevolent outreach and in its social involvement. At one time it provided assistance to Catholic widows and orphans, primarily. In 1948 it inaugurated a program explaining Catholic doctrine and beliefs by placing advertisements in newspapers and magazines.

More recently (1960s and 1970s) the order has sponsored religious radio broadcasts, contributed to deaf work, aided missionaries, given to relief programs, established scholarships, assisted senior citizens, helped Vietnamese refugees, underwritten medical research, conducted blood donor drives, and still more recently it has been very active in the pro-life movement. In 1968 the KC absorbed the Catholic Benevolent Legion of Brooklyn, New York.

Structurally, the order conducts its affairs on three levels. The national level is known as the "Supreme Council." Its officers are the Supreme Knight, Supreme Chaplain, Deputy Supreme Knight, Supreme Secretary, Supreme Treasurer, Supreme Advocate, Supreme Physician, and Supreme Warden. The Supreme Council also has a board of directors, present and past state officers, and elected delegates when the Supreme Council is in convention. On the state or district level, there is a similar group of officials. On the local or chapter level the KC has subordinate councils. Its officers bear the titles of Grand Knight, Grand Secretary, and the like. There are over 6,000 subordinate councils. The headquqarters are in New Haven, Connecticut.

Background literature on the Knights of Columbus is provided in the order's weekly publication, *Knights of Columbus News*, and a monthly periodical, *Columbia*. The society has also published occasional pamphlets: *We Hold These Truths* (1976); *These Men They Call Knights* (1972).

KNIGHTS OF EQUITY. This society was a secret fraternal group of Catholics, formed n 1895 in Cleveland, Ohio. Its purpose was to recruit Irishmen in the United States in order to bring them more closely together so that national traditions might be perpetuated. Meetings were held in "Courts." REFERENCE: *DSOS*.

KNIGHTS OF HONOR (KOH). This society was organized on June 30, 1873, in Louisville, Kentucky, by men from the Ancient Order of United Workmen* and also from the Independent Order of Odd Fellows.* Upon being founded, the KOH had as one of its objectives to provide fraternal unity and benevolent assistance for white men of sound moral character and good physical health. The KOH differed from most fraternal societies in that its candidates did not take an oath in the initiation rite. They merely promised to obey the regulations of the society and to help a "brother" in need.

In 1875 the society created a ladies' auxiliary degree, but in 1877 the supreme lodge repealed its resolution of 1875, apparently because few auxiliaries were formed during the two years from 1875 to 1877. The repeal led to the formation of a new, independent beneficiary order: The Order of Protection of Knights and Ladies of Honor. Later this group changed its name to Knights and Ladies of Honor.*

The KOH was one of the more successful fraternal benefit groups. By 1898 it had 90,335 members. But when the order upgraded its method of collecting fees for the insurance fund, many dropped their membership because insurance cost more. This was a common occurrence in other fraternal organizations too. Many members would not accept the changes that led to better actuarial methods. By 1916 the society was forced to disband.

Membership was drawn exclusively from white males, who professed belief in a supreme being. Each prospective member also had to be "able to earn a livelihood for himself and his family." Every member was to keep the affairs of the society secret so that "intruders and unworthy men" could not falsely obtain benefits from the society.

The seal or emblem of the KOH was a shield, depicting a knight with his shield arm raised. On the main shield was a triangle with the letters O.M.A.

Organizationally, the KOH was a three-tiered structure, like almost all fraternal societies. The local units were called "Subordinate Lodges." State or regional groups were referred to as "Grand Lodges," and the national authority was known as the "Supreme Lodge."

Additional information may be found in Myron W. Sackett, *Early History of Fraternal Beneficiary Societies in America* (1914). Another source is Albert Stevens, *Cyclopedia of Fraternities* (1907), which this account relies on for a number of key points. Terence O'Donnell, *History of Life Insurance* (1936), also makes some observations concerning the KOH.

KNIGHTS OF JERICHO (KOJ). The society was formed in 1850 as a total abstinence secret organization. It was founded in Utica, New York, by Daniel Cody, who in 1842 helped found the Sons of Temperance. In 1851 the KOJ changed its name to Good Templars.* A year later (1852) a disgruntled member formed a rival fraternal order known as the Independent Order of Good Templars. This rival group merged with the Good Templars before the year 1852 had passed. When the merger resulted, the name Independent Order of Good Templars was adopted, the name of the former seceding order.

For additional information, see the discussion of the International Order of Good Templars in the present volume.

KNIGHTS OF KHORASSAN, DRAMATIC ORDER OF (DOKK). If the Masons and Odd Fellows can have a "fun" group, why not also one for the Knights of Pythias?* Thus members of the Knights of Pythias in 1894 organized the Dramatic Order of the Knights of Khorassan.

Colloquially the members of the DOKK are called "Dokeys." They meet in "Temples," and their activities are very much oriented toward fun. One of the order's publicity brochures says: "The Dokeys pride themselves on fancy Drills, Zouaves, Color Guards, Parades, Oriental Costumes, Drum and Bugle Corps, and Brass Bands." Like the Shriners,* the Dokeys wear Arabic fezzes. Another statement in the brochure states: "Dokeys are happy people, but they are happiest where they are able to share with 'deserving' children and adults, who are afflicted and need help."

Members are exclusively drawn from the Knights of Pythias, and like the Knights of Pythias, the Dokeys have declined in membership over the years. In the 1920s the society had about 100,000 members. Today (1979) it has 15,000 members in 110 temples. The Dokeys also sponsor a ladies' auxiliary, Nomads of Avrudaka.

Being a fraternal secret society, the DOKK has a secret ritual that contains two degrees: the Temple degree and the Imperial degree. The former is given in the local meeting place(s) of the society. The latter is conferred only by the national body, known as the "Imperial Palace." According to the official literature of the order, the "ritual teaches valuable lessons of life. The scene exemplifying the motto, 'Lift Up The Fallen,' is rated one of the finest ritualistic parts ever written." Upon being initiated, each candidate receives an official fez.

The Dokeys like to believe that they are "geared to the future," especially with regard to humanitarian concerns. Each temple is required by Imperial Law (a national resolution) to take up some humanitarian cause, and each temple must have its own humanitarian committee. The committee seeks out some permanently disabled sufferer, often selecting a child, whom it can help support. On the national level the society has donated equipment to fifteen nonsectarian children's hospitals.

The emblem of the order is a crescent standing on its side with three stars embossed on it. The letters D.O.K.K. continue on from the crescent to form a circle. The head of a bengal is surrounded by the crescent and the letters D.O.K.K. The three watchwords of the order are "Humanitarianism, Education, Enjoyment."

Structurally, the order operates on two levels: the local and national. As already noted, local units are called "Temples." The national authority, the "Imperial Palace," meets in convention biennially. The chief officer of the imperial palace is known as "Imperial Prince." Headquarters are located in Des Moines, Iowa.

Additional background on the DOKK may be gained by reading the society's official periodical, *The Dokey-Nomad Herald*. It is published quarterly. Other information may be found by reading pamphlets and brochures printed by the society. The *Constitution and Statutes* are also quite helpful in understanding the Dokeys as an organization.

KNIGHTS OF LIBERTY. Founded in 1923 in New York, this secret society was an anti-Ku Klux Klan organization. The founder, Andrew J. Padon, was an expelled member of the KKK. Apparently Padon had opposed the undesirable members that the KKK was attracting in the early 1920s. Headquarters were in the city of New York. REFERENCE: *DSOS*

KNIGHTS OF LUTHER. A secret society formed in 1912 in Des Moines, Iowa, "for the purpose of fighting the Romanist Church with weapons like those with which it fights." By 1915 the order reportedly had 128,000 members. The society seems no longer to exist today. REFERENCE: *DSOS*.

KNIGHTS OF MALTA, THE ANCIENT AND ILLUSTRIOUS ORDER (KOM). This order considers itself to be the most ancient fraternal order in existence, tracing its origin back to A.D. 1048, when the order was established as a charitable and religious organization. The next notable date was 1099, when it entered Jerusalem in the Crusades. Whether its linkage to the Crusades is authentic is open to question.

The present order was introduced to the United States in 1870 by receiving a charter from the Scottish Commandery in Scotland. The KOM, not to be confused with the Masonic group called the Order of Knights of Malta, states that it is

a band of Protestant Christian men, bound together by secret ties, for the promotion of Protestant Christianity, Good Fellowship, Mutual Aid, Ritualistic Instruction, and Preservation of a Sound Christian Moral Fiber, which will preserve for us and for our children the Blessings of our North American Way of Life!

The KOM also sees itself in existence "to defend the Protestant faith against all foes whatsoever; to ever defend civil and religious liberty; to exercise the fullest toleration and charity toward all men; to practice benevolence; and to maintain a universal Protestant fraternity."

Critics have seen the KOM as being strongly prejudiced against the Catholics. Some evidence exists showing that not only are Catholics excluded from its membership, but also Protestants married to Catholics are barred.

Membership requirements make up a quite lengthy list. The individual must be a white male, not less than eighteen years old; have no physical or mental infirmities; be a "True Protestant in Religion"; be able to read, write, and speak English; be known to be law-abiding; and be "competent to pursue some useful and lawful occupation." Applicants for membership are investigated before being accepted. Each applicant must be proposed by a member of the order, who must have known the applicant for at least two years so that his moral and religious beliefs can be verified as being acceptable. Over the past decade the order has suffered a drastic loss in members. In the late 1960s there were 10,000 knights, but by 1979 the figure had declined to 2,000, a loss of 80 percent.

The KOM prides itself on being a secret, ritualistic order. "To expose our secrets to the world would be to destroy the Order as we know it today. The world at large would suffer from its loss, far more than the present members would suffer." There are twelve degrees available, but after the candidate has received the second degree he is a full-fledged member. Each of the twelve degrees conveys given teachings taken from Bible stories.

The insignia of the KOM is a Maltese, eight-cornered, cross with an eagle perched between the four arms of the cross. The center of the cross displays a ring with a Latin cross and the words "IN HOC SIGNO VINCES." This slogan is also used by the Knights Templar.*

Declining in membership, the order still owns and maintains a home for its aged members in Granville, Pennsylvania. It is known as the Malta Home.

Having been brought to the United States in 1870, the order reorganized itself in 1889. The national organization is known as the "Supreme Grand Commandery," which meets annually in convention. State structures are called "Grand Commanderies." Each grand commandery has its own constitution and headquarters. On the local scene the KOM calls its gatherings "Commanderies." Currently there are thirty-six commanderies in Canada, New York, Ohio, Pennsylvania, and the New England states. Headquarters for the Supreme Grand Commandery are in Reading, Pennsylvania.

For further information the reader may obtain the booklet, *What Does the Ancient and Illustrious Order Knights of Malta Have to Offer Christian Men Today?* (n.d.). Another source is the *Malta Bulletin*, a monthly periodical published by the order.

KNIGHTS OF PETER CLAVER (KPC). This order had its origin in the deep-seated racial discrimination prevalent in the United States during the late 1800s and early 1900s. When the Knights of Peter Claver were founded in Mobile, Alabama, in 1909, black citizens were not permitted to join white fraternal societies. Catholic fraternal groups were no exception. Thus four Josephite priests and three laymen organized a Catholic fraternal order for blacks. In 1911 the order became incorporated.

Objectives of the KPC are to provide faithful service to God and the church and to promote the brotherhood of man through works of charity and kindness. During the 1960s the order took an active part in getting black citizens registered so that they would not be denied the right to vote. The order operates a beneficiary insurance program, as well as a department that furnishes mortgage loans. However, the order does not sell insurance as do most fraternal benefit societies. It has no agents promoting and selling insurance. The society sees itself as a fraternal order that does not rely on its insurance for new members.

Over the years the KPC has undergone a considerable amount of organizational change. In 1917 the order created a fourth-degree division. It formed the Junior Knights, an order for boys under the age of eighteen, also in 1917. In 1922 a ladies' auxiliary was established, and in 1930 the Junior Daughters came into being for girls under eighteen years of age. The constitution has been revised a number of times since the order was launched.

The KPC, unlike many other fraternal groups, has been growing. In 1959 it had 13,000 members; ten years later it had about 18,000; and by 1979 it had 25,000 members. This figure includes the ladies from the order's female auxiliary. Approximately 25 percent of the membership consists of white members.

Philanthropically, the KPC gives aid to its sick members from a fund established and run by the councils (local chapters) for such benefits. The order also has its members engage in various helping activities in their respective parishes. Scholarships are awarded to deserving students.

The KPC operates in nineteen states. Its local units are known as "Councils." The ladies' auxiliary calls its local groups "Courts." The society on the national level meets in convention once each year. Its headquarters are in New Orleans, Louisiana.

For further information, see the society's bimonthly publication, *The Claverite*. Other information may be obtained by consulting the brochures issued by the KPC.

KNIGHTS OF PYTHIAS (KOP). The founder of this order was Justus H. Rathbone, a member of the Freemasons* and the Red Men.* On February 19, 1864, Rathbone and several federal government clerks founded the Knights of Pythias in Washington, D.C. By April of that same year the Grand Lodge for the District of Columbia was organized, and by 1868 the Supreme Grand Lodge of the World (the national structure) was established.

Rathbone once directed a school play that portrayed the loyal friendship between Damon and Pythias (originally an erroneous spelling for Phintias), two Syracusans who lived during the fourth century B.C. Phintias was condemned to death for opposing Dionysius, tyrant of Syracuse from 405 to 367 B.C. Damon offered himself as security so that Phintias, his friend, could go home to see his wife and children. The time for Phintias's execution drew near, but he had not returned. Damon held true to his promise, permitting himself to be led to the place of the planned execution, when suddenly Phintias rushed forward embracing his friend. Dionysius was so moved by this incident that he released both men and asked if he could join their friendship.

The school play seemed like an ideal story out of which a ritual could be developed. Rathbone also borrowed ritual parts from some of the other existing fraternal orders to which he belonged, Masonry and the Red Men society, for example.

Basing its ritual on the story of Damon and Pythias, this society accents the principles of friendship, charity, and benevolence. In fact, the Pythian motto is: "Be Generous, Brave, and True." Pythian literature says that after the American Civil War Rathbone felt the United States urgently needed these principles "to rekindle the brotherly sentiment which had been all but stamped out under the merciless heel of human passions. . . ."

Membership is open to any white man in good health. Until 1875 the order did not admit maimed individuals. All applicants must also believe in a supreme being. Black applicants were denied membership in the KOP even before the constitution contained the "white-male" clause. The clause made its appearance after 1871. It should be noted, however, that some agitation with the all-white clause occurred in 1964 at the national (Supreme Lodge) convention. The convention referred the matter to appropriate committees. In 1966 the issue was again referred to committees, and in 1968 the matter failed to appear on the convention's agenda. Black citizens in 1869 formed their own group, Knights of Pythias of North America, Europe, Asia, and Africa.*

Once an applicant has been accepted for membership by ball ballot, he is, as in so many fraternal groups, required to go through the mandatory initiation rites. In preparation for the first rank (degree), the candidate is blindfolded and required to kneel before an open coffin, containing a skeleton. He is asked a number of questions, and finally in the oath of secrecy he vows: "I solemnly promise that I will never reveal the password, grip, signs or any other secret or mystery of this rank . . . I will obey the laws . . . heed the teachings of this rank . . . So help me God—and may He keep me steadfast." For the second and third ranks an oath or "obligation" is required again.

The KOP also has a uniformed contingent, similar to the Knights Templar in York Rite Freemasonry* or the Patriarchs Militant in the Independent Order of Odd Fellows. The uniformed group is under the control of the supreme lodge, and only members with the rank of Knight (third degree) are eligible to join the Uniform Rank. This group on occasion participates in public parades and processions.

The KOP, like some other fraternal orders, has a "fun" group, the Dramatic Order of Knights of Khorassan* (DOKK, commonly referred to as "Dokeys" by the Pythians). This order was founded in 1894. Its regalia in many ways resembles that of the Shriners. Only KOP members may join this society.

Women are ineligible to become members of the Knights of Pythias, but the order helped women form an auxiliary group in 1888, now known as the Pythian Sisters.* For the male youth the KOP has the Junior Order of Princes of Syracuse.* Boys from fourteen to twenty-one are eligible to join this group. For young ladies there is the junior group known as Sunshine Girls.*

The insignia of the KOP is an inverted triangle that has four smaller triangles within it, three inverted and one upright. The inner, upper left-hand triangle displays the letter "F," the inner, upper right-hand triangle reveals the letter "C," and the bottom inner triangle portrays the letter "B." The fourth inner triangle, in the upper middle of the larger triangle, depicts the bust of a medieval knight with armor, sword, and axe. The letters F. C. B. stand for friendship, charity, and benevolence.

In 1877 the KOP introduced its Endowment Rank, a fraternal insurance department. This rank became the fourth degree, a voluntary one. In 1930 this insurance degree separated from the KOP by becoming a mutual life insurance company. Today it is known as American United Insurance Company, headquartered in Indianapolis, Indiana.

Philanthropically, the KOP has for a number of years embraced a major benevolent project, the Cystic Fibrosis Research Foundation. It has provided financial assistance "to worthy Pythians in distress" and given aid to national or sectional emergencies in case of disasters and calamities. Kiddy Kamps are operated for unfortunate children who would ordinarily have no vacation or outing opportunities. Recently the KOP also has been promoting highway safety programs. A number of Pythian homes are maintained for aged members and their wives and children. The order has also conducted blood banks and provided scholarship funds for winners of public-speaking contests held in colleges or universities.

When one examines the history of the KOP, he cannot help but note that this fraternity is a classic example of the rise and fall of a fraternal order. With a few minor exceptions, the KOP prospered and grew for a number of decades. By the early 1920s the society had almost 1,000,000 members. It once had the ability to attract members from other fraternal groups. Masons, Odd Fellows, Red Men, Elks, and others were commonly numbered among the Pythians. In 1936 the KOP was honored by having Franklin D. Roosevelt join its fellowship. Today, however, the KOP has less than 200,000 members. In fact, the fraternity is facing what appears to be a gloomy future. Many of the society's lodges have over the last two decades closed their doors, and many of those still open often are located in buildings that require repair and upkeep. In some geographic areas the KOP still has lodges with enthusiastic members, but they seem to be becoming fewer each year.

The deteriorating situation is recognized by officials of the order. For instance, the *Pythian International* (Summer, 1978) said in an article concerning membership: "Inactive lodges create a stale-mate and an astigmatism on the Order." The article continued:

Lodges are not doing their part. Their house is not in shape so that one could ask a person to join the Order. In many instances if applications were secured, the lodge in that area would not be in a position to initiate those seeking to become members. We have to start at the bottom and get our house in order.

The organizational structure of the KOP is three-tiered. The national convention is under the auspices of the "Supreme Lodge," which meets every two years. The chief executive officers of the supreme lodge are the Chancellor, Vice Chancellor, Prelate, Secretary, Treasurer, Master at Arms, Inner Guard, and Outer Guard. State groups are called "Grand Lodges." Local units used to be called "Castles," but in recent years they seem to be referred to as "Subordinate Lodges." The national headquarters are located in Stockton, California.

For further information see P. C. Kibbe, *Damon and Pythias* (1930); Jon Van Valkenburg, *The Knights of Pythias Complete Manual and Textbook* (1887); *Brief History of the Knights of Pythias* (n.d.); *The Pythian Story* (n.d.). The latter two items are pamphlet publications issued by the KOP. Additional information may also be obtained by reading the order's *Journal of Proceedings*. The *Ritual for Subordinate Lodges of the Knights of Pythias* (1945) gives a detailed, illustrated view of the KOP ritual and opening ceremonies. The *Pythian International* is published quarterly by the KOP.

KNIGHTS OF PYTHIAS, IMPROVED ORDER OF (IOKP). After the national conventions of the Supreme Lodge of the Knights of Pythias in 1892, 1894, and 1895 declined to allow various lodges to print the ritual of the order in any language but English, a number of German members of German American lodges seceded to form the IOKP. The seceding lodges were accustomed to conducting their sessions in German.

The new order was formed in June of 1895 in Indianapolis, Indiana. The IOKP was essentially a carbon copy of the parent body. The IOKP never really prospered in terms of membership growth. The advent of World War I eventually forced the order to dissolve. REFERENCE: *Cyc. Frat.*

KNIGHTS OF PYTHIAS OF NORTH AMERICA, EUROPE, ASIA, AND AFRICA (KOP). This is the black fraternal society that modeled its order upon the white organization, Knights of Pythias.* This black order was founded in 1869 in Richmond, Virginia. Current information was not obtainable regarding the present status of the KOP.

KNIGHTS OF ST. JOHN (KSJ). Organized in the United States in 1879, this order sees itself as "a modern counterpart of the Knights of St. John Hospitalers who were founded in the City of Amalfi in the Kingdom of Naples in the year 1048." The objective of the KSJ is summed up in the following words: "The medievel [sic] knight fought well for God and the Church, but the modern knight chose a spiritual field, wherein they [sic] could strive to capture men's hearts and minds for God by promoting among its members a filial devotion to Holy Mother, the church and a profound respect for her authority."

The KSJ is a semimilitary society. Thus its members commonly wear uniforms in celebrating parish events such as participating in processions of first communions, confirmation, first Masses, anniversaries, and the like. The order also sees itself as a benevolent fraternity, providing benefits ranging from parish involvement to paying death benefits to its members' beneficiaries. Another prominent activity sponsored by the society is its national sports program. Each year gold and bowling tournaments are conducted by the program.

Membership requirements specify that one must be a "practical Catholic gentleman" between sixteen and fifty-five years of age. Individuals who are merely social members (holding no right to insurance benefits) may join even if over fifty-five years of age. Total membership in 1978 was 7,144 knights in 172 commanderies (local units). The society has twenty-seven commanderies in West Africa, five in Togo, and eight in Trinidad and Tobago. The remaining commanderies are in the United States.

The KSJ has a secret ritual that contains the usual fraternal rites and ceremonies. Recently (April 1977), however, the order discontinued the use of its password. One reason for dropping the password was that it was too time-consuming to inculcate it into the members. The order also said it had "no appreciable organizational value. . . ."

The society's insignia consists of the Maltese cross, with two swords forming an X-shaped design over the cross. In the center of the cross is a picture of a medieval knight's head armor. The word "Knights" appears on the upper vertical arm of the cross, and "St. John" is inscribed on the lower vertical arm.

As has already been stated, the order calls its local units "Commanderies," of which there are 172. The regional structures are known as "Grand Commanderies." On the international level the society calls its organization the "Supreme Commandery." Head offices are in Parma, Ohio.

Additional information on the KSJ may be found in the order's quarterly publication, *Knight of St. John*. This periodical is really the only source that contains information about the order. For instance, the September 1978 issue contains a brief history of the order.

KNIGHTS OF ST. JOHN, SUPREME LADIES' AUXILIARY (SLA).
The Supreme Ladies Auxiliary, Knights of St. John, was founded in 1900 in Philadelphia, Pennsylvania; and in September of the same year the society was incorporated in the state of New York. Some of the society's objectives are to foster fraternalism among Catholic women, to develop patriotism, to provide support for the Catholic Church, and to assist the Knights of St. John.* The Virgin Mary is the patron saint of the order.

The SLA conducts several fraternal activities. One noteworthy activity is sponsoring a uniformed drill team that performs at state and national conventions of the society. Another activity of the organization pertains to mission work, assisting the church's work in mission areas. Still another activity of the society is assisting the junior auxiliaries, the youth department.

In terms of benefits, the women operate a death benefit fund for its members. For nonmembers the society helps support the Red Cross, American Heart Association, Muscular Dystrophy Association, National Foundation of Infantile Paralysis, and the American Cancer Association. Contributions are also made to other charity projects.

Requirements for membership specify that applicants must be "practical Catholic ladies between the ages of sixteen (16) and fifty (50) years." Applicants who are over fifty years of age or who fail to pass the medical examination may join the society as social members. Young ladies between eight and fifteen years may join the junior auxiliary of the SLA. In April of 1978 the society's membership roster had 14,251 members in 189 local units.

As a typical fraternal order, the SLA has a ritual which it keeps secret from nonmembers. The ritual contains an initiation ceremony and other rites. The emblem of the society is a Maltese cross encircled by a laurel wreath.

Local units are referred to as "Subordinate Auxiliaries," of which there are 161 in the United States and twenty-eight in foreign countries. A subordinate auxiliary is composed of three or more local units. State structures are called "Grand Auxiliaries." These groups meet annually. The Supreme Convention, the highest authority, meets biennially. Head offices are located in Rochester, New York.

For further information the reader is confined to brochures and data provided by the head office. The society does not publish a periodical.

KNIGHTS OF THE ANCIENT ESSENIC ORDER. This fraternal order was founded in 1888 in Olympia, Washington. The society really was a semimilitary fraternal benefit group. Its benefits were not of the insurance variety, but rather more of the relief and aid nature. The society had 35,000 members in the late 1890s. REFERENCE: *Cyc. Frat.*

KNIGHTS OF THE BLUE CROSS OF THE WORLD. This group was formed in Homer, Michigan, in 1888. It functioned as a fraternal benefit group by means of a mutual assessment plan. In the event of sickness or death, it paid weekly benefits to the beneficiaries. By 1900 the society seemed to have been dissolved. REFERENCE: *DSOS*.

KNIGHTS OF THE FLAMING CIRCLE. In order to counter the Ku Klux Klan, this order was founded in 1923 in Pennsylvania. Each member had to wear a robe in his initiation. On his left breast he wore a flaming red circle, symbolizing truth. It welcomed Catholics, Jews, and blacks to its membership roster. Protestants were excluded. REFERENCE: *DSOS*.

KNIGHTS OF THE GLOBE (KOG). Prominent among the founders of this organization were men from Freemasonry,* the Odd Fellows,* the Royal Arcanum,* the Ancient Order of the United Workmen,* the Grand Army of the Republic, and Woodmen of the World.* The order was organized in 1889, in Chicago, Illinois, as a fraternal benefit group that had strong patriotic sentiments.

Both men and women were able to become members; however, women had to enter by first joining the Daughters of the Globe, an auxiliary of the KOG. The society went out of existence in the early 1900s.

While it functioned, the KOG had a four-degree ritual and ceremony. The four degrees were named Volunteer, Militant, Knight, and Valiant Knight. Much of the ritual showed the influence of Freemasonry and Odd Fellowship.

The order's members resided mostly in Illinois. Headquarters were maintained in Chicago, Illinois.

For additional information, see Albert C. Stevens, *Cyclopedia of Fraternities* (1907). The present report is largely based on Stevens' volume.

KNIGHTS OF THE GOLDEN EAGLE (KGE). This fraternal benefit society was founded in Baltimore, Maryland, in 1872. Being a semimilitary society, the KGE founded its rituals and ceremonial rites on the history and pageantry of the medieval Crusaders. The order's objectives were to provide mutual relief for its members in finding employment and aided them while unemployed.

The KGE ritual had three degrees, each symbolically referring to a medieval soldier. The first degree accented the pilgrim role; it taught the candidate fidelity to God and man. The second rite took the medieval knight as a model; here the member was taught to revere religion, fidelity, valor, charity, courtesy, and hospitality. The third degree revolved about the symbolism of the crusader; it equipped the member against the evil of his enemies. The order's motto was "Fidelity, Valor, and Honor."

Membership requirements of the KGE required the applicant to be a believer in a supreme being, a white male at least eighteen years old, free of mental or bodily handicaps, able to write and support himself, a law-abiding citizen, of sound moral character, and a believer in the Christian faith. These requirements were the same as those demanded by the Order of Heptasophs.* For the ladies the KGE had an auxiliary organization, Ladies of the Golden Eagle. The women took the Temple degree upon being initiated.

The KGE was popular during the latter part of the nineteenth century. The Odd Fellows* took an interest in the order and helped it get established in Philadelphia in 1875. Similarly, the Knights of Pythias* (at that time a highly respected group) helped the KGE get a foothold in 1880 in Massachusetts. Thus by the early 1920s the order had 73,000 members in twenty-six states. With the advent of the 1930s the order began to experience numerical decline. By 1965 it had less than 15,000 members, and most of these were in Pennsylvania. It appears that the society has in recent years become extinct, as the author was unable to locate an address for the organization.

The KGE's local groups were known as "Castles." The castles were governed by the state structures called "Grand Castles." The national government was named "Supreme Castle." The latest site for the KGE headquarters was in North Wales, Pennsylvania.

For additional information, see Albert C. Stevens, *Cyclopedia of Fraternities* (1907). This report is largely drawn from Stevens' work.

KNIGHTS OF THE INVISIBLE COLORED KINGDOM. This was an anti-Ku Klux Klan society founded in Tennessee in August of 1923. The order's purpose was to organize "male members of the Negro race into grand and subordinate organizations and teaching them the principles of good citizenship and their political duties and possibilities." The society no longer exists. REFERENCE: *DSOS.*

KNIGHTS OF THE KU KLUX KLAN. See Ku Klux Klan, Knights of the.

KNIGHTS OF THE LOYAL GUARD. This fraternal benefit group was founded in Flint, Michigan, in 1895. The society admitted men and women into its membership. About ten years after its formation the society had 5,000 members in lodges in 104 communities. REFERENCES: *Cyc. Frat.*; *DSOS.*

KNIGHTS OF THE MYSTIC CHAIN, ANCIENT ORDER OF (AOKMC). This secret society was founded upon the traditions and legends of King Arthur and the Knights of the Round Table. The AOKMC was organized by Freemasons* in 1871 in Reading, Pennsylvania. Because it was started by Freemasons, the society, of course, had some Masonic characteristics. The all-seeing eye and placing the Bible on the lodge altar are but two examples.

The AOKMC had three degrees that every member had to attain. This requirement also reflected Masonic influence. The first degree was known as the Esquire or White degree. Its basic lesson pointed to the Good Samaritan of the New Testament days. The Sir Knight's or Blue degree was based on the chivalry of King Arthur's era. The Round Table or Red degree impressed the candidate with the certainty of life and death. A fourth degree was also available. It was a military-rank degree requiring all holders of this degree to wear military-like costumes. There was also a Mark degree, given only to all past officers of subordinate units, called Castles. The national structure, the Supreme Castle, conferred the Supreme degree. In 1890 a degree was introduced for women. It was called the Naomi or Daughters of Ruth degree. At first this degree was under the supervision of the Supreme Castle, but before long it was permitted to conduct and legislate its own affairs.

When the AOKMC was founded, it was a fraternal secret society without any insurance benefits. In 1889, however, the order did enter the fraternal insurance arena. In addition to providing benevolent features, the society also sought to foster love for the member's home, country, and brotherhood. The order once enjoyed a membership of 40,000 members.

The society's emblem was a pentagon. Each side of the pentagon symbolized a specific value. The first was white and portrayed an open book. The second was blue and depicted a shield and spear. Red was the color of the third side, displaying the skull and crossbones. The fourth was also red with crossed swords. The fifth side was black, showing the all-seeing eye. "Loyalty, Obedience, and Fidelity" was the slogan of the AOKMC.

The AOKMC conducted its activities on three levels. The local units were known as "Subordinate Castles." State or regional groups were referred to as "Select Castles," and the national structure was called the "Supreme Castle." The latter, of course, was the highest authority.

For additional information the reader may wish to consult Albert C. Stevens, *Cyclopedia of Fraternities* (1907). The present writer made liberal use of Steven's volume with regard to the AOKMC.

KNIGHTS OF THE RED CROSS. Formally the name of this fraternal benefit group was Order of the Red Cross and Knights of the Red Cross. It was founded in 1879 by members of the Ancient Order of United Workmen and some other fraternal group members. Its motto was *"Omnia pro caritate"* (everything for charity). The ritual was based on Biblical incidents, and it also showed a strong resemblance to Freemasonry. REFERENCES: *Cyc. Frat.*; *DSOS*.

KNIGHTS OF THE RED CROSS OF CONSTANTINE (KRCC). Although this order knows that its historical link to the Order of Knights of the Red Cross of Constantine in the early fourth century is legendary, it nevertheless identifies with that group founded by the Emperor Constantine in A.D. 312. Constantine, the Roman Emperor, was converted to Christianity on October 27, 312. His conversion was triggered by the vision he saw in the sky, which revealed a golden cross with the inscription of "IN HOC SIGNO VINCES." According to tradition, Constantine selected a group of fifty young knights of proven bravery to guard the emperor's newly fashioned labarum, which consisted of a banner bearing the letters I.H.S.V. and the monogram of Christ.

The Masonic Order of the Red Cross of Constantine in the United States was introduced on November 12, 1783, when the "Red Cross" degree was conferred on a class of eight men in Charleston, South Carolina. The first conclave (local chapter) was not organized until 1870 in Washington, Pennsylvania. The Grand Imperial Council of Pennsylvania was formed in 1872 in Reading, Pennsylvania. Officially, the KRCC considers 1872 as the year of its origin in the United States. By June 1, 1875, a number of representatives met in a Masonic lodge in New York City and organized the Sovereign Grand Council of the United States.

Initially, the Sovereign Grand Council had very limited power and jurisdiction over the grand councils on the state level. In 1896, however, all state grand and imperial councils ceased to exist, and all conclaves were placed under the direct jurisdiction of the Sovereign Grand Council. This new power and authority given to the Sovereign Grand Council soon brought intraorganizational conflict. A number of state organizations (jurisdictions) went their separate ways. Some even changed their order's name. The Grand Council of Illinois in 1911, for example, changed its name to the Grand Imperial Council of the Imperial Ecclesiastical and Military Order of the Red Cross of Constantine for the United States of America. In 1935 the Grand Jurisdiction from the Grand Imperial Council of Pennsylvania changed its name to the Grand Imperial Council of Knights of the Red Cross of Constantine (and Appendant Orders) for the United States of America, Empire of the East. Not until 1958 did the different groups come together to form a union.

The KRCC has several objectives: (1)To form a closer Masonic bond among its members. (2) To "purify the system of Masonic science, extend its limits, and increase its influence. . . ." (3) Preserve and prevent perversion of Masonic institutions. (4) Oppose "infidelity and treason under whatever form" it may exist. (5) Promote the "social happiness and external welfare of our fellow creatures."

The official emblem is the Greek cross with the Chi Rho symbol superimposed upon it. Each arm of the cross bears one letter forming the abbreviation for *In Hoc Signo Vinces*. The Greek cross is red, and the letters and Chi Rho are gold-colored.

Being a Masonically linked fraternal group, the KRCC has a secret ritual. The degrees given are: Knight of the Red Cross of Constantine; Knight of the Holy Sepulchre; Knight of St. John the Evangelist. On the Grand Imperial Council level the order bestows: Chapter of Knights Grand Cross (limited to fifty recipients); Grand Senate of Sovereigns (limited to Coroneted Sovereigns); Grand College of Viceroys (limited to Coroneted Sovereigns and Consecrated Viceroys).

Membership is exclusively drawn from the Masonic York Rite. After an individual has attained the seventh (Royal Arch Mason) degree, he may join the KRCC. Membership is only open by invitation. Since only white males are eligible for the Royal Arch Mason degree, the KRCC also has only white members. The current (1979) membership roll has about 5,800 knights. A decade ago there were about 5,000 members.

Local units are known as "Conclaves." The order has conclaves in the United States and Canada. The highest authority structure is the "United Grand Imperial Council." It meets in convention annually. Headquarters are in Chicago, Illinois.

About the only materials available on the KRCC are brochures and pamphlets issued by the order.

KNIGHTS OF THE YORK CROSS OF HONOUR, THE CONVENT GENERAL (KYCH). The idea of this order was conceived by John Raymond Shute II, a native of Monroe, North Carolina. It was his intent to form an organization of past presiding officers of the four bodies (the Blue Lodge,* the Royal Arch Chapter,* the Royal and Select Master Council,* and the Commandery of the Knights Templar*) of the York Rite.* On March 13, 1930, Shute assembled four "brethren" to organize the Knights of the York Cross of Honour. On June 6, 1930, the Convent General (similar to a grand lodge structure) was formed, also in Monroe, North Carolina.

The KYCH is an honorary degree that exists to promote friendship and helpfulness among its members. Its membership is drawn from those who have presided in the Blue Lodge, Chapter, Council, Commandery, or Preceptory (so named in Canada) of the York Rite. Its members all are past presiding officers of the several York Rite divisions, where only white males may join. Thus the KYCH also has only white members. The current (1978) membership was approaching the 11,000 mark.

The emblem of the KYCH is a crown, embroidered with the insignia of the square and compasses, the upright triangle, the upright triangle with its broken base, and the crown and Latin cross. Respectively, these represent the Blue Lodge, Royal Arch Masonry, the Council of Royal and Select Masters, and the Commandery.

The ritual of the KYCH has two degrees. The first one is the Initiatory or Reception of the Candidate degree. The second degree is known as the Knight York Grand Cross. Each degree has an oath, resembling other Masonic vows.

On the charity circuit, the KYCH is not overly involved. It operates a medical research foundation, primarily to fight leukemia.

Structurally, the KYCH calls its national (really international) administration the "Convent General." It meets annually in a convention known as a "Conclave." The convent general offices are the Grand Master-General, Deputy Grand Master-General, Grand Warder of the Temple, Grand Registrar-General, Grand Seneschal, Grand Marshall, Grand Sentinel, and Grand Prelate. Regional structures are known as "Priories." These priories also function as local groups in that members meet in the town or city that serves as the headquarters of each priory. The priory meetings are also referred to as "Conclaves." The priory's main offices are Prior, Deputy Prior, Warder, and Registrar. The KYCH has sixty-eight priories in Canada, Australia, the Philippines, and the United States. The national headquarters of the KYCH are in Hastings-On-Hudson, New York.

Information on the KYCH may be found by reading the order's annual publication, *The Quaternion*. Brief references to the KYCH may be found in R. F. Gould, *History of Freemasonry Throughout the World* (1936).

KNIGHTS TEMPLAR, GRAND ENCAMPMENT OF THE UNITED STATES (KT). Not long after Pope Urban II had approved and proclaimed the first Crusade in 1095, there arose a military monastic order in 1119 in Jerusalem that did not live in cloisters but sought to protect the Holy Sepulcher and defend the Crusaders. The order at first was limited to nobles who took vows of poverty. The King of Jerusalem billeted the order in his palace, which was erected on the site of King Solomon's temple. From this site the order received the name "Poor Knights of the Temple," which soon became Knights Templars. The order grew and became wealthy, possessing property throughout Europe. Ruling princes, hard pressed for money, envied the Templars. Philip IV of France (reportedly denied membership in the Templars) with the help of Pope Clement V succeeded not only in having the Pope disband the order but also in having its grand master, Jacques de Molay, burned at the stake in 1314. The Grand Encampment of the Knights Templar of the United States takes its legend, titles, ritual, and symbolism largely from the medieval order.

There are several legendary accounts that seek to link the present KT to the Templars of the Middle Ages. However, well-versed Masonic scholars assert there is no link between the present KT and the order led by Jacques de Molay. The earliest account for the origin of the KT goes back to 1769, where, in Boston, the Knight Templar degree was first conferred upon William Davis. An encampment of the Knights Templar was organized in Charleston, South Carolina, in 1780. However, the present grand encampment office located in Chicago lists 1816 as its date of origin, which represents the formation, adoption, and ratification of the KT constitution. The

KT is a uniformed group wearing regalia reminiscent of the medieval Knights Templars. The order is part of the York Rite* in Freemasonry.

Among Masons, the KT is frequently referred to as "Commandery." Its ritual contains three degrees: the Order of the Red Cross, the Knights of Malta, and the Knights Templar. Once the Royal Arch degree (the seventh degree in the York Rite) has been received, two routes are available to become a Sir Knight, as its members are known. The Royal Arch Mason may go via the Council of Royal and Select Masters (eighth and ninth degree, respectively), or he may go directly on to the Order of the Red Cross (eighth degree), from this degree to the Knights of Malta (ninth degree), and then to the Knights Templar. The latter is the "highest" degree in the York Rite. However, before any of these degrees may be pursued, the individual must become a member of the Blue Lodge* as a Master Mason.

Secrecy to the KT, as with other fraternal groups, is very important. Having been accepted for membership, the candidate takes a long oath (obligation), invoking corporeal death upon himself should he violate any secrets or other Templar obligations. Part of the obligation requires the candidate to say: "I furthermore promise and vow, that I will wield my sword in defense of innocent maidens, destitute widows, helpless orphans, and the Christian religion." This and other promises he is to carry out "under no less penalty than to have my head struck off and placed on the highest spire in Christendom. . . ." Reputedly the KT is an order for Christians only. And since "none but Christians can be admitted, consequently it cannot be considered strictly as a Masonic body," according to one Masonic writer.

The emblem of the KT is an eight-cornered Maltese cross, covering the front part of an armored knight from his shoulders down. In the center of the cross is an inner and outer circle. The former contains IN HOC SIGNO VINCES; the latter displays the Latin cross encircled by a crown.

The KT conducts various programs and activities. It publishes "Guidelines on Patriotic and Civic Activities" to encourage its members to become active in civic affairs. The Knights Templar Eye Foundation, Inc., in operation since 1957, allocates money for eye research and for surgical and hospital expenses. The order's educational foundation furnishes loans for vocational, professional, and graduate study. In some localities the KT sponsors Easter sunrise services. One of the official publications urges its members to attend such Easter services: "The Grand Encampment [the national structure] especially encourages every Sir Knight to attend the church of his choice on that great day and join with other millions of professing Christians in celebrating the great victory of Christ over death." In 1976 the Knights were actively engaged in supporting the Bicentennial of the United States.

As already noted, in order to become a member of the KT the individual first must become a Master Mason in the Blue Lodge. Membership can only be acquired by white males, because no one may enter Masonry in the United States unless he is white. The current (1978) membership consists of approximately 368,000 Sir Knights. This represents a drop since 1968, when there were 398,000 members.

The Knights Templar had ten senators on its membership roster in 1977. Of the fourteen United States presidents who were Masons, Andrew Johnson, Warren Harding, and William McKinley also were members of the Knights Templar.

On the national scene, the KT refers to its structure as the "Grand Encampment of the U.S.A." The state or regional groups are known as "Grand Commanderies." When three or more commanderies are established in a state, they form a grand commandery. Local groups also are called "Commanderies." Each commandery usually has twelve officers: Eminent Commander, Generalismo, Captain-General, Prelate, Senior Warden, Junior Warden, Treasurer, Recorder, Warden, Standard-Bearer, Sword-Bearer, and Sentinel. On the grand commandery and grand encampment level the officers have the same titles, except that the term "Grand" precedes the designations. The national offices are in Chicago, Illinois.

For further information, the reader may consult various historical accounts of the medieval Knights Templars, bearing in mind that the link between the modern order and the one led by Jacques de Molay is nonexistent. The KT booklet, *Charting The Course* (1975), gives a brief view of the order's activities. The triennial convention proceedings provide a good picture of how the order functions and views itself. *Knight Templarism Illustrated* (1904), published by Ezra A. Cook, Chicago, Illinois, yields helpful information with regard to the order's ritual and symbolism. Albert Mackey's *Encyclopedia of Freemasonry* (1946), pp. 427-434, offers a short account of the modern Knights Templar.

KU KLUX KLAN, KNIGHTS OF THE (KKK). The KKK was founded by Judge Thomas M. Jones in 1865 or 1866 in Pulaski, Tennessee. Jones, together with six Confederate Army veterans, was eager for some fun and amusement, which they sought to achieve by creating an organization that would provide them with fraternal companions. In seeking amusement the members used bed linen for disguises to ride through towns and neighborhoods. By 1867 and 1868, given the considerable lawlessness following the social changes after the Civil War, vigilante-minded individuals began to control the KKK. The vigilantes found the KKK produced for them at least three desirable effects: Its disguised night rides provided amusement by frightening the illiterate former black slaves; the KKK was a convenient vehicle for checking lawlessness; and it helped keep blacks in "their place."

In forming the KKK, mystical titles, rituals, and secrecy were chosen for the organization. All of these elements were common in nearly all American fraternal organizations. In the search for titles and names the Greek word *kuklos* (circle) was corrupted by deriving Ku Klux from it. The word "Klan" was added apparently because it gave an appealing alliterative sound.

The KKK operated mostly in nine southern states from about 1867 to the early 1870s. Many analysts believe that attempts by the United States Congress during the latter 1860s to provide civil rights for the former slaves served as a stimulus for the growth of the KKK, in that its secrecy was a convenient way to practice prejudice and discrimination. In fact, one of the order's primary objectives was to maintain the supremacy of the white race. Membership was limited to those who opposed social and political equality for black people.

The KKK began to decline in the early 1870s, largely due to three civil rights laws (often referred to as the "Ku Klux Klan laws") that provided penalties for some of the activities engaged in by the KKK. Congress in 1871 also appointed a committee, the Joint Select Committee on the Condition of Affairs in the Late Insurrectionary States, to investigate the terrorizing tactics of the klan.

The KKK was revived in 1915 by "Colonel" William Joseph Simmons. He obtained a state charter for what appeared to be another fraternal benevolent group called Knights of the Ku Klux Klan. This revival of the KKK is commonly referred to as the second phase of the klan's existence in the United States.

Simmons was an ex-soldier who had served in the Spanish-American War. After the war he became a circuit rider for the Methodist Episcopal Church. This position lasted for about ten years. He next turned to selling and other jobs, not being able to hold any job for long. He even had a position as an instructor at Lanier University in Atlanta for a while.

In reorganizing the klan, Simmons showed his bent for understanding fraternal orders. He was a member of a number of fraternal groups: the Masons, the Great Order of Knight Templars, and others. Simmons selected new titles for the klan's officers and symbolism, and one of the group's objectives was to spread belief in white supremacy. Anti-Semitism and anti-Catholicism were soon added to the klan's prejudicial menu. The latter two objectives were not part of the original KKK in the 1860s and 1870s.

One of Simmons fraternal strongpoints, so to speak, was his familiarity with lodge rituals and symbolism. Some believe that he wrote the klan's ritual, which had an initiation rite, oath, and secrecy. Some, however, believe that Albert Pike, the renowned Freemason, was also a member of the KKK and that he wrote the ritual. The ritual and the klan's constitution were incorporated in 1921, and the official name of the group was Knights of the Ku Klux Klan. The ritual spelled out four degrees: Order of Citizenship, Knights Kamellia, Knights of the Great Forest, and Knights of the Midnight Mystery. These degrees were also known as K-Uno, K-Due, K-Trio, and K-Quad, respectively. The ritual is replete with special klan language and terms. The following are but a few examples: Klectokon (initiation fee), Klonverse (convention in a "Province"), Kloran (manual of rituals, rules, and regulations), Klavery (local meeting unit), and Kloncilium (advisory board).

The klan's secrecy exceeds that of any other secret fraternal society in the United States. The Klarago (inner guard) and Klexter (outer guard) have been known to use two-way radios to safeguard the secrecy of meetings from "aliens," nonklansmen. Klaverns commonly maintain secrecy with regard to finances, rituals, special projects, and even the identity of their officers. In some instances the KK has created secret "action groups," who have frequently been engaged in extralegal activities.

The oath taken by the klansman consists of four parts: Obedience, Secrecy, Fidelity, and Klanishness. Part of the secrecy oath reads: "I most solemnly swear—that I will forever—keep sacredly secret—the signs, words and grip—and any other and all other—matters and knowledge—of the [KKK]. . . ." Another portion requires the candidate to say:

I most sacredly vow—and most positively swear that I will never yield to bribe—flattery—threats—passion—punishment—persecution—persuasion—nor any enticements whatever—coming from or offered by—any person or persons—male or female—for the purpose of obtaining from me—a secret or secret information—of the [KKK]—I will rather die than divulge same—so help me God—.

The KKK values its seven symbols: the Bible, Cross, Flag, Sword, Water, Robe, and Hood. The Bible signifies that there is a God. Every klavern has the Bible lying on an altar and opened to the thirteenth chapter of Romans, which speaks about the Christian's responsibility to government and how he is to live a humble, loving life. Every Klansman is told that he should read this chapter every morning and then live by it during the day. The cross signifies sacrifice and service. The KKK has added fire to the cross to signify "CHRIST THE LIGHT OF THE WORLD" [emphasis in the original]. The flag is a symbol of the suffering of American heroes and of the Constitution of the United States, as well as of free speech, free press, free schools, and freedom of worship. The red color in the flag stands for the blood of American heroes, the white for the purity of American womanhood, and the blue of America's unclouded sky. The stars represent the undefeated states of the Union. The sword signifies law enforcement and the powers of military and government. Water represents the "purity of life and unity of purpose." Klansmen are to be as useful to humanity as water is to life. The robe indicates that the klan does not judge a man by the clothes he wears. "There is no rich, or poor, high or low, in Klankraft. As we look upon a body of Klansmen robed in white we are forcibly reminded that they are on a common level. By this means we also help to conceal our identity, which is an essential principle of Klankraft." The hood is intended to be a symbol of unselfishness. The KKK also sees the hood as symbolizing the power of secrecy. "We are a great secret organization to aid the officers of the law and we can do our best work when we are not known to the public."

The constitution and laws of the United Klans of America, Inc., Knights of the Ku Klux Klan, states the membership requirement in the following words: "An applicant must be a white male Gentile person, a native-born citizen of the United States of America . . . have attained the age of twenty-one years . . . a believer in the tenants of the Christian religion . . . whose allegiance, loyalty and devotion is to the government of the United States of America. . . ."

No one outside the KKK has ever known the true membership count of the klan, primarily because of the klan's secrecy. Yet, it is known that its membership has been yo-yo-like. It prospered during its first phase (1860s and early 1870s). Then it virtually vanished until it was revived in 1915 by "Colonel" Simmons for the klan's second phase. During this period the klan made some successful membership appeals. In 1917 it took on the unassigned role of hunting down draft dodgers and defending the nation "against alien enemies, slackers, idlers, strike leaders, and immoral women, . . ." (see David M. Chalmers, *Hooded Americanism*, 1965). This type of involvement caught on with other likeminded individuals, and so the KKK began to grow and spread to other states. Chalmers states: "the rank and file turned to the Klan by the thousands, and the Scottish Rite Masons and Orange Lodges were particularly rich hunting grounds." In the 1920s the klan attracted members by promoting itself as an organization founded by "consecrated business brains." The KKK again declined in the 1930s and early 1940s. In fact, the klan officially dissolved.itself on April 23, 1944, largely as a result of repeated attempts by the bureau of Internal Revenue to collect unpaid taxes. By the mid-1950s, however, the order of white-hooded, crossburning men entered its third phase or cycle. Again it attracted members and took on new life, primarily because some people reacted to the civil rights movement of that time, when demonstrations and "freedom" rides were held in the southern states.

It was during the KKK's third cycle of existence that it probably received the most adverse publicity, because of acts of terror and violence directed against black citizens and white civil rights workers. In 1965 the 89th Congress had the Committee on Un-American Activities (a standing committee in the House of Representatives) conduct an investigation into the violent and conspiratorial acts of the KKK. The Committee on Un-American Activities published a lengthy, detailed report: *The Present-Day Ku Klux Klan Movement* (1967). After a thorough investigation of the KKK one Congressman of the subcommittee said:

We are, therefore, forced to the conclusion that the traditional, ugly image of the Ku Klux Klan is essentially valid—preaching love and peace, yet practicing hatred and violence; claiming fidelity to the Constitution, yet systematically abrogating the constitutional rights of other citizens. . . . Their [KKK] record seems clearly one of moral bankruptcy and of staggering hypocrisy.

Another Congressman stated:

Any group that engages in organized, large-scale intimidation in the political, economic and social fields and terrorizes individuals and groups, attacks the very root of the democratic process. It does so because it destroys freedom and, without free citizens, our representative form of government is not secure and cannot be preserved.

During the last decade—since the late 1960s—the klan again seemed to have declined. Very little was heard about the KKK in recent years, except for an occasional newspaper article in various localities. However, in 1979 the klan appeared to gain new life once again. Reports of the society's resurgence appeared in northern and southern states. Various parades were held in the summer of 1979, as some KKK leaders tried to project a nonracist posture.

The organizational structure of the KKK is four-layered. The national or overall jurisdiction is known as the "Invisible Empire." Its convention is known as "Imperial Klonvokation." The invisible empire is headed by the Imperial Wizard. Territorial divisions of the invisible empire are named "Realms." These usually correspond to state boundaries. Realms are led by "Grand Dragons." A realm is divided into "Provinces," which usually are Congressional districts. Provinces are headed by "Grand Titans." The convention of a province is known as a "Klonverse." The fourth organizational unit is the "Klan," which meets in a "Klavern." This is the local chapter group or subordinate body. Its leader is the Exalted Cyclops. Sessions on the local level are termed "Klonklaves."

On the invisible empire level the following officers exist: Imperial Wizard (Supreme Chief Executive), Imperial Klaliff (Supreme Vice President), Imperial Klokard (Supreme Lecturer), Imperial Kludd (Supreme Chaplain), Imperial Kligrapp (Supreme Secretary), Imperial Klabee (Supreme Treasurer), Imperial Klarago (Supreme Inner-Guard), Imperial Klonsel (Supreme

Attorney), Imperial Night Hawk (Supreme Courier), and five Imperial Klokann (a board of auditors, advisors, and trustees).

Literature on the KKK is quite plentiful. In addition to the two publications already cited, the following are very good sources: Arnold C. Rice, *The Ku Klux Klan In American Politics* (1962); Edward Price Bell, *Creed of the Klansman* (1924); Winfield Jones, *The True Story of the Ku Klux Klan* (1921); John Moffat Mecklin, *The Ku Klux Klan: A Study of the American Mind* (1924); and J. C. Lester and D. L. Wilson, *Ku Klux Klan: Its Origin, Growth and Disbandment* (1905).

L

LADIES OF THE MACCABEES. See Maccabees, Ladies of the, of the World.

LADIES ORIENTAL SHRINE OF NORTH AMERICA (LOSNA). Formally this order came into being on June 24, 1914, but informally the society had its beginning about ten years earlier. According to the Masonic Service Association's report on allied Masonic groups, the idea for the women's order was born in Wheeling, West Virginia, as the wives of Shriners were entertaining visiting Shriners' wives. Earlier meetings were held in private homes. By June 24, 1914, a governing body was created and named the Grand Council of Ladies' Oriental Shrine of North America. Incorporation, however, did not occur until 1954.

The objective of the LOSNA, according to Voorhis (see his *Masonic Organizations and Allied Orders and Degrees*, 1952), was fellowship and pleasure, but now its emphasis is largely on assisting the Shriners in their work with crippled children. However, when the women meet they are still able to have a good time, in spite of their interest in the Shriners' hospitals.

Membership requirements call for the applicant to be a Shriner's relative. A wife, mother, daughter, or sister of a Shriner is eligible for membership. As of 1977 the order had 30,000 members, compared to 24,000 about ten years earlier. Only white females are accepted as members.

Local units are known as "Courts." The national structure is named the "Grand Council." It meets annually in convention, always on the third Wednesday in May. Headquarters are located wherever the Grand Recorder resides.

Additional information on the LOSNA is sparse. The reader may wish to consult Harold V. B. Voorhis, *Masonic Organizations and Allied Orders and Degrees* (1952). The mimeographed copy of "Allied Masonic Groups and Rites" (1978), produced by the Masonic Service Association, is also helpful.

LADIES' PENNSYLVANIA SLOVAK CATHOLIC UNION (LPSCU). Founded in 1898, this fraternal benefit society has been faithful in providing fraternal benefits for female Slovak members of the Catholic faith. As a Catholic fraternal group, the KPSCU is strongly supportive of the Catholic Church and related activities. For instance, the society helps support the Slovak Seminary in Rome, Italy. It contributes to the Slovak Catholic Federation, an organization that coordinates religious activities of Slovaks. Donations are also made to other Catholic religious institutions.

In 1978 the society had approximately 16,000 members. This was also the membership count of the organization in 1965; however, the membership was slightly higher in the late 1960s and early 1970s.

The number of local units in 1978 was 267, a decline from the 281 of 1972. The society sells insurance in eight states outside Pennsylvania. The national headquarters are maintained in Wilkes-Barre, Pennsylvania.

LADY ELKS (LE). This female fraternal group, like other lady Elks auxiliaries, has never received official recognition from the Benevolent and Protective Order of Elks* (BPOE). The LE seems to vary from place to place with regard to its activities. Apparently the society has no published or printed ritual. For the most part, the society espouses the general principles promoted by the Elks, who have essentially ignored the Lady Elks. The author was unable to ascertain the date or place of the society's origin. No published material seems to be available on the society.

The fact that the LE has never received official recognition from the BPOE shows that the Elks take their national resolution of 1907 very seriously. That resolution said: "There shall be no . . . adjuncts or auxiliaries. . . ."

The Lady Elks apparently operates only on the local level. No national or grand lodge structure appears to be operative.

LEGION OF THE RED CROSS. Organized in 1885 in Maryland by members of the Knights of the Golden Eagle.* The society was a fraternal beneficiary group that had a ritual based on the legends of the medieval Crusades. In 1905 the society had about 3,100 members. By 1910 its membership dropped to 2,300, and by 1915 no record of the society can be found in *Statistics, Fraternal Societies*.

LIONS, ROYAL ORDER OF. This fraternal benefit society was organized by William P. Woods, a physician, in 1911 in Evansville, Indiana. The order had a ritual with six degrees. Three of the degrees were given in the "Subordinate Den." The fourth degree was conferred on the state level ("Grand Den"), and the fifth was worked on past officers of the grand lodge. The sixth, and final degree, was given to select members of the fifth degree. In the early 1920s the society operated in twenty-three states with 300,000 members. As far as can be determined, the order no longer exists today. Headquarters were in Evansville, Indiana. REFERENCE: *DSOS*.

LITHUANIAN ALLIANCE OF AMERICA (LAA). This relatively small fraternal benefit society was founded in 1886 in Shenandoah, Pennsylvania, during the time immigrants from Eastern Europe flocked to the United States. Most immigrants were frequently in need of fraternal fellowship as well as in need of insurance assistance. The IAA provided both for Lithuanians.

The first move to form fraternal societies for Lithuanians in America began with an appeal in the American Lithuanian newspaper, *Lietuwiszka Gazieta*, which appeared in New York on August 16, 1879. The paper pointed out that other ethnic groups, for example, the Germans, the English, and the Jews, had all formed fraternal societies providing benefits in the form of insurance. The newspaper article urged Lithuanian immigrants to form and organize fraternal societies in the local Lithuanian and Polish parishes.

The constituting convention took place on November 22, 1886, in Plymouth, Pennsylvania. This convention had delegates from Polish and Lithuanian parish societies, which in effect meant that the Lithuanian Alliance at first consisted of two bodies under one organizational name. In 1888 the first twin alliance was ended when a heated discussion in the convention decided that American Lithuanians were "badly in need of de-Polonized churches. . . ."

The society later experienced additional conflict. In 1905 a faction of radical Socialists, who later became Communists, formed an alliance of their own. Prior to 1905, conflict brewed off and on between the clergy and the lay members of the society. Other tensions and conflicts followed the year of 1905. By 1912 the society began to move to greater unity and harmony. The harmony showed itself by a membership of 9,401 in 1916. However, in 1920 the organization again encountered opposition from Communists within its membership. In 1925 "the executive board mailed out a circular warning lodges against Communist infiltration and disruptive tactics." In the 1930s the "progressives" in the society brought unsuccessful litigation against the organization. When the litigation failed, the Communists "managed to disrupt a score of lodges . . . on the local level.'' Today (1979) the society, although reduced in membership compared to the past (in 1930 it had 22,000 members), seems to operate with organizational calm and stability. The present membership roster lists about 6,563 members. In the mid-1960s the society had about 10,000 members. Membership is open to individuals of Lithuanian ancestry.

Fraternally, the LAA renders aid to widows and orphans, provides relief for victims of natural disasters, and awards scholarships to eligible members who are students. The society also contributes to Lithuanian cultural programs.

The LAA presently has 209 local lodges, a decline of sixty-one since 1972, when it had 270 local units. The society is licensed to sell insurance in ten states, primarily in the northeastern section of the country. The national convention assembles every two years. Headquarters are housed in the city of New York.

For additional information, see *Tevyne*, a bimonthly newspaper, published in Lithuanian and in English. The organization's constitution also provides helpful information. In 1976 the LAA published a book on its history: *Susivienijimas Lietuviu Amerikoje, 1886-1976*. This lengthy volume is published in Lithuanian and English.

LITHUANIAN CATHOLIC ALLIANCE (LCA). This group was founded in 1889 to provide economic aid and insurance for its members at a time when countless other fraternal orders were being formed for similar purposes. As a fraternal beneficiary organization, the LCA maintains and oprates charitable, benevolent, and educational activities for the benefit of its members and their families. Each year the society also grants some scholarships to worthy members attending college. Prior to 1975 the society was known as the Lithuanian Roman Catholic Alliance of America.

As a Lithuanian organization, the LCA promotes cultural relations between the United States and Lithuania. For the most part, these cultural relations focus on Lithuanian customs and traditions, which the society ardently tries to keep alive for its members. These activities range from providing Lithuanian cookbooks to special film and radio programs on festivals. The society also supports various community affairs such as the Community Chest, blood donor clinics, Catholic youth programs, Catholic Social Services, and youth camps.

Membership in the LCA has been declining for some years. In 1965 the society had more than 7,000 members. Now in 1978 the roster shows only about 4,000 members. Membership is open to males and females alike, providing they are Roman Catholics.

The number of local units also have declined. In 1972 there were 163 lodges, whereas by 1977 there were only 147. The national convention takes place triennially. Head offices are in Wilkes-Barre, Pennsylvania.

Ten times per year the society publishes *Garsas*, a periodical issued in

Lithuanian and in English. The reader may also wish to consult the constitution of the organization for further information.

LITHUANIAN WORKERS, ASSOCIATION OF (ALW). This relatively small fraternal benefit society has been in existence since 1930. It has members in eight states. The ALW conducts fraternal, social, and cultural activities for its members. Women's groups in the society are called "Sororities." The sororities carry out much of the society's charity work. Each year the ALW awards three college scholarships to student members of the society.

The ALW in its native language is known as the *Lietuviu Darbininku Susivieniimas* (LDS). Its membership is drawn from Lithuanians or those of Lithuanian descent. Currently (1979) the society has about 1,000 members. This count shows a decline since 1965 when there were 4,555 members.

The ALW presently has eighty local units, declined from 100 since 1972. The national convention, which is the supreme authority, meets biennially. Headquarters are maintained in Ozone Park, New York.

About the only additional information available is the back issues of the monthly periodical, *Tiesa*. It is usually published in two sections, one in English and the other in the Lithuanian language. The society's constitution and biennial proceedings may also be consulted for further background on the ALW.

LOCOMOTIVE ENGINEERS MUTUAL LIFE AND ACCIDENT INSURANCE ASSOCIATION, THE (LCMLAIA). Four years after the Brotherhood of Locomotive Engineers (BLE) was organized in 1863, the LCMLAIA was founded to provide insurance protection for the BLE. The association presently issues "life insurance to spouses, surviving spouses, sons, daughters and grandchildren of the B. of L.E. members."

Membership eligibility means belonging to the Brotherhood of Locomotive Engineers and being in good physical condition. Wives, widows, children and grandchildren of BLE members may also join the LCMLAIA. A third category of membership is for "persons, their wives and eligible children who are represented under contracts for group insurance coverage between the Brotherhood of Locomotive Engineers and the railroad industry. . . ." Currently (1979) there are about 20,000 members in Canada and the United States. This figure represents a one-third drop since 1968, when the association had 30,000 members.

The chief governing entity is the national convention, which meets every four years. Local groups are known as branches. Headquarters are maintained in Cleveland, Ohio.

The association publishes no periodical, nor does it have a separately published history. Its *Constitution and By-Laws* is helpful in providing additional information.

LOYAL AMERICAN LIFE ASSOCIATION (LALA). Founded in 1896 in Illinois, the society was a fraternal benefit organization. It admitted men and women to its membership roster. Like most fraternal benefit groups, the LALA also had a social membership in addition to the beneficial category. The society began with the assessment plan. Over the years, however, it adjusted and changed its assessments to better and more accurate actuarial methods. According to *Statistics, Fraternal Societies* (1923), the LALA had 15,851 members in 1923. Headquarters were in Chicago, Illinois, during the latter years of the society's existence. Prior to 1911 Springfield, Illinois, served as the headquarters city. REFERENCE: *DSOS*.

LOYAL CHRISTIAN BENEFIT ASSOCIATION (LCBA). When this group was founded on April 9, 1890, in Titusville, Pennsylvania, it was known as the Ladies Catholic Benevolent Association. The society was formed to further the specific purposes of insuring only Catholic women and supporting the clergy's objectives for developing the parish community, in which the new society organized local branches. The venture into life insurance for women in 1890 was almost unique, since people thought it unnecessary to insure them. Only men or husbands were insured according to the existing social norms. The new insurance plan was curiously watched by many to see whether it would fail or succeed.

As the years went by, the LCBA continued to grow. By 1927 insurance coverage was extended to sons and daughters of the members. Any offspring from birth to sixteen were eligible for fraternal insurance. In 1960 Catholic husbands, brothers, and nephews were also permitted to join the order as insured members. In 1969 the society changed its name to Loyal Christian Benefit Association.

The LCBA has given millions of dollars to Catholic churches, hospitals, orphan asylums, schools, colleges, foreign missions, religious orders, and to the aged. Since 1945 the society has adopted a national project of providing spiritual and practical aid to the deaf. Several institutions for the deaf are given aid. During 1978 the LCBA gave particular attention to family life by studying legislation affecting the family's well-being. The order also monitored the TV industry and its programs pertaining to family life. Funds also are given to the Catholic Communications Foundation (C.C.F.). An orphan's benefit program has been instituted for the children of deceased members. On the local level various projects exist: visiting the sick, comforting the bereaved and their families, aiding senior citizens, helping the blind, and assisting exceptional children.

The association conducts a rite of initiation when receiving new members, and every initiate also is required to take an obligation, pledging faithfulness to the LCBA. Along with the ritual ceremony, the society has its selected guards, who make certain no one but members attend association meetings. Marshalls also are utilized on the national and local organizational levels.

The emblem of the association is a ring with a shield in its center. The shield is decorated by laurel-like leaves on each side and a Latin cross on its face. The letters LCBA are imprinted on the arms of the cross. Toward the outer edge of the ring is the society's name, Loyal Christian Benevolent Association.

Membership qualifications, according to the constitution, call for someone of the Christian faith, good moral character, and in good health. The LCBA has two adult categories of membership: the nonbenefit or social member and the benefit member. Both types of members must be initiated. In December of 1978 there were 51,369 members. In 1967 the society had 85,000 members. Thus a loss of 38 percent of the membership resulted during the last ten to twelve years.

The LCBA operates on the national and local level. The national organization is known as the "National Council," and the local meetings are conducted in "Branches." In 1978 the LCBA had branches in twenty-eight states and in one Canadian province. National headquarters are in Titusville, Pennsylvania.

For additional information the reader may see the association's bimonthly magazine, *The Fraternal Leader*. See also the *Constitution and By-Laws* of the Loyal Christian Benefit Association.

LOYAL KNIGHTS OF AMERICA. Founded in Wilkes Barre, Pennsylvania, in 1890, this society arose from a schism in the American Protestant Association. The Loyal Knights were an anti-Catholic secret fraternity. Its membership never was very large. REFERENCE: *DSOS*.

LOYAL KNIGHTS AND LADIES. This secret fraternal beneficiary group arose as an offshoot of the Knights and Ladies of Honor.* It was founded in 1881 in Boston, Massachusetts. The ritual closely resembled that of the parent order. REFERENCE: *DSOS*.

LOYAL LADIES OF THE ROYAL ARCANUM. This group became an auxiliary of the Royal Arcanum,* a male fraternal beneficiary group, in 1923. This date was primarily a formal ratification of the female auxiliary, which had been in existence since 1909 when a group of women organized themselves in Springfield, Massachusetts. Headquarters were in Bridgeport, Connecticut. REFERENCE: *DSOS*.

LOYAL MYSTIC LEGION OF AMERICA. Founded in 1892 in Nebraska, this fraternal benefit society had a membership of about 5,000 in 1910. Ten years earlier it had just under 6,000 members. By 1920 the society appears to have discontinued its operations and activities. Headquarters were located in Hastings, Nebraska.

LOYAL ORANGE ASSOCIATION [CANADA] (LOA). The origins of this society go back to Ireland where in 1795 a group of Protestants loyal to the British crown founded a fraternal order in honor of William III, Prince of Orange. In Canada the society began in 1830, when Ogle Robert Gowan called a general meeting of Orangemen on January 1, 1830, in Brockville, Ontario. This meeting resulted in the formation of a grand lodge of the Loyal Orange Association (Canada). A grand lodge was formed in the United States in 1870.

During the early 1800s, when the law in England outlawed all fraternal secret societies, except Freemasonry, the British Orangemen met in Masonic lodges. In some instances they operated under the cover of Masonic warrants and charters. This close past association with Masonry in part explains the many similarities of the society's ritual with that of Masonry. The LOA ritual lists four degrees in its ceremonies.

From its beginning, Orangeism has had a strong anti-Catholic orientation. In fact, the fraternity was frequently seen as synonymous with anti-Catholicism. Today the anti-Catholic posture has been somewhat mitigated. However, Canadian Orangemen reportedly oppose Catholicism in the context of resisting French Canadian values. One of the society's pamphlets currently reads: "Protestantism is not simply anti-Roman Catholic, nor is the Orange Order, any more than the Order is anti-Buddhist, anti-Unitarian or anti-Semitic (though Buddhists, Unitarians and Jews, etc., are not members of the Order because they are not Christian)." The society also says it "is politically militant in that it is devoted to the preservation of the Monarchy and the British System of Government [*sic*]. . . ."

Eligible candidates desiring to join the order must be eighteen years of age, believe in the Trinity, profess to being a Protestant, attend church regularly, read the Bible, and be upright citizens. Most of the society's members reside in Canada, where its roster numbers about 100,000. In the United States the memberships are primarily in the northeastern part of the country. California has the next largest American contingent.

For some time, Orangeism has had two faces. One conforms to the fraternal secret society pattern, and another follows the fraternal benefit model. In 1891 the society in part assumed the latter function, while also retaining the fraternal secret society objectives. The fraternal benefit arm enables the society to service its members with a variety of fraternal insurance benefits. The order maintains several homes for children, as well as a senior citizen's home.

Like other fraternal groups, the LOA has a female auxiliary, the Ladies Orange Benevolent Association. Although the women have a separate auxiliary, they do hold full membership privileges in the male order.

Structurally, the society functions on four levels. On the national scale the order is known as "Grand Lodge." The provincial level in Canada is referred to as "Provincial Grand Lodge." Local units are called "County Lodges." In some areas the county lodge has units known as "Primary Lodges." The principal officer on the national level is referred to as Most Worshipful Master. Headquarters are located in Toronto, Ontario, Canada.

Additional background may be found by consulting the order's annual proceedings. Ten times each year the organization publishes *The Sentinel*. Hereward Senior's *Orangeism: The Canadian Phase* (1972) gives a good modern portrait of the society. This same author also has written *Orangeism in Britain and Ireland* (1966). See also Senior's "The Genesis of Canadian Orangeism," *Ontario History* (June 1968).

LOYAL ORDER OF BUFFALOES. See Buffaloes, Loyal Order of.

LOYAL ORDER OF MOOSE. See Moose, Loyal Order of.

LOYAL SONS OF AMERICA. Founded as a "non-sectarian and non-political patriotic, ritualistic fraternal Order," the society was formally organized in 1920. The society paid sick, disability, and funeral benefits. It also operated a free employment bureau for its members. The order was very meticulous as to whom it selected for membership. Upon being founded, the society had set a goal of attaining 5,000,000 members. The society did not even reach 5,000 before its demise in the 1930s. REFERENCE: *DSOS*.

LOYAL WOMEN OF AMERICAN LIBERTY (LWAL). Founded in Boston, Massachusetts, in 1888, this society was a semisecret patriotic organization. Its membership was composed entirely of Protestants who were very much concerned about keeping church and state as separate institutions. The society did not admit Roman Catholics. Protestant women whose husbands were Roman Catholic were also ineligible for membership. All members pledged "not to assist the Roman Catholic clergy or their institutions." The society had many similarities to the Lady Orange Association of British North America. The LWAL is no longer extant. It apparently faded from the scene in the early 1900s. REFERENCES: *Cyc. Frat.*; *DSOS*.

LUTHERAN BROTHERHOOD (LB). A group of Norwegian Lutherans in Minnesota persuaded the Norwegian Lutheran Church of America, which held a convention in 1917, to give approval for an "aid society." This society was to provide sick, accident, and life insurance to members of the Norwegian Lutheran Church. There was opposition on the part of some because it was felt the church should not become involved in the insurance business. To some it indicated a lack of trust in God. One argument that squelched opposition to the aid society was the assertion that contended the new society would prevent many Norwegian Lutherans from joining unacceptable secret fraternal benefit societies, or "lodges" as Lutherans commonly referred to these organizations. (Conservative Lutheran synods in the United States had always instructed their members not to join "lodges.")

In the original articles of incorporation the aid society was officially named the Luther Union. On September 18, 1918, the society was legally licensed by the state of Minnesota. It was also in September of 1918 that the Luther Union began negotiations for some form of cooperation with the Lutheran Brotherhood of America, a fraternal benefit society founded in Des Moines, Iowa. Two years later in 1920 the two groups merged and adopted the name Lutheran Brotherhood.

Membership is open only to Lutherans. Since the society's beginning the membership roster has experienced a rather steady growth. Today (1979) the LB has about 900,000 members. In 1965 there were some 550,000 members.

The philanthropy practiced by LB is directed to its members and the Lutheran Church. In some instances the society helps establish new congregations through its Church Extension Fund. Scholarship aid is given to Lutheran colleges and seminaries. One phase of the scholarship program enables parish pastors to enroll in summer school courses. Recently, in January of 1979, the LB sponsored a seminar in Houston, Texas, on "The Church in Future Society." This session had Alvin Toffler as one of the principal speakers.

Although the LB operates on the lodge system, it has no lodge rituals, secrets, or oaths. The absence of such fraternal society paraphernalia in the LB is largely due to the influence of conservative Lutheranism, which founded the organization. In fact, the society has never used the word "lodges" because that was too reminiscent of the deistic features commonly a part of most American fraternal organizations. Local units therefore have always been called branches.

The official emblem of the LB is a circular medallionlike insignia that has Luther's coat of arms in the center of the emblem. Surrounding the Luther symbol are the words: Loyalty To Home Church And Country. These words in turn are encircled by the following: Lutheran Brotherhood, Minneapolis, Minnesota. The society has no ritual.

Organizationally, the LB operates through local units called branches. Three types of branches (A-1, A-2, A-3) are in existence. The A-1 branch is affiliated with some Lutheran congregation; A-2 is usually sponsored by a group from within a Lutheran parish; A-3 is a geographic branch. The latter accommodates members who have left the Lutheran denomination. On the national level the LB meets in convention every four years. During the interim a board of directors expedites the society's business. Headquarters are situated in Minneapolis, Minnesota.

Sources for further information on the LB consist of its monthly periodical, *Bond*, and a brief history known as *Pioneers in Security: History of Lutheran Brotherhood* (n.d.). Outside of these sources very little has been published about the society.

LUTHERAN LIFE INSURANCE SOCIETY OF CANADA (LLISC). This is one of the more newly formed fraternal benefit societies. It came into being with the merging of the Aid Association of Lutherans* and the Lutheran Brotherhood* in 1972. The society was the result of the desire to have an indigenous Canadian fraternal benefit society for Lutherans.

The LLISC has the usual array of fraternal life insurance. It also provides scholarships to Canadian Lutheran educational institutions as well as to individual society members. Special fraternal grants are given to churches and church-related organizations and projects. The society also makes available mortgage funds at reduced rates to Lutheran churches.

When the society came into being it had about 30,000 members. In 1979 it had 37,500 members. Membership is only open to those who hold membership in a Lutheran church.

Local units are called "Branches," of which there were 120 in 1979 in the Dominion of Canada. The members, through the branches, elect a board of directors, which makes key policy decisions. The society has its headquarters in Kitchener, Ontario, Canada.

Further information may be obtained by reading the society's quarterly, *Lutheran Life News*. A number of brochures and pamphlets also provide informative material about the society. There is no scholarly history on the group.

M

MACCABEES, THE. In a kerosene-lit room of a jewelry store in London, Ontario, M. J. McGloghlon in 1878 assembled a few men who founded the Knights of the Maccabees of the World. The order used the traditions and history of the ancient Maccabeans, who had Judas Maccabeus as their leader in the second century before the birth of Christ. As the order was founded by McGloghlon, a plan called for each member to contribute 10 cents to the widow of a deceased "brother." No widow, however, could receive more than $1,000. The remaining contributions were placed in deposit with the treasurer of the fraternity. A constitution and ritual were soon adopted and by August 7, 1878, the organization held its first grand convention.

The order prospered in terms of memberships. By 1880 there were 10,000 members holding "endowment certificates," assuring the members that in the event of death their wives and children would receive $1,000. In spite of its growth the order was experiencing factional strife and actuarial difficulties. Thus in 1881 and 1883 the order was essentially reorganized under the leadership and influence of Major N. S. Boynton, naming the group Supreme Tent, Knights of the Maccabees of the World. In 1914 the society changed its name to The Maccabees, dropping the name Knights. One year later, in 1915, the order had 331,756 members.

In 1886 a proposal was made to form a ladies' auxiliary, Ladies of the Maccabees.* By 1890 the ladies' group adopted a constitution and elected officers, but in 1892 a schism occurred that led to the formation of the Ladies of the Modern Maccabees. In 1926 the original ladies' group merged with the men, adopting their name. In 1941 the society absorbed Michigan Union Life Association. The society had also absorbed the Slavic Progressive Beneficial Union in 1937.

After the order reorganized in the early 1880s its progressiveness and success became widely known, not only for providing for widows and orphans, but also for its accident and sickness benefits. By 1911 the order moved forward again, this time by adopting the National Fraternal Congress Tables. The latter had a sounder actuarial basis than had the assessment plan. The American Mortuary Table of Rates was adopted by the Maccabees in 1920. In 1961 the order, as a result of a "Supreme Review" in 1958 decided to become a mutual life insurance company. This change was effected in 1961. Although the organization is now a mutual firm, it retained the lodge system for those who were members before the change to a mutual company occurred. Thus the head office presently houses both a mutual operation and a fraternal benefit structure. The fraternal benefit operation had a membership of about 10,000 in 1978.

The emblem of the Maccabees was a globe with the Stars and Stripes on one side and the Union Jack on the other. The order's name, The Maccabees, appeared on the face of the globe.

Organizationally, the "Supreme Tent" was the legislative and governing body of the society. The head officer was the Supreme Commander. The district or regional division was known as "Great Camp." The local chapters were referred to as "Subordinate Units." Detroit, Michigan, is where the order had its national head offices. Since 1965 it has been located in Southfield, Michigan.

For further information the reader may consult the former publication of the order, *The Maccabees Bee Hive*. It was published quarterly. The constitution, known as "Laws of the Maccabees," is not published but only mimeographed. The fraternal society segment of the Maccabees no longer issues a periodical.

MACCABEES, LADIES OF THE, OF THE WORLD (LMW). Reputedly this society was the first fraternal benefit group to have been managed by women. It came into being around 1885 in Muskegon, Michigan. At first the society was a local auxiliary to the Knights of the Maccabees.* However, by 1886 the Muskegon group applied to the Great Camp for Michigan (the supreme authority of the Knights of the Maccabees) for official recognition as an auxiliary that would aid local "Tents" of the Maccabees. The request was denied by the men, both in 1886 and in 1887. In 1887, however, the ladies did receive recognition. This led to the formation of a statewide organization in 1888, and in 1892 a national structure was created, known as the Supreme Hive of the Ladies of the Maccabees of the World.

The society, like numerous other fraternal groups, suffered a schism, in 1892. The splinter group took the name of Ladies of the Modern Maccabees. This group currently is known as the North American Benefit Association.*

The LMW prospered in spite of the schism of 1892. By 1915 it had 179,716 members.

State groups were called "Great Hives." Local units were known as "Hives," and the national organizational structure was referred to as "Supreme Hive."

Some of this information was selected from Albert C. Stevens, *Cyclopedia of Fraternities* (1907). Additional items were gathered from materials furnished by the Maccabees.*

MAIDS OF ATHENA, THE. This order, comprised of young women, originally was known as "Sparta." It was founded in Tacoma, Washington, on July 5, 1930. The first charter was issued in 1937 by the Order of Ahepa,* which at first also governed the young women's order in that the Ahepa had written the constitution and ritual.

During the order's formative years (1930 to 1952) the name Maids of Athens replaced the former name, Sparta Chapter. The order held its first national conference in Houston, Texas, in 1953. At this conference the secret ritual was rewritten to conform to the ritual of the Daughters of Penelope.* A manual of instructions was also approved. The next year (1954) the society elected its first slate of officers for its grand (national) lodge. Since 1950, the order has been the junior auxiliary of the Daughters of Penelope.

In order to join the Maids of Athena, as it is now called, the female candidate must be between the age of fourteen and twenty-one. Greek descendancy is also required. If a young lady joins at age twenty-one, she may remain in the order until age twenty-three. The order in 1977 had 1,300 members distributed over 155 chapters in the United States and Canada.

The years 1965 to 1972 were very progressive years for the Maids of Athena. It had several grand presidents who visited numerous local chapters and encouraged the members. During this seven-year span the group again revised its ritual, provided a new code of ethics, and also issued a new manual of instructions pertaining to the ritual. New chapters were formed, and old ones were reactivated. In 1968 the order began observing "Maids Sunday," a holiday celebrating the founding of the Maids of Athena. This Sunday was first observed on November 18. On this Sunday every member participated in communion in her home church.

The Maids of Athena, during the late 1960s and early 1970s, also showed concern for others. It began providing volunteer work for mental health clinics. Aid was sent to an orphanage in Vietnam; overseas servicemen of the Greek Orthodox denomination received letters from the Maids; a booklet was printed for Greek immigrants listing all facilities available in New York City; money was gathered to help support St. Basil's Academy (an Ahepan institution for orphan children) in Garrison, New York; and funds were raised for multiple sclerosis research. The Maids also became concerned about helping solve social problems. To this end the members established an Ecology Education and Action Program. Drug abuse gained the order's attention, especially as it related to working with mental health clinics.

The Maids of Athena meet annually in conference on the national level. Its national structure is referred to as the "Grand Lodge." The grand lodge convenes at the same time and location as do the supreme lodges of the Daughters of Penelope, the Order of Ahepa, and the Sons of Pericles.* The grand lodge officials are Grand President, Grand Vice President, Grand Secretary, Grand Treasurer, two grand governors, and a national advisor. The latter is a member of the Daughters of Penelope. On the district and chapter levels the array of officers is essentially the same, except the title of "Grand" is not employed. Headquarters are in Washington, D.C.

Published information on the Maids of Athena may be found by reading the order's periodical, *Charisma*. A newsletter, *Eleftheri Zoe*, is also of interest. The reader may also consult George J. Leber's volume, *The History of the Ahepa* (1972), which contains one chapter on the Maids of Athena.

MASONIC LIFE ASSOCIATION. In 1872 American Freemasons organized this association in order to provide benefits similar to those provided for by the fraternal benefit societies. The association was reorganized in 1919 to give it a more sound financial and actuarial basis. The author has been unable to determine whether the association still exists today. REFERENCE: *DSOS*.

MASONIC RELIEF ASSOCIATION OF THE UNITED STATES AND CANADA (MRA).

This relief association was organized in 1885 in Baltimore, Maryland. The group has five objectives: (1) To detect and publish in *The Bulletin* the names of "unworthy Masons and imposters preying upon the Fraternity." (2) Coordinate and correlate Masonic relief programs throughout the United States and Canada. (3) Promote prompt and effective means of expediting cases in interjurisdictional relief. (4) Serve as the agent in organizing Masonic relief in times of national disaster "when such services are requested by any Grand Lodge. . . ." (5) Provide a meeting place to discuss various problems of Masonic relief.

The MRA is made up of the majority of the fifty-eight grand lodges (state or regional structures) in Canada and the United States. Hence, the association serves about 3,000,000 Masons. The MRA has no degree work or rituals.

The officers of the MRA are a president, two vice-presidents, an executive secretary, and a treasurer. It also has an executive board. Conventions are held biennially. The head office is in Sioux Falls, South Dakota.

The association publishes *The Bulletin* on a bimonthly basis. This publication regularly prints lists of missing Masonic persons whose addresses have become unknown to respective Masonic lodges. *The Bulletin* also notes lost receipts and frauds pertaining to "imposters preying upon the Fraternity." The "imposters" are those who seek "unlawful" assistance from Masonic lodges.

MASONIC SERVICE ASSOCIATION (MSA).

In 1919 American Freemasons saw a need for a united effort to serve Masons in the Armed Services of the United States so that relief and assistance could be provided to needy servicemen. The association was founded in Cedar Rapids, Iowa.

The association provides various information. Some of the documents issued (usually in mimeograph form) are "Allied Masonic Groups and Rites," 1978; "Grand Lodge Facts and Figures," 1955; and "An Introduction to the Problems of Declining Memberships and Poor Attendance," 1961.

Membership consists of the grand lodge of the United States. No degrees are offered. Headquarters are located in Silver Spring, Maryland.

MASSACHUSETTS CATHOLIC ORDER OF FORESTERS. See Catholic Association of Foresters.

MECHANICAL ORDER OF THE SUN, LEAGUE OF FRIENDSHIP (MOS). It was this order that disappointed "Father" Upchurch with its beneficiary efforts. Thus in 1868 Upchurch organized the Ancient Order of United Workmen.

The MOS was largely a blue-collar order, having attracted mechanics, firemen, railroad men, and the like. Its basic objective was "to advance and foster the interests of its members by cooperating in effort and financial assistance wherever called upon to serve a worthy and approved cause." Each member was initiated and pledged to organizational secrecy. The society disbanded before 1900. Headquarters were housed in Meadville, Pennsylvania.

The present account is based on M. W. Sackett, *Early History of Fraternal Beneficiary Societies in the United States*, 1914; Arthur Preuss, *Dictionary of Secret and Other Societies*, 1924.

MECHANICS, INDEPENDENT ORDER OF. This fraternal benefit society was formed in Baltimore, Maryland, in 1868. Its name "Mechanics" really had no connection with mechanics. All white men between eighteen and fifty were admitted as members. "Friendship, Truth, and Love" was the order's motto. The society had 10,000 members in 1897. It apparently disbanded in the early 1900s. Home offices were in Baltimore, Maryland. REFERENCES: *Cyc. Frat.*; *DSOS*.

MENNONITE MUTUAL AID ASSOCIATION (MMAA). Prior to the actual formation of the MMAA, the Mennonite General Conference (a denomination) in the 1930s undertook paying for members' hospital bills, survivors' expenses, and other costs. Then in 1945 the denomination approved the organizing of the Mennonite Mutual Aid. Its chief objective was to provide loan aid to returning civilian public service men at the end of World War II. (The expression "civilian public service men" stems from the Mennonite policy of not permitting its members to serve as armed soldiers.) Following 1945, there were a number of benevolent efforts made by the Mennonite General Conference to assist its members. In 1961 the Mennonite Aid Insurance, Inc., was formed. This organization provided health and survivors' aid programs. Five years later, in January 1966, the 1961 organization commenced business as a fraternal benefit society under the name of Mennonite Mutual Aid Association, its present name. The society is presently operating in twelve states.

Programs supported by the MMAA include providing assistance for individuals in local communities with unusual needs, helping local families with emergency needs, giving aid to local church projects, and helping the uninsurable in Mennonite congregations. Educationally, the association sponsors seminars on church leadership, family life training, estate planning, financial counseling, youth leadership, and family communications. Recently the society has supported conferences for black and Hispanic women. Scholarships are given for theological training that will aid Mennolatino churches. Not to be overlooked are the contributions that the association has in conducting studies on peace, peacemaking, and the creative arts.

Both sexes may join the MMAA, providing they are sixteen or older and hold membership in a Mennonite church. Two categories of membership are available, as is true in many other fraternal benefit groups. The "insurance membership" indicates that the member holds an insurance certificate. The category of "general membership" has no insurance benefits. As of February 1979, the MMAA had 4,984 insured members. The society has been growing rather steadily since its founding in 1966.

The emblem of the society is a circle around a triangle symbolizing the front of a modern church building. Down the middle of the triangle (church building) are two people, apparently exercising their faith and displaying brotherhood. The society has no ritual.

Local units are known as "Branches." Before a branch may be formed at least twenty members need to be present. In most instances, the branches are affiliated with the congregations of the Mennonite General Conference. Each branch is required to meet at least twelve times annually. The highest authority is the "Biennial Conference." Intermediate between the branch and the biennial conference is the district conference. Goshen, Indiana, serves as the site for the society's national headquarters.

For further information, see *Sharing*, the society's quarterly periodical. No history has been published. There is, however, a brief mimeographed history available from the head offices. Also available is the society's *Constitution and Bylaws*.

MODERN AMERICAN FRATERNAL ORDER. Founded in Effingham, Illinois, in 1896, the order paid death, old-age, and disability benefits to its members who contributed to the order's fund on the basis of mutual assessments. The order was somewhat blue-law oriented in that it did not even permit subordinate lodge officers to be installed on Sundays. REFERENCES: *Cyc. Frat.; DSOS.*

MODERN BROTHERHOOD OF AMERICA. This fraternal benefit society was founded in Tipton, Iowa, in 1897. It admitted men and women. The society had a "Duofold Protection" plan, one that paid life insurance and savings for old age. Both were given for the price of one. In 1898 the membership of the society stood at 9,853 with 430 local lodges. However, by 1905 the order seems to have disbanded. REFERENCE: *DSOS.*

MODERN KNIGHTS' FIDELITY LEAGUE. Members of the Royal Arcanum* and National Union Woodmen of the World* helped organize this fraternal benefit group in 1891 in Kansas. Like most societies its membership requirements had age limitations. Prospective members had to hail from the more healthful areas of the country. Both men and women between eighteen and fifty-six years were able to join. Along with maintaining a reserve fund, the society paid sickness, accident, and death benefits. The society had a three-degree ritual, which to a large extent was based on Don Quixote and his companion Sancho Panza. Local lodges were called "Councils," and the regional groups were known as "Grand Councils." The national body was referred to as "Supreme Council." Home offices were maintained in Kansas City, Kansas. REFERENCE: *Cyc. Frat.*

MODERN KNIGHTS OF ST. PAUL. This group was organized for boys and young men who had been "converted" by Billy Sunday's evangelistic campaigns. It was formed in Detroit, Michigan, in 1971 by D. H. Jemison, a Methodist clergyman. The order conferred three degrees: Order of Jerusalem, Order of Damascus, and Order of Rome. These degrees resembled the first three degrees of Freemasonry. Parents were asked not to question the boys about their secret vows. REFERENCE: *DSOS*.

MODERN ORDER OF CHALDEANS. See Chaldeans, Modern Order of.

MODERN ROMANS (MR). Michigan was the state where this fraternal benefit group was organized in 1904. Both men and women were admitted as members. The society never provided insurance membership for juveniles. Like most other fraternals the Modern Romans were pledged to secrecy and used a ritual in organizational meetings. The name Modern Romans was chosen because the founders felt the ancient Romans represented fidelity and permanency. In 1927 the society had 2,146 adult members, a loss of about 500 members since 1919. By 1935 the membership had declined to less than 1,000. It appears that the society did not survive the 1930s. Headquarters were maintained in Manistee, Michigan.

MODERN SAMARITANS, THE (TMS). This fraternal benefit organization was founded in 1897 in the state of Minnesota. For the first twenty-five years years the society was conflict-ridden over political arguments among the members. This strife did not help the organization's prosperity. Had it not been for its devoted leaders the society would have folded early in its existence. In 1920 the TMS had 6,061 benefit members in ninety-three local lodges. By 1935 the membership had dwindled to 2,918. In 1936 the society changed its objectives and its name when it became known as the Samaritan Life Association. Headquarters were located in Duluth, Minnesota.

MODERN WOODMEN OF AMERICA (MWA). The primary founder of this fraternal benefit society was Joseph Cullen Root, the man who later was expelled from the MWA because of a feud he had with the order's head physician. Root listened to a sermon one Sunday in which he heard about "the pioneer woodmen clearing the forest to provide for their families." This sermon statement was seen to have symbolic value by Root in that the new society would clear away problems of financial security for the members' families. And so on January 5, 1883, Root organized the Modern Woodmen of America as a fraternal assessment society. The question of adopting a reserve fund first arose in 1897. It kept coming up at every convention for more than twenty years and was always defeated. Today the MWA is indeed a legal reserve fraternal life insurance society. Although founded in Lyons, Iowa, the MWA has always been incorporated in the state of Illinois.

The ritual which Root prepared had a "strange mixture of Roman dignity and forest freedom. . . ." Root also prepared a separate ritual for the ladies' circle. The ritual, of course, was secret. The emblem consisted of the axe, beetle (mallet), wedge, five stars, and branches of palm, all displayed on a shield. The order's motto was (still is) *Esto Perpetua*.

When the society was founded, it barred prospective members in the following occupations: "railroad brakemen, firemen, engineers, switchmen, miners, employees in gun powder factories, wholesalers and manufacturers of liquor, saloon keepers, bartenders, balloonists, sailors on lakes and seas, plow grinders, brass workers, and professional firemen and baseball players." The society wanted low-risk members as well as residents from the twelve healthiest states in the United States. Residents of large urban centers (e.g., Chicago, Detroit, St. Louis, Milwaukee, and Cincinnati) were excluded from membership.

The society always has had a fair amount of benevolence work under its supervision. Much of the benevolent work is done on the local (camp) level. An orphan benefit plan provides monthly income and makes scholarships available to young people of the MWA, as part of the society's insurance scheme. A variety of civic programs also are sponsored, ranging from community Easter egg hunts to ecology awareness.

The society began as an all-male group, but it helped organize a women's group: Royal Neighbors of America* in 1895. New members in the MWA are accepted by balloting. Three negative votes bar the applicant of gaining admission. Those who do not meet the health requirements of the society may become social members. Social members, however, are not eligible to hold elective offices or serve as delegates to the national convention. Minimum age for joining is sixteen years of age. In 1979 there were approximately 500,000 members. This represents an increase of about 40,000 during the past ten years.

Organizationally, the MWA has its members assemble in "Camps" on the local level. Regional groups are called "Districts." The national convention is the highest authority, and it meets every four years. National headquarters are located in Rock Island, Illinois.

For further information see the society's periodical, *The Modern Wood-*

men, published bimonthly. The MWA also has a two-volume history, *Modern Woodmen of America*. The first volume was published in 1927 and the second in 1935.

MOOSE, THE LOYAL ORDER OF (LOM). About forty miles west of Chicago, Illinois, in the beautiful Fox River Valley on 1,200 acres, lies a rather unique constellation of over 100 buildings in Mooseheart, Illinois. This village not only is the headquarters for the LOM, but also exists as a home for children who have lost one or both parents. "Child City," as it is often called, is operated by the LOM to take in children from the smallest tot to a high school senior. All children (about 500) are the offspring of male Moose members. In some instances the mother moves to Mooseheart with her child(ren).

This "model village," as it is sometimes called, offers formal, accredited education from nursery school through high school. It also has a hospital, a post office, stores, a large chapel (wherein Protestant and Catholic services are held by two chaplains who live at Mooseheart), fieldhouse, a swimming pool, a sports stadium, a vocational training center, a skating rink, a lake, a bank, and some forty residential halls. The halls house a minimum of eight to a maximum of twenty-four children. Each hall has house parents.

The Loyal Order of Moose was organized in Louisville, Kentucky, in 1888 by a physician, John Henry Wilson. Soon after its founding, the order failed to prosper. In 1906, the organization got a new lease on life when James J. Davis joined its ranks. Davis came to the United States from Wales as a young boy. In Pennsylvania he worked as a puddler in an iron-works plant. Later he entered labor activities and politics, and during President Harding's administration he served as Secretary of the Department of Labor. As a member of the Moose, he traveled thousands of miles recruiting members for the order. In 1911 the Moose convention in Detroit instructed Davis, then Director General of the LOM, to acquire property for purposes of establishing a "Moose College," "Institute," or "School," as the resolution phrased it.

News of the convention's action in Detroit spread, and offers began pouring in from all over the country. By December 1912, it was decided to buy a dairy farm near Aurora, Illinois; and in 1913 an additional adjoining 1,000 acres were purchased. Today the 1,200 acres is known as "Mooseheart," a name adopted by the Moose in 1913. Mooseheart is an incorporated village that appears on the map, just as any other town.

The Loyal Order of Moose presently has thirty-six state groups and over 4000 local lodges. Like so many other fraternal groups, it places a high value on its ritual. A new member takes an obligation promising:

I, . . . , promise,—that I will not—in any manner,—communicate or disclose or give any information—concerning anything—I may hereafter hear, see or experience in this lodge or in any other Lodge—of the Loyal Order of Moose—unless it be—to one whom I know to be a Loyal Moose—in good standing.—By this vow I bind myself for all time.—Amen.

This vow is taken only after the candidate replied affirmatively to the question, "Do you believe in a Supreme Being?" After the vow the governor (one of the main leaders in the initiation ceremony) instructs the new member, telling him about the use of passwords, how to enter the lodge room, and how to keep lodge matters within the confines of the membership. After the instruction the new member participates in the Nine O'Clock ceremony. Here every Moose lodge in session has its members face toward Mooseheart with bowed heads and folded arms and say in silent prayer: " 'Suffer little children to come unto me and forbid them not for such is the Kingdom of Heaven.' God bless Mooseheart."

Another noteworthy part of the ritual has the prelate advance to the altar before reading the ten "thou shalts." These enjoin the candidate to believe in God; love his country; protect the weak; love fellow Moose; avoid slander; tolerate the weakness of others; be true, pure, just, kind; and practice humility.

Near the end of the initiation rite, the prelate offers a prayer. A song also is sung to the tune: "Nearer, My God, To Thee," and then the governor, with his right arm outstretched, speaks to the new member: "By virtue of the power vested in me by this Lodge, I create you and each of you a Loyal Moose."

Members may also choose to receive the second, third, and fourth degree: Mooseheart Legion of the World, Fellowship, and Pilgrim, respectively. Women cannot become members. They may as relatives of Moose members join the Women of the Moose. Social memberships that omit the initiation rite are not available. The current (1979) membership stands at 1,323,240.

Although Mooseheart is the hub of the LOM, it also operates Moosehaven, a senior-citizens home, sixteen miles south of Jacksonville, Florida. Here sixty-eight acres and twenty-five buildings offer a haven for Moose members and their wives in their sunset years. The primary emphasis in Moosehaven is on "companionship." The community provides the 500 residents with indoor and outdoor games, sports, tournaments, and prizes. A library is available for reading books, magazines, and newspapers. Many residents have the opportunity to work on the premises. Some forty different job classifications permit working up to three hours per day. Every member in the work program draws a monthly allowance. Those unable to work receive a "Sunshine Allowance."

In addition to taking care of its members and children of its members, the LOM also supports several charity efforts: March of Dimes, muscular dystrophy, heart fund, cancer research, and cerebral palsy research. It also has lent support to Boy Scout and Girl Scout programs.

In many areas of the United Staes the LOM operates country club activities, offering golfing, swimming, tennis, and dining opportunities where liquor may be had. In operating clubs the order has recently had its whites-only policy revealed. For instance, in June 1972 a legal decision was handed down by the Supreme Court of the United States that the Moose Lodge in Harrisburg, Pennsylvania, could not be denied a state liquor license for refusing to serve a black guest at its club. Although the court's ruling was not detrimental to the LOM, it brought to the nation's attention that the LOM was another fraternal group practicing racial discrimination in the 1970s. It may be noted that the racial discrimination in the LOM is as old as the organization.

Like some other fraternal groups, the LOM has been involved in inter-organizational conflict. In 1925 it brought legal suit against the black Moose, which called itself Independent, Benevolent and Protective Order of Moose (IBPOM). The LOM tried to obtain a legal order to keep the IBPOM from using the name, the Moose emblem, the ritual, the name "Moose," and titles of its officers, which were all similar to those of the LOM.

Structurally the LOM is organized on three levels. On the national level the Supreme Lodge of the World meets annually. Its officers bear the title of Supreme Secretary, Supreme Governor, Supreme Past Governor, and so on. On the state level the order is known as the "State Association"; on the local scene the term "Lodge" is commonly employed. Sometimes the society refers to its entire membership as the "Moose Domain." Its official emblem is the moosehead surrounded by a circle displaying the initials P.A.P. (these stand for "Purity, Aid, Progress") and the inscription Loyal Order of Moose.

The Moose organization has been one of the few fraternal orders that has experienced continued growth in the 1960s and 1970s. Many other well-known fraternal orders, for instance, the Masons* and Odd Fellows,* have suffered considerable membership losses during the last two decades.

Some sources available on the LOM are the order's annual proceedings. Robert W. Wells, *Mooseheart: The City of Children* (1962) provides a good account of Mooseheart. Periodically the society issues publicity brochures. The order publishes ten issues annually of *Moose Magazine*. The LOM ritual published in its volume *Enrollment Ceremony* is not publicly disseminated.

MOOSE, WOMEN OF THE (WOM). Some twenty-five years after the Loyal Order of Moose (LOM) was founded as an all-male fraternal secret seciety, the women (mostly wives of the LOM) formed the Women of the Moose. The group from its beginning has always functioned as a ladies' auxiliary to the LOM.

Unlike some of the other women's auxiliaries that are not recognized by their male counterparts, the WOM are officially accorded recognition by the LOM. The Women of the Moose are commonly permitted to use the lodge halls of the LOM.

Since the order's origin in 1914, the membership has grown to 377,282 in 1979. This figure represented a gain of 4.8 percent from the previous year. WOM has 1,824 local chapters.

The society has a ritual that confers three degrees. The first degree is known as Co-worker; the second is called Academy of Friendship; and the third degree is called College of Regents. Conferral of the first degree qualifies the candidate for full-fledged membership. The remaining two degrees are essentially given on the basis of merit. When the society engages its members in formal attire, the women wear black Geneva gowns, similar to those worn by high school graduates or church choirs. Officers wear stoles of different colors.

On the national (really international) level the society calls its offices by the name of "Supreme Chancellor," "Supreme Recorder," and so on. On the state level the term "Grand" is employed. The WOM meets on the supreme level once each year. Headquarters are in the same town and building where the LOM is housed, namely, in Mooseheart, Illinois.

For further information the reader may consult the *Moose Magazine*, which is published ten times annually. Most of this account is based on a personal interview with a WOM officer.

MOSAIC TEMPLARS OF AMERICA. A fraternal benefit society of blacks that was founded on May 22, 1883, in Little Rock, Arkansas. Up until the 1920s the society paid $1,000 to the beneficiaries of deceased members. It also paid sick and disability benefits. The order was a secret society, but did not accent secrecy as much as other groups. REFERENCE: *DSOS*.

MUSCOVITES, IMPERIAL ORDER OF (IOM). This order used to be the "playground" for the Independent Order of Odd Fellows.* It was organized in Cincinnati, Ohio, in 1894. In 1924 the society merged with four other organizations (the Veiled Prophets of Bagdad, the Oriental Order of Humility and Perfection, the Knights of the Oriental Splendor, and the Ancient Order of Cabirians) to form the Ancient Mystic Order of Samaritans.*

When the IOM functioned as an independent order, it admitted only Odd Fellows to its ranks. All members were pledged to secrecy. The membership never was very large.

Local units of the IOM were called "Kremlins." The principal officer of the national structure was known as Supreme Czar.

MUTUAL BENEFIT ASSOCIATION OF RAIL TRANSPORTATION EMPLOYEES, INC. (MBA). This fraternal benefit group was founded on June 2, 1913, in Pittsburgh, Pennsylvania. Its first name was The Mutual

Benefit Association of Pennsylvania Railroad Employees. The society, although composed of railroad workers, followed the established patterns of other fraternal benefit groups in that it set the minimum age for membership at sixteen, paid benefits to its members, and adopted the lodge method.

Membership is only available to employees of rail transportation companies. The age range for eligibility is from sixteen to sixty years. Both beneficial and nonbeneficial memberships are available. The latter holds no insurance in the society. Each member is required to go through an initiatory ceremony, which has the candidate take a pledge that is brief and simple. The 1979 membership of the MBA stands at 14,190. This is a slight gain since 1965, when the society had 13,885 members.

The MBA conducts the usual fraternal activities and programs found in most fraternal benefit organizations. For instance, it offers scholarships, contributes to leukemia research, donates to the United Fund, sponsors a blood donor campaign, and engages in various civic programs. It also offers aid to disaster victims in distress. Local units carry on such activities as visiting sick and bereaved members. Numerous social events are also part of the society's life. On Flag Day the society furnishes flags to various groups in order to promote patriotism.

Local groups are called "Local Assemblies." The national body, which represents eight states and the District of Columbia, is known as the "General Assembly." It meets in convention biennially. Headquarters are maintained in Philadelphia, Pennsylvania.

For additional information, see the society's published book, *History of the Mutual Beneficial Association of Penn Central Employees, Inc.* (1970). The bylaws are also helpful for the interested reader. The society publishes a monthly periodical, *Mutual*.

MUTUAL GUILD OF GRAND SECRETARIES (MGGS). This association consists of grand secretaries, grand recorders, and grand commanderies. The guild exists to promote closer ties of fraternal fellowship among the various recording officers in the grand jurisdictions of the different masonically oriented orders. The MGGS was founded in 1900, and prior to 1948 the group was named Masonic Grand Secretaries Guild.

The guild has no local or subordinate units. Its only meetings take place on the national level every three years. Headquarters are located in San Francisco, California, where the secretary of the guild resides.

MYSTIC BROTHERS, INDEPENDENT ORDER OF. Founded in Boston, Massachusetts, in 1882, the order was known for paying sick benefits to its members on a weekly basis. The order apparently had a very short life span, less than ten years. REFERENCE: *DSOS*.

MYSTIC WORKERS OF THE WORLD. Founded as a fraternal benefit society by members who were Masons,* Odd Fellows,* Woodmen,* and Knights of Pythias,* the society began in Fulton, Illinois, in 1892. It admitted both men and women. It once (in 1919) had more than 95,000 members. Charity was the central theme of its ritual. Individuals engaged in hazardous occupations were ineligible for membership. In 1930 the society changed its name and function when it became Fidelity Life Association. REFERENCE: *DSOS.*

_ N

NATIONAL ASSOCIATION OF HAYMAKERS. See Haymakers, National Association of.

NATIONAL BENEFIT SOCIETY. Founded in Kansas City, Missouri, in 1894 as a fraternal benefit group, the society no longer exists today. Headquarters were in Kansas City, Missouri.

NATIONAL DEFENDERS. Organized in Knoxville, Tennessee, in 1919 as a fraternal benefit and patriotic order. One of its primary goals was to unite white males who were eighteen or older. All applicants for membership were required to believe in a supreme being. Members were also expected to be opposed to Bolshevism. Its motto was *Finis coronat opus* (the end crowns the work). The slogan for the order was "God, Country, Home." The ritual was ornate and secret. The ladies' auxiliary was named National Co-Defenders. REFERENCE: *DSOS.*

NATIONAL FEDERATED CRAFT (NFC). On June 3, 1929, a constitution was adopted to complete the organization of the National Federated Craft, a society that seeks to bring Freemasons, who work or have worked in the United States government service, into a closer bond with each other. The chief founder and organizer was Archibald R. Crawford. Part of the NFC constitution, in its preamble, reads: "We pledge our devotion to Almighty God, our Allegiance to the Constitution of the United States and our Country; and that through the fulfillment of these principles Equality, Justice and Right may be meted out to all."

Eligibility for joining the NFC is confined to Master Masons; those "in good standing who are in, or have been honorably separated from, any branch of the Services of the United States Government, shall be eligible to consideration for membership." Presently (1979) the society has 1,250 members in twenty-nine cities of the United States.

Community services sponsored by the NFC include hospitals, orphan homes, and other deserving agencies. To help the fraternally minded, the NFC lends much of its support to Masonic youth organizatons such as the De Molay,* Job's Daughters,* and the Rainbow Girls.* These three organizations are supported nationally.

Local units within the NFC are called "Crafts." All crafts are numbered in chronological order as they are chartered. Currently there are 165 crafts in six districts. The districts are numbered. On the national level the NFC holds a convention every year for four days. Women attend as guests. National headquarters are housed in Anderson, Indiana.

For information, see the society's magazine, *National Federated Craft News*, published five times per year. See also the *National Federated Craft Constitution and By-Laws* (1976).

NATIONAL FRATERNAL CONGRESS OF AMERICA (NFCA). Initially, at the time of its founding in 1886, this group was known as the National Fraternal Congress. Although the NFCA is not a fraternal insurance or benevolent organization, it cannot be overlooked when fraternal benevolent societies are discussed. In the 1880s, when more and more fraternal insurance societies were experiencing financial problems due to the absence of actuarial or scientific methods, sixteen fraternal insurance societies, with a combined membership of 535,000 and about $1,200,000,000 worth of insurance, organized the National Fraternal Congress in Washington, D.C., on November 17, 1886. The purpose in forming this congress was to promote uniform legislation in all states where fraternal societies sold insurance. The first meeting in Washington, D.C., was urged by the Ancient Order of United Workmen, the group that is often credited with being the first society to enter the fraternal life insurance arena.

In 1913, in Chicago, the NFCA and the Associated Fraternities of America (a group formed in 1901 to oppose the efforts of the National Fraternal Congress) merged, and the present name was adopted. Today (1979) the NFCA embodies about ninety-five legal reserve fraternal benefit societies. Its current objectives are: "1. To promote the general welfare of the Fraternal Benefit System [sic] in all matters of mutual concern and public interest. 2. To disseminate to the general public information regarding the Fraternal Benefit System. 3. To render service to its members."

The NFCA has done much for the preservation of American fraternal benefit societies. It adopted the Uniform Bill in 1893, compiled a mortality table in 1899, formed the Mobile Bill in 1910—together with the National Convention of Insurance Commissioners (a nonfraternal organization)—

and in 1912 it refined the Mobile Bill that resulted in the New York Conference Bill. All of these actions helped hundreds of fraternal benefit societies attain actuarial soundness and financial solvency. Both of these qualities were sorely lacking in all fraternal benefit groups during the latter part of the nineteenth century.

The emblem of the NFCA is a circular design with a number of fraternally clasped hands forming a ringlike border. In the center of the insignia is a shield with a blazing torch positioned between the letters NF and CA. Encircling the shield are the words National Fraternal Congress-America.

Membership is open to any fraternal society that meets the *Uniform Code* requirements, namely, having no "capital stock, carried on solely for the mutual benefit of its members and their beneficiaries and not for profit; having a lodge system with a ritualistic form of work and a representative form of government, and which shall make provision for the payment of death, sickness or disability benefits or both."

The NFCA meets in convention annually. The head office with a staff of three persons is maintained in Chicago, Illinois.

Each year the NFCA publishes *Statistics, Fraternal Benefit Societies*. From 1895 to 1975 this annual volume was a separate issue of the *Fraternal Monitor*. If the reader wishes to obtain a quick glance of a specific fraternal benefit society's assets, number of insurance certificates in force, amount of insurance in force, premium income, and the like, then this volume is very helpful. The reader may also wish to note that the NFCA is mentioned at some length in the discussion of the Fraternal Context in the present volume.

NATIONAL FRATERNAL LEAGUE. Founded in Green Bay, Wisconsin, in 1902, this fraternal benefit organization began with very inadequate assessment methods. In time these methods were improved. In 1919 the order merged with the Beavers Reserve Fund Equity and the Beavers National Mutual Benefit. REFERENCE: *DSOS*.

NATIONAL FRATERNAL UNION. Members from Freemasonry,* the Independent Order of Odd Fellows,* and the Knights of Pythias* helped form this fraternal benefit society in Cincinnati, Ohio, in 1889. The ritual embodied three degrees, and the order's emblem was a six-pointed star complemented by the monogram letters N.F.U. The society seems to have become extinct in the early 1900s. REFERENCES: *Cyc. Frat.*; *DSOS*.

NATIONAL FRATERNAL SOCIETY OF THE DEAF (NFSD). In the 1890s and up to the year 1907 there existed a fraternal order known as Coming Men of America. Its founder and organizer was a Freemason. This fraternal order sought to inspire high principles of patriotism, honor, and manhood. Before it became extinct, it penetrated a school for the deaf in Flint, Michigan, where a lodge was founded among the older deaf boys.

From the lodge in Flint, Michigan, a number of individuals moved to Chicago upon graduating from the school for the deaf. In the summer of 1901 a handful of these men met in Chicago to plan a fraternal insurance society, since deaf people had a rather difficult time obtaining insurance in those days. The new order was really founded during a reunion at the Flint school on June 12, 1901. By August, 1901, the group was officially incorporated in Illinois. Upon its organization, the society was largely a fellowship group with only meager benevolent benefits, which had a rather haphazard assessment plan for gathering funds. (Such a plan, however, was quite common among most fraternal benevolent groups at that time.) Until 1907 the order was known as the Fraternal Society of the Deaf. Since 1907, the group has had the word "National" added to its name.

Over the years the NFSD became more sophisticated in its insurance programs by adopting better actuarial methods and insurance tables. By 1936 the society moved into its first permanent home office in Oak Park, Illinois. In 1975 it moved to an ultramodern office in Mount Prospect, Illinois. A training program for its insurance agents was begun in 1968, and the following year its office automated its business methods by adopting data processing procedures. The NFSD also sells automobile insurance to its members.

For a fraternal insurance group, the NFSD has a considerable amount of ritual and ceremonial trappings. It adopted a degree system in 1947. Past members received degrees according to their past records and services to the order. Every new member must be initiated and take an obligation (vow): "I hereby solemnly and sincerely promise that I will obey the constitution and laws of this society . . . that I will not reveal to any non-member the business transacted at its meetings or discuss affairs with non-members. . . ." The fifth degree, which is really the second, requires an oath of membership, initiation, and having held a subordinate division (local chapter) office for one year or two committee chairmanships; the tenth degree requires the membership oath, initiation, and two years in some office; the fifteenth degree requires an oath of membership, initiation, and being an officer for three years; the twentieth degree again requires the oath of membership, initiation, and being an officer for five years; the twenty-fifth degree involves the membership oath, initiation, being an officer for five years, and passing a written examination on the laws and history of the order; the thirtieth degree applies to the grand (national) officers only, who must have been grand officers for at least one year; the thirty-fourth degree, in addition to the oath and initiation, requires passing a written examination of the laws and history of the society and accumulating 100 to 200 points. Any member may earn points by performing extraordinary service in addition to holding an office.

The society also has a "Mobile Division," which requires each member to wear a fez, similar to that of the Shriners. The mobile division participates in various parades and celebrations.

The official emblem is a ring with a white background upon which a smaller ring is embossed. The smaller ring displays a blue five-pointed star that is surcharged with a small square, outlined in gold and portraying the letter "F." Around the outside, upper half of the smaller circle are the letters "N.F.S.D.," and the letters "W.A.E." on the lower half. Encircling the letters and inner design is a chain of gold links attached to two hands clasped together. At the bottom of the emblem is a small black shield, charged with the letter "P."

Membership is open to any deaf man or woman between eighteen and sixty years of age. If individuals are not healthy enough to become regular members with insurance benefits, they may become "social" members. Normal hearing people may also become social members. The NFSD also has had a ladies' auxiliary group since 1952. Total membership figures for 1979 were 13,000. In the late 1960s the NFSD had slightly more than 10,000 members.

In terms of charity contributions, the NFSD donates clothing and incidentals to the aged deaf and to hospitals. Toys and clothing are regularly given to needy children. Many members also participate in community projects of various kinds.

Civic affairs are commonly the concern of the society's national board of directors. This group has taken firm stands against proposals and legislation that are detrimental to the deaf. The NFSD has also fought to prevent discrimination against the deaf in employment and other basic American rights.

Organizationally, the NFSD's supreme governing body is known as the "Grand Division." The grand division meets in convention every four years. It must meet in a state or province wherein the society has at least two subordinate divisions (local chapters). In 1979 the NFSD had 126 subordinate divisions in Canada and the United States. The grand division is headquartered in Mount Prospect, Illinois.

Additional information may be found in the society's official publication, The Frat, a handsomely designed magazine, issued bimonthly. See also Constitution and Bylaws of the National Fraternal Society of the Deaf (1975). Other helpful information was acquired from the head offices in Mount Prospect, Illinois.

NATIONAL FRATERNITY. Founded as a fraternal beneficiary society in Philadelphia, Pennsylvania, in 1893 by members of the Ancient United Order of Workmen, the society enrolled both men and women between eighteen and fifty years of age. The ritual revolved about the history of the United States. Like many other fraternal benefit societies, this society apparently ceased to exist in the early 1900s. Home offices were in Philadelphia, Pennsylvania. REFERENCES: *Cyc. Frat.*; *DSOS*.

NATIONAL HOME GUARD. Organized in 1907 in Pennsylvania, this fraternal benefit group offered insurance benefits for men and women members. According to *Statistics, Fraternal Societies* (1921), the society had 1,249 members in 1921. REFERENCE: *DSOS*.

NATIONAL LEAGUE OF MASONIC CLUBS, THE (NLMC). On April 20, 1905, the League of Masonic Clubs was formed in Syracuse, New York. The league was (and still is) an affiliation of Masonic clubs of different rites throughout the United States. At the league's first convention in 1906 the name was changed to National League of Masonic Clubs. The group was incorporated in 1922 under the laws of the District of Columbia. The league has four basic objectives: (1) Subscribe to the "Declaration of Principles" adopted by the Grand Masters Conference in 1939. (2) Foster patriotism and promote universal brotherhood. (3) Promote closer fraternal and social ties with the member clubs. (4) Encourage the study of Americanism, as well as promote science, literature, art, history, and other areas of knowledge. The league convention in Atlantic City, New Jersey, in 1922 adopted a resolution saying "the United States of America is a Masonic nation, and we will ever strive to keep it as such."

The league engages in a number of "public Masonic ceremonies." Every year it honors its deceased "brother," George Washington, at the U.S. Sub-Treasury Building in New York City's Broad and Wall Streets. Here thousands view the annual ceremony. Another past "brother," Benjamin Franklin, is honored annually in Philadelphia. This ceremony is conducted in historic Christ Church and ends by laying a wreath on his grave. Since 1951, the NLMC has been bestowing its Meritorious Service Award Medal upon individuals who have benefited humanity. Some of the recipients have been Admiral Byrd, General Le May, J. Edgar Hoover, and Admiral Rickover.

The league's official emblem is a circle with the name "The National League of Masonic Clubs" in circular-border form. The inner portion of the emblem displays a lamp of knowledge, surrounded by "Organized April 20, 1905, incorporated September 15, 1922." The NLMC also has adopted an official flower, the cherry blossom. The cherry blossom has significance for the league each year in spring when the cherry blossom is distributed throughout member clubs and worn by Masons across the country in honor of George Washington. The league has no ritual or degrees.

To conduct its affairs nationally, the NLMC elects national officers: president, deputy president, vice-presidents, secretary-treasurer, and a board of directors. A similar slate of officers is elected for the state organizations. The league's headquarters are in Hicksville, New York.

The league prints brochures and pamphlets periodically that may be obtained by writing to its headquarters. The *Constitution and By-Laws of The National League of Masonic Clubs* (1972) provides a good understanding of how the league operates on the state and national levels. The *League News* is published ten times each year.

NATIONAL MUTUAL BENEFIT (NMB). The origin of this fraternal benefit group go back to 1902 when the society was known as Beavers' Reserve Fund Fraternity (BRFF). The BRFF was founded to provide "social outlet as well as low cost life insurance protection to the population of the [Stoughton, Wisconsin] area." In 1916 the Beavers National Mutual Benefit (BNMB) was organized as a separate organization to overcome the insufficient income of the flat-rate assessment. The latter group operated a legal reserve system. Members of the BRFF were permitted to transfer their inadequate rate policies to BNMB. In 1931 the word Beavers was dropped to form the present name. Currently the society has 80,000 members.

In 1931 the NMB absorbed the Farmers' Life Insurance Association, and in 1945 the United Danish Society of America was also incorporated into the NMB. Prior to 1913 the society was headquartered in Stoughton, Wisconsin. Now Madison, Wisconsin, serves as the headquarters site.

The present report is based on mimeographed material received from NMB headquarters. The reader may also wish to consult the society's ritual, known as *Ritual and Rules for Colony Meetings* (1940).

NATIONAL ORDER OF COWBOY RANGERS. See Cowboy Rangers, National Order of.

NATIONAL ORDER OF VIDETTES (NOV). Frequently this society was known as the Order of Thirteen. It was formed by Texas farmers in 1886 to protest unfavorable agricultural conditions. In this regard, the NOV resembled the Patrons of Husbandry.* The society grew rapidly, but in 1900 it was virtually extinct, even though it had had about 500,000 members in 1888. The order was organized on a semimilitary basis. State structures were called "Brigades." These were divided into "Regiments" and "Companies." REFERENCE: *Cyc. Frat.*

NATIONAL PROTECTIVE LIFE ASSOCIATION. Founded in 1891 as a fraternal beneficiary society, the society initially was called National Protective Legion when it was organized in the state of New York by members of Freemasonry. The society sought to unite acceptable men and women in one fraternal group, as well as provide them with benevolent insurance protection. One feature that the society had that was not common in its time was a semi-endowment plan. Two membership classes were available, benefit and social. According to *Statistics, Fraternal Societies* (1923), the order had a total membership of 18,000. Waverly, New York, served as the society's headquarters. REFERENCES: *Cyc. Frat.*; *DSOS*.

NATIONAL SLOVAK SOCIETY OF THE U.S.A. (NSS). This fraternal benefit society was founded by Peter P. Rovnianek, a onetime theological student who was expelled from a divinity schol in Budapest for promoting "Pan-Slavism." After Rovnianek came to the United States in 1888, he enrolled in an American seminary but left after one year to become a newspaper editor. On February 15, 1890, he formed the National Slovak Society with the hope of uniting all Slovaks, regardless of their religious affiliation. The formation of the National Slovak Society, which stood for union among all Slovaks, was not well received by the Magyarone Slovaks, loyalists of Hungarian royalty. Most notably, the new society was opposed by some Catholic priests who had been trained in Magyar seminaries in Hungary. These priests even refused to pronounce absolution to any member of the society. In fact, clergy of other denominations also frowned upon the National Slovak Society because they felt it would make the members too materialistic and cause them to lose their faith.

The NSS lists seven objectives for its members: (1) Fraternally unite Slovaks and those of Slovak ancestry. (2) Uphold Slovak traditions and language. (3) Preach and practice the "gospel of fraternity, charity and benevolence." (4) Uphold the American Constitution. (5) Help European kinsmen to make their homeland free. (6) Publish and distribute "Slovak literature and . . . patronize Slovak arts and sciences." (7) Protect its orphans, widows, disabled, sick, and aged.

The NSS speaks of its members being "humanitarians . . . who strive in a spirit of brotherhood for the betterment of their fellowmen. Its members are Christian gentlemen and gentlewomen—Christian in the sense of being practicers [*sic*] of the teachings of Him who taught that 'we should do unto others as we would have them do unto us' and 'to love our neighbors as ourselves.'" Scholarship awards are given to deserving college students who belong to the NSS.

Fraternally and socially, the NSS conducts spelling bees and Christmas parties for its juvenile members. Financial aid is given to softball, baseball, and dartball teams sponsored by local assemblies. Also through local assemblies, the NSS conducts dances, dinners, bazaars, and other kinds of celebrations.

Membership is open to any person of either sex between sixteen and sixty-five years of age. The constitution states membership eligibility requires individuals to be "a Christian of Slovak or Slavic birth or ancestry and their non-Slav friends and relatives of sound health and good moral character. . . ." The society has suffered a substantial membership loss over the last decade. In the late 1960s there were 35,000 members. By 1979, however, the figure had dropped to 21,000, a decline of 40 percent.

The emblem of the society is an eight-cornered cross, surrounded by two rings. Between the two rings are the words SVOBODA ROVNOST BRATSTVO, LIBERTY-EQUALITY-FRATERNITY. The center of the cross displays an eagle mounted on a shield that depicts a double-armed cross. The society confers no degrees, but it does have a ritual. Basically, the ritual is a brief "worship" form that contains an opening and a closing prayer along with a loyalty pledge. The new member vows "in the presence of Almighty God, the Searcher of all hearts, that [he] will always protect, defend and advance the welfare and the interests of the NATIONAL SLOVAK SOCIETY; that [he] will always help, protect and assist the widow and the orphan, the aged and the distressed brethren of the society. . . ." The slogan of the society is "One for All and All for one."

On the local level the NSS refers to its meetings as subordinate assemblies. Regional groups are known as district assemblies. The national structure is called the "Supreme Assembly." It meets every four years. National headquarters are situated in Pittsburgh, Pennsylvania.

For additional reading the reader may wish to consult the society's official organ, *The National News*. It is published in newspaper format on the first and fifteenth day of each month. The Slovak name of the paper is *Narodne Noviny*. In preparation for each national convention the NSS publishes a convention journal that contains advertisements, greetings from national and state dignitaries, and some short articles. The society issues a number of informative brochures.

NATIONAL SOJOURNERS, INC. (NS). The roots of the National Sojourners, an organization of active and retired Masonic military officers, go back to 1898 when the North Dakota Regiment of Volunteer Infantry landed in Manila, Republic of the Philippines. Some officers of the regiment petitioned for a dispensation from the Grand Lodge of the State of North Dakota to operate a field lodge in Manila. The field lodge, however, had to be disbanded the next year as the regiment left, taking the dispensation along. Between 1899 and 1907, the Masonic military officers stationed in the Philippines met and called their informal group the "Sojourners Club." In 1907, the Masonic Sojourners Association was organized in Manila. One of its principal goals was to assist fellow Masons, who as military transients often found themselves in need. Following the formation of the Sojourners, no continuity of the club was maintained for an entire decade. Not until 1917, in Chicago, did the group become renewed. A number of officers of the armed forces felt there was a need to establish and renew acquaintances with their Masonic "brethren" who were "thrown together from various parts of the county." The officers in Chicago held a number of informal meetings; and on February 28, 1918, the Sojourners Club (then only a Chicago group) was organized with elected officials. It was not until 1920, however, that the proposal was made to form a national club, separate from the Chicago group. In 1921 the first regular annual meeting of the National Sojourners Club was held.

In recent years the NS has worked to prevent any weakening of the United States' national defense. This objective corresponds closely with one of the group's original purposes, namely, to bring together past and present military officers to further the country's national security.

Candidates eligible for membership must be Master Masons and be active or retired commissioned or warrant officers in the American armed forces. Since American Masonry doesn't admit nonwhites as members, they are ineligible for membership, even if they are American military officers. The current 1978 membership of the NS is about 10,000.

The NS has two ritualistic ceremonies: the Reception Ceremony and the Heroes of '76. The former requires participation of every new member, and the latter is really a "side" degree with fun as its major objective. In fact, this side degree, when acquired, makes its holders members of the order known as Heroes of '76.*

Like most Masonically allied orders, and like Masonry itself, the NS spices its activities with a certain amount of religious values. For instance, a speech given by one of the club's national vice-presidents during the last decade contains religious references throughout. The following are some excerpts: "[P]ower of prayer must be second nature to all of us in National Sojourners. As General George Washington was unashamed to do, so should we make prayer a vital part of our power for peace." "The God-centered origin of our Republic must be reaffirmed." "The ideological war is basically the struggle between the God-fearing and the Godless." Other instances could be cited.

The emblem of the NS is ornate and full of symbolism. It is an oval shield (in upright position) portraying the Masonic insignia (square and compass) which stands behind the American eagle. Both symbols stand below the words of the NS motto, EX ORIENTE LUX, and are surrounded by thirteen stars. Regarding the symbolism of the thirteen stars, the designer of the emblem said, they remind "us that our Masonic forefathers, by their patriotic efforts, brought this country of ours into existence in the shape of the thirteen original states. . . ." Concerning the American Eagle and the Square and Compass, the designer said: "it was the Masonic power and ideals that was back of our American Eagle . . . That so long as our country was governed and controlled by Masonic ideals we progressed in a manner that astonished the world. . . ."

Structurally, the NS functions on two levels, the national and the local. The officials on the national scene consist of President, First Vice President,

Second Vice President, Third Vice President, Secretary-Treasurer, Chaplain, Judge Advocate, Surgeon, and Historian. A similar array of officers exists on the chapter level. There are 175 local chapters. Headquarters are in Washington, D.C.

For further information see Lavon Parker Linn, *Fifty Years of National Sojourner's* (1970). Helpful insights also can be gleaned from the National Sojourner's magazine *The Sojourner*, a bimonthly publication.

NATIONAL TRAVELERS CLUB FOR MASONS (NTCM). In 1966 a few interested Masons organized a club for Masons who in their recreational pursuits use campers and recreational vehicles. By 1978 there were fifty-five chapters in thirty-two states. Each year the club holds a national rally. There are no degrees or rituals. The national director currently resides in Orchard Park, New Jersey.

The present information was largely gathered from the Masonic Service Association's "Allied Masonic Groups and Rites" (mimeographed, 1978).

NATIONAL UNION ASSURANCE SOCIETY (NUAS). Organized in Mansfield, Ohio, in 1881, this fraternal benefit group was noted as one of the more progressive societies in the fraternal arena. The society operated with the graded assessment plan, which considered the member's age and the increasing cost of insurance with one's age. Thus it employed a "step-rate" method that had the member pay from year to year the actual cost of the insurance promised. This method meant that the society's solvency did not depend on taking in new, young members.

The NUAS took in only white males between twenty and fifty years of age. All prospective members had to be in good health and morally, socially, and intellectually acceptable as well. In 1896 the society had 48,000 members. Many of these were professional and business men. By the early 1920s the society had declined to 35,000 members.

The ritual of the society was considered to be secret. The American flag played a key role in the ritual ceremonies.

When the NUAS was founded, its name was National Union. In the early 1900s it was changed to National Union Assurance Society. The organizational government was based on that of the United States. The national or supreme body was called the "Senate." State groups were known as "Assemblies" or "Legislatures." Local units were referred to as "Councils." Headquarters were maintained in Toledo, Ohio. REFERENCES: *Cyc. Frat.*; *DSOS*.

NATIVE DAUGHTERS OF THE GOLDEN WEST (NDGW). The author had difficulty obtaining up-to-date information on this society in that its head offices did not respond to several written requests. It is known, however, that the society was founded in 1886, apparently as a female counterpart to the male society, Native Sons of the Golden West.*

The society admits only women who were born in California. Currently (1979) its membership stands at approximately 20,000.

The NDGW primarily seeks to promote the child welfare program known as the Children's Foundation. It also assists in marking and restoring historic landmarks, as well as participating in civic affairs that interest the organization. The society operates a home for its aged members in San Francisco. Each year the organization makes itself known publicly by entering a float in the Tournament of Roses.

As a fraternal insurance society, the organization also has a secret ritual. Like most fraternal groups, the society takes the ritual quite seriously. A separate committee is charged with the supervision of the ritual.

Local groups are referred to as "Subordinate Parlors." The grand lodge structure is called "Grand Parlor." The grand lodge convention takes place annually. Headquarters are in San Francisco, California.

For further information see *Constitution and Laws*, issued by the society. There does not appear to be a scholarly history of the NDGW.

NATIVE SONS OF THE GOLDEN WEST (NSGW). Founded on July 11, 1875, by General A. M. Winn and several associates, as a fraternal order that would provide beneficiary insurance to its members, the society was founded in San Francisco. Ever since its origin, it has restricted its membership to native Californians. The society's purpose is to preserve the history and landmarks of the American West and California.

The author was unable to get any response from the society with respect to up-to-date information. Thus some of the present report is not completely current. For instance, the society once had a secret ritual for initiating its members. It apparently still has a ritual.

A few years ago the membership of the NSGW was near 16,000. In the past the membership contained a number of high-status individuals from within the state of California. Membership is open only to males. The females have their own organization known as the Native Daughters of the Golden West.*

The NSGW is confined to the state of California. Its structure operates on two levels only, the local units and the statewide organization. The statewide organization meets annually in convention. San Francisco, California, is the society's headquarters city.

NEIGHBORS OF WOODCRAFT (NOW). When the Woodmen Circle assembled for its supreme (national) session in St. Louis in 1897, delegates from nine western states passed a resolution to withdraw from the Woodmen Circle to form a new and separate order. The delegates were led by

Mrs. C. C. Van Orsdall. Initially, the Neighbors of the Woodcraft chose the name Pacific Circle, Women of Woodcraft. In 1917 the society changed its name to Neighbors of Woodcraft. The order began as a fraternal insurance group. Its first office was in Leadville, Colorado, managed by the "Grand Clerk." In 1905 the grand clerk's office was moved to Portland, Oregon, where it is located to this day.

Although the NOW is predominantly a fraternal insurance group, it nevertheless has a strong ritual orientation. Its 1977 constitution states: "The Grand Guardian shall be the custodian, interpreter, and instructor of the secret, ceremonial, and ritualistic work of the Association." The order also issues to its members an annual password. The initiation of new members requires taking an obligation. In fact, once each year an "Obligation Night" is held that requires all members present at the meeting to repeat the obligation in unison. The individual in charge of the local unit (circle) is called "Magician." During initiation and other ceremonies the order has an Inner Sentinel and an Outer Sentinel at work. The latter individual guards the outer door at all sessions of the circle (local chapter).

NOW has five membership classifications: benefit, social, junior benefit, junior social, and family affiliate members. A benefit member is one who contributes to the Benefit Fund of the order and is insured by the order. The social member does not contribute to the Benefit Fund and ordinarily is not eligible to hold key offices. Junior benefit members are similar to the benefit memberships, except that they are under age and require the parent to sign for the insurance contract. A junior social membership is for someone under age sixteen who does not qualify for a junior contract of insurance. Family affiliate applies to a benefit member's child whose life is insured on a family rider plan. The Neighbors of the Woodcraft has no clause in its consultation pertaining to racial discrimination. Its 1978 membership roster had approximately 25,000 "neighbors," which represents a loss of about 17 percent since the late 1960s. Fifty years ago (1927), the order had more than 77,000 members.

From the late 1920s to 1952 the order operated the Woodcraft Home in Riverside, California. In 1952 the home was moved to Hood River, Oregon. The home serves aged members of NOW. The society also provides scholarship assistance through its Grand Circle Scholarship Program. Any son, daughter, or grandchild of a member of the order is eligible. The NOW operates primarily in California, Colorado, Idaho, Montana, Nevada, Oregon, Utah, Washington, Wyoming, and Alaska.

The grand circle is the centralized administrative authority. District circles encompass regional areas, and the local groups are referred to as circles. Circle officers are the Guardian Neighbor, Past Guardian Neighbor, Adviser, Magician, Clerk, Banker, Attendant, Captain of Guards, Flag Bearer, Musician, Inner Sentinel, Outer Sentinel, three Managers, Correspondent, and Senior Guardian. The headquarters of the grand circle are in Portland, Oregon.

A quarterly magazine, *Pacific Echo*, is published by the order. It provides news of the order's fraternal functions. The reader may also wish to consult *Constitution of Neighbors of Woodcraft and By-Laws of Circles* (1977). Another publication of help is Keith L. Yates, *History of the Woodcraft Home* (1975). The order's quadrennial proceedings may also be consulted.

NEW ENGLAND ORDER OF PROTECTION. Formed in 1887 in Massachusetts as a fraternal beneficiary society, the society was an offshoot of the Knights and Ladies of Honor. It was organized by members of Freemasonry,* Royal Arcanum,* Knights of Pythias,* and others. In 1927 the order had attained a membership of 26,219, a figure that included social and benefit members in 278 local lodges.

NEW ERA ASSOCIATION. A fraternal benefit society formed in 1897, the association drew members from Michigan and Illinois. Both men and women were admitted to membership. Its membership in 1927 stood at 35,216, with 256 local lodges. The ritual of the society was not considered to be so secret as that of some other fraternal groups. Grand Rapids, Michigan, was the society's headquarters site.

NORTH AMERICAN BENEFIT ASSOCIATION (NABA). This women's fraternal society was founded in 1892. It assumed the name of Ladies of the Modern Maccabees. In reality, the order arose as the result of a schism in the Ladies of the Maccabees of the World,* which was founded in 1885, a female auxiliary of the Knights of the Maccabees.* The leading figure of the new society was Bina M. West.

Having seen penniless widows and orphaned children put to work in factories and shops, the youthful schoolteacher was moved to organize a group that would provide women some insurance protection. One day in October 1892, without the approval of the Ladies of the Maccabees of the World, West obtained a $500 loan to set up a small office in the basement of a house in Port Huron, Michigan. Part of the loan was used to travel to Ohio, where she went to woo people to join the new fraternal benefit society. By the end of the society's first decade there were 100,000 members. The next decade saw the membership climb to 150,000.

By the early 1920s the society, which changed its name in 1915 to Women's Benefit Association from the former name of Ladies of the Modern Maccabees, had local units in every state but Massachusetts and South Carolina. Its membership in 1927 was 271,952. This number also included the members in Canada. Today (1979) the roster shows 145,000 members in 700 lodges.

The society changed its name again in 1966, this time adopting the present name, North American Benefit Association. A number of other changes have been made too. In 1931 the society voted to admit men, hoping to establish a family fraternity. A fraternal benefit program with broader effects was introduced in 1966. This program assists eligible members in five areas of personal misfortune: aid to orphans, education benefits, blindness retraining, cancer, and natural disaster. Also in 1966 the society created a marketing department that supplements field sales activities by placing more emphasis on specially trained representatives with the hope of expanding membership and benefits.

Unlike many fraternal benefit societies, the NABA never encountered any real financial difficulties over the decades such as many fraternals on the assessment plans experienced. In fact, in 1915, when many societies were striving to overcome difficulties, the NABA built a beautiful headquarters building. One reason for the continued financial solvency of the order was its willingness to heed the advice and counsel of the National Fraternal Congress,* of which it was a member. The relationship to the National Fraternal Congress was so cordial that in 1925 Bina West became the first woman president of the congress. Today the society, although it has fewer members than it once had, is still quite prosperous with assets of $80 million.

Throughout the years the NABA has had very friendly relaitons with the Knights of Maccabees. In 1919 the society challenged the Maccabees to a three-year membership contest. The ladies won the contest decidedly each of the three years.

The society has a ritual that it considers secret, to be kept from nonmembers. In this sense the NABA is more serious about its ritual than are many fraternal benefit societies that have freely shared their rituals with the present writer. The emblem of the NABA consists of a shield, cradled in a laurellike wreath. In addition to a circle in the shield's center, displaying a female figure upholding a green branch, the shield is divided into eight parts, each depicting a separate symbol.

As with most fraternal benefit societies, the NABA has a junior membership department for individuals under fifteen years of age. These junior members may be insured, provided they receive parental or other adult approval. Individuals over fifteen years of age who are mentally, physically, and morally sound are eligible for benefit membership.

When a local unit is entirely composed of women members, it is known as a "Review." Sexually mixed groups are called "Clubs." The NABA now has no state organizations, but every four years given states conduct district conventions from which delegates are chosen for the national convention. The national structure, when in convention, is referred to as the "Supreme Review." National headquarters are located in Port Huron, Michigan.

Information on the society was obtained from sources provided by the NABA. Some additional items were gathered from back issues of *Statistics, Fraternal Societies*.

NORTH AMERICAN SWISS ALLIANCE (NASA). Prior to the formation of this fraternal benefit society, the Swiss society known as *Gruetli Verein* of St. Louis, Missouri, lent the advice and assistance of its members to help organize a Swiss alliance, known as the *Gruetli Bund der Vereinigten Staaten von Nord Amerika*. This alliance, with a German name, was founded on June 14, 1865, in Cincinnati, Ohio. As the society was organized, it took for its motto the words "One for All, and All for One." The first headquarters were housed in St. Louis, Missouri, from 1865 to 1867. From 1867 to 1869 Cincinnati, Ohio, served as the headquarters city. Washington, D.C. was the main office site from 1869 to 1874. Then from 1874 to 1877 St. Louis again was the headquarters location. Buffalo, New York, had the main office spot from 1877 to 1885. The next move was to Cleveland, where the society had its head offices from 1885 to 1889. The years from 1889 to 1898 Chicago was the headquarters city. The society kept moving its head offices every few years. Currently (1979) the headquarters are in Cleveland, Ohio.

In July of 1911, at the society's national convention, the organization changed its name to *Nordamerikanischer Schweizerbund*. The name of its periodical was also changed. Instead of *Gruetlianer*, it was now called *Der Schweizer*. In 1940 still another name change occurred when the organization changed its name to North American Swiss Alliance, its present designation. Over the years the society also changed its insurance programs to more varied certificates (policies) and better actuarial methods.

Membership is open to Swiss or those who are Swiss descendants. Individuals married to someone who is Swiss are also eligible to join NASA. The membership has in recent years grown slightly. In 1965 the society had a combined membership roster of 2,000 benefit and social members. The latter comprised about one-seventh of the total roster. The figures for 1978 show a total membership count of about 4,000 members.

The emblem of the society is a shield displaying the letters N.A.S.A. above a white cross in the center of the shield. Behind the shield is a knight's axe and fasces.

Local units are called "Branches," although the society's literature will also employ the word "lodges" on occasion. The national convention meets every four years.

For additional information, see the society's *Jubilee Book, 1865-1965*. Also consult the organization's monthly, *The Swiss American*.

NORTH AMERICAN UNION LIFE ASSURANCE SOCIETY (NAU).
Organized in 1893 in Chicago, Illinois, this socity initially was known as

North American Union. It was incorporated in 1895, and in 1925 it adopted the present name by adding Life Assurance Society.

The objectives of the organization were "To protect the home and promote the fraternal, social and material interests of its members." Another goal was "To unite fraternally on the broad, liberal plane of humanity all white persons between the ages of sixteen and sixty years . . . who are physically and morally acceptable." While the society barred nonwhites, it did have a more open posture regarding religious affiliations. Protestants, Catholics, and Jews were able to join.

The order still has a ritual which it considers to be secret from nonmembers. The ritual contains the customary fraternal rites pertaining to initiation of new members and installation of officers.

Membership at one time was only open to white males. Today females also belong to the organization. However, the ladies have their own councils, as do the men. Whether the society still bars nonwhites, the writer was unable to ascertain. Currently (1979) the society has approximately 7,000 members. This number has remained fairly constant over the last five years. Like most fraternal benefit groups, the NAU contributes to civic and other charities. Local units provide recreational and leisure activities.

Local units are known as "Councils." The highest governing authority is called the "Supreme Council." It meets in convention every four years. Headquarters of the society are maintained in Chicago, Illinois.

Additional information may be gathered by consulting the society's periodical, *The North American Union Monthly News*. This publication has been issued for eighty-five years. *The Constitution and Laws of the North American Union Life Assurance Society* gives a brief history of the organization.

NORTH STAR BENEFIT ASSOCIATION. Founded in 1899, this fraternal benefit society operated on the flat-rate assessment plan. Its main features were offering disability, accident, and old-age benefits. Its principal officer was called "Chief Astronomer." In the early 1920s the society had fewer than 7,000 members. Moline, Illinois, served as the headquarters city. REFERENCE: *DSOS*.

NORTHWESTERN LEGION OF HONOR. The graded assessment plan was what this fraternal benefit society used to collect its insurance funds. The society was founded in Iowa in 1884, as an offspring of the American Legion of Honor.* Men and women between eighteen and fifty years of age were eligible for membership, if they were white and did not hold a hazardous job. The society's ritual accented benevolence. Its motto was "We Work Together." Administrative affairs were conducted only on two levels, the subordinate council and the grand council. REFERENCES: *Cyc. Frat.*; *DSOS*.

O

OCCIDENTAL MUTUAL BENEFIT ASSOCIATION. Founded in 1896, this organization functioned as a fraternal benefit society, providing benefits to men and women. The society had about 4,000 members in 1922. Shortly after it disbanded. Headquarters were in Salina, Kansas. REFERENCE: *DSOS*.

ODD FELLOWS, GRAND UNITED ORDER OF, IN AMERICA (GUOOF). In order to understand the background of the GUOOF, a black fraternal group, it is necessary to go back to the United Order of Odd Fellows, which existed in England since the latter part of the eighteenth century. Whether the United Order's roots go back to 1745, when the first lodge of Odd Fellows was formed in England, is not certain.

Although drunkenness was common in most working class lodges, one lodge in Manchester, England, objected to the drunken conviviality prevalent in the United Order. The objectors seceded from the United Order in 1813 and called themselves Independent Order of Odd Fellows, Manchester Unity. This group soon had a large following.

In 1819 the Independent Order of Odd Fellows, Manchester Unity, was introduced to the United States by Thomas Wildey, a blacksmith. Soon the Grand Lodge of Odd Fellows of the United States was organized in 1825. Thomas Wildey was the first grand master. This American order of Odd Fellows, which began as an all-white fraternal organization, received its charter from the Manchester Unity in England the previous year, 1820. The GUOOF, on the other hand, received its charter from the United Order (also known as the Grand United Order) in England in 1843.

The black Odd Fellows, upon receiving their charter, formed their first lodge in New York City in 1843. The following year they organized the Grand United Order of Odd Fellows, incorporating the name of the old English order. The GUOOF tried to be loyal to its English ancestor in other ways as well. For instance, all signs, passwords, and rituals were taken over from the United Order in England.

The same year (1843) that the GUOOF received its charter to organize in the United States the white grand lodge withdrew from the Manchester Unity in England. Frequently it is asserted that the withdrawal was prompted by the English Odd Fellows granting a charter to the black Odd Fellows. The GUOOF literature disputes this argument, however, primarily because the GUOOF was chartered by the United Order, whereas the Wildey group was chartered by the Manchester Unity.

The prime organizer of the black Odd Fellows was Peter Ogden, a black sailor, who was initiated into Odd Fellowship in England. Ogden received a charter for the GUOOF from the Grand Lodge of Odd Fellows in England.

In many ways, Ogden was to the GUOOF what Thomas Wildey was to the IOOF.

Membership eligibility has never been restricted to black males; however, because of widespread racial prejudice in American fraternal secret societies, whites did not join the GUOOF. Even today the GUOOF has only a handful of white members. Presently (1978) the membership roster has approximately 108,000 members, comprising six regional groups. The order's auxiliary group is known as the Heroines of Jericho.

In addition to the order's fraternal activities, it also supports various charities. Seminars and professional training sessions are conducted for interested members from the business community. The order also maintains a library in Philadelphia.

Local groups are called "Lodges," and the national structure is known as the "Grand Lodge." National conventions are held every two years. Headquarters are maintained in Philadelphia, Pennsylvania.

For further information, see the order's quarterly publication, *Bulletin*. A good historical source is Charles H. Brooks, *The Official History and Manual of the Grand United Order of Odd Fellows in America* (1902, reprinted in 1971).

ODD FELLOWS, INDEPENDENT ORDER OF (IOOF). Like Freemasonry,* the Odd Fellowship did not originate in the United States but rather in England. There is some evidence indicating that an Odd Fellows lodge existed in England as early as 1745. Yet as Albert Stevens said in his *Cyclopedia of Fraternities* (1907), the real "origin of the society of Odd Fellows will probably remain obscure." However, once the nineteenth-century literature appears, information about the Odd Fellows is quite clear. By the early 1800s, records show, the United Order of Odd Fellows (also known as Grand United Order) existed in England. Also during this time several schisms occurred in the United Order, the primary and most notable being the one that resulted in the group calling itself Independent Order of Odd Fellows, Manchester Unity. This group, in Manchester, England, seceded from the United Order in 1813 because of the widespread conviviality present in Odd Fellowship in that era.

In 1817 an Odd Fellow, Thomas Wildey, immigrated to the United States; and on April 26, 1819, he organized an Odd Fellows lodge in the Seven Stars Tavern in Baltimore, Maryland. This lodge was chartered by the Duke of York Lodge, Preston, England, one of the lodges in the Manchester Unity group. It should be noted, however, that the lodge founded by Wildey was not the first Odd Fellows society in the United States. Records show that an unchartered lodge had appeared in Baltimore as early as 1802 and one in New York in 1806. But since Wildey's effort received a formal charter from the English Odd Fellows, the credit and honor for establishing Odd Fellowship in the United States goes to him.

By 1821 a grand lodge was formed in Maryland; and by 1825 the Grand Lodge of Odd Fellows of the United States was organized, holding a convention the same year. Thomas Wildey became Grand Sire of this grand lodge. The following year in 1826 he journeyed to England, where he was honored for having formally brought Odd Fellowship to the United States. Wildey's leadership was highly effective, for by the time he died in 1861 there were forty-two grand lodges (state jurisdictions) and more than 200,000 Odd Fellows in the United States.

The Odd Fellows severed their formal ties with their English "brethren" in 1843. One argument frequently heard is that the American Odd Fellows broke from the Manchester Unity because the black Odd Fellows had received a charter that same year. The black Odd Fellows, known as the Grand United Order of Odd Fellows (GUOOF),* however, dispute this contention. They assert that the white Odd Fellows had no reason to contest the blacks being chartered because not the Manchester Unity but rather the Grand United Order extended that right. Since 1843, the white Odd Fellows have called themselves Independent Order of Odd Fellows.

The IOOF was the first American fraternal order to offer its members financial benevolencies with regard to relief of the sick, distressed, and orphans and burial of deceased members. Whether the benevolent features or other organizational qualities appealed to the people is not easy to determine. Whatever the reason, the IOOF, even after Wildey's death, flourished immensely. Albert Stevens notes in his *Cyclopedia of Fraternities* (1907) that from 1830 to 1895 the IOOF had initiated 2,012,840 members. This is striking when one remembers that the population of the United States was relatively sparse during those sixty-five years.

Odd Fellowship, often referred to as "the poor man's Masonry," in many ways resembles Masonry. Like Freemasonry, it teaches its members secret passwords, signs, and grips; it hoodwinks (blindfolds) the candidate during initiation; it votes by ball ballot when admitting the candidate; it requires belief in a supreme being; it accents certain moral lessons in its ritual; and until 1971 its constitution allowed only white males to become members.

The candidate, in addition to being hoodwinked, is also put in chains, symbolizing darkness and helplessness as the members form a funerallike procession and then march around the lodge room. After the procession the candidate's blindfold is removed and he is invited to meditate on death as he views a human skeleton illuminated by two torches.

In the oath (obligation) the candidate promises that he "will never communicate to anyone, unless directed to do so by a legal lodge, the signs, token or grips, the term, traveling or other password. . . . Nor . . . expose or lend any of the books or papers relating to the records or secret work of the Order . . ." (*Revised Odd Fellowship Illustrated*, 1951).

The Odd Fellows confer three degrees in addition to the initiatory degree. These are known as Friendship, Love, and Truth, symbolized by three chain links joined together. The three links also are the official emblem of the IOOF. The letters F, L, T are illustrated in the three links, one letter per link.

Members who desire to attain "higher" degrees may join the Encampment Lodge of the IOOF. It works three degrees in addition to the four received in the subordinate lodge. The parade unit of the society is known as Patriarchs Militant. The IOOF also sponsors a youth group, Junior Lodge, Odd Fellows.*

Membership is open only to adult males, and as already noted, until the 1970s only white males were admitted. The IOOF, however, has a female order, the Rebekah Assemblies,* which was organized in 1851. Men from the IOOF may join the Rebekah Assemblies, but the reverse is not possible. Currently (1978) the society has approximately 243,000 members. This figure represents a remarkable decline from a roster of 3,400,000 that the order once boasted in 1915.

Local units are known as "Lodges." Regional groups are called "Grand Lodges," and the national structure, which includes Canada as well as the United States, is referred to as the "Sovereign Grand Lodge." The sovereign grand lodge meets annually in convention. Headquarters are maintained in Baltimore, Maryland.

Additional information may be acquired by reading the following: T. G. Beharrell, *Odd Fellows Monitor and Guide* (1894); Theodore A. Ross, *Odd Fellowship: Its History and Manual* (1897). The annual *Journal of Proceedings of the Sovereign Grand Lodge* are very helpful in terms of the detail they provide for a good understanding of the IOOF. Not to be overlooked is the order's monthly publication, *International Odd Fellow*.

ODD FELLOWS, JUNIOR LODGE. The senior members of the Independent Order of Odd Fellows* commonly call their junior organization "Junior Lodge." The society was organized in 1921. The Junior Lodge is intended to provide a place for young men interested in becoming members of the Odd Fellows upon reaching adulthood. The ritual and ceremonies are supervised by the senior lodge. At one time the order was known as Loyal Sons of the Junior Order of Odd Fellows.

While current (1979) membership figures were not available to the writer, it is known that in 1970 the Junior Lodge had 4,873 members. The society has been slowly declining in membership in recent years.

Additional information may be gleaned by consulting the annual proceedings of the Sovereign Grand Lodge of the Independent Order of Odd Fellows.

ORDER KNIGHTS OF FRIENDSHIP. This group was organized as a fraternal, benevolent, social, and patriotic society in Philadelphia, Pennsylvania, in 1859. The society's ritual embodied three degrees: Knight Junior, Knight Bachelor, and Knight Errant. According to *Statistics, Fraternal Societies* (1923), the order had 20,000 members in 1920. Today it is no longer in existence. Headquarters were in Reading, Pennsylvania. REFERENCES: *Cyc. Frat.*; *DSOS*.

ORDER OF AEGIS. See Aegis, Order of.

ORDER OF AMARANTH. See Amaranth, Order of.

ORDER OF AMERICUS. This fraternal benefit society was founded in 1897 in the state of Pennsylvania. The society began as a graded assessment fraternal insurance concern. Women were admitted on the same basis as men. Headquarters were maintained in Greensburg, Pennsylvania.

ORDER OF ANCIENT OAKS. See Ancient Oaks, Order of.

ORDER OF ANTI-POKE-NOSES. See Anti-Poke-Noses, Order of.

ORDER OF B'RITH ABRAHAM. See B'rith Abraham, Order of.

ORDER OF BUGS. See Bugs, Order of.

ORDER OF THE BUILDERS. See Builders, Order of.

ORDER OF CAMELS. See Camels, Order of.

ORDER OF CHOSEN FRIENDS. See Chosen Friends, Order of.

ORDER OF DE MOLAY. See De Molay, Order of.

ORDER OF DESOMS. See Desoms, Order of.

ORDER OF EASTERN STAR. See Eastern Star, Order of.

ORDER OF EQUITY. See Equity, Order of.

ORDER OF GOLDEN CHAIN. See Golden Chain, Order of.

ORDER OF GOLDEN KEY. See Golden Key, Order of.

ORDER OF GOLDEN LINKS. See Golden Links, Order of.

ORDER OF IRON HALL. See Iron Hall, Order of.

ORDER OF THE AMERICAN UNION. See American Union, Order of the.

ORDER OF THE BATH OF THE UNITED STATES OF AMERICA (OOB). On June 21, 1921, in Red Bank, New Jersey, nine Masons got together and formed the Wahoo Band. The order held this name until 1930, when it was changed to the Order of the Bath. According to Harold V. B. Voorhis, *Masonic Organizations and Allied Orders and Degrees* (1952), the order's purpose is to bring together Freemasons* in mutual meetings, promote charity, and to confer the Order of the Bath on fellow Masons.

Membership is only open to Master Masons. The membership has never been large. Voorhis shows the order having had a total of 217 members in 1950. Current membership figures were not available.

The OOB has no subordinate bodies or units, although at one time local groups were called "Bands." Presently the chief officer, Commander General, resides in Cresskill, New Jersey. The secretary, known as Keeper of the Bath Records, lives in Glassboro, New Jersey. Thus the "headquarters" are in New Jersey.

ORDER OF THE CONSTELLATION OF JUNIOR STARS. See Junior Stars, Order of the Constellation of.

ORDER OF THE CONTINENTAL FRATERNAL UNION. See Continental Fraternal Union, Order of.

ORDER OF THE DAUGHTERS OF SCOTIA. See Daughters of Scotia, Order of the.

ORDER OF THE GOLDEN ROD. See Golden Rod, Order of the.

ORDER OF THE HEPTASOPHS. See Heptasophs, Order of the.

ORDER OF THE LITTLE RED SCHOOL HOUSE. August 1895 was the founding date of this fraternal, patriotic fraternity. Its birthplace was Boston, Massachusetts. Through its ritual the order sought to inspire its members to have a greater love for "Old Glory" and a greater reverence for the "Little Red School House," the public school. Membership was open to all: whites, blacks, Jews, Catholics, Protestants, or Mohammedans. All members were required to take a "solemn oath." State Groups were called "Seminaries," and local units were known as "Schools."

ORDER OF HOMEBUILDERS. See Homebuilders, Order of.

ORDER OF HOUN' DOGS. See Houn' Dogs, Order of.

ORDER OF IROQUOIS. See Iroquois, Order of.

ORDER OF KNIGHT MASONS. See Knight Masons, Order of.

ORDER OF MUTUAL PROTECTION. This fraternal benefit order was formed in St. Louis, Missouri, in 1878 as an offshoot of the Order of Mutual Aid. Local lodges employed a ritual embodying religious elements. An oath of secrecy was commonly required of all benefit members. In 1905 the society had 8,184 members. By 1927 the membership had declined to about 5,000, and by 1930 it appears to have disbanded.

ORDER OF PATRONS OF HUSBANDRY. See Patrons of Husbandry, Order of.

ORDER OF PENTE. See Pente, Order of.

ORDER OF RED EAGLE. See Red Eagle, Order of.

ORDER OF SCOTTISH CLANS. See Scottish Clans, Order of.

ORDER OF SHEPHERDS OF BETHLEHEM. See Shepherds of Bethlehem, Order of.

ORDER OF SHIELD OF HONOR. See Shield of Honor, Order of.

ORDER OF SONS OF HERMAN. See Sons of Herman, Order of.

ORDER OF SONS OF PERICLES. See Sons of Pericles, Order of.

ORDER OF SONS OF ST. GEORGE. See Sons of St. George, Order of.

ORDER OF SPARTA. See Sparta, Order of.

ORDER OF UNITED AMERICANS. See United Americans, Order of.

ORDER OF UNITED COMMERCIAL TRAVELERS OF AMERICA, THE. See United Commercial Travelers of America, The Order of.

ORDER OF UNITY. See Unity, Order of.

ORDER OF THE WHITE SHRINE OF JERUSALEM. See White Shrine of Jerusalem, Order of the.

ORIENTAL ORDER OF HUMILITY AND PERFECTION. This was a side degree of the Independent Order of Odd Fellows. It was commonly known as the "playground" of Odd Fellowship. In 1924, together with several other groups, it formed the Ancient, Mystic Order of Samaritans. REFERENCES: *Cyc. Frat.*; *DSOS*.

ORIOLES, THE FRATERNAL ORDER (FOO). When this fraternal society was organized in Rochester, New York, in 1910, it was to be called the Order of Owls.* But as there already was a society by that name, a court injunction restrained the founders from employing the existing name. The court order led the organizers to call their society the Fraternal Order Orioles. Although the FOO chose its own name, it did, however, imitate many of the ritualistic features of the Order of Owls.

The FOO has four watchwords: liberty, integrity, fraternity, and equality. Some of the order's principal objectives are to lessen "the burdens of their fellow Orioles. . . . advance the welfare of all brother Orioles in business life. . . . assist our members who are candidates for public office. . . . outline and promulgate civic, humanitarian and educational programs of national and international scope. . . ." With regard to lessening the burdens of a fellow member, the society has provisions in its constitution that make available donations or benefits in the event sickness, accidents, or injury strike. These benefits, it should be noted, are not the result of a given members' holding an insurance certificate, as would be the case if he were a member of a fraternal life insurance group. The benefits received are really the result of fraternal charity because the order is not obligated to pay benefits or make donations.

The FOO has a ritual which resembles the rituals of many other fraternal societies. The lodge ("Nest") floor plan has an altar in the center of the room, and several religious features are evident in the presence of a chaplain, prayers, and a Bible. As part of the initiation, the candidate, in part, promises: "I will not—reveal the secrets or work—of the Order—to any person or persons—who shall not—be known to me—as fully initiated members—of the Order."

New members are received by ball-ballot vote. Three or more blackballs reject a prospective member. The successful candidate goes through an initiation rite in which he receives the Initiatory degree. There are three types of memberships available: the good standing, the social, and the honorary membership. The good standing member is eligible for benefit or donations in the event of sickness or accident. The social member may not receive any financial benefits. An honorary member is one who resides in a community where the society has no nest, a local unit. Ladies are eligible to join the order's auxiliaries. An auxiliary is officially called "Ladies' Auxiliary, Nest No._____, Fraternal Order Orioles."

In addition to the Initiatory degree, the FOO has two other degrees. The second degree is the Supreme degree, which is conferred by the supreme convention, as is the Invincible degree, the third rite. The emblem of the order is an oriole perched on a tree branch upon which the letters LIFE appear, representing the watchwords of the society.

The FOO presently (1979) has 12,649 members in fifty-seven local units, which are called "Subordinate Nests." In the early 1920s the society had more than 140,000 members. State or provincial organizations are known as "Grand Nests." The national structure is referred to as the "Supreme Nest." The supreme nest meets in convention annually. The principal officer on the supreme level is the Supreme Worthy President. In the local nest the head officer is the Worthy President. Headquarters of the FOO are in Reading, Pennsylvania.

For further information, see *The Oriole Bulletin*, a quarterly publication. Also helpful for understanding the FOO is the *Supreme Constitution of the Fraternal Order Orioles*. The society's ritual reveals the order's fraternal values.

OWLS, INDEPENDENT INTERNATIONAL ORDER OF. This was a Masonically related group that organized itself in 1890 in St. Louis, Missouri. Its objectives were to promote recreation and sociability among the members. Only Master Masons were eligible to join. Its local units were called "Nests." The head officer of each nest was known as "Sapient Screecher." The national body was called "Supreme Nest of the World." REFERENCE: *Cyc. Frat.*

OWLS, ORDER OF (OOO). South Bend, Indiana, was the city where this "animal" lodge was born. John W. Talbot and a small group of his associates in November of 1904 formed this fraternal group. When it was founded, the order sought to assist its members in business and in employment, provide help to the widows and orphans of the deceased members, and to enjoy mutual fellowship with one another. This order has no relationship with the onetime Masonically related group, the Independent Order of Owls, that was organized in St. Louis, Missouri, in 1890.

The OOO has four degrees, plus the presence of a ritual, passwords, and fraternal grips. The ritual, as in most fraternal orders, is intended to be secret. The OOO publications (e.g., brochures) contend that its ritual has no religious elements. An older edition of the ritual states: "We advocate no creed. We know there are so many gods, so many creeds, so many paths that wind and wind. We believe that the art of being kind is all this world needs."

Membership has been open only to white males. During the early 1920s the OOO had over 600,000 members in 2,148 local lodges, called "Nests." Since the 1920s, the order has been losing members rather significantly. Its present (1979) membership roster has about 40,000 members.

Local units, as noted, are called "Nests." The national governing body is known as the "Supreme Nest." Its main officer is named "Supreme President."

Additional information may be gained by consulting William Whalen, *Handbook of Secret Organizations*, 1966; Arthur Preuss, *A Dictionary of Secret and Other Societies*, 1924. Back issues of the society's periodical, *The Owl*, are also helpful.

__P

PANCRETAN ASSOCIATION OF AMERICA (PAA). This society had its origin in Chicago, Illinois, when on October 1, 1916, a group of Cretans organized themselves as a fraternal group. The organization was called the Cretan Brotherhood of Chicago. In 1929 the society became known as the Pancretan Association of America, after Cretans were called together from various parts of the United States to hold a national convention. It was at this convention that the organization elected its first president. A year later (1930) the society organized chapters for female members, and since then the PAA has also formed youth chapters.

The constitution of the PAA states that the society shall "promote and develop social and phyletic relationship and mutuality among all of the Cretans and their descendants residing in the United States and Canada." The organization also seeks to assist fellow Cretans by providing scholarship funds and contributing to Cretan philanthropic institutions. Members also receive encouragement and inspiration to be loyal and faithful citizens of their respective country. Since the society's inception, the organization also has been quite enthusiastic about assisting the Greek Orthodox Church.

Membership is open to individuals who have at least one parent, grandparent, or spouse who hails from the Greek Island of Crete. The number of members in July of 1978 was about 3,300 in forty chapters, which comprise men, women, and youth groups.

The emblem of the PAA consists of a circle that is enveloped by the words Pancretan Association of America. Inside the circle is an island representing the Greek Island of Crete. Three other symbols complete the insignia, a laurel wreath, two crossed mallets, and a cross. The society has no ritual.

The forty chapters on the local level send delegates to the national convention every two years. During the interim the society conducts its affairs through the elected officers, district governors, and a board of trustees.

There are seven districts in the PAA. National headquarters are in Ceres, California.

For additional information, see the society's monthly publication, *KPHTH* (Crete). Much of this periodical's content is printed in the Greek language. To observe its fiftieth anniversary, the society in December of 1978 published a special issue of *KPHTH*. The *Constitution and By-Laws of the Pancretan Association of America* (1965) may be obtained from the head offices in Ceres, California.

PATRIARCHAL CIRCLE OF AMERICA. Founded in 1880 in Milwaukee, Wisconsin, this order was a fraternal benefit society. Originally, the order was an Odd Fellows'* society, intended to confer new degrees for its Uniformed Patriarchs division. The Patriarchal Circle of America had a ritual with three degrees: Preparatory, Perfection, and Patriarchal Feast and Knighthood. Sometime during the early 1900s the order ceased to exist. REFERENCES: *Cyc. Frat.*; *DSOS*.

PATRIOTIC AND PROTECTIVE ORDER OF STAGS OF THE WORLD. This order was organized on New Year's Eve in 1911 in Chicago, Illinois. The society had a ritual with signs, passwords, and grips. Local units were called "Droves." Each drove paid its own fraternal benevolencies. The "Supreme Drove" was located in St. Louis, Missouri. REFERENCE: *DSOS*.

PATRONS OF HUSBANDRY, ORDER OF (POH) [The Grange]. The War Between the States was over. The South was particularly exhausted economically, especially in its agriculture. President Andrew Johnson's administration sought to restore the fertile farms of the South. This resulted in Isaac Newton (the nation's first Commissioner of Agriculture) sending a governmental clerk, Oliver Hudson Kelley, from the Bureau of Agriculture to the South for a firsthand report. As Kelley surveyed southern agriculture in 1866, he felt that one of the key problems that beset farmers was their lack of unity and organization. Upon returning to Washington, he suggested a fraternal organization for farmers. As a member of the Masonic lodge, he felt that farm fraternalism would provide unity and organization. On December 4, 1867, Kelley and six friends (William Saunders, John R. Thompson, William M. Ireland, Aaron B. Grosh, John Trimble, Francis M. McDowell) founded the Order of Patrons of Husbandry. It was Saunders— a man with organizational ability—who gave the new fraternity its name. Instead of calling the meeting place "lodge," Saunders suggested the name "Grange." The term soon gained a broader connotation, often referring to the entire order as well as the local meeting place. For many people the term "Grange" is the only name they know for the order.

When the Grange was founded in 1867, there was no Department of

Agriculture, no agricultural research, no university extension service, no agricultural voice in the press, no effective farm program. One Grange publication said: "Big business and cities looked upon agriculture as something to exploit. People believed there was no end to free land and soil fertility." Thus in the order's Articles of Incorporation, it stated that one of its primary objectives was "the promotion of agriculture and other kindred pursuits by inducing cooperation among farmers and those alike interested for their mutual benefit and improvement." The POH also asserted: "We desire a proper equality, equity, and fairness; protection for the weak; restraint upon the strong; in short, justly distributed burdens and justly distributed power."

The Patrons of Husbandry was the first fraternal organization in America to admit women as full-fledged members. It was Caroline Hall, Kelley's niece, who persuaded the seven founders to enroll women by saying: "Your organization will never be permanent if you leave women out." As early as 1885 a resolution passed at the order's national convention read:

Resolved, that one of the fundamental principles of the Patrons of Husbandry, as set forth in its Declaration of Purposes, regulating membership, recognizes the equality of the two sexes. We are therefore prepared to hail with delight any advancement in the legal status of woman, which may give to her the full right of the ballot-box, and an equal condition of citizenship.

Enthusiastic over the new order, "Father" Kelley resigned his government post on April 3, 1868, and set out to promote the organization. He organized Fredonia Grange No. 1, Fredonia, New York, but this was Kelley's only success in several weeks of traveling. He came home to his Minnesota farmstead distraught and penniless, having borrowed money from Masonic friends in Madison, Wisconsin, in order to get home. Had it not been for his wife, Temperance Lane Kelley, the POH might have died that first day of May, 1868. She not only encouraged her husband but gave him the $500 that she had just received as a legacy from a relative.

Kelley's second traveling effort bore fruit. By February, 1869, a statewide grange was organized in his home state, Minnesota. Two years later, Iowa formed a state organization. By 1875 the Grange was established in thirty-six of the thirty-nine states then in the Union. It has over 850,000 members. Farmers saw the Grange as their spokesman. It presented their cause.

In the 1880s the Grange came upon difficult times. Its membership suffered losses, not only because of an economic depression but also as a result of competing farmers' groups. One such group was the Farmers' Alliance, a secret political organization. Grangers, who were impatient with their order's efforts to educate farmers and legislators and its nonpartisan posture, joined the Farmers' Alliance and similar groups. By 1890, however, the Grange once more began to prosper.

Even though the Grange has always been a nonpartisan organization, in that it has never supported any particular candidate or political party, it nevertheless has been very active in promoting legislation favorable to the agricultural community. It prides itself on having been instrumental or influential in accomplishing the following: the university-based agricultural extension service, removal of federal tax on fuel for "on-the-farm" use, free rural mail delivery, the parcel post system, Cabinet rank for the Secretary of Agriculture, implementation of the Rural Electrification Administration, a rural telephone program, farm cooperatives, antitrust laws, Social Security for farmers, tariff and trade reforms, soil conservation programs, school lunch programs, Food for Peace, the farm-parity concept, and others.

Very important to the Grange is its elaborate and highly symbolic ritual. At Kelley's urging the order adopted a secret ritual with several degrees, signs, passwords, and regalia. The Grange has retained its ritual to the present day. Every member must acquire at least four degrees. All four degrees employ symbolism derived from nature and agricultural life. The first degree is named "Degree of Preparation," which teaches the lesson of "Faith." The candidate for this degree is called "Laborer or Maid." The ritual setting is a farm scene in spring. The candidate is hoodwinked, seeking employment, and "traveling in search of light and knowledge." The candidate vows not to reveal the Grange's secrets, to obey the laws of the land, to be impartial in suggesting names for new members, and not to defraud a fellow member. Violations may lead to suspension or expulsion from the order. A brief address is given by the Grange Master, who removes the hoodwink, but before doing so he says: "My friends, to primeval darkness, covering the face of the deep, came the command, 'Light be!' " The hoodwink is suddenly removed, and the candidate hears, "and light was!" The second degree is the "Degree of Culture," sought by a "Cultivator" or "Shepherdess," who will receive the lesson of "Hope." The setting of this degree is a farm scene in early summer. The third degree, "Harvest," is given in a farm setting at harvest time. The candidate for this degree is a "harvester" or "Gleaner," who will be taught the lesson of "Charity." The fourth degree is given in a setting of a farm home in winter. This is the "Home Degree," which teaches the lesson of "Fidelity." Pursuers of this degree are "Husbandmen" or "Mastons." All four degrees require separate vows.

The degrees are worked (a common expression in fraternal groups) in the subordinate (local) grange meetings. Officers in a typical meeting are the Grand Master, Gate Keeper, Overseer, Steward, and Chaplain. Their titles are derived from the old English estate. A lecturer (Worthy Lecturer), not drawn from the English estate, is in charge of education.

The Patrons of Husbandry also works a fifth (Pomona), sixth (Flora), and seventh (Ceres or Demeter) degree. These are given on the district (county), state, and national levels, respectively. The district assembles quarterly, and the state and national groups meet annually. The seventh degree interprets "all of the ritualism of the Subordinate, Pomona, and State Granges . . . [and] is drawn from the most spectacular agriculture ritual in all the world's history." The Assembly of Demeter (holders of the seventh degree) is the Grange's "Supreme Court," where charges against officers of the Grange on the national level can be heard.

Religion plays a big role in the life of the Grange. All its meetings are opened and closed with prayer in the presence of an open Bible lying on an altar. In administering the four degrees on the subordinate level, at least forty-three Bible passages are quoted. One of the order's publications proudly notes: "It is often said that no other association has within it so much of religion with so little sectarianism. . . ."

As has been noted, the Grange has always admitted men and women as members who are fourteen or older. For the youth, ages five to fourteen, the POH conducts a Junior Grange that has its own ritual, degree work, educational programs, social activities, and community projects.

In addition to having affected new farm programs, policies, and legislation, the Grange has also been very active in community service. It has helped construct community buildings, donated medical equipment, remade and refinished hundreds of toys for Christmas, developed recreation parks, and provided scholarships.

Over the years the Grange has been quite responsive to organizational change, especially in adopting new goals. Since the 1960s, the order has actively been encouraging and promoting private enterprise. In 1914 it entered the life insurance business, calling its operation Farmers National Life Insurance Company. Today it is known as Farmers Traders Life Insurance Company. The National Grange Mutual Insurance Company was organized in 1923. The Grange Mutual Life Company, designed to help Grange members in economic need, was begun in the 1930s. To provide a clearing house for the reinsurance of risks by member companies, the National Federation of Grange Mutual Insurance Companies was founded in 1934. These insurance firms were organized after two previous companies, Patrons Mutual Insurance Company of Connecticut and Grange Insurance Association, had already been founded in 1887 and 1894, respectively. The latter was confined to the state of Washington.

More recently (1960s and 1970s), the Grange has added family unity as one of its objectives. It believes family unity can be practiced in part by families as members of the Grange. One of its publications asserts: "The Grange is one of the very few places where the whole family—all ages—may attend together for sociability, education, and to meet other families on a common level of understanding." The order also selects a "Young Couple of the Year" from one of its granges.

Sensitive to the increasingly urban way of life in the United States, the Grange now admits to its membership anyone who is interested in agriculture. Farming or rural residence is no longer a membership prerequisite.

In its long history, the Grange has received many noteworthy recognitions from high-status individuals. Every president of the United States, from Ulysses Grant to Gerald Ford has publicly praised the Grange. Franklin D. Roosevelt and Harry S. Truman not only lauded the organization but held membership in it as well. Numerous governors, over the years, have paid tribute to the order by declaring one week in April as Grange Week.

Organizationally, the Grange conducts its business on local, district, state, and national levels. The national Grange has a "Grand Master," and there is no limit on the number of years he may serve as head of the national structure. The national offices are headquartered in Washington, D.C.

The Grange emblem is a shield with seven corners (presumably one corner for each of the seven degrees available in the POH). In the center of the shield is a wheat sheaf, flanked by a "P" on its left and an "H" on its right, with "of" between the two letters. Just below these letters a band, bearing the word GRANGE, stretches across the shield.

Information on the Patrons of Husbandry is quite abundant in comparison to some other fraternal groups. An excellent source, although somewhat dated, is Solon Justus Buck's book, *The Granger Movement: A Study of Agricultural Organization and Its Political and Social Manifestations, 1870-1880* (1903, republished 1965). See also W. L. Robinson, *The Grange, 1867-1967* (1966). A booklet, *The Grange Blue Book*, published by the POH, gives a nutshell account of the organization's 100 years of history.

PENELOPE, DAUGHTERS OF (DOP). Seven years after the Ahepa* was organized in 1922 to promote fellowship and good citizenship and to advance better understanding of the Greeks and their culture, twenty-five women relatives of Ahepans met in San Francisco, California, in 1929 to form a ladies' auxiliary to the Order of Ahepa. The founding ladies met in the home of Dr. Emmanuel Apostolides, a deputy supreme governor in one of the Ahepan district lodges. Mrs. Apostolides, well versed in Greek culture, thought the new order should be called "Daughters of Penelope" in honor of the virtuous and faithful wife of Ulysses (Odysseus) in Greek mythology.

In organizing themselves, the Daughters of Penelope leaned heavily on two sources: the constitution of the Order of the Eastern Star* (an auxiliary to Freemasonry) and *Robert's Rules of Order*. The Eastern Star served the new order well in terms of developing its ritual.

The organization has prospered quite well in terms of membership growth. By 1939, ten years after the order's birth, it had grown to 5,000 members in ninety-five chapters. During the World War II years the order suffered a decline, but by 1947 the membership roster began to grow again, so that by 1953 the membership stood over 5,600. Its 1977 membership roll boasted 14,000 "daughters" in 314 chapters.

In benevolency efforts, the society sometimes assists the Ahepa. For instance, during World War II they rallied to the side of the Ahepans in selling war bonds. However, there are numerous benevolent projects that the women have carried out by themselves. From 1949 to 1971 over $37,000 was given in scholarships for female students. The order has contributed to relief funds, medical projects, cancer research, and cultural programs. Much of the society's charity dollar goes to projects that are part of the "Ahepan family," as they refer to themselves and to the Ahepans. St. Basil's Academy (a grammar school for orphans operated by the Ahepans), the Penelopean Shelter Home in Greece, Ypsilanti Greek Theatre, and the Patriarchate Fund are examples of projects in which the "Ahepan family" has vested interests.

Members of the Daughters of Penelope, officially adopted by the Ahepans in 1934, do not resent being an auxiliary group of the all-male order. One past grand president of the DOP in 1972 said: "We who are Daughters of Penelope are truly fortunate to be part of the AHEPA family, and we hope we have lived up to the expectations of the Ahepans. . . ." The Daughters' national headquarters in Washington, D.C., is at the same address as that of the Ahepans. Moreover, the ladies hold their national (supreme lodge) conventions simultaneously with those of the Ahepans.

Structurally, DOP operates on three levels, as does its "brother" society, Ahepa. While the Ahepans call their national organization "Supreme Lodge," the Daughters call theirs the "Grand Lodge." The state or territory lodges are known as "Districts," and the local lodge level is referred to as "Chapter." Each chapter usually carries a distinctive name, for example, "Hellas," "Hermione," or "Eos." On the grand lodge level most officers bear titles very similar to the Order of Ahepa. The top grand lodge level position is the Grand President, followed by the Grand Vice President, Grand Vice President of Canada, Grand Secretary, Grand Treasurer. There are also three governors and a national advisor. The grand lodge meets in convention once each year.

Literature on the Daughters of Penelope is sparse. George J. Leber's book, *The History of the Order of Ahepa* (1972), contains one chapter on the DOP as well as a number of references in his discussion of the Ahepans.

PENNSYLVANIA SLOVAK CATHOLIC UNION (PSCU). On June 24, 1893, in the town of Pittston another American fraternal benefit group was born. The organizers of this society were Slovak miners from the anthracite coal region of Pennsylvania. The society, like so many other fraternal groups, was formed to provide some economic assurance for the members and their families in the event of sickness, disability, or death. These objectives are still primary with the society.

Membership is open to males and females who are "of Slavonic origin or descent, not less than sixteen (16) years of age, of sound body and mind, of exemplary habits, of good moral character and a practical Roman or Byzantine Catholic, residing in the United States." Presently (1979) the PSCU has approximately 10,000 members. This represents a decline from 13,095 that the society had in 1965. Each member is required to take an oath of allegiance to the society. The oath is simple and unencumbered.

Similar to most other fraternal benefit groups, the PSCU conducts a number of fraternal activities for its members on the local, district, and national level. The society supports religious and literary projects that promote good citizenship and ethnicity. Member families receive financial aid when hit by natural disasters.

The officers of the society bear titles similar to those of many other fraternals. The chief national officer is known as the "Supreme President." Being a Catholic group, the organization has a "Supreme Chaplain." Local groups also have a chaplain. The chaplain is seen as the final authority relative to religious questions and issues.

Local groups are called "Branches." Regional structures are referred to as "Districts." The highest authority is the national convention. A board of directors meets between conventions. Headquarters are maintained in Wilkes-Barre, Pennsylvania.

For additional information, see *By-Laws of the Pennsylvania Slovak Catholic Union* (1974). The monthly newspaper, *Bratstvo*, which is published in Slavic and English, also provides news and details about the society.

PENTE, ORDER OF. This fraternal benefit group was founded in 1888 in Philadelphia, Pennsylvania. The name "Pente" (five) was derived from the society's practice of issuing short-term, five-year certificates instead of paying death benefits. Men and women were able to become members. Its headquarters was located in Philadelphia, Pennsylvania. REFERENCE: *Cyc. Frat.*

P.E.O. SISTERHOOD (PEO). Of all the fraternal secret societies, the PEO is without a doubt the most secretive. The order has even kept the meaning of the letters P.E.O. secret; however, it is believed that they stand for Protect Each Other. A few things are known about the society, in spite of its secretive stance. For instance, the society was founded at Iowa Wesleyan College on January 21, 1870, by seven senior coeds. A "Supreme Chapter" was formed in 1883. It is the only female fraternal group that is unaffiliated with any male order.

The PEO is not a fraternal life insurance group. Its primary function is social and educational. In conformity with its educational interests, the order supports Cottey Junior College, Nevada, Missouri.

As a fraternal secret socity, the PEO has its secret ritual. Lodge sessions, in conformity with the ritual requirements, are conducted quite solemnly. Prayer and Bible readings reportedly are a regular part of a given lodge meeting. One of the society's officers is a chaplain. The official flower of the PEO is the marguerite. Its emblem is a five-pointed star.

Membership is open to white females who believe in a supreme being. Most commonly the order appeals to Protestant ladies from the upper end of the social status continuum. In the mid-1960s it had 130,000 members. The writer was unable to obtain the 1979 membership count.

The present report is largely based on William Whalen, *Handbook of Secret Organizations*, 1966. Other sources of information are difficult to obtain.

PHILALETHES SOCIETY, THE (TPS). The word philalethes is derived from two Greek words: *philos* (meaning "friend") and *alethia* (meaning "truth"). Thus the TPS is a society organized by Freemasons who desire to learn more about the "truths" conveyed by Masonry. The TPS was organized on October 1, 1928. In addition to being an organization engaged in studying and researching the many facts of Freemasonry,* the society also attempts to form "a bond of union for isolated Masonic writers and also to protect editors of Masonic publications from undeserved aggression of some 'dressed in a little brief authority.' "

The idea for the Philalethes Society was spawned by a California Masonic editor who also has been a member of the Boston Press Club. The TPS now is an international organization of Freemasons "who *seek more Light and . . . who have more Light to impart.*" The society also encourages individuals to write accurate and interesting articles for its periodical, *The Philalethes*, a bimonthly publication.

Membership is open only to Master Masons (third-degree members of Freemasonry). A recommendation from a member of the society is necessary. The society has the following classes of membership: (1) Regular Members—those who are Master Masons in good standing; (2) Fellows—regular members who have been honored by the society for outstanding service to Freemasonry and TPS; (3) Subscribers—individuals or organizations who are ineligible for membership but wish to receive the TPS publications.

The TPS sponsors a Masonic workshop during Masons Week in February of each year. The workshop is an informal get-together in Washington, D.C. It is during the Masonic Week that the TPS also holds its annual convention. TPS also encourages small groups of its members (as few as two or three) to meet and cultivate their interests when and wherever feasible. There were 2,100 members of the society in 1979.

The TPS has no degrees or rituals. It does, however, designate certain members as "Fellows" from time to time. These individuals write the letters F.P.S. behind their names. The Fellows are referred to as the "Forty Immortals of Masonic Scholars."

The emblem of the society consists of an inner and outer circle on which appears: THE PHILALETHES SOCIETY . . . INTERNATIONAL . . . FOUNDED 1928. In the center of the smaller ring is the Masonic compass and square with a burning lamp in the center. Behind the upper part of the compass is an open book (presumably the Bible), which has the words FIAT LUX above it. Beneath the compass and square is the Latin word VERITAS.

Organizationally, the TPS has no subordinate bodies. It has a slate of seven officers: President, First Vice President, Second Vice President, Executive Secretary, Treasurer, Editor of *The Philalethes Magazine*, and Editor Emeritus. The latter is John Black Vrooman, a well-known Masonic scholar. The society's business and communication are executed by the executive secretary, who presently (1979) resides in Columbia, Maryland.

The best, and really the only, information on the TPS is the society's publication, *The Philalethes*. The reader may obtain copies of this magazine in Masonic libraries or by subscribing to it.

PILGRIM FATHERS, UNITED ORDER OF (OPF). This organization was founded in 1878 in Lawrence, Massachusetts, by members of several other fraternal orders. When the order was founded, it had intended only to confine itself to the New England states. Its fraternal insurance was based on the graded assessment plan by the 1890s. By 1910 the membership had decreased to 18,000 from 23,000 in 1898.

Local units were known as "Colonies." The highest authority structure was called "Supreme Colony."

Information pertaining to the OPF was primarily drawn from Albert C. Stevens, *Cyclopedia of Fraternities* (1907). Some items were also selected from back issues of *Statistics Fraternal Societies*.

PIONEER FRATERNAL ASSOCIATION. This fraternal benefit group was organized in 1892 in Manitoba, Canada. It provided aid to retarded children and awarded scholarships. Its membership in the 1960s was about 1,600, including juvenile members. In 1972 the society merged with The Wawanesa Mutual Life Insurance Company, Winnipeg, Manitoba. Former headquarters were also in Winnipeg, Manitoba, Canada.

POCAHONTAS, DEGREE OF (DOP). In 1885 in Elmira, New York, a ladies' auxiliary of the Improved Order of Red Men* was authorized by the Red Men, and in 1887 the first council (local chapter) was begun in Philadelphia, Pennsylvania. The newly founded group was given the name Degree of Pocahontas in honor of an Indian princess. The DOP has as its objectives teaching kindness, love, charity, and loyalty to one's country. More specifically, the Red Men's auxiliary stands for: (1) love and respect for the American flag, (2) preserving the American way of life, (3) keeping alive the legends and customs of the American Indian, (4) creating and inspiring greater patriotism, (5) joining its members together in love and friendship, and (6) providing organized charity for those in need.

The order has a secret ritual with password and secret signs. New members are required to go through the order's initiation ceremony, and a fee also is assessed. Membership figures for 1977 showed 22,827 members. This represented a decline of 1,731 from the previous "two Great Suns," as the society expresses the period of two years since it held its previous national convention.

The emblem of the Pocahontas displays the portrait of an Indian maiden with two American flags on each side of her. On her chest is a shield bearing the words Degree of Pocahontas.

Most of the charity programs operated by the DOP are frequently also those of the Red Men. Its project called AID (American Indian Development) is a national health and education care program for American Indian children. Financial support for braille books for the blind is another altruistic venture of DOP. Another charity project is the Retarded Children's Program. The Indian Affairs Project furnishes food, clothing, and other items of necessity to Indian reservations.

Concerning civic affairs, the DOP honor the unknown soldiers and those who have died in defense of the United States by joining the Red Men at Arlington National Cemetery each year for a memorial service. The order also provides financial support to fight communism. Each year on December 16th the ladies participate with the Red Men in commemorating the Boston Tea Party of 1773. This day is commemorated because the individuals who tossed the tea overboard were white men disguised as Indians. Many believe these "Indians" were from the Sons of Liberty and also from Freemasonry*. In recent years the Pocahontas have been promoting a national program for safe driving.

The Pocahontas publicize their order as "Pocahontas Have Fun, Too!" There are a number of social activities that each council (local chapter) sponsors. These activities are dances, cookouts, picnics, sports, and socials.

Indian names are used for various terms and titles. "Council," a local lodge; "Tepee," a meeting place; "Pocahontas," president of a local lodge; "Powhatan," male counselor; "Prophetess," immediate past president; "Kindling the Council Fire," opening the meeting.

As an auxiliary, the Pocahontas have a national organization known as the National Degree of Pocahontas. This group is made up of Past Great Pocahontases (state presidents). This national group, however, is under the supervision and authority of the Great Council of the United States of the Improved Order of Red Men. The national group has a Board of Great Chiefs, which is elected from Past Great Pocahontas who attend the national sessions. The Board of Great Chiefs consists of seven officers. The state organization is similar to the structure of the national organization, and the local council is similar to the state group. The executive officer's address for the Pocahontas is in Oakley, California.

The writer knows of no separate book that has been published on the Degree of Pocahontas. The interested reader may obtain brief pamphlets concerning the order, or he may gather information in a piecemeal fashion by consulting the published proceedings of the national conventions. Helpful insights may also be obtained by reading the IORM magazine, *Red Men*.

POLICE AND FIREMAN'S INSURANCE ASSOCIATION (PFIA). This association was founded in Indianapolis, Indiana, in 1913 by a group of policemen and firemen. A series of catastrophies that resulted in large numbers of casualties in both occupational groups left a number of families financially destitute and prompted the formation of the PFIA. The association's initial objective was to be in a position to provide "immediate assistance in times of adversity due to sickness, injuries, or death." In addition to providing financial assistance to its members when disabled, the present (1976) constitution states: "The object of the Association shall be to create a Supreme Lodge and Subordinate Branches for the purpose inculcating principles of friendship and brotherhood among Police Officers and Fire Fighters [*sic*]."

When the PFIA was organized, there was no intention to have the association be anything but a local group. In time, however, the association's effectiveness and popularity spread to other American cities and states. Thus today the PFIA has members in thirty-nine states and the District of Columbia. It is the largest organization in the world whose membership is limited to policemen and firefighters. Like other fraternal benefit groups, the PFIA is nonprofit and nonpolitical in its orientation. The insurance program is supervised by the Indiana Department of Insurance.

The association's constitution specifies membership requirements as follows: "Any man or woman of good moral character and good general health, and between the ages of eighteen and forty-nine. . . ." The prospective candidate for membership must also be a member of a police or fire department. Currently (1979) the PFIA has 14,000 members. This membership count is a significant drop (a loss of 63 percent) from the 38,000 members the association had in 1967.

The association has no formal or secret ritual, but it does open its supreme (national) convention proceedings with a processional hymn and other religious trappings. The emblem of the society is a circle with a smaller circle inside. This forms a border containing the inscription: Police and Firemen's Insurance Association. Inside the smaller circle are two shields, one bearing the letter "F" and the other the letter "P." Above the two shields is an eagle with outstretched wings, and below the shields are two hands clasped in fraternal friendship.

The slogan or motto of the PFIA is "Each Other's Keeper." In line with this slogan, each local unit is required to have a Relief Committee that is to visit the sick and injured members. The committee is also called on to "approve or disapprove or correct all claims for benefits and otherwise represent the members of the Section [local unit] in all business matters with the Association."

Local groups, as noted, are called "Sections." Each section is required to meet at least once per month. The highest level of authority is the national convention, known as the "Supreme Legislative Body." The supreme body meets quadrennially. Its staff is headquartered in Indianapolis, Indiana.

The only background material on the PFIA are its convention proceedings and its *Constitution and By-Laws*. These are available from the head office in Indianapolis.

POLICE, FRATERNAL ORDER OF (FOP). This fraternal order was organized on May 14, 1915, in Pittsburgh, Pennsylvania, by twenty-three men of the Pittsburgh Police Department. The same day the order was founded the Superintendent of Police became quite angry upon hearing that the FOP came into being. The superintendent was so upset that he said "heads are about to fall." He accused one of the main organizers of creating turmoil in the police department.

One of the main objectives of the newly founded order was "for the purpose of bettering existing conditions for Policemen . . . for advancing Social, Benevolent and Educational undertakings among Policemen." The new constitution also said "Race, Creed or Color shall be no bar." By 1918 the FOP decided to become a national organization.

The FOP in its constitution says:

The Fraternal Order of Police shall not strike or by concerted action cause a cessation of the performance of police duties, or induce other members or lodges to do likewise. The penalty for such action by any member or subordinate lodge, shall be immediate expulsion from the Fraternal Order of Police.

While the antistrike article is still part of the society's constitution, it has not been enforced since 1967, for its was in 1967 that the FOP in Youngstown, Ohio, refused to have its members work during a salary dispute with the city. In 1974 and 1975 the FOP decided that it would not take action against members who violate the antistrike article until all efforts were exhausted on the local and state lodge level. Since 1975, other police strikes have taken place in which the FOP was implicated. Yet the antistrike clause remains in the order's constitution even though the society has in recent years become quite actively involved in unionlike methods.

The present constitution also asserts that the order is "strictly non-political, non-sectarian, and shall have no affiliation, directly or indirectly, with any labor union, congress, federation or committee of like nature or political action committee, or similar organization by whatever name known."

In the 1960s the FOP strongly opposed police review boards, first advocated by Robert F. Kennedy, the Attorney General in President John F. Kennedy's administration. In fact, one letter from the society's national president in 1962 called review boards a "sinister movement against law enforcement." The American Civil Liberties Union has also not met with favor, apparently because it has taken strong stands against police brutality. The FOP has seen the police brutality issue as a liberal attempt to discredit the police. In the early 1970s the order was heartened by President Nixon's emphasis on law and order.

The insignia of the FOP consists of a five-pointed star imposed on a circle. Each of the upper three star points display the letters F. O. P., respectively. The lower left point depicts the all-seeing eye, and the lower right point portrays the fraternal handclasp. In the center of the star appear the words *Jus, Fidus, Liberatum*. It might be noted that it was not until 1967 that it was revealed to the FOP that the insignia's word *Jus* should be spelled *Ius* to be correct Latin. Moreover, *Fidus* was incorrectly translated as "friendship" by the order for years. If the society wanted the Latin word for friendship, it should have chosen *Amicitia*. And finally, *Liberatum* was not to be translated as "equality," which the organization also had been communicating erroneously to its members. The order's leadership learned upon consulting Latin specialists that *Jus* could be translated "law" instead of "justice." *Fidus* (an adjective) could read as "trustworthy" or "safe," and *Liberatum* (the genitive case) could be translated "of liberty" or "of freedom." The FOP retained the incorrect spelling of the Latin on all its stationery and other mementos. However, the national board meeting in 1968 voted unanimously to change the English translation of the motto to read: "Law Is A Safeguard of Freedom." To change the Latin spellings was seen as too expensive.

Members are required to be initiated according to a ritual. The ritual, among other things, has an oath which requires the members to pledge secrecy so that nonmembers do not discover the "secrets" of the society: "I will not divulge any of the secrets of this Order to any one not entitled to receive them." As in most rituals, the FOP ritual has its religious elements. A lodge chaplain commonly speaks the prayers. One prayer reads:

Our Father, who art in Heaven, we ask Thee to bless this meeting. Endow us with Thy Spirit. May all our actions be guided by Thy hand that we may be fair and just to all. Bless the Order and all members everywhere. We ask it in Thy name. Amen.

Currently (1978) the FOP has 138,472 members in thirty-four state groups. There are about 1,250 local units throughout the thirty-four state structures. Local groups are called "Lodges." The national structure is known as the "Grand Lodge." Headquarters of the order are housed in Indianapolis, Indiana.

The interested reader may obtain additional information by reading Justin E. Walsh, *The Fraternal Order of Police, 1915-1976* (1977). This volume was written by a professional historian. Other sources are the order's periodical, *Fraternal Order of Police Journal*, and the order's *Grand Lodge Minutes*.

POLISH BENEFICIAL ASSOCIATION, THE (PBA). As was true of countless European immigrants who had come to the United States in the latter part of the nineteenth century, the Poles in the Philadelphia area, like others who formed fraternal benefit societies, realized that they needed some insurance for their beneficiaries and some means of providing aid when sickness, accidents, and old age became a fact of life. This realization led to the founding of the Polish Beneficial Association in 1899.

Looking back on the origin of the society, one of the order's publications said concerning its golden jubilee: "Where else would have been cultivated our Polish manners, and customs? Where else could have been found the 'at-home' atmosphere? Where, the Polish language, that language of our daily lives, essential holy, beloved, so dear to the heart of our ancestors? Where, the Polish priest." This type of ethnic pride is still quite charactristic of the PBA. The society's official newspaper, *Pol-Am Journal*, carries statements in bold type such as "The Pleasure of Being Polish," "The Pole has been defeated, but he has never been conquered, because he never surrenders," and so forth.

As a fraternal benefit society, the PBA offers its members the usual life insurance certificates and fraternal benefits. Members may obtain cash value, extended term, and full-paid insurance certificates. Juvenile certificates are available for individuals under fifteen years of age.

Requirements for membership stipulate that the individual be "of good moral reputatation, Polish, Lithuanian or Slavic descent, Roman, Byzantine or Greek Catholic faith." The constitution also states that persons "not of Polish or Slavic descent who are related by marriage to a Polish, Lithuanian or Slavic person and who are of the Roman, Byzantine or Greek Catholic faith may become members of . . ." the PBA. Two classes of membership are available: active (insured) and honorary. The latter "may be a person who has rendered a great service to the Association, to our faith, to our country, to mankind, or to people of Polish origin." The minimum age for joining the society is sixteen years. Once accepted for membership, the candidate "shall sign and orally pronounce the oath by the Central Committee." Juvenile members are exempted from taking the oath. Presently (1979) the PBA has 16,000 members in 105 local units. This represents a loss since 1967, when the society had 24,500 members on its roster.

The PBA is quite active in fraternal and charitable activities. Individuals from local units visit the disabled, sick, and handicapped members. Scholarships are awarded to college students. Various recreational activities are offered for the youth. Folk dances, polka parties, ballroom dances, Halloween frolics, and other leisure activities are sponsored by the society on a regular basis.

The PBA is quite close to the Roman Catholic Church. In fact, the society is under the patronage of St. John Cantius, a fifteenth-century saint who once taught theology at the Jagiellonian University in Cracow. Legend has it that he diligently transcribed Latin and Greek manuscripts into the wee hours of the night so he could sell them and give the money to needy university students. The society keeps religious activities alive for its members by holding Masses, services for the living and deceased members, and an annual pilgrimage to the National Shrine of Our Lady of Czestochowa in Doylestown, Pennsylvania. This latter activity is sponsored by all local units of the society.

The emblem of the society is a white eagle with a shield on its breast. The shield is divided into four parts. One part displays the fraternal handclasp; one portrays the American flag and also the Polish flag; the third section has a cross and a sacred heart; the fourth portion shows the portrait of a Polish patriot. Below the shield and eagle are the words: Polish Beneficial Association. The society has no secret ritual.

Local gatherings are called "Groups." Nationally, the society refers to itself as the "Association." The highest authority is the national convention, which occurs quadrennially. The head offices of the PBA are in Philadelphia, Pennsylvania.

Additional information on the PBA is largely confined to the society's official periodical, *Pol-Am Journal*, and its constitution and bylaws. The society has published two very brief histories, one for its golden jubilee and one for its seventy-fifth anniversary. Both are available from the national offices.

POLISH FALCONS OF AMERICA (PFA). This group first received its charter in Chicago on May 1, 1894, although it had organized its first "nest" (local chapter) in 1887. By the time it received its first charter in 1894 the order had twelve nests in operation. The name at the time of being chartered was Alliance of Polish Turners of the United States of America.

The PFA was founded as a "fraternal and physical culture organization" with its inspiration being the Latin Maxim: *mens sana in corpore sano* (sound mind in a sound body). In 1914 the former name was changed to Polish Falcons Alliance of America. Its objectives were at this time also modified. Specifically, the order stated: "The object of the Polish Falcons Alliance of America is to regenerate the Polish race [*sic*] in body and spirit and create of the immigrant a national asset, for the purpose of exerting every possible influence towards attaining political independence of the fatherland."

The objectives of 1914 remained until 1924 when the group was rein-corporated in Pennsylvania. ʿThe 1924 objectives now sought "To maintain private parks, club houses, and the facilities for skating, boating, trotting and other innocent and athletic sports, including clubs for such purposes in order to improve the physical, mental and social condition of its members." On March 30, 1928, the order changed its name again, this time to Polish Falcons of America; and again its purposes were altered. The new objectives spoke of accumulating and maintaining a fund for sickness, accident, and death benefits, along with promoting social and physical culture.

In order to join the PFA one must be between sixteen and sixty years of age, of good moral character, mentally and physically sound, and of Polish or Slavic descent. Spouses of Polish or Slavic descents may join regardless of their ethnic origin. There are two types of memberships: beneficial and social. The former has insurance with the Falcons, whereas the latter does not. In 1978 there were 26,346 beneficial members and 2,867 social members. The latter have no voice or vote relative to insurance concerns.

All members are initiated according to the ritual of the order. Part of the ritual requires each candidate to take the Falcon oath:

I, (give full name), having become acquainted with the knightly ideals of the Polish Falcons of America, join its ranks knowingly and voluntarily and solemnly swear before God and those present to faithfully serve the Falcon order, conscientiously defend it precepts [*sic*] and follow its rules and regulations, so help me God.

The emblem of the PFA is the falcon with wings outstretched and clutch-ing a barbell in his talons. The PFA usually displays the emblem on a banner.

The Falcons' activities, for the most part, focus on developing and main-taining social, educational, and physical qualities. Most of the order's 160 nests conduct gymnastic classes. Golfing and bowling tournaments are held nationally each year, as well as district tournaments. Track and field events are held biennially on the district level. Summer camps are operated for hundreds of youngsters. Scholarships are available for deserving college students, but they must major or minor in physical education or possess proven athletic talent, as well as participate in Falcon gym classes. The order also maintains a museum.

On the local scene the PFA calls its gatherings "Nests." Each nest has the general array of officers found in other fraternal and benevolent groups. The regional structures are known as districts. Each district must have at least 500 members. The national organization meets in convention every four years. Pittsburgh, Pennsylvania, has been the national home of the PFA since 1912.

For information see *Constitution and By-Laws of the Polish Falcons of America* (1973). The semimonthly newspaper, *Sokol Polski*, which is published in Polish and English, gives news of the order. Other information in pamphlet and brochure form may be obtained from the national office.

POLISH NATIONAL ALLIANCE OF BROOKLYN, U.S.A. (PNA). This is one of several Polish fraternal benefit groups in the United States. It was founded in 1903. Although it has a local name, the society has members in Connecticut, Michigan, Minnesota, New Jersey, and New York. It is licensed to sell insurance in all of these states. In 1960 the society absorbed the Polish American Workmen's Aid Fund.

The PNA, like a number of other Polish fraternals, is quite serious about providing support to the Catholic Church. It contributes yearly grants to the Catholic Foundation and also to theological seminaries. On the local level it regularly offers Masses to the members.

Currently (1978) the membership stands at approximately 12,000 members. This figure represents a substantial loss when compared to the membership roster of 1965. At that time the society had 21,413 members. The number of lodges also declined significantly. In 1972, for instance, there were 155 local units, but by 1978 the count had dropped to eighty-seven lodges.

The society publishes the *Polish-American Journal*. The reader may wish to consult this newspaperlike publication for further information. See also *Statistics, Fraternal Societies* (1978).

POLISH NATIONAL ALLIANCE OF THE UNITED STATES OF NORTH AMERICA (PNA). On February 14, 1880, a group of Poles, recent immigrants, gathered in Philadelphia to issue an appeal for organizing a national alliance. By September, 1880, delegates assembled in Chicago for the first convention of the Polish National Alliance. The new society formed with several objectives in mind, namely, to provide for the material and moral growth of Poles in the United States, offer protection for the Polish immigrant, enlighten the Polish immigrants politically so that they would become effective citizens, and commemorate Poland's historic anniversaries. The PNA also sought to be free of religious biases or involvement.

When the PNA was founded, it adopted the American model of most fraternal orders, namely, lodges, the initiation of new members, and a ritual. Presently (1979) the bylaws of the PNA require every applicant to "be inducted in accordance with the Ritual of the alliance."

As a fraternal, benevolent society, the PNA had by 1891 paid out $49,000 in death benefits, but the society did more than provide death benefits. In 1891 it also allocated funds for a library in Washington, D.C., which was later moved to Alliance College, a four-year liberal arts school founded by the PNA in 1912. In 1909 the PNA purchased the Polish Immigrants' Home in New York to provide aid, counsel, and protection for the immigrants from Poland. During World War II nearly a quarter million dollars were donated to the Red Cross for the aid of war casualties in Poland.

The PNA has been one of the few fraternal, benevolent groups that granted women full membership rights as early as 1900. The society takes great pride in this early action.

Today the PNA is engaged in supporting a wide variety of civic projects and activities. It provides support for youth endeavors by conducting a biennial youth jamboree on the Alliance College campus. Scholarship grants and subsidies are given to students attending Alliance College in Cambridge Springs, Pennsylvania. In addition, local lodges have their members engage in benevolent acts in their respective communities.

The PNA has two types of memberships, benefit and social members. The benefit member is one "on whose life a benefit certificate is in force." The social member has no benefit certificate and they have no voice in the government of the society. Membership qualifications require individuals to be sixteen years or older, "good moral character, physically and mentally sound, who by birth, descent, or consanguinity, are of Polish, Lithuanian, Ruthenian or Slovak nationality, and the husbands and wives of members regardless of nationality." During the past ten years the membership has slightly declined from 326,000 in 1967 to 300,000 in 1979.

The emblem of the PNA is a shield divided into three parts. The upper left portion pictures the white eagle on a red background; the upper right section portrays a mounted white knight on a blue background; the lower segment depicts Michael Archangel on a white background. The three symbols were once representative of Poland, Lithuania, and Ruthenia, respectively. Perched on the shield's top are two hands clasped together and a band bearing the letters P.N.A.

Administratively, the national convention is the highest authority. Five executive officers and a board of directors carry out the convention's resolutions and decisions between conventions. Locally its gatherings are known as "Lodges." Headquarters are maintained in Chicago, Illinois.

For additional information the reader may consult a pamphlet by the PNA, *In the Mainstreams of American Life* (1977). The society's bimonthly publication *Zgoda* provides news about the society. The *By-Laws of the Polish Alliance* are published by the organization.

POLISH NATIONAL UNION OF AMERICA (PNU). In February of 1908 some twenty-five Polish residents met in Scranton, Pennsylvania, to form Sponjnia, as the fraternal benefit society is still known to the Poles. The society was formed in the parish hall of St. Stanislaus Cathedral. By the end of 1908 the society received its charter. The first constitution of the organization declared that "Religious, political and social convictions may not hinder the admission of candidates to the P.N. Union." At the first convention of the society in 1909 the ladies were authorized to form their own branches. The PNU has always been "closely tied to the rise of the Polish National Catholic Church."

In 1923 the society moved toward a stronger actuarial base by adopting the American Experience Table, which had the effect of increasing the insurance certificates by seven percentage points. This change greatly aided the PNU; even its membership grew, so that by 1931 there were 20,000 members.

In 1929 the society purchased a farm that it developed into a home for aged and disabled members. The institution is affectionately known as Sponjnia Farm, located in Waymart, Pennsylvania. The PNU also operates Warsaw Village in Thornhurst, Pennsylvania. This village was begun in 1948 and operates as a vacation area, where tourists may rent facilities during the summer months.

Over the years the PNU has always shown great concern for Poland. This concern has especially been pronounced during the two world wars. Since 1945 the society has continued its interest in Poland, always adding a religious dimension to its efforts. For instance, the Church of Our Lady of Perpetual Help, built near the village of Zarki, Poland, was largely made possible by PNU funds.

Membership is open to males or females who are sixteen years old or older. The 1975 constitution does not specify that members must be Polish or Polish descendants. Each member is required to take a pledge that is simple and free of religious elements. It reads:

I [name and surname] solemnly promise that I will faithfully fulfill the duties of a member of the Polish National Union. I shall abide by the statutes of our Union and the enactments of the Branch. I shall always and everywhere defend the rights of my nation. I will spread brotherly love, peace and unity and propagate the principles upon which the Polish National Union is founded.

The society has no ritual or secrecy. Currently (1979) the PNU has 31,649 members in 210 branches. This represents a slight decrease since the mid-1960s when its membership was 32,142 in 247 branches.

Local units are known as "Branches." Within the society's national structure there are regional groups called "Districts." The national convention, the highest body of authority, meets quadrennially. The head offices are located in Scranton, Pennsylvania.

Additional information may be gained by reading the society's *Sponjnia: Past and Present*. It appears in pamphlet or booklet form. See also the society's newspaper, *Straz/The Guard*.

POLISH ROMAN CATHOLIC UNION OF AMERICA (PRCUA). This fraternal benefit society was founded in 1873. The group has a number of objectives, namely, strengthen and preserve spiritual values of Polish culture and heritage; foster cultural relations between the United States and Poland; encourage good citizenship and loyalty to the United States; promote Catholic action; support the clergy and the Catholic Church; sponsor sports teams; support the Polish Museum of America; aid communities; and give recognition to prominent Americans of Polish descent in the various fields of learning.

The PRCUA operates on the lodge system as a fraternal insurance group. In 1978 it had a total of 815 local lodges compared to 887 in 1972. It has lodges in twenty-five states. Chicago, Illinois, serves as the national headquarters.

For additional information, the reader may see the society's official organ, *Narod Polski*, a biweekly newspaper. It contains articles in Polish and English.

POLISH UNION OF AMERICA (PUA). Founded in 1890, this fraternal benefit society resembles many other ethnic fraternal insurance organizations. The society is very active in antidefamation efforts, trying to curb prejudice against Polish culture, tradition, and its descendants. Like many other fraternals, the PUA provides colleges scholarships; it also contributes to churches and charities, as well as to educational foundations.

The society's White Eagle Young Adults Club is actively engaged in promoting the preservation of Polish culture and values. The order also sponsors a weekly radio newscast giving Polish-American informational items.

Membership consists of individuals of Polish ancestry. In 1979 the membership count stood at about 10,000. Headquarters are maintained in Buffalo, New York.

For additional information, see the organization's monthly publication: *PUA Parade*. Other information may be obtained from brochures and pamphlets issued by the society.

POLISH WOMEN'S ALLIANCE (PWA). May 22, 1898, was the founding date of this Polish fraternal beneficiary group. The site of the organization's origin was Chicago, Illinois. The society began as a group to serve primarily local Polish women. Today, however, it is a national concern, doing fraternal insurance business in seventeen states.

In the PWA's eighty years of service the society has not only dispensed fraternal insurance to its members but also tried to preserve Polish traditions and customs in the United States. The society sponsors Polish language, literature, folklore, history, folkdance lessons, festivals, and youth conferences. In recent years the PWA has also worked diligently to improve women's rights in the United States.

Like so many fraternal benefit groups, the PWA each year contributes tens of thousands of college scholarship monies to eligible members of the organization. A fraternal aid fund is maintained to help needy members. Several religious, hospital, and children's institutions receive financial assistance in Poland. One of these institutions is a home for blind children in Laski, Poland.

Membership in the society has continued to grow so that today it has 90,000 members. Membership is open to women of "Polish extraction and/or conviction."

Officers in the society are known as Honorary President, President, Vice President, Secretary General, and so on. Regional groups are known as "Councils," while local units are called "Groups." Headquarters are housed in the Chicago suburb of Park Ridge, Illinois.

The interested reader may wish to consult the society's semimonthly publication, *Glos Polek* (Voice of Polish Women). The paper is printed in Polish and in English.

PORTUGUESE CONTINENTAL UNION OF THE UNITED STATES OF AMERICA (PCUUSA). After a number of meetings were held in several towns in Massachusetts during the summer of 1925, interested individuals of Portuguese birth organized the PCUUSA, as a fraternal benefit society. The society was somewhat slow in getting fully established, apparently because just prior to 1925 two fraternal societies had folded in the Massachusetts area. Nevertheless, the society organizers did not give up, and so by 1930 the first annual convention took place in Plymouth, Massachusetts.

When the society was organized, only men born in continental Portugal or their male descendants were eligible for membership. At the 1930 convention, however, it became permissible for "men and women of Portuguese birth or descent, white race regardless of their origin . . ." to join the PCUUSA. But women were not able to receive disability benefits. The 1938 convention added another dimension to the society by creating a juvenile insurance department. In 1958 the society adopted the following resolution:

To unite fraternally all persons of Portuguese ancestry, whose ages are not under 16 and not over 60 years, of good moral character, mentally and physically able to earn their livelihood, born in any part of the world and residents of the United States of America or any other country where this Society [sic] maintains subordinate lodges, and any other persons who, by reasons of language, marriage, education or culture may be integrated in the Portuguese Community.

Current (1979) membership stands at about 9,000 members in seventy lodges.

The PCUUSA, like most fraternal benefit socieites, has a ritual it keeps secret from nonmembers. In line with a secret ritual the society elects an inner guard whose task it is to keep nonmembers away from society meetings. The emblem of the society is a Maltese-like cross with a circle and a shield superimposed upon the cross.

Since the late 1960s the society has been awarding scholarships to students of Portuguese ancestry. Other activities sponsored by the PCUUSA include studying and analyzing social problems pertaining to the Portuguese-American community so that some solutions might be implemented. Various leisure activities are also conducted: outings, movies, dances, parties, parades, and picnics. A Peter Francisco Award is given to honor any person who makes a notable contribution to the Portuguese-American culture and well-being of the members of the Portuguese-American community.

On the local level the society refers to its units as "Subordinate Lodges." Regional groupings are known as "Districts," and the national authority is called "Supreme Lodge." The convention itself is called "Congress of Delegates." Headquarters are in Boston, Massachusetts.

About the only source available on the PCUUSA is the golden anniversary book that was published in 1975. It was obtained from the national headquarters.

PORTUGUESE UNION OF THE STATE OF CALIFORNIA (UPEC). The letters U.P.E.C. represent the Portuguese name for the society, UNIAO PORTUGUESA DO ESTADO DA CALIFORNIA. The origin of the UPEC dates back to August 1, 1880, when thirty Portuguese immigrants organized the society in San Leandro, California. One of the society's publications reads: "Even though times have changed drastically in the past 94 years, the objectives of U.P.E.C. are still the same; unity among its members, protection through up-to-date insurance plans, and charity with justice to those in need." The UPEC is the oldest domestic fraternal insurance order in California.

The society got started in 1880 by thirty men who were compelled to take up a collection to bury one of their fellow Portuguese immigrants. The UPEC began, like most fraternal benefit groups, with the assessment method. When a member died, each was assessed $1.00. In 1896 the society created a sick benefit fund, and in 1928 a charity fund, started informally in 1890, was established on a permanent basis.

As an ethnic fraternal insurance society, the UPEC has been less nationalistic than most, for in 1888 it admitted its first non-Portuguese member.

The policy of admitting non-Portuguese has only briefly been interrupted, one such period was from 1889 to 1892. The society takes considerable pride in its policy. Its present (1979) membership is 12,000.

From the order's beginning, it has been a society that has valued its ritual. Thus the UPEC has the usual array of officers who are charged with given ritualistic duties. The ritual, however, is quite brief, devoid of mythical legend. As presently constituted, the ritual has several agendas, pertaining to the initiation of new members, installation of officers, ceremonies for the organization of subordinate councils, rites for the dedication of new UPEC buildings, funeral oration, pledge of allegiance, American national anthem, and God Bless America. Until 1937 the ritual work was conducted in the Portuguese language.

Over the years the UPEC has been approached by other fraternal benefit groups to form mergers or consolidations. The first merger request came from the Portuguese Society of Queen Saint Isabel (SPRSI) in 1901. The UPEC, however, declined. In 1927 a second appeal was made by the SPRSI, and again the petition was declined. Other fraternals have tried to merge with the UPEC, but thus far none have occurred.

The UPEC is quite supportive of a number of cultural projects and programs. Serious efforts are made in promoting bilingualism and in preserving the Portuguese culture. The society houses some 4,000 books on Portuguese history, available to the public interested in Portuguese studies. Most of the newspapers published by the Portuguese in California are also housed in the society's library. The society also maintains a small museum of Portuguese artifacts.

Local groups or units are known as "Subordinate Councils." There are seventy-seven councils in the society, which operates only in California and Nevada. The national authority is referred to as the "Supreme Council." It meets in convention annually. Head offices are situated in San Leandro, California.

An excellent source for further information about the UPEC is the book by Carlos Almeida, *Portuguese Immigrants* (1979). This book was written to celebrate the society's centennial. Other helpful materials are the organization's ritual, known as *Ceremonial of the Subordinate Councils of the U.P.E.C.* (1962). The bylaws of the order may also be consulted. Finally, the reader will find helpful information concerning the UPEC in its quarterly publication, *Life*.

PRAETORIANS, MODERN ORDER OF (MOP). Organized in 1898, the society in many ways resembled the Modern Woodmen of America.* As a fraternal benefit society, the MOP had a secret ritual in the typical fashion of fraternal orders. Local groups were known as "Councils," and the national governing body was called the "Supreme Senate." The MOP maintained its head offices in Dallas, Texas. In 1957 the society became a mutual life insurance company.

PRESBYTERIAN BENEFICIAL UNION (PBU). Founded in 1901 in Pennsylvania by a group of Presbyterian Calvinists, this fraternal benefit society today has several objectives. It seeks to be "a truly fraternal social order, with all its connotated benefits among members of Presbyterian churches." Other objectives are to cultivate "wholesome humanitarian brotherhood" and "to share in the benefits derived from denominational mutual insurance." Throughout the existence of the PBU it has always been a church-affiliated society, made up of "staunch Presbyterians."

As a fraternal benefit group, the PBU offers the typical fraternal insurance program found in most other fraternal benefit societies. Its members are eligible for loans. For instance, presently (1978) members may obtain mortgages for thirty years at 9 percent interest. Juveniles up to sixteen years of age may also obtain fraternal insurance from the juvenile department.

Membership eligibility, according to the constitution reads: "The requisites for adult beneficial membership in the Presbyterian Beneficial Union shall be Protestant faith, sound health, and good moral character." The age range is from sixteen to sixty years for adult membership. Currently the membership roster lists 1,350 members.

In the past the PBU occasionally published pamphlets dealing with religious topics in the Slovak language. This practice was to serve the members, who for many decades were of Slovak origin. Also, back in the 1940s the society published a hymnal in Slovak for its older members.

Structurally, the PBU refers to its local membership units as "Subordinate Assemblies." The national body is known as "Supreme Assembly." This group meets in convention quadrennially. Between conventions the board of directors establishes given policies. Headquarters are in Philadelphia, Pennsylvania.

Additional information may be found by consulting the society's constitution, plus a number of pamphlets and brochures. The society also publishes a monthly journal known as *Calvin*.

PRINCE HALL FREEMASONRY (PHF). In surveying Prince Hall Freemasonry, one discovers first hand what effect racial prejudice and discrimination has had in American society, even among fraternal orders. For instance, PHF came into being because the white Masons barred black citizens from joining white Masonic lodges.

Prince Hall, a black man, was born in 1748 in the British West Indies. In 1765 he came to the United States and soon became a clergyman serving a congregation in Cambridge, Massachusetts. For some reason, he was intent on becoming a Freemason. Thus one day in March, 1775, he courageously approached a British military camp in Boston with one purpose in mind: to become a Mason. The British Army Lodge (Lodge No. 441) accepted him and made him a member of the ancient craft. On July 3, 1775, he opened a Masonic lodge of black men, dedicated to St. John. This was the first black lodge in the United States.

Prince Hall, however, wanted the black Masons to be recognized and accorded the privileges of the white lodges. With this in mind, he petitioned the Provincial Grand Master of Modern Masons of Massachusetts for a charter. His petition was rejected on the basis of color. Not too long after the rejection he petitioned the Grand Lodge of England for a charter on March 2, 1784. The British Masons accepted his request and thus the black Masons received formal, official Masonic recognition. In fact, they received their Masonic legitimation from the same Grand Lodge of England that established the white Masonic lodges in the United States.

The document, which granted the charter on September 29, 1784, designated the lodge founded by Prince Hall as African Lodge No. 459, meaning that it was the 459th lodge chartered by the Grand Lodge of England. The British charter appointed Prince Hall as "Master" of the lodge. By 1808 the first grand lodge was formed, the African Grand Lodge of Boston, later known as Prince Hall Grand Lodge of Massachusetts. A second grand lodge was organized in Pennsylvania in 1815, and soon after a third was established, called the Hiram Grand Lodge of Pennsylvania. By 1847 the three grand bodies formed a national grand lodge. This national grand lodge existed only for a few years, apparently as a defense against slavery.

In spite of Prince Hall Masonry having received its fraternal legitimation from the same source that the white American Masons received theirs, white Masonic lodges have not only refused to recognize Prince Hall Masonry but have often referred to it as "clandestine."

How the term "clandestine" developed with respect to black Masonry is not known to the present writer. It could be that the term had its origin during the slave era when some state governments forbade black Masons to assemble in their lodges. The fact that Masonic lodge sessions were secret and unsupervised by whites made some state governments fearful. Because black Masons continued to meet, even though forbidden to do so, it could very well be that this led to their being labeled "clandestine."

The statement made some years ago by Albert Pike, the leading Masonic spokesman, is frequently cited by Masons and others relative to how Prince Hall Masonry is viewed by the white Masons. Pike said: "I took my obligations from white men, not from negroes. When I have to accept negroes as brothers or leave Masonry, I shall leave it. Better let the thing drift" (Cited in Delmar Duane Darrah, *History and Evolution of Freemasonry*, 1967). It should be recalled that Pike not only wrote the well-known Masonic work, *Morals and Dogma* (1881), and was instrumental in getting Scottish Rite

Masonry established in the United States, but he also once held the rank of general in the Confederate Army.

Prejudice against Prince Hall Masonry, however, is not confined to one or two persons in Masonry. Not at all! Whenever attempts have been made (and there have been several) to recognize black Masonry, it has met with rebuff on the grand lodge level. For instance, in 1898 the Grand Lodge of Washington entertained the question of possibly recognizing Prince Hall Masonry as legitimate. Although the report was favorable to the black Masons, stating that Prince Hall Masonry was indeed legitimate, the Grand Lodge of Washington took no specific action relative to recognizing black Masonry. This rather innocuous report set off a flurry of condemnations by other American grand lodges, all directed against their fellow grand lodge in Washington. Some of the grand lodges severed their ties with the Grand Lodge of Washington. (See Roscoe Pound, "The Data of Masonic Jurisprudence" in *Little Masonic Library*, Book I, 1946.) The Grand Lodge of Illinois in 1899 said in response to the Masons in Washington:

We know that Masonry is not only close in fellowship, but it is perfect in morals and intricate in Science. And we know that the Negroes of the South are wholly incompetent to embrace it. They are ignorant, uneducated, immoral, untruthful, and intellectually they are more impotent than minority or dotage—both of which we exclude. (See *Proceedings of the Grand Lodge of Illinois*, 1899.)

Given the well-entrenched prejudice of white American Masonry against Prince Hall or black Masonry, there is, however, one curious anomaly to be found. In Newark, New Jersey, there exists Alpha Lodge No. 16, which, as a white lodge, has black members. Moreover, this lodge is affiliated with the Grand Lodge of New Jersey (a white Masonic group). Because the Grand Lodge of New Jersey has over the years tolerated the Alpha Lodge, it has been censured by other grand jurisdictions. In fact, some grand lodges even severed their relations with the New Jersey Masons, as, for example, the Grand Lodge of Oklahoma did in 1940. Two years later, however, the ties were restored.

The Alpha Lodge has been in existence since 1791, with the absence of one year, 1871, when it had its charter revoked over the issue of enrolling black members. In 1872 its charter was restored, and the group has had an integrated membership ever since then.

A number of white Masons, it must be noted, have over the years strongly disagreed with American Masonry's white face. William H. Upton, a former Grand Master of the Grand Lodge of Washington, presented a lengthy report to his grand lodge in 1898 showing that Prince Hall Masonry was Masonically legitimate. Upton later published a pamphlet, *Light on a Dark Subject* (1899). In 1902 Upton wrote *Negro Masonry: A Critical*

Examination. Upton believed that a small group of Masons in the Grand Lodge of Washington tried to prevent an unbiased examination of Prince Hall of black Masonry. The Grand Lodge of Massachusetts in 1947 gave a special committee report on black Masonry. While neither the committee nor the grand lodge formally recognized black Masonry as legitimate, it noted: "The real opposition to Negro Freemasonry is rather social than legal." The report also noted that racial discrimination, practiced by so many American Masons, was inconsistent with the tenets of Freemasonry and that "we should practice our teachings" (see *Proceedings of the Grand Lodge of Massachusetts*, 1947).

There have been other white Masons who have not accepted the "official" view regarding black Masonry. For instance, Marshall Field, the famous Chicago businessman, was initiated into Masonry in a Prince Hall lodge in Chicago. More recently a white Mason, Harvey Newton Brown, has chided his Masonic colleagues for their prejudicial view of black Masonry. Brown writes: "one might suspect that the 'spiritual home' of many Southern Masons (and some Northern, too) is the Klan, rather than in the Masonic Fraternity" (see his *Freemasonry and Negroes and Whites in America*, 1965).

Finally, regarding Prince Hall Masonry vis-à-vis white Masonry in the United States, it should be said that some officials in Prince Hall Masonry feel that white Masonry is becoming more receptive of black Masonry. As noted earlier in the present volume under Freemasonry,* no official acceptance announcements have been made by white Masonry, but some black Masons think that they are slowly being seen as a legitimate part of the ancient fraternity and that they are no longer really considered "clandestine."

With reference to the use of ritual, degrees, signs, and oaths the black Masons differ very little from the white lodges. In fact, the Scottish Rite degree ritual, from the first to the thirty-third degree, was given to the Prince Hall Ancient and Accepted Scottish Rite by Albert Pike. Apparently Pike, who felt white Masons were to be segregated from the black members, did not see it amiss to supply the black Masons with his works. For a description of each of the degrees, the reader is asked to see Freemasonry, the Scottish Rite, in the present volume.

Prince Hall Freemasonry, it must be remembered, is over 200 years old. During these years the order, similar to the Blue Lodge among white Masons, has overcome a number of setbacks. The latest one confronting PHM is its membership decline. Over the generations, the order has with few exceptions grown in numbers. From 1900 to 1930 it probably experienced its finest decades. Then came the Great Depression, which sent memberships downward. The late 1940s and 1950s again brought increases to the black craft. The 1960s, however, seemed to end the hope that the 1950s had foreshadowed. Since the 1960s memberships have been declining, a trend very similar to Masonry among white Americans. In 1976 the total American membership of all grand lodges in PHM stood at approximately 265,000.

True to the white traditions and "landmarks" of Freemasonry, PHM also does not permit women to join its brotherhood. Women belong to auxiliary organizations. Some of these are discussed in the present volume.

The organizational structure of Prince Hall Masonry is very similar to that of white Masonry in the United States. Like its white counterpart, PHM has no national grand lodge. All grand lodges usually are confined to state boundaries. Grand Lodges usually meet once a year as the supreme authority. Between grand lodge sessions the Grand Master exercises considerable authority and power. This also is very much the way it is in white grand lodges.

For additional information pertaining to Prince Hall Masonry, see William H. Grimshaw, *History of Freemasonry Among the Colored People in North America* (1903); Donn A. Cass, *Negro Freemasonry and Segregation* (1970); Harry E. Davis, *A History of Freemasonry Among Negroes in America* (1946); William H. Upton, *Negro Masonry: A Critical Examination* (1902); Harry A. Williamson, *Negroes and Freemasonry* (1920); and Harry Williamson, *Prince Hall Primer* (1946). Recently a helpful volume was published by William A. Muraskin, *Middle-Class Blacks in a White Society* (1975). This volume illustrates the functions that Prince Hall Masonry has provided for the middle-class black citizen in the United States. See also Harold V. B. Voorhis, *Negro Masonry in the United States* (1940). Another interesting book is also authored by Harold V. B. Voorhis, namely: *Our Colored Brethren: The Story of Alpha Lodge New Jersey* (1971).

PRINCES OF SYRACUSE, JUNIOR ORDER OF (JOPS). This fraternal society is the junior order for the Knights of Pythias,* the white society. As a junior order it serves to interest young men in the senior order so that upon reaching adulthood they might join that group. The ritual and ceremonies are supervised by the adult Knights of Pythias.

The writer was unable to obtain any pertinent information concerning the present status of the society. Most likely the order is declining in members, as are the Knights of Pythias.

PROTECTED HOME CIRCLE (PHC). Organized as a fraternal benefit society in Sharon, Pennsylvania, in 1886, the organization admitted men and women to membership on equal terms. By 1929 the society had more than 131,000 members. Like numerous other fraternal groups, the ritual had a sprinkling of Biblical passages. In addition to the Initiatory degree, the society conferred the Kibosh degree, which was intended to accent the lighter side of life. The national structure was called the "Supreme Circle." In 1964 the PHC converted to a mutual life insurance company. Presently it is known as the Protected Home Mutual Life Insurance Company. Headquarters were in Sharon, Pennsylvania. Information was gleaned from several issues of *Statistics, Fraternal Societies*.

PROTESTANT KNIGHTS OF AMERICA. Founded in St. Louis, Missouri, in 1895, this fraternal benefit society was to be to Protestants what the Knights of Columbus was to the Roman Catholics. As far as can be determined, the order became extinct during the early 1900s. REFERENCE: *DSOS*.

PROVIDENCE ASSOCIATION OF UKRAINIAN CATHOLICS IN AMERICA (PAKC). This society organized itself as a fraternal benefit group in 1912. The society gives aid to needy members and grants low-interest mortgage loans to religious institutions. Parochial schools are especially favored in terms of receiving loans. Each year the society awards scholarships to needy student members.

Membership is open to "Any Catholic subject to the Pope of Rome, of sound mind and body, and good character, performing his Catholic religious duties. . . ." Members are told "to send their children to school in accordance with the laws of the Church." Presently (1979) the membership stands at approximately 18,000 members. In 1965 the society had 16,994 members.

The society has 210 local lodges in Pennsylvania and New Jersey only. It does not sell life insurance outside of these two states. The legislating body (the convention) meets annually, always in Philadelphia, Pennsylvania. The headquarters also are in Philadelphia.

The society has four basic objectives: moral, material, religious, and civic. PAKC seeks to assist its members so that these objectives may be realized. The civic objective includes instructing the members about Ukrainian history and culture.

Growth in the order was slow for some time. By the 1930s the society had 11,000 members, including juvenile members. The Great Depression of the 1930s, as with so many other societies, did not benefit the organization. By 1942 the society's membership was down to 8,000. However, after World War II, the society began to grow again.

For additional information, see the society's newspaper, *America*. This paper is published in a Ukrainian section and also in an English edition. A published history of the organization appears in the *Jubilee Book: 1912-1972*. Most of this book is in Ukrainian, with the exception of pages 93-110, which give an English account of the fraternity.

PRUDENT PATRICIANS OF POMPEII OF THE UNITED STATES OF AMERICA. This was the first fraternal beneficiary society incorporated by an act of Congress in 1897. Prominent members from the Elks,* Odd Fellows,* and the Royal Arcanum* were instrumental in organizing this society. Membership was open to both sexes, but only if they were white. In addition to the sick and death benefits, the order offered its members an annuity plan. Members upon reaching seventy years of age no longer had to pay any assessments, but rather received an annual 10 percent of their certificates' face value. The head offices were maintained in Saginaw, Michigan. REFERENCE: *DSOS*.

PURITANS, INDEPENDENT ORDER OF. This was a fraternal benefit society based in Pittsburgh, Pennsylvania. It provided the usual death, sickness, old-age, and accident benefits. It also paid monthly annuities. The *Fraternal Monitor* of March, 1919, reported the order's membership at 11,136. REFERENCE: *DSOS*.

PYRAMIDS, ANCIENT ORDER OF. Topeka, Kansas, was the site where this fraternal benefit society was organized in 1895. The order apparently had a short life span. No record of its existence could be found by the author after 1900. Headquarters were housed in Springfield, Missouri. REFERENCES: *Cyc. Frat.*; *DSOS*.

PYTHIAN SISTERS (PS). The history of the present-day Pythian Sisters is complicated by the fact that the present order is the result of a consolidation that occurred in 1907. In 1888 the Supreme Lodge of the Knights of Pythias* approved Joseph Addition Hill's ritual for a women's order. The women, however, preferred their own ritual written by Mrs. Alva A. Young. The latter ritual was accepted when the first assembly of the Pythian Sisterhood was organized in Concord, New Hampshire, on February 22, 1888. That same year the first temple of the Pythian Sisters of the World was organized in Warsaw, Indiana. Mr. Hill was again involved; in this instance he was the prime organizer of the latter society.

The Pythian Sisterhood (the Concord group) differed from the Pythian Sisters (the Warsaw group) in that the former order did not permit the Knights of Pythias to join its ranks, whereas the latter did. In 1894 the Warsaw "sisters" were in danger of losing their male (honorary) members because the Supreme Lodge of the Knights of Pythias did not permit any of its members to belong to an organization that used the name "Pythian" but was not under the male order's jurisdiction. This rule prompted the Pythian Sisters to change their name to Rathbone Sisters of the World.

In 1906 the Knights of Pythias permitted its members to belong to groups employing the name "Pythian." As a result of this action, the two women's orders consolidated in 1907 and adopted the new name of Pythian Sisters. This is the society that is presently in existence.

Membership qualifications are stated in the constitution of 1964:

To be eligible for membership for initiation in a Temple [lodge], the person must be over sixteen years of age, of good character, and speak the English language, and be the wife, widow, sister, half-sister, sister-in-law, mother, stepmother or mother-in-law of a Knight of Pythias in good standing. . . . Persons having Negro blood in their veins or unable to speak the English language are not eligible. . . . A Knight of Pythias must have taken the Rank of Page, Esquire and Knight before he is eligible to membership in a Temple. . . .

Similar to its male counterpart, the Knights of Pythias, the Pythian Sisters are losing members. In 1966 the society had 90,000 "sisters," but by 1979 the number had declined to less than 60,000.

By comparison, the PS have several things in common with the Order of the Eastern Star* and the Rebekah Assembly*: (1) neither group is accorded the status that is given to their counterpart male lodges, even though each of the female groups was organized by a Knight of Pythias, a Mason, and an Odd Fellow, respectively; (2) neither group may initiate someone who is not related to a male lodge member; (3) all three orders have a ritual patterned to some degree after the male rituals; (4) all three support their respective male lodges in an auxiliary capacity; and (5) all three do not appear to resent being subordinate or dependent on deriving their identity in large measure from the male orders.

The administrative or organizational structure operates on the national, state, and local level. The national structure is known as the "Supreme Temple." It meets biennially when the Knights of Pythias meet. State organizations are referred to as "Grand Temples," and local units are "Temples." The national or Supreme Temple offices are located wherever the Supreme Secretary resides. Presently the secretary lives in Lonaconing, Pennsylvania.

Additional information on the PS may be found by reading Ida M. Jayne-Weaver and Emma D. Wood, *History of the Order of Pythian Sisters* (1925). The biennial proceedings are a helpful source in understanding the Pythian sisters. Finally, publicity brochures are also available.

— *R*

RAINBOW GIRLS, INTERNATIONAL ORDER OF (IORG). The official name for this group is International Order of Rainbow for Girls. This group, which was founded in 1922 in McAlester, Oklahoma, is to the Order of the Eastern Star* what the De Molay* is to Freemasonry.* Freemasonry hopes to draw many of its stalwart members from its "farm system," the De Molay. In a similar manner the Order of the Eastern Star hopes to recruit from the Rainbow Girls.

The IORG was founded by W. Mark Sexson, a clergyman, who was Masonic chaplain of Freemasonry's Grand Lodge of Oklahoma at that time. Since its formation, the order had grown to 300,000 girls by 1975, but by 1978 it had dropped to about 215,000 members. The order also lists 1,000,000 "majority members," who are either married or over twenty years of age. This brings the total to 1,215,000 members. Ten years ago, in the late 1960s, the IORG had a membership total of 1,217,000.

Eligibility for membership consists in being recommended by a Freemason or Eastern Star member. A girl friend of the Masonic or Eastern Star girl may also be admitted. Each applicant applying for membership must be white and between the ages of twelve and twenty years. Balloting is done by the ball-method. White balls indicate acceptance; black balls mean rejection.

Regarding the order's whites-only policy, a considerable amount of publicity was aired in the fall of 1976. An Associated Press article was carried by papers across the country. The article noted that when the Indianola, Iowa, chapter admitted a twelve-year-old girl of biracial parents to the IORG the national officials of the order expelled Iowa's 136 Rainbow assemblies and their 5,000 members for admitting the girl. This was not the first time the IORG has been in the news for its racist stance. On September 21, 1972, the *New York Times* noted an incident that occurred in Worcester, Massachusetts, where a Mrs. Anderson resigned her twenty-year membership in the Order of the Eastern Star because the Rainbow Girls who admitted blacks were officially suspended.

True to the traditional practice of fraternal orders having secret rituals and ceremonies, the IORG also has its secret ritual. Two degrees, the initiatory and the Grand Cross of Color, are given to qualified candidates. One edition of the ritual depicts the candidate being initiated as in search of the pot of gold at the end of the rainbow. During the ceremony all members kneel and the chaplain, facing a white altar, prays: "Go with this sister every step of this initiation, show her that we teach Thy Truth, not only for this moment, but for life eternal. Amen."

The ritual endeavors to teach the young ladies ten "outstanding things": belief in the existence of a supreme being, the great truths in the Bible, good character, a conception of higher values in life, leadership, church membership, patriotism, cooperation among equals, love of home, and service to humanity. Since the order uses the name "Rainbow," it uses the seven colors of the rainbow to teach the ten "outstanding things" by way of symbolism. During a typical initiation ceremony, prayers are said and hymns are sung. The religious qualities of the ritual are reinforced by requiring each local assembly to attend some church service in its respective community. This compulsory church attendance takes place each year on the Sunday nearest April 6th, the order's day of origin.

The ritual was authored by W. Mark Sexson. One IORG account has referred to Sexson as having been "divinely inspired for this work [the ritual] for which he was peculiarly fitted." Only members of the Masonic order and the Eastern Star may view the working of the order's ritual.

The IORG emblem depicts a rainbow bearing the letters B.F.G.L. with an R at the bottom center of the bow's base, which has a chain attached to a pot of "gold." It might be noted that in the ritual the pot of "gold" contains the following items: the Bible, the American flag, the Declaration of Independence and the Constitution of the United States, a list of presidents who were Freemasons, and a miniature lambskin apron.

The IORG conducts its affairs on three levels: international, regional, and local. On the international scale the order has branched out to Japan, Australia, Mexico, the Philippines, Canada, and Guam. The order calls its international structure the "Supreme Assembly." Regional structures are known as "Grand Assemblies," and local chapters are called "Assemblies." The Supreme Assembly meets biennially. Headquarters are in McAlester, Oklahoma.

To the writer's knowledge no scholarly work has been published on the Rainbow Girls. The ritual of the society, although available, is difficult to obtain, since the IORG considers it to be secret. An unpublished copy of "The Rainbow Story" is also available in some libraries. The reader may also consult the order's proceedings.

RATHBONE SISTERS OF THE WORLD. This fraternal secret society in reality had been in existence since 1888 when it was founded in Warsaw, Indiana, adopting the name of Pythian Sisters of the World. By 1894 the society ran into opposition from the Knights of Pythias,* who ruled that its members were not permitted to belong to another group bearing the Pythian name. This prompted the name change to Rathbone Sisters of the World. The Knights of Pythias changed its mind in 1906 and permitted its members to join a group using the Pythian name. This change brought the Rathbone Sisters together with the Pythian Sisterhood (also founded in 1888) in 1907 to form a consolidation, called Pythian Sisters.* Thus the Rathbone Sisters, as a separate order, ended with the merger of 1907.

For further information, see Ida M. Jayne-Weaver and Emma D. Wood, *History of the Order of Pythian Sisters* (1925).

REBEKAH ASSEMBLIES, INTERNATIONAL ASSOCIATION OF (IARA). This order, which once was known as the Daughters of Rebekah, is to the Independent Order of Odd Fellows (IOOF)* what the Order of the Eastern Star* essentially is to Freemasonry.* Today the IARA in fraternal circles is commonly known by the name "Rebekahs." The order was founded in 1851 by Schuyler Colfax (an Odd Fellow) of South Bend, Indiana.

Colfax had received approval to prepare a ladies' degree from the Grand Lodge convention in 1850. Colfax, who later became vice-president of the United States, wrote most of the ritual and lectures for the Rebekah degree, and in the following year (1851) his work was adopted by the Grand Lodge of the IOOF.

All members of the IARA take only one degree, the Assembly degree. The ritual of the degree refers the candidate to "the beautiful and graceful Rebekah, whose kindness and hospitality to a humble unknown servant [Abraham's major-domo, Eliezer] portrays the grandeur of her character. . . ." The obligation, taken by the candidate during initiation, stresses secrecy and faithfulness to the order's laws, rules, and regulations. The ritual also contains a sign of recognition, and, in typical fraternal fashion, there is the utterance of prayers.

The IARA is an auxiliary order of the Independent Order of Odd Fellows. The ladies, along with the Odd Fellows, sponsor the Educational Foundation, which provides loans to members. The order also participates in the World Eye Bank, another project that the Odd Fellows also support. For the youth group, Theta Rho Girls' Club, the IARA regularly conducts and sponsors pilgrmages. The society is proud of the fact that, together with the IOOF, it was the first fraternal organization to establish homes for the aged and orphans. The first home was founded in 1872 in Pennsylvania. Many of the homes are largely supported by the grand lodges (state groups).

The IARA sees the letters of the name Rebekah spelling out the following qualities of the society:

R—Rendering your service above self
E—Ever mindful for all to remember of your Love and Devotion [sic]
B—Represents our Bible for which you are a part of—representing our degree
E—your—Ever striving to please God and your people
K—is for Kindness—one of your many outstanding traits
A—Always striving to live up to God's teachings
H—Represents your hospitality shown an humble unknown servant.

Membership eligibility requires the applicant to believe in a supreme being, to be a relative of an Odd Fellow, of good moral character, and at least eighteen years of age. Presently the membership roster of the IARA is larger than that of the IOOF. In 1977 there were 331,844 members, plus 34,337 male members from the IOOF. Males from the IOOF may join the Rebekahs, but the converse is not permitted by the Odd Fellows. Since 1972 membership has constitutionally removed the barrier to blacks and other nonwhites. The revised constitution (Code of General Laws) says in part: "All women of good moral character who have attained the age of 18 years. . . ." are eligible to join the Rebekahs.

The IARA, similar to the IOOF, has been declining rather continuously in membership for some years. The combined Rebekah and Odd Fellows once had three and a half million members in 1915. Today it seems the order is struggling to survive with only a combined membership of 575,000. In fact, the Odd Fellows now have fewer members than the Rebekahs.

The emblem of the IARA is a circle with the three Odd Fellow chain links in the center. The letter "R" is directly below the three links.

Local units are known as "Lodges," of which there are 6,300 in Canada and the United States. On state or regional level the chief officer is addressed as "Noble Grand." On the international level the title is "Sovereign Noble Grand." The IARA meets in convention annually, usually at the same time that the Sovereign Grand Lodge of the Odd Fellows meets. The Rebekahs maintain their headquarters in Minneapolis, Kansas.

Additional background may be obtained by reading the literature mentioned in the discussion pertaining to the Odd Fellows in the present volume. The *Revised Rebekah Ritual Illustrated* (1948) is published by Ezra A. Cook Publisher of Chicago, Illinois. This publication provides a good understanding of the IARA's ritual and the order's degree. The order's *Journal of Proceedings*, published annually, is also a good source for further information.

RECHABITES, INDEPENDENT ORDER OF (IOR). If any fraternal order could have called itself "Ancient," it would have been appropriate for the IOR to have done so. The Old Testament scriptures in Jeremiah 35 speak of the Rechabites having totally abstained from wine and that they lived in tents instead of houses.

The IOR was a descendant order of the Independent Order of Rechabites, Salford Unity, that was founded in England in 1835. The IOR began in the United States in 1842. Both the English and the American order were total abstinence societies that practiced secret fraternalism. The IOR essentially functioned as a fraternal benefit society along with its abstinence philosophy.

Membership in the IOR was limited to white males between sixteen and fifty-five years of age. They were also required to believe in a supreme being, plus sign a pledge of total abstinence. Individuals over fifty-five were able to become honorary members. Females over twelve years were permitted to form their "Tents." Males under sixteen years had their juvenile tents. In the early 1900s the society had 990,000 members.

As a fraternal society, the IOR had a ritual with three degrees. The Knight of Templiance was the first degree. Knight of Fortitude was the second degree, and the Covenanted Knight of Justice was the third degree rite. The ritual, as in most fraternal orders, was intended to be secret and solemn. Some of the ritual features resembled the rites of Freemasonry.*

As noted, local groups were called "Tents." The national structure was known as the "High Tent." Headquarters for the IOR were in Washington, D.C.

For additional information, see Albert Stevens, *Cyclopedia of Fraternities* (1907). This report is in part based on Stevens' volume. Some information was also obtained from *Statistics, Fraternal Societies*.

RED EAGLES, ORDER OF. This group was a benevolent, protective, and patriotic society, reportedly founded in Germany in 1705. It was incorporated in Michigan in 1912. At the time of incorporation the order really separated itself from the old German society. The new order claimed to be 100 percent American. Headquarters were in Kalamazoo, Michigan. REFERENCE: *DSOS*.

RED MEN, IMPROVED ORDER OF (IORM). This fraternal society claims to be the oldest secret order founded in America. It bases this claim on being the continuation of certain secret societies that were in existence prior to the American Revolution. Notable among these societies were the Sons of Liberty and the Sons of Tamina. The IORM literature says it was originally (1763) known as the Sons of Liberty whose members "worked 'underground' to help establish freedom and liberty in the Early Colonies." After the American Revolution the name was changed to the Order of Red Men. Whether the present IORM is a definite descendant of the Sons of Liberty cannot be ascertained positively, for the IORM as it is known today was founded in 1834, and by 1847 the "Great Council of the United States" (the national structure) was organized in Baltimore, Maryland.

After having organized itself on the national level in 1847, the IORM grew, as so many fraternal orders did in the latter part of the 1800s and early part of the 1900s. By 1921, the Red Men had over 519,942 members in forty-six states. Today (1978), the IORM has only 31,789 members in thirty-two states. One official report in 1977 showed that, from 1960 to 1975, the Red Men suffered a net loss of 19,776 members. The order which once, according to its claims, had Theodore Roosevelt, Warren G. Harding, and Franklin D. Roosevelt as members currently has more problems keeping its members, let alone gaining new ones.

The IORM has a secret ritual that in many ways shows the influence of the Masonic Blue Lodge* ritual. It has three basic degrees: Adoption, Warrior, and Chief. A fourth degree is given for insurance purposes, the Beneficiary degree.

The organizational and ritual terminology is almost exclusively derived from language attributed to the American Indian. The local lodge is known as "Tribe;" "Paleface" means nonmember; "Wigwam" is a meeting site; "Sachem" is president or head of a lodge; "Senior Sagamore" is the first vice-president; "Chief of Records" means secretary; "Raising up of Chiefs" stands for installing officers; "kindling the council fire" is to open a meeting; and "twigging" is the act of voting.

In receiving the Adoption degree the candidate is seen as a paleface who stumbles upon a camp of warriors and braves. They take him to the tribe, where he is tied to the stake and threatened with death. The prophet (an IORM official) intercedes by asking the tribe to adopt him. The vow for the first degree promises secrecy and conformity to the order. It concludes with the statement: "So help me, Great Spirit." The Chief's degree enacts a scene where the candidate is given a peace pipe, then shared by the lodge officers. Among the paraphernalia given to the new "chief" is a tomahawk, which has the emblem of the order engraved: an eagle whose wings bear the stars and stripes of the American flag, as well as the letters TOTE (totem of the eagle) on its breast.

The IORM employs a number of religious expressions in its rituals, lodge sessions, and general communication. Some prayer expressions are: "O Thou Great Spirit," "Hear Us, O Great Spirit," "O Thou Great Spirit of the Universe." Departed members are referred as having gone to the "happy hunting grounds." At one time (during the 1890s and early 1900s) the IORM had a German edition of its ritual.

The watchwords of the IORM are "freedom," "friendship," and "charity." It sees these as characterizing the ideals of the American nation. Thus the IORM is presently a fraternal group that holds to a conservative social and political philosophy. The order opposes federal welfare, communism, and waste in government. Its official magazine, *Red Men*, periodically prints articles conveying the order's conservative stance. Each year the society conducts an annual pilgrimage to Faith of Our Fathers Chapel in Valley Forge, Pennsylvania. This pilgrimage is designed to "renew and strengthen our beliefs in the American Way of Life."

During the heyday (1880s and 1890s) of American fraternal orders, the Red Men had a uniformed rank or contingent, known as the Knights of Tammany. It also once had the Chieftain's League, which was made up of members who had "been exalted to the Chief's Degree, and in good standing in their respective Tribes."

Membership to the Red Men is not open to women, although there is an auxiliary order for women known as the Degree of Pocahontas.* Until 1974, the order's bylaws stipulated that candidates for membership had to be white. Native red men (American Indians) were not eligible to join the Red Men. However, in 1974, at its 106th session, the Great Council of the United States eliminated its all-white requirement. The order refers to this session as the "turning point of our order." For the boys who are eight years or older there is the junior order known as Degree of Hiawatha.* A counterpart order exists for girls in the Degree of Anona.* Adult females are eligible for the Degree of Pocahontas, an auxiliary to the IORM.

In recent years the IORM has supported the American Indian Development program, which is designed to aid American Indian children by providing education and health care. By 1976 (three years after the order embarked upon the program), the organization had a total of 212 sponsored adoptions of Indian children. The order also has come to the defense of the American Indian. One issue (December 1974) of the magazine, *Red Men*, said: "The American Indian, seeking a return to more acceptable means of managing his native stands of maiden timber and clean, sparkling waters now seeks support from all of us to fully practice 'Americanism.' . . ." Financial support has been given to aid and promote books for the blind. Some assistance has also been given to the Association of the Retarded.

Structurally, the IORM is organized in three levels. The "Great Council" of the United States is the national administration. It consists of the national president, known as Great Incohonee, and a Board of Great Chiefs. These are the Great Senior Sagamore, Great Junior Sagamore, Great Chief of Records, Great Keeper of the Wampum, and Prophet. The latter is the immediate past president. The state level ("Reservation") is very much like the national structure. It has a great sachem (president) and a great council or board of chiefs, who are elected from the former chiefs of local "Tribes" (lodges). Each tribe has a sachem and a board of officers similar to the state and national organizations. The national headquarters currently are located in Waco, Texas.

Published information on the IORM includes the order's official magazine, *Red Men*. Charles M. Skinner's *Myths and Legends of Our Own Land*, 1896, is an old source that provides interesting details. The ritual of the IORM can be read by consulting *Red Men Illustrated: The Complete Revised Ritual Adopted by the Great Council of the United States of the Improved Order of Red Men, Comprising the Adoption Degree, Warrior's Degree, and Chief's Degree*, 1903. An interesting pamphlet, "What Every American Should Know About The Order of Red Men," was obtained from the Great Chief of Records in Waco, Texas. The national proceedings, known as the *Record*, are helpful for understanding the functions of the IORM. The *Constitution and General Laws* are also quite useful in providing information about the Red Men.

RED MEN, INDEPENDENT ORDER OF. German members of the Improved Order of Red Men seceded and formed the Independent Order of Red Men in 1850. According to Albert C. Stevens, *Cyclopedia of Fraternities* (1907), the order had 12,000 members in 1896. Today it is extinct.

ROSICRUCIAN FRATERNITY [also known as THE FRATERNITATIS ROSAE CRUSIS] (RF). This society claims that its date of origin is 1614, the date that Rosicrucians say the book *Fama Fraternitatis Bendicti Ordinis*

Rosae-Crucis appeared in Germany. For a more detailed account of this work, commonly referred to as *Fama*, see the discussion on the Rosicrucian Order, the San Jose group.* The American founding date is listed as 1858 by the RF.

The RF has many similarities with the other Rosicrucian groups, for instance, the Rosicrucian Order.* The RF society, as its related fraternities, believes that it possesses special, esoteric knowledge. One statement reads that its initiates "know the Grand Secret, and [are] able to teach awakening mankind many things concerning the body, the will, concentration of mental energy, prolongation of existence here on earth, and the potencies and glories of the Soul seldom dreamed of by the thinkers of earlier centuries."

The society says it operates the largest known library of arcane books, with 10,000 such volumes. The library is located in Quakertown, Pennsylvania.

The author was unable to determine the society's membership. Both males and females are eligible to join the fraternity.

For further information, see the following books published by the society: *The Book of Rosicruciae* (three volumes); *The Rosicrucians: Their Teachings*; and *The Philosophy of Fire*. See also *The Confederation of Initiates*, issued by the RF.

ROSICRUCIAN ORDER, THE [also known as THE ANCIENT, MYSTICAL ORDER ROSAE CRUCIS] (AMORC). In terms of legend the AMORC traces its roots back to the mystery schools of learning that existed as far back as 115 B.C. in Egypt. Chronologically, however, the order is first mentioned in Germany in A.D. 1115. In the United States the Supreme Council of the Martinist Order and Synarchy was legally incorporated on August 3, 1938. This group is a fraternal affiliate of the Rosicrucian Order in Europe.

Prior to 1938 the Rosicrucians established a foothold in New York in 1915 through the efforts of H. Spencer Lewis, who was instrumental in promoting the society across the United States. Lewis customarily signed his name with a Ph.D., even though he never earned a single credit from a university or college. One of the AMORC books, *Rosicrucian Manual*, Volume 8 (renewed copywrite date of 1978), also pictures Lewis with the letters Ph.D. following his name. In 1939 his son Ralph Lewis succeeded him as "Supreme Autocratic Authority" and "Imperator for North America, Central, and South America, the British Commonwealth and Empire, France, Switzerland, Sweden and Africa."

Some Rosicrucian accounts, similar to those in Freemasonry,* love to trace their organizational roots back to antiquity. Some Masonic writers attempt to trace Freemasonry back to King Solomon's temple era. The AMORC says that in terms of tradition or legend Rosicrucian teachings go back to the mystery schools of learning that were started by Pharoah Thutmose III, around 1500 B.C. More specifically the Rosicrucians point to Thutmose's descendent Akhnaton of the fourteenth century B.C. Akhaton is seen as the first Grand Master of the order. More accurately, however, the origins of the order go back to the early seventeenth century, following the appearance of the publication *Fama Fraternitatis Bendicti Ordinis Rosae-Crucis* (1614), commonly abbreviated as *Fama*. Some evidence exists, however, that the *Fama* was already in circulation as early as 1610.

Fama portrays the peregrinations of one Christian Rosenkreuz, who traveled to Arabia, Damascus, Egypt, and Fez, where he learned about philosophy, medicine, magic, cabalism, Gnosticism, and even spirit communication. What he reportedly learned placed him beyond the knowledge of his contemporaries in the West. Upon returning from his journey to the East, he formed a brotherhood that would practice and safeguard the knowledge he brought back. The brotherhood was named the Society of the Rose and Cross, in honor of Christian Rosenkreuz. Some have suggested that the *Fama* was written by Johann Valentin Andreae, a seventeenth-century Lutheran theologian, and that he was Christian Rosenkreuz. However, a rather exhaustive study by John Warwick Montgomery (see his *Cross and Crucible*, Volumes I and II, 1973) shows that Andreae did not produce the *Fama*. Those who credit Andreae with writing *Fama* say he intended the work to counteract alchemy, astrology, and even Roman Catholicism. Rosicrucians credit Sir Francis Bacon as having written the *Fama*.

One of the basic teachings of the AMORC is the doctrine of reincarnation. The society is careful to distinguish reincarnation from the transmigration of souls. By reincarnation the order believes that the human soul, a divine essence, manifests itself

in the human body during its earthly life as the ego or character of the person, and at transition [death] moves on and into the cosmic plane along with the Soul Essence. There it remains until the right time for another incarnation with the Soul Essence in another physical body, for more and different experiences, which are added to the personality memory and remain intact there as the accumulating knowledge and wisdom of the inner self.

As a fraternal organization, the AMORC has a ritual and an oath similar to many other fraternal groups. The AMORC, however, differs from most fraternal orders in that it places high value on occult activities. In fact, one of its publications, *Rosicrucian Manual* (1978), defends occultism by saying: "Occultism affirms that man has powers which are subliminal (beyond the level of his normal consciousness, and of which he is ordinarily unaware), and which are just as much a part of his being as his sight, his hearing, or his powers of speech."

Membership is open to any law-abiding individual "of either sex and eighteen years of age or over, with an expressed desire to learn more about himself and the universe. . . ." Unlike Freemasonry, which does not solicit members, the AMORC frequently places advertisements in newspapers or magazines asking interested persons to enquire, presumably to get them interested in joining the order. One of the order's publications says: "It is a traditional custom with the Rosicrucian Order . . . to *invite* a seeker or a worthy person to come into the circle of its activities and share in its unusual benefits." Currently (1978) the AMORC has about 120,000 members.

Since 1917 the order has inaugurated what it calls a "Sanctum Membership." This type of membership is by correspondence only. In fact, "All members of the Grand Lodge of AMORC in the Worldwide Jurisdiction (the Americas, Australia, Europe, Africa, and Asia) are Sanctum members. . . ."

Before new members are initiated into the order, they are required to engage in preliminary studies for a period of six weeks. This period of study is intended to prepare the candidate by means of "correspondence and . . . psychic contact through Rosicrucian methods." These studies are "preliminary to the higher Temple Degree monographs, and provide the means by which the Neophytes can qualify for these Temple Degrees and receive them for study in their own home in the same manner as the introductory Degrees."

While there are several Rosicrucian societies, the best-known group is the one whose headquarters are in San Jose, California. This group maintains Rose-Croix University, which houses physics, chemistry, light, radio, and photography laboratories, as well as a science museum and planetarium. An art gallery and a library is also part of the university setup in San Jose.

The AMORC has a staff of over 200 in its San Jose offices. Local groups number about 285. The society convenes every year to conduct convention business. The 1979 convention was held in Quebec City, Quebec, Canada.

Additional information on the AMORC may be obtained by reading the society's *Rosicrucian Digest*, a monthly publication. See also Arthur Edward Waite, *The Brotherhood of the Rosy Cross* (1924). This work is an exhaustive treatment by a man well-versed in Freemasonry and related societies. Another helpful source is Montgomery's two volumes, cited earlier. The AMORC also publishes its *Rosicrucian Manual* (1978, 25th edition).

ROYAL ARCANUM (RA). Like so many other orders, this group was founded by men who belonged to Freemasonry,* the Ancient Order of United Workmen,* and the Independent Order of Odd Fellows.* The order was founded by Darius Wilson in June, 1877, in Boston, Massachusetts. Wilson founded the RA primarily because the Knights of Honor, whom he also had organized, refused to adopt the graded assessment plan.

From the beginning the society operated with the graded assessment plan relative to its insurance funds. Presently its objectives are:

To unite fraternally all eligible male and female persons of sound bodily health and good morale standing, who are socially acceptable and between sixteen and twenty years of age . . . Boys and Girls [sic] from birth to 15 years and 11 months of age. . . . To give all moral and material aid in its power to its members and those dependent upon them. To teach morality without religious distinction, patriotism without partisanship and brotherhood without creed or class. To educate the members socially, morally and intellectually; and assist the families of the deceased members. To establish funds for the payment of Death, Disability, Old Age Benefits, Educational Loans, Retirement Income Annuities, and Weekly Hospital Indemnity Benefits.

In addition to the benefits just listed, the RA also offers other insurance plans. Some of these are twenty-payment life certificates, home-protection life plans, limited payment life plans, and others.

The RA promotes itself as being a family fraternity that does not cater to a certain class of individuals. It is "non-sectarian, non-political and thoroughly cosmopolitan in character." The order makes no apologies in saying that it is "highly selective, and every applicant must conform to a definite social, moral and financial standard."

Concerning basic principles, the RA says it teaches "good citizenship, love of country, home and friends; the Fatherhood of God and Brotherhood of Man; faithfulness in performance of the obligations of the home; honor in your dealings with mankind; generosity with those less fortunate than yourself; sympathy, kindness and consideration for the bereaved and distressed."

The order still very much believes in the value of having a ritual. In one of its publicity brochures it defends its ritual by saying: "The ritual service is dignified and impressive." The ritual, although revised twice in the history of the order, is still quite elaborate. The RA makes much of the number 1105, which has some special esoteric meaning known only to its members. The words "Mercy, Virtue, Charity" are the society's motto. The ritual, it should be noted, requires a rather lengthy obligation or oath at the time of initiation.

The official insignia is a royal crown within a circle. On the circumference of the circle are ten small Maltese crosses.

Membership at one time was confined to men only. Now women also are admitted to the local councils. In 1919 the RA had more than 135,000 members. The current (1978) membership of the society is approximately 28,000 members. This figure represents a decline from 1965, when there were 36,000 members.

Each year the society awards scholarships to students who are in high school and who have been members of the Royal Arcanum for at least three years. Free scholarships are regularly awarded to Royal Arcanum orphans. Student loans are available also.

The RA operates in Canada and in the United States. Local chapters are known as "Councils." Regional (state or provincial) structures are referred to as "Grand Councils." The highest legislative body is known as the "Supreme Council." This group meets biennially. National headquarters in the United States are situated in Boston, Massachusetts.

For further information the reader may wish to consult M. S. Sackett, *Early History of Fraternal Beneficiary Societies in America* (1914). This volume has a brief history of the RA up to 1914. For more recent information, brochures and pamphlets are obtainable from the head office in Boston, Massachusetts.

ROYAL ARCH MASONS, INTERNATIONAL GENERAL GRAND CHAPTER OF (GGC). Once one becomes a Master Mason (third degree) he may elect to obtain additional degrees by going the route of the Scottish Rite* or the York Rite.* If he chooses the York Rite, the fourth, fifth, sixth, and seventh degrees are what Masons call the "Chapter Degrees." The Grand Royal Arch Chapter of the Northern States of America was organized in 1797 in Boston, Massachusetts. In 1799 the name was changed to General Grand Chapter of Royal Arch Masonry for the United States of America. This name was changed again in 1946 to The General Grand Chapter.

Basically, the GGC functions as a supervisory body seeing to it that uniformity prevails relative to the chapter degrees. These degrees are the Mark Master Mason, Past Master Mason, Most Excellent Master Mason, and Royal Arch Mason. Only Master Masons may enter the GGC.

Subordinate units are called "Chapters." State or regional groups are named "Grand Chapters," and the supreme authority is known as the "International General Grand Chapter." The international structure meets every three years in convention. Headquarters are located in Lexington, Kentucky.

For further information, see the discussion in the present volume pertaining to the York Rite.* The Mason Service Association's "Allied Masonic Groups and Rites" (mimeographed, 1978) also is helpful. Most published articles focusing on the York Rite in Masonic periodicals will provide further insight into the GGC or "Chapter Degrees."

ROYAL BENEFIT SOCIETY. This fraternal benefit society was founded in the city of New York in 1893. Its founders were members of the Masons,* Odd Fellows,* Knights of Pythias,* the Royal Arcanum,* and other fraternal orders. The society offered its members sickness, death, and accident benefits. Its ritual was reputed as being plain and businesslike. Home offices were quartered in New York City. REFERENCES: *Cyc. Frat.*; *DSOS*.

ROYAL HIGHLANDERS. Organized in 1896 as a fraternal benefit society, this order admitted men and women to its ranks on equal terms. Two classes of membership were available, benefit and social. The ritual, which was secret, was based on Scottish history and intended to teach "Prudence, Fidelity, Valor." These latter three were the watchwords of the society. All members took a vow of secrecy. The society invested extensively in Nebraska farm lands. In 1930 the society had approximately 17,000 members. The order reincorporated in 1937 to become a mutual life insurance company, and in 1946 it changed its name to Lincoln Mutual Life Insurance Company. Head offices were in Lincoln, Nebraska. REFERENCE: *DSOS*.

ROYAL LEAGUE (RL). This fraternal benefit order was founded as an offshoot of the Royal Arcanum.* It was organized in 1883 in Chicago, Illinois, to modify the then rather advanced cooperative life insurance offered by the Royal Arcanum. The Royal League customarily offered debates, the reading of papers, and other forms of social interaction in its lodge meetings. These practices were borrowed from the parent order. The female auxiliary was called Ladies of the Royal League. In 1932 the RL absorbed the Order of Mutual Protection.

The RL, like so many other fraternal groups, experienced financial difficulties. Thus in 1923 the society had to levy a special assessment of $1.00 per member. If a member brought a new member to the society, his special assessment was cancelled. This was one way in which the RL sought both to bolster its general fund and to enlarge its membership roster.

In 1904 the society opened the Fellowship Sanatorium in Black Mountain, North Carolina. This institution was the first of its kind to be operated by a fraternal society. In 1920 the institution was destroyed by fire, which led the RL to replace the complex with new, modern facilities. In 1970 the Royal League merged with Equitable Reserve Association.*

Membership was open only to white males. Females had to join the Ladies of the Royal League. In 1923 the society had 22,000 benefit and social members.

Local units were known as "Councils." State groups were called "Advisory Councils" in that they served in the advisory capacity to the national body, the "Supreme Council." Headquarters were located in Chicago, Illinois.

For further information the reader will find the back issues of the society's official organ, *Royal League News Letter*, helpful. See also Albert C. Stevens, *Cyclopedia of Fraternities* (1907).

ROYAL NEIGHBORS OF AMERICA (RNA). In 1888 the Royal Neighbors of America was founded as a social group, but by March 21, 1895, it was chartered as a fraternal benefit society for ladies. From 1888 to 1895 the group was really an unofficial auxiliary group of the Modern Woodmen of

America,* and until 1890 its name was "The Ladies Auxiliary of Hazel Camp No. 171, MWA." Even as a social group, the ladies had adopted a secret ritual as early as 1889. Meetings were purely social and were held only occasionally. All ladies were either wives or sisters of the Modern Woodmen.

In 1890 the ladies chose the name of Royal Neighbors of America. By 1891 the RNA voted to admit men as members, and by 1895 the order, as a chartered fraternal benefit society, had a total of 4,000 members.

The RNA has always held its ritual in high regard. Early in the order's life, a drill team was organized with each member wearing appropriate regalia. The 1978 constitution shows that the ritual and secrecy are still greatly valued: "No member shall expose any of the secret work of this Society by publishing or sending out any circulars containing printed words or illustrations relative to the same. . . ." In fact, the constitution notes that revealing any ritual secret is an offense that demands disciplining the offending member. The society issues an annual password to each member.

Membership is open to "Any person who is not less than sixteen (16) nor more than seventy (70) years of age. . . ." Two classes of membership are available, beneficiary and social. The social member, as in other societies, does not qualify for beneficiary status. Current (1979) membership (which includes adult, junior, and social members) stands at 289,075. This compares to 420,000 members in the late 1960s, a loss of about 31 percent over a period of ten years. Although the society admits men as members, it is predominantly a female organization.

The RNA maintains a national home for its aged members in Davenport, Iowa. Back in 1902 the society voluntarily contributed money to the Temple of Fraternity in St. Louis, Missouri, in which the RNA set up "headquarters for use of those members of the Society who visited the Louisiana Purchase Exposition held there in 1904," as part of the World's Fair. The RNA also sponsors a national "Help-to-Hear" project. Aid has been given to orphans and to needy members in times of public disasters. A college scholarship program provides assistance to worthy students. The sick and bereaved are visited through the activities of local units.

The society has adapted itself to the times where and when necessary. Having begun as an fraternal assessment order, it is today a solvent legal reserve insurance group. It holds membership in the National Fraternal Congress of America. In 1918 it organized a juvenile department, enabling young people to benefit from insurance plans. The ritual has been revised a number of times during the society's existence.

The Royal Neighbor emblem is a white rose. Each of the five petals has a separate design symbolizing the society's five principles: faith, unselfishness, courage, endurance, and modesty. The organization's motto is EX FIDE FORTIS (through faith we are strong).

Local subordinate units are called "Camps." Regional groups are referred to as "State Camps." The highest voice of authority in the society is the Supreme Camp, which meets in convention every four years. Between conventions the board of directors makes key decisions. Some of the supreme officers still have the exotic-sounding titles so characteristic of fraternal orders of the past. The RNA has its Supreme Oracle, Supreme Recorder, Deputy Supreme Oracle, and the like. The Supreme Oracle is president of the organization. The supreme headquarters are located in Rock Island, Illinois.

For further information see *Royal Neighbors of America 75th Anniversary*, a society publication that was issued in 1970 in commemoration of the group's seventy-fifth anniversary. It provides a rather detailed history of the society. *The By-Laws and Articles of Incorporation* (1978) also gives a good understanding of how the RNA functions. A monthly periodical, *The Royal Neighbor*, carries articles, news, and recipes.

ROYAL ORDER OF LIONS. See Lions, Royal Order of.

ROYAL ORDER OF SCOTLAND, THE (ROS). Although this order's origin goes back to the mid-eighteenth century in Europe, the organization was not founded in the United States until May 4, 1878. At first the order limited its membership to 150, with a margin of twenty-five above the limit. Eventually this restriction was removed. Now the society has about 6,000 members. Membership requirements call for a minimum of five years as a Freemason and "a firm belief in Christianity." Two degrees are conferred: the Heredom of Kilwinning and the Rosy Cross.

Subordinate bodies are called "Provincial Grand Lodges." The ROS meets once each year in conjunction with the Supreme Council of the Scottish Rite.* One year it meets with the Northern Jurisdiction, and the next year with the Southern Jurisdiction. Headquarters of the Provincial Grand Lodge are in Kensington, Maryland.

For information, see Albert C. Stevens' brief discussion in his *Cyclopedia of Fraternities* (1907). See also the Masonic Service Association's capsule-like summary in its "Allied Masonic Groups and Rites" (mimeographed, 1978).

ROYAL PURPLE, ORDER OF, AUXILIARY OF THE B.P.O. ELKS OF CANADA (OORP). Like its male counterpart (the Benevolent and Protective Order of Elks of Canada), the OORP was founded in Vancouver, British Columbia. The date of organization was in June 1915.

The aims and purposes of the OORP are "To inculcate the principles of Justice, Charity, Sisterly Love and Fidelity; to promote the welfare and enhance the happiness of its members; to quicken the spirit of women toward a pure and noble citizenship; to cultivate good fellowship. To seek as a fraternal organization to become potent in the realm of Purpledom throughout Canada." The society also seeks to assist the Elks, as a true and loyal auxiliary.

The OORP is very serious about its ritual and its various elements. Concerning its fraternal signs, the order requires that "Signs must not be used before the Bible is opened or after it is closed." The society also has passwords, regalia for formal dress, and a floral emblem. The initiation oath for new members in part reads: "I, . . . , voluntarily . . . do solemnly promise that I will never divulge any of the secrets of this Order to anyone." The candidate also promises to defend every worthy member's reputation, not to wrong a member, to aid and assist needy members, and not to join an order that uses the name Order of the Royal Purple unofficially. The membership obligation follows the chaplain's prayer and the singing of an ode, "In Charity's Sweet Name."

New members are accepted or rejected by means of cube balloting. Three or more black cubes spell rejection for an applicant. A second ballot may be ordered by the Honored Royal Lady, head of a local lodge. Membership is open to women who believe in a supreme being, are eighteen years or older, and "have a husband, father, brother, half-brother or son who is a member in good standing in the B.P.O. Elks. . . ." The society also admits "A mother, sister and a daughter of a member. . . . also a lady who has no male relative, or ladies may be accepted whose male relatives are not members of B.P.O. Elks, up to 25 percent of the total membership of the lodge." Every new member must pay an initiation fee.

The insignia of the OORP is diamond-shaped. Inside the corners of the diamond are the letters O.O.R.P., reading from the nine o'clock to the six o'clock position. In the center is the picture of an elk's head.

Local units are called "Lodges." The national organizational structure is known as the "Supreme Lodge." Headquarters of the society are maintained in Brandon, Manitoba.

Additional information may be found by reading the society's *Constitution and Statutes*. The ritual referred to here was taken from the 1958 edition. The proceedings may also be consulted.

ROYAL AND SELECT MASTERS, INTERNATIONAL GENERAL GRAND COUNCIL OF (RSM). This organization of Masons in the York Rite* or American Rite is often referred to by Masonry as "the Council." It was organized June 12, 1872, in New York City by fifteen grand councils, who were intent on forming a general grand council. The constitution was adopted at the fifth convention in Detroit on August 23, 1880. According to one Masonic report, the constitution's avowed "purpose is to control the three Cryptic Degrees." The three "Cryptic Degrees" are the Royal Master,

Select Master, and Super-Excellent Master degrees. (Each of these is discussed in the present volume under the York Rite.) The Super-Excellent degree is optional in all grand councils.

In order to become a member one must have attained the seventh (Royal Arch Mason) degree in the York Rite. A Royal Arch Mason, however, need not join the "Council." He may elect to go directly on the Order of the Red Cross, Order of the Knights Malta, and the Knights Templar.* In 1950 the RSM had 250,000 members. Present membership figures were unavailable to the writer.

The oaths for the degrees in the Council are remarkably similar to those in the Masonic Blue Lodge.* The Select Master's degree, for instance, requires the candidate to swear: ". . . binding myself under no less penalty, besides all my former penalties, to have my hands chopped off at the stumps, my eyes plucked out from the sockets, my body quartered, and then thrown among the rubbish of the Temple. . . . So help me God, and keep me steadfast in the same."

The organizational structure is very similar to the grand lodges of the American Blue Lodge. The officers, however, bear different titles. The five principal officers are The Most Puissant Grand Master, Deputy Grand Master, Grand Puissant Conductor of Works, Grand Recorder, and Grand Treasurer. Subordinate units are called "Councils." The supreme structure is known as the "General Grand Council." It meets in convention every year.

For additional information, see Albert G. Mackey, *Encyclopedia of Freemasonry* (1946). The society's constitution also is helpful for gaining a better understanding of the order. Finally, the reader may profit by consulting the proceedings of the RSM.

ROYAL SOCIETY OF GOOD FELLOWS. See Good Fellows, Royal Society of.

ROYAL TEMPLARS OF TEMPERANCE, THE (RTT). Founded in 1870 in Buffalo, New York, this fraternal group was at first primarily interested in closing saloons. By 1877 the society revised its constitution, which provided for a fraternal benefit assessment system.

The RTT permitted women to join on equal membership basis with the men. Membership once was drawn from Canada and Scandinavia, as well as from the United States. In the 1890s the society had about 50,000 members. Of this number about 30,000 were social members who were not eligible for insurance benefits. In 1903 the society disbanded.

Local units were known as "Select Councils." State or regional groups were referred to as "Grand Councils." The highest authority was called the "Supreme Council."

For additional information, see Albert C. Stevens, *Cyclopedia of Fraternities* (1907).

ROYAL TRIBE OF JOSEPH. Founded in 1894, this society functioned as a fraternal beneficiary organization. As its name implies, the society took Joseph of the Old Testament era as its model. In fact, the ritual was based on morals drawn from Joseph's life and experiences. The order's leadership referred to Joseph's storing-up of food to overcome the seven-year famine as the "first life insurance" effort exercised on a large scale. The ritual conferred one degree only. Statewide structures were known as "Grand Lodges." The chief governing unit was the "Supreme Lodge." Apparently, the society ceased to operate in the early 1900s. Headquarters were housed in Sedalia, Missouri. See Albert C. Stevens, *Cyclopedia of Fraternities* (1907), for more information.

RUSSIAN BROTHERHOOD ORGANIZATION OF THE U.S.A. (RBO). This society was founded in 1900 and incorporated in 1903. As a fraternal benefit society, the organization has always had strong interests in preserving Russian culture and heritage. Many of 365 lodges of the society are connected with parishes. The close association between the society lodges and the parishes of the Greek Catholic rite have been particularly beneficial to the churches, especially in that many parishes have received financial support from the RBO.

The society, like most fraternal benefit groups, grants scholarships to selected member students attending college. Contributions also are made to needy, destitute, and disabled members. Local lodge members frequently visit sick members. Grants are also given to parochial schools in Alaska and other stateside territories. Civic and charitable institutions also frequently receive assistance from the RBO.

Culturally, the society supports Russian art, music, theatrical works, and ballet. Local lodges in many areas organize choral groups for purposes of preserving liturgical and folk music, along with balalaika orchestras and folk dancing. District lodges have built sports and cultural centers.

Currently (1978) the membership in the RBO stands at less than 9,000, a decrease from the 12,000 members that the society had in the mid-1960s. Members primarily reside in Connecticut, New Jersey, New York, Ohio, and Pennsylvania.

The society has about 365 local lodges. This number is down from a few years ago. For instance, in 1972 it had 386 local units. The national convention takes place every four years. Headquarters are in Philadelphia, Pennsylvania.

Additional information may be acquired by consulting the society's monthly newspaper, *The Truth*. Brochures and pamphlets produced by the society provide added information. There appears to be no scholarly history of the RBO.

RUSSIAN INDEPENDENT MUTUAL AID SOCIETY (RIMAS). This small fraternal benefit group was formed in 1931. As a Russian ethnic society, the organization has always had, and still has, a close relationship with the Orthodox Catholic Church. Local units work hand in hand with parishes. Many of the RIMAS members volunteer time and effort to church work.

The society supports a number of cultural events such as the study of the Russian language, music, folk dances, and customs. Many local units sponsor annual picnics, banquets, dances, concerts, dramatic presentations, and other social events.

Membership in the RIMAS is continuing to go downward. In 1965 the society had 1,475 members, but in 1978 it had fewer than 900 members. The membership is essentially confined to Illinois and Michigan.

Local units are commonly known as "Branches." The national convention takes place every two years. Headquarters are situated in Chicago, Illinois.

RUSSIAN ORTHODOX CATHOLIC MUTUAL AID SOCIETY OF THE U.S.A. (ROCMAS). Founded in 1895, this society, as its name indicates, is a fraternal benefit society for Americans of Russian descent, who are members of the Orthodox Catholic Church. Closely associated with the church, the society regularly contributes to the church's theological seminaries. The society also assists members who are hit by disaster. Other recipients of aid are the Boy Scouts of America, the Girl Scouts, and the American Red Cross.

The society's membership has been declining. In 1965 the organization had 2,777 members, but by 1978 the count had dropped to about 1,500. Similarly, the society's local units have also dwindled. For instance, in 1972 there were 170 local lodges, but by 1977 there were only 152.

Conventions of the ROCMAS take place every four years. Headquarters are maintained in Wilkes-Barre, Pennsylvania.

Since the ROCMAS failed to furnish the writer specific information, this organizational sketch is of necessity brief. The interested reader, however, may obtain additional information by consulting the society's bimonthly periodical, *Svit* (The Light).

RUSSIAN ORTHODOX CATHOLIC WOMEN'S MUTUAL AID SOCIETY (ROCWMS). This small fraternal benefit society, which in 1965 had 2,425 members, has currently (1978) about 1,700 members. The society was formed in 1907 to provide fraternal benefits for women in the Russian Orthodox Catholic community.

Today the society, small as it is, grants college scholarships to eligible members. Each year donations are made to St. Tikhon's Seminary and Monastery. It also provides aid to St. Vladimer's Seminary, as well as to the Orthodox Monastery of Transfiguration. Other recipients of ROCWMS financial aid are the Orthodox Herald Press, the Alaskan Fund, and the Children's Hospital of Pittsburgh Annual Appeal Fund Drive.

Currently (1978) the society has about fifty local lodges, all of which are located in Pennsylvania. The organization holds a convention quadrennially. Head offices are in Pittsburgh, Pennsylvania.

For further information, see the society's semiannual newsletter. Its constitution and several publicity brochures are also helpful sources of information concerning the society.

__ S

SAINT JOHN OF JERUSALEM, SOVEREIGN ORDER OF (OSJ). This society asserts that it is the only authentic and legal order founded in A.D. 1048 in Jerusalem. "All other groups parading under different settings of the same words are simply provincial imitations, and as such, do not deserve any recognition." So reads one of the official brochures issued by the OSJ. Occasionally, the society is also known by the name of Sovereign Order of St. John of Jerusalem (Knights of Malta).

The society apparently was founded in a Roman Catholic monastery that was dedicated to Saint John the Baptist. The monks of this particular monastery were called Brothers of Saint John. Some also called them hospitalers. The latter name arose due to the order having been engaged in caring for the sick. When the Crusades got underway, the order became a rival of the Knights Templar.* The OSJ inherited some of the property of the Templars when they were disbanded in the early fourteenth century. Taking over the Templars' property was in some ways the beginning of the OSJ's wealth and power, which later made itself felt throughout Europe.

From 1048 to 1291 the ancient order resided in Jerusalem. During this time the Bull of Pope Innocent II in 1150 lauded the OSJ for defending the Eastern Church. After the Saracens captured the Holy Land, the order moved to Cyprus, where it existed from 1292 to 1310. From Cyprus the society went to the island of Rhodes. Here it remained from 1311 to 1523. When the Turks conquered Rhodes, the order moved on to Malta. It stayed here until 1798. According to the OSJ literature, the order moved from Malta to Russia, where it stayed from 1798 to 1907. And in 1908, says the OSJ, it migrated to the United States, where it still is in existence. Most historians note that after Napoleon Bonaparte conquered Malta in 1798, the order soon lost its glory, wealth, and power. Today the society has a meager membership of approximately 500.

While the order once was an exclusive group of Roman Catholics, today its membership consists of Baptists, Lutherans, Methodists, Presbyterians, Episcopalians, and Orthodox, as well as Catholics. This heterogeneous membership apparently has led the society to adopt its present slogan: "As we are united in Christ, we are united with one another."

Today (1979) the order displays a significantly different posture from that it had 900 years ago. For instance, it is promoting the virtues of cosmic energy, which the order says not only can be used to control the weather but also help "maintain normal physical health."

To join the OSJ the applicant must be "a practicing Christian" and submit a biography of himself relative to "date and place of birth for self and parents, education, career, names and ages of children." To acquire and maintain membership a "substantial voluntary contribution or gift, according to the conscience and ability of the applicant . . ." is requested. Membership is not solicited. There are three ranks in the order, namely, Knight, Knight Commander, and Knight Grand Cross.

The traditional emblem of the OSJ is a white Maltese cross. The four arms represent four cardinal virtues: prudence, justice, fortitude, and temperance. Each of the eight points on the cross stands for a particular beatitude: spiritual joy, to live without malice, to weep over one's sins, to humble oneself before those who injure, to love justice, to be merciful, to be sincere and pure of heart, and to suffer persecution.

Currently (1979) the OSJ has twenty priories in countries outside of the United States. The highest authority in the order is the "Supreme Council," and the highest officer is known as the Grand Chancellor. World headquarters are situated in Shickshinny, Pennsylvania.

Additional information may be acquired by consulting the order's official periodical, *The Maltese Cross*. A number of brochures and pamphlets are also available from the head office of the order.

ST. PATRICK'S ALLIANCE OF AMERICA (SPAA). Founded in 1868 as a fraternal beneficiary association, the society paid sick and death benefits to its members, who mostly were Roman Catholics. The ritual of the society accented freedom of religion and denounced bigotry. Its emblem was a disk portraying the letters S.P.A. of A. It also had a picture of the "Tree of Life." In many of the society's practices it had borrowed fraternal customs from the Foresters. The society's headquarters operated out of Newark, New Jersey, the home of its secretary. REFERENCE: *Cyc. Frat.*

SAMARITANS, ANCIENT MYSTIC ORDER OF (AMOS). If the Masons can have a "playground" or "fun" order, why not one for the Odd Fellows?

This is precisely what the AMOS is for the Independent Order of Odd Fellows (IOOF).* The AMOS came into existence in 1924 when a number of Odd Fellow "fun groups" formed a consolidation. The largest order that helped make up the new order in 1924 was the Oriental Order of Humility and Perfection. Others in the merger were the Imperial Order of Muscovites,* the Veiled Prophets of Bagdad, the Knights of Oriental Splendor, and the Ancient Mystic Order of Cabirians.

This group, which in many ways resembles the Ancient Arabic Order of Nobles of the Mystic Shrine,* has never been officially approved by the Sovereign Grand Lodge of the Odd Fellows. The lack of such formal recognition, however, is not uncommon. For instance, the Knights of Columbus* have never officially recognized the Order of Alhambra,* the "playground" society for the Knights of Columbus. Other instances could be cited.

The titles of the AMOS officers and other terms have Arabian-sounding names. The chief officer on the national level is Supreme Monarchos. Some of the other leaders are the Supreme Kalifah, the Supreme Ali-Baba, and the Supreme Muezzin. The members, like the Shriners, wear fezzes.

The fun orientation of the society is not just confined to its meetings or public appearances. In one of his letters to the author, the Supreme Secretary displayed some wholesome humor when instead of ending the letter with the customary "Yours truly" or "Sincerely," he wrote: "In *A Mile Of Smiles*," and then signed his name.

The order's insignia consists of a crescent cradling an Egyptian pyramid and three palm trees. The pyramid bears the letters AMOS and also carries the name XERXES. A scimitar portraying the message WE NEVER SLEEP is balanced on the point of the pyramid. The scimitar also has a wide-eyed owl perched on its center.

Two degrees are available in this order. The Humility degree is given to all who become regular members. The Perfection degree is only given to those attending a supreme or divisional convention.

Only members in good standing in the IOOF are eligible to join the AMOS. Currently (1979) the order has 3,953 members. This represents a loss of about 2,000 (or one-third of the members) since 1967, when the organization had about 6,000 members.

The AMOS, along with the IOOF, in recent years has opened its membership rolls to nonwhites. In one of his letters to the author the Supreme Secretary, Mr. Harold T. Swindler, wrote: "I have registrars who are proud to announce they have a Brother of the IOOF that has been accepted in their Sanctorum who is red, yellow, or black. . . . Yes, we do have very active 'colored' members."

A Samaritan Act Program is operated to help support mental retardation programs. The Samaritans prefer to call this program S.H.A.R.P. (Samaritans Help All Retarded Persons). Members who contribute to the SHARP program receive a certificate that portrays the Samaritan giving aid to his stricken "enemy" found by the wayside. Any member who gives as little as $5.00 receives the certificate. No funds are solicited from the general public.

Administratively, the AMOS operates on three levels: national which includes Canada, regional, and local. The national business of the order is transacted in the "Supreme Sanctorum" sessions. These sessons are held annually, usually in a city or town where there is an active local chapter which the AMOS calls "Sanctorum." The nine regional groups are referred to as "Divisional Sanctorums." The national headquarters are situated in Morgantown, West Virginia.

For additional background the reader may consult the order's mimeographed newsletter, "A.M.O.S. Realm." It is issued quarterly. Another source is the society's constitution and bylaws.

SANHEDRIMS, ANCIENT ORDER OF. A fraternal benefit society founded in 1895 in Richmond, Virginia, the society was an outgrowth of the Ancient Order of Knights of the Orient. The latter was a side degree of the Knights of Pythias.* Headquarters were situated in Richmond, Virginia. REFERENCE: *Cyc. Frat.*

SCIOTS, ANCIENT EGYPTIAN ORDER OF (AEOS). San Francisco, California, was the site where this order was formed in 1905. A group of Freemasons gathered to organize a society that would enable them to be "free from the restraint of the lodge room, yet organized for the purpose of furthering Masonic teachings and applying, in a practical way, in everyday business affairs, the teachings of the fraternity." At the time of its formation the society was known as the Boosters. In 1910 the name of the order was changed to Ancient Egyptian Order of Sciots, in honor of the island Scio in Asia Minor.

The AEOS uses "Boost One Another" as its motto. Its government is vested in a "Supreme Pyramid, composed of representatives of its various local units, called "subordinate pyramids." Presently (1979) the order has seventeen pyramids in California and Arizona.

A number of activities and programs are sponsored by the AEOS. Once monthly, the order holds a "social night," during which dinners, dances, lectures with movies, and other entertainment are provided. Since 1923 the society has sponsored De Molay* chapters whenever asked. Bands and drill teams also are a regular part of the order's activities. A widows-and-orphans fund is operated that provides a benefit of $1,000 to the beneficiary in the event of a member's death. Funds for this program are collected by assessing each member $1.20 upon the death of a member.

The ritual of the AEOS is based on an event that supposedly occurred in

1124 B.C., or sixty years after the fall of Troy. The Sciots at that time were under Greek rule and well known for their strong emphasis on democracy, which resulted in their forming "A League of Neighbors." As "neighbors," they practiced true fraternity. This behavior so impressed the Pharaoh of Egypt that he invited the Sciots to visit his palace. Soon a great friendship developed between the Egyptians and the Sciots. Thus every "third moon the Sciots would journey to the palace, where they received a warm welcome and were entertained with much feasting and merry-making." As the ritual revolves about this legend, the AEOS calls its degree "League of Neighbors."

Membership is open to any Master Mason in good standing. In order to join, the applicant is required to petition and to promise that he will attend his Blue Lodge at least once a month. As of March, 1979, there were 1,800 members in the AEOS. This figure represents a notable decline from the 3,000 members that the order had in the mid-1960s. Membership is confined to Arizona and California.

The emblem of the order is a pyramid that bears the portrait of a Sphinx. The Sphinx denotes past Toparchs, and the pyramid symbolizes past Pharaohs. The uniforms and regalia of the society closely resemble those worn by the Shriners.*

Local units, as already noted, are called "Subordinate Pyramids." The highest authority is the "Supreme Pyramid." It meets in convention annually. Head offices are in Sacramento, California.

Additional information may be obtained by reading the *Sciots Bulletin*. It is published ten times per year. Pamphlets and brochures were obtained from the head offices.

SCOTTISH CLANS, ORDER OF (OSC). This society of Scotsmen and Scotswomen was organized in 1878 in St. Louis, Missouri, by James McCash and some of his Masonic friends. Its objectives were (1) to unite fellow Scotsmen who were between eighteen and fifty-five years of age; (2) to establish death benefits for the deceased member's family; (3) to relieve the financial burdens of sick members by establishing a relief fund; and (4) to strengthen Scottish bonds and cultural heritage.

The ritual of the OSC was based in part on the Danes trying to capture the Castle Slanes and their defeat. The Battle of Bannockburn also played a part in the order's ritual. The emblem of the society was the Scottish thistle with the motto: *Nemo Me Impune Lacessit.*

In the 1920s the order experienced actuarial insolvency in the state of Missouri, where it was incorporated. In 1971 the society merged with the Independent Order of Foresters (IOF).*

Membership originally was open only to Scottish male descendants. During the latter years of the order's existence, Scottish females were also eligible for membership. Before the OSC merged with the IOF, it had about 16,000 members.

Structurally, the order operated on three levels: local, regional, and national. Local units were known as "Subordinate Clans," and the national group was referred to as the "Royal Clan." The latter group met in convention every two years. Headquarters were in Boston, Massachusetts.

Additional information may be had by consulting Albert C. Stevens, *Cyclopedia of Fraternities*. This report in part is based on Stevens' work.

SCOTTISH RITE FREEMASONRY. See Ancient Accepted Rite of Freemasonry for the Northern Masonic Jurisdiction of the United States of America. Also see Ancient and Accepted Scottish Rite of Freemasonry for the Southern Jurisdiction of the United States of America, The Supreme Council 33°, Mother Supreme Council of the World.

SERB NATIONAL FEDERATION (SNF). The history of this fraternal benefit society dates back to 1901 when the group was known as Srbobran-Sloga. In 1929, when Sloboda and Srbobran-Sloga merged, the newly formed organization chose the name of Serb National Federation, making it the largest Serbian fraternal group in North America.

The society is a typical fraternal beneficiary organization, serving American Serbians who are between sixteen and sixty years of age. The SNF seeks to keep "alive the finest traditions of the Serbian people . . . fosters and perpetuates 100 percent Americanism. . . ." Various programs are also sponsored such as cultural events, sports programs, and social gatherings for the members. In a number of instances the society has helped finance church buildings, plus halls for social, humanitarian purposes.

Membership is open to individuals of Serbian or Slav origin. Children under sixteen are accepted (insured) in the auxiliary called "Junior Order." Presently (1979) the SNF has approximately 20,000 members. Membership groups exist in ten states and in Canada. Headquarters are maintained in Pittsburgh, Pennsylvania.

A bilingual newspaper, *The American Srbobran*, is published by the SNF. The reader may wish to consult it for additional information. Pamphlets and brochures are also issued by the society.

SEXENNIAL LEAGUE. A fraternal benefit organization chartered under the laws of Pennsylvania in 1888, the league was founded by members from the Royal Arcanum,* Ancient Order of United Workmen,* Independent Order of Odd Fellows,* Freemasonry,* and other secret societies. The society offered the rather distinctive feature of permitting members to terminate their membership after six years. Such members could rejoin, and in another six years again terminate their membership. This plan was intended to create a financial reward for persistent membership. The ritual was based on the life of Archimedes, with special reference to his statement about having a place to stand so that he could move the world. Head offices were situated in Philadelphia, Pennsylvania. REFERENCES: *Cyc. Frat.*; *DSOS*.

SHEPHERDS, ANCIENT ORDER OF. This organization functioned as a fraternal benefit group, while in reality it was also the third degree of the Foresters of America. The order was founded in 1902. Both men and women were admitted. Membership was never large. In 1905, for instance, the society had 708 members. Head offices were located in Chicago, Illinois.

SHEPHERDS OF BETHLEHEM, ORDER OF. Founded in Trenton, New Jersey, in 1896, this society was a fraternal beneficiary society. It admitted men and women to its membership roster. Men addressed the woman member as "Lady," and women referred to the male member as "Sir." The secret ritual contained three degrees: Light, Shepherd, and Disciple degrees. Headquarters were in Camden, New Jersey. REFERENCE: *Cyc. Frat.*

SHIELD OF HONOR, ORDER OF. This fraternal order was organized in Baltimore, Maryland, in 1877 as a beneficiary society. The society admitted only white males to its ranks. In 1896 the membership count was 14,000. By 1910 its membership was down to 9,942 and by 1923 the count dropped to a total of 3,500. By 1930 the organization appears to have gone out of existence. The ritual of the society was considered to be secret. The home office was in Baltimore, Maryland.

SHRINE, ANCIENT ARABIC ORDER OF THE NOBLES OF THE MYSTIC (AAONMS). In spite of the Shrine's foreign-sounding name, it is as American as apple pie. This "playground for Masons," as it is often known, was founded by two American citizens: Walter M. Fleming, a medical doctor, and Billy Florence, an actor. William J. Whalen, *Handbook of Secret Organizations* (1966), says Florence was an indifferent Mason and a delinquent Catholic, who renounced Freemasonry* only hours before his death in 1891.

The idea to create a "fun" order of Masons basically was Fleming's, but to give it an Arabian flavor was Florence's doing. In 1867, while Florence was in Marseilles, France, he was invited by an Arabian diplomat to view a musical comedy that concluded by making its viewers members of a secret society. It is from this experience that Florence later in 1870 developed the first draft of the Shrine ritual.

Once the ritual was drafted, Dr. Fleming publicized the newly created fraternal order. In fact, he "let it be known that the Shrine ritual had been written by the great Persian poet, Alnasafi the Hafiz." So reads one of the Shrine's own accounts.

Fleming, however, did more than provide publicity for the order. He also designed the society's costumes, emblem, and its "jewel" which is the crescent, now usually made of the claws of the Bengal tiger. The crescent is an oriental religious symbol that has commonly signified a higher and purer source of knowledge. Fleming also created the Shrine salutation, "*Es Selamu Aleikum*" (peace be with you) to which there is the response, "*Aleikum es Selamu*" (with you be peace).

The familiar red fez, which everyone associates with the Shrine, apparently served to attract members during the order's early years. Some historians believe that this headgear dates back to A.D. 980. However, the name "fez" or "tarboosh" first appears in Arabic literature in the fourteenth century. One of the earliest references to the term fez is found in "Arabian Nights."

The first temple (similar to a lodge or chapter) was formed on September 26, 1872, in New York City. The Imperial Grand Council was organized on June 6, 1878. This council is the order's international administrative structure.

Early in the Shrine's existence, it was decided that membership should be restricted to thirty-second-degree Scottish Rite* Masons. This means that an individual must not only be a Master Mason with three degrees from the Blue Lodge,* but he must acquire an additional twenty-nine degrees. Masons in the York Rite who are in the Commandery of the Knights Templar* (tenth degree) may also become members of the Shrine. All members are white, as nonwhites are barred from the lower-degree rites. Three blackballs are required to reject applicants for membership. The 1978 membership roster had close to 1,000,000 "Nobles," as the order calls its members. The order has, with the exception of the years from 1927 through 1941, experienced a net increase in its membership each year.

Its wide involvement in the crippled children's hospital work has bolstered the Shrine's social public image during the past fifty years. But that is not all. The AAONMS can also point to some high-status individuals who have come to its temples. For instance, Franklin D. Roosevelt, Harry S. Truman, Gerald Ford, and John Diefenbaker (former Canadian Prime Minister), as well as some United States senators and a number of governors have conferred status upon the Shrine.

Who in the United States and Canada does not know about the Shriners' hospitals for crippled children! This indicates that the order has been very successful in public relations. Prior to 1920 the Shrine had no humanitarian projects. To take care of "friendless, orphaned, and crippled children" was the idea of W. Freeland Kendrick, an "Imperial Potentate" (the highest national officer). Thus at the Shrine's 46th Imperial council session in 1920, Kendrick's proposal for a Shriners hospital for crippled children was adopted. Part of the resolution required every Noble to pay $2.00 each year to help underwrite the humanitarian venture. Today (1978) the assessment is $5.00 per member. This assessment raises less than 20 percent of what it costs to run the twenty-two hospitals in Canada and the United States. Some of the costs also are paid from the One Hundred Million Dollar Club, a Shrine endowment fund. The annual East-West football games also help provide hospital monies. Each year about 31,000 patients receive medical care; of these 8,000 are in-patients. Since 1962, the Shrine has extended its medical charity to treating burn-injured patients in several of its hospitals.

Being the playground for Masons, the Nobles frequently participate in parades, funfare, and hoopla. One can observe them, especially during their conventions, engaging in such activities as kissing unknown ladies in the street, chasing college coeds on campus and then making them drink from nursing bottles, carrying toilet paper and calling out: "Evening Paper." One Imperial Potentate once said: "Little boys play cops and robbers. Shriner's play Moslems and infidels."

The ritual of the Shrine has both serious and burlesque features. In true Masonic fashion, each candidate takes a vow of secrecy not to reveal the "Secrets" of the order. The good Noble promises:

In willful violation whereof may I incur the fearful penalty of having my eyeballs pierced to the center with a three-edged blade, my feet flayed and I be forced to walk the hot sands upon the sterile shores of the Red Sea until the flaming sun shall strike me with a livid plague, and may Allah, the god of Arab Moslem and Mohammedan, the god of our fathers, support me to the entire fulfillment of the same. Amen, Amen, Amen.

The burlesque features of the ritual take place during the initiation ceremonies. For instance, the candidate is tricked into a boxing match with an experienced Noble, who soon complains of being robbed. This prompts an investigation of the candidate. Previously placed items are found in some "guilty" candidate's clothing. Punishment ensues by stripping him of his clothes, blindfolding him, and seating him on a large sponge filled with ice water. When the news comes saying he is exonerated because of his good character, he is permitted to put on his clothes.

Another portion of the initiation requires the candidates to experience the Bung Hole test, which has two blindfolded candidates enter a large metal cylinder (lying on its side) from opposite ends. In the middle they bump heads. One of the Nobles yelps like a small dog. Another squirts a few drops of warm water on the blindfolded candidates' faces. At that moment another Noble shouts: "Take that dog out of here. He has just p_____ in the face of Mr._____!"

Administratively, the Shrine's national (really international) structure is known as the "Imperial Council." Its officers bear exotic sounding titles: Most Illustrious Grand Potentate, Illustrious Grand Rabban, Illustrious Grand High Priest. The AAONMS is headquartered in Chicago, Illinois, and meets in convention annually in different locations each year. Its local meetings take place in "Temples," of which there presently (1978) are 180. Temple officers bear similar titles to those of the imperial council, except the term "Imperial" is not employed.

The emblem of the AAONMS is the scimitar, which holds the crescent, and between the dropping horns of the crescent hangs a five-pointed star. The crescent also displays the portrait of the Egyptian Sphinx.

To obtain further information the reader may consult the booklet by George M. Saunders, *A Short History of the Shrine* (n.d.). This is published by the AAONMS. The *Mystic Shrine: An Illustrated Ritual of the Ancient Arabic Order Nobles of the Mystic Shrine* (1968) may be bought from Ezra A. Cook Publications, Inc. This volume also contains the order's constitution. The reader may also consult Fred Van Deventer, *Parade to Glory: The Story of the Shriners and Their Hospitals for Crippled Children* (1959).

SHRINE, ANCIENT EGYPTIAN ARABIC ORDER OF NOBLES OF THE (AEAONS). This is a black order of Shriners, organized on June 10, 1893, in Chicago, Illinois. The claim has been made that the order was founded by the visiting Grand Council of Arabia, whose representatives were in Chicago attending the World's Fair in 1893. Originally, the order was named Ancient Arabic Order of Nobles of the Mystic Shrine of North and South America.

The AEAONS is very similar to the Ancient Arabic Order of the Nobles of the Mystic Shrine, the white fraternity. Its ritual reportedly is the same as the white Shriners' version. The ritual revolves about Arabic legends, and it is kept secret from nonmembers. The regalia of the AEAONS also resembles the formal dress of the white Shrine. Members in public appearances wear the fez and other colorful garb.

Membership is open to thirty-second-degree Masons and Knights Templar. Until rather recently the order had only black members. Now the society reportedly has some white members on its roster. The membership has been growing. In the mid-1960s the AEAONS had 15,000 members. Now (1979) there are about 31,000 black Shriners.

The AEAONS is a fraternal secret society in that it does not offer its members fraternal life insurance, as is the practice in fraternal benefit societies. Its members enjoy the social and fraternal activities largely as an end in themselves. However, it must be noted that the society also supports research hospitals, contributing funds to medical research pertaining to diseases that tend to afflict blacks more commonly.

Local units are called "Temples," and the ladies' auxiliary (Daughters of Isis*) groups are known as "Courts." On the national level, the AEAONS refers to its structure as the "Imperial Temple." The national group meets annually in convention. Headquarters are in Detroit, Michigan.

For further information, see the order's quarterly publication, *The Pyramid*. The annual proceedings also provide further insight into the AEAONS.

SHRINE DIRECTORS ASSOCIATION OF NORTH AMERICA (SDANA). This association was founded in 1919 to bring together all the directors from every white Shrine temple in North America. The association conducts safety research and sponsors educational programs. It also provides assistance to the Shriners' hospitals for crippled children.

Membership consists of the 180 directors, one from each Shrine temple in North America. Only Shriners may belong to the SDANA.

The association meets in convention annually. Its headquarters are maintained in Jacksonville, Florida.

SHRINE RECORDERS ASSOCIATION OF NORTH AMERICA (SRA). This association does not function as a fraternal order, as most orders ordinarily do. The group meets annually to render assistance to those who hold the position of recorder in the White Shrine* organization. It has no ritual or degrees. There are no head offices. The individual who is elected secretary-treasurer of the SRA serves as the "head office" in his home town.

SLAVONIC BENEVOLENT ORDER OF THE STATE OF TEXAS (SPJST). The letters SPJST form the abbreviation of the society's name (Slovanska Podporujici Jednota Statu Texas) in Czech. The SPJST began with twenty-five Czech Texans meeting in La Grange on December 28, 1896, to form a fraternal, benevolent society. By June 1897 the first convention, with twenty-two lodges represented, was held in La Grange, Texas.

The society lists several objectives, namely, encourage individual and group social responsibility, provide economic security and benevolent assistance to members and their families, encourage and promote American patriotism, and study and retain the Czech language, as well as honor its traditions and culture.

Like most fraternal groups that are predominantly engaged in insurance, the SPJST has some type of initiation requirement, but the austere religious trappings of the more traditional fraternal societies are lacking. Signs, secrets, and passwords also are not part of the fraternal paraphernalia.

Membership is open to men and women, provided they enjoy good health. All prospective members must be citizens of the United States. Five negative votes are necessary to reject a candidate for membership. Initiation of new members is done once each year, and the date for the event is set by each local lodge. In 1979 the SPJST had 54,000 members. Ten years ago the society had 35,000 members on its roster.

The emblem of the society is a five-pointed star with the letters SPJST encircling the star. A laurel wreath encircles the star and the letters SPJST.

Altruistically, the order supports two ultramodern homes for the elderly. One home is in Taylor, Texas, and the other in Needville, Texas. During World War II the society bought enough bonds to purchase a B-24 Literator bomber. This aircraft bore the name "SPJST of Texas."

Administratively the SPJST has a "Supreme Lodge," seven districts, and 130 local lodges. The supreme lodge meets quadrennially. Local lodges are required to meet monthly. The supreme lodge is headquartered in Temple, Texas.

Reading material on the SPJST is limited. A good primary source is the society's weekly paper, *Vestnik*. The *Constitution and By-Laws* (1976) provide a good understanding of how the order functions and operates. Various pamphlets and brochures may be obtained from the head office in Temple, Texas.

SLOGA FRATERNAL LIFE INSURANCE SOCIETY (SFLIS). Organized in 1908, this fraternal benefit group was known as South Slavic Benevolent Union "Sloga" until 1968. Since its origin, the society has served Slovanians. However, in recent years non-Slovanians also are eligible for membership. Unlike many Slavic fraternal organizations, the SFLIS does not require its members to be Catholic.

In typical fraternal benefit manner, the SFLIS awards scholarships to eligible members. Other fraternal projects of the society range from conducting blood banks to athletic events such as bowling, golf, and softball. Members are also encouraged to contribute to various community charities, for example, United Fund and Easter Seals.

Membership in 1978 numbered approximately 1,400. This number has remained relatively constant over the last few years.

Because of the organization's small membership the number of local lodges also is quite small. There were fourteen in 1978. Wisconsin is the only state in which the society is licensed to sell insurance. Conventions take place every four years, and headquarters are in Milwaukee, Wisconsin.

SLOVAK CATHOLIC SOKOL (SCS). When first organized in 1905, this group was named the Roman and Greek Catholic Gymnastic Union Sokol. The society chose St. Martin, Bishop of Tours, as its patron saint. Its motto was picked to be "For God and Nation," in Slovak: *"Za Boha a narod."*

Early in the organization's existence gymnastics were introduced. This feature helped attract new members. Thus by 1921 the society had 19,025 members with close to a quarter million dollars in assets. The SCS has always been closely associated with the church. It has participated in the 26th International Eucharistic Congress in the 1920s, and other ecclesiastical involvement is characteristic of the order.

The Great Depression of the 1930s did not seem to affect the SCS. Its membership continued to grow. By 1936 there were more than 42,000 members. The only slowdown that occurred was during World War II, when the society held no conventions or *Slets* (gymnastic exhibitions). Right after the war, the society resumed regular activities. Its membership in 1946 was 44,243.

The SCS is a fraternal benefit society, even though it is extensively engaged in gymnastic activities and events. As a fraternal benefit organization, it provides the usual life insurance programs and other fraternal benevolences. Each year the society donates thousands of dollars to charitable organizations, churches, and emergency funds. Financial assistance is also provided to missionaries and to individuals preparing for the priesthood. The society also is active in awarding scholarships. Every year twenty scholarships of $500 each are given to qualified applicants. On the local level, the order assists members in distress and sickness.

The SCS insignia is a golden eagle with outstretched wings. Each claw is upholding the end of a barbell. On the eagle's breast is a blue shield displaying a double-armed cross. Below the shield appear the letters SCS. A laurellike wreath forms an oval-shaped design around the eagle.

The SCS, which strongly believes in the slogan, "A sound mind in a sound body," had approximately 50,000 members in 1979. The society is organized into five districts, eighteen "Groups," and 537 senior and junior assemblies (local units). Its headquarters are in Passaic, New Jersey.

Additional information may be obtained by consulting the society's weekly newspaper, *Katolicky Sokol*. It also publishes a periodical, *Children's Friend*. The latter is issued monthly. The society also has available a mimeographed copy of its history, covering the period from 1905 to 1976.

SLOVAK GYMNASTIC UNION SOKOL OF THE UNITED STATES OF AMERICA (SGUS). The word *sokol* in Czech language means falcon, a bird symbolizing love of freedom, strength, courage, and agility. Sokols to Czechs since 1872 have come to be identified with physical education and physical fitness. In 1862 a university professor (Dr. Miroslav Tyrs) at Charles University in Prague and a businessman (Jindrich Fuegner) interested in the arts and music organized a program of physical fitness (a Sokol) that stemmed from the philosophy of a sound mind in a healthy body. The idea of organizing Sokols soon spread to the United States. In March of 1865 the first Sokol group was organized in St. Louis, Missouri. By 1892 the first Slovak Sokol fraternal lodge was formed in Chicago, Illinois, and in 1896 the Slovak Gymnastic Union Sokol of the United States of America was founded as a fraternal benefit society. In 1944 the society absorbed the Tatran Slovak Union. That same year it also absorbed the Slovak Evangelical Society.

The SGUS, as a fraternal insurance organization, offers the usual kinds of fraternal insurance plans to its members. The society also is true to its name by accenting physical fitness through gymnastic competitions and exhibitions known as *Slets*. The latter are competitive festivals consisting of sports, calisthenics, dances, games, gymnastics, and the like.

In addition to the physical fitness programs and insurance, the society also maintains camps and homes in several states. Scholarships are awarded to worthy members who are in college.

Membership is open to those of Slovak descent or by marriage to a Slovak descendant. Currently (1979) the membership of SGUS is in the vicinity of 23,000. The society has approximately 200 local units and twelve district groups. The national body convenes in convention every four years.

For further information, see the society's weekly publication, *Slovensky Sokol*. Leaflets and brochures from the organization will provide additional background.

SLOVENE NATIONAL BENEFIT SOCIETY (SNBS). Three days after the society was formed in Chicago on April 6, 1904, it held its first convention on April 9. Incorporation of the SNBS, however, did not occur until June 17, 1907. The incorporation was delayed over one year because Illinois insurance law required that a fraternal benefit society had to have a minimum of 500 members. When the society began, it offered death benefits of $500 per member. The assessed fee was $1.00 per capita regardless of age. Only males were insured. Today the society is a legal reserve insurance group, affiliated with the National Fraternal Congress of America.

The present constitution of the SNBS states that the society is "founded on a free-thought basis." It "grants to its members personal freedom of religious, philosophical, ethical and political creeds." This posture of the organization can only be changed by a three-fourths majority vote. The free-thought basis of the society has its origin from the days prior to the organization's actual formation when many Slovene immigrants in the United States felt that some of the existing Slovene fraternal groups were too closely linked to the church. When the SNBS was organized it assumed the posture of being relatively free of religious ties and influence. The constitution also says the object of the SNBS is "to unite eligible persons of both sexes of sound mind, health and good moral character in a fraternal beneficiary society for the sole benefit of its members and their beneficiaries and not for profit. . . ." In recent years the society also has been very supportive of organized labor.

Membership eligibility calls for the individual to be "of sound mind, health and good moral character, not below the age of 16 and not above the prescribed maximum age as established by the National Board. . . ." Male and female are welcome. Like most fraternal organizations, the SNBS constitution provides for disciplining members when they transgress the society's principles. In the SNBS possible offenses range from the intemperate use of alcohol or drugs to attempting to bring into the society someone who is immoral or physically unsound. Current membership stands at 56,000 in 350 lodges located in twenty states. In the late 1960s the society had 68,000 members. Thus during the last ten years the society has incurred a membership loss of 18 percent.

The SNBS has a ritual, but there is no great secrecy pertaining to it. The ritual contains rubrics covering installation of officers, initiation of new members, the organizational pledge, and funeral rites. The initiation pledge is simple and unencumbered. The candidate promises to be faithful to the constitution of the society, defend the reputation of the lodges in the SNBS, and in no way bring harm to the society. No one may attend society meetings prior to being initiated. The ritual is published in English and the Slovene language: the first half is in English and the second half in the society's native tongue.

Apart from the benevolence provided through fraternal insurance, the SNBS has the usual array of benevolent activities, ranging from awarding scholarships to providing a recreation center for its members. The society also is very youth-conscious. It sponsors an annual youth roundup and a biennial convention for youth and young adults.

The official colors of the SNBS are red, white, and blue. These colors are boldly visible in the society's emblem which consists of two rings. Within the smaller circle are two laurellike branches, two hands clasped in fraternal friendship, and the American flag. Between the inner and outer ring are two white stars, the Slovene abbreviation for the society's name: S-N-P-J, and the founding date: 1904.

Local units or chapters are known as "lodges" in the SNBS. Each lodge initiates its own members and has supervision over them. The supreme authority, as with most fraternal groups, lies with what the SNBS calls its "National Legislative Body," the national convention which meets quadrennially. Between conventions the National Board transacts various decisions. Headquarters of the SNBS are in a Chicago suburb, Burr Ridge, Illinois.

Not much has been published by or on the SNBS, except for its ritual, constitution, and two periodicals. One periodical is directed to the youth; it is a monthly magazine: *The Voice of Youth*. For the adult members the society publishes a newspaper, *Provesta*. This paper also publishes the society's convention proceedings.

SOCIAL ORDER OF THE BEAUCEANT. See Beauceant, Social Order of the.

SOCIEDADE PORTUGUESA RAINHA SANTA ISABEL (SPRSI). While the preceding name is the official designation of the society, it is also known as the Portuguese Society Queen St. Isabel. The society was founded in 1898 at St. Joseph's Catholic Church in Oakland, California. Its original purpose was to be an altar society, as well as to render material assistance to the members in time of need. The female society chose as its motto "Sociability and Protection." White and blue were selected as the official colors.

In May of 1900 the organization left behind its ecclesiastical altar purposes and became a fraternal benefit society. The supreme council (national body) was formed on January 20, 1901.

Like most fraternal beneficiary societies, the SPRSI involves itself in various community and civic affairs. In the early 1950s the order began awarding scholarships to eligible members who were students.

The constitution of the SPRSI states that membership eligibility consists of being "in good health; to be a good Catholic or a good Christian and of good Moral Character [sic]; and not more than fifty-five years and five months of age, or less than fifteen years and five months. . . ." Membership is open only to females. Currently (1979) the society has 13,386 members in 116 subordinate units, seven junior groups, and two intermediate groups.

Local units are known as "Subordinate Councils." The national body is called "Grand Council." The grand council meets annually in convention. Headquarters are maintained in Oakland, California..

For further information, see the society's *Constitution and General Laws* (1977). A mimeographed copy of the order's history was obtained from the head office in Oakland, California. The society also publishes a monthly newspaper, *Boletim da S.P.R.S.I.*

SOCIETAS ROSICRUCIANA IN CIVITATIBUS FOEDERATIS (SRCF).

This society was founded in the United States on April 21, 1880, in Philadelphia, Pennsylvania, by members of the society from Scotland. The primary purpose of the SRCF is to keep alive the study of the esoteric philosophy derived from the Kabaloh and the teachings of Hermes Trismegistus, especially as it relates to Freemasonry.*

The order has three categories of degrees, commonly referred to as first, second, and third order. Each order has more than one degree. The degrees in the first and second order are conferred on the subordinate level. The third order degrees are only offered by the High Council, the governing unit of the society.

Only Masons may join the SRCF, and then only by invitation. The current (1979) membership figures were unavailable to the writer.

Subordinate groups are called "Colleges." The national and highest authority structure is known as the "High Council." The principal officer of the high council is the Supreme Magus. Headquarters are in Summit, New Jersey.

For additional information, see Harold V. B. Voorhis' brief discussion in his *Masonic Organizations and Allied Orders and Degrees* (1952).

SOCIETY OF BLUE FRIARS, THE (SBF). This rather atypical fraternal organization was formed in Monroe, North Carolina, on July 1, 1932, by John Raymond Shute II. Until 1944 the society conducted its affairs by correspondence and had no formal meetings. Since 1944, however, the society has an annual meeting in Washington, D.C.

The society has no ritual, no degrees, no local lodges, no fees, no dues, no printed proceedings, no constitution, and no magazine. According to the Masonic Service Association's mimeographed document "Allied Masonic Groups and Rites," the society honors one Masonic author each year by making him a "Blue Friar." The document goes on to say that "Upon the death of a Blue Friar, the vacancy is filled by an additional Blue Friar if the total number is less than twenty." This figure apparently has changed, because one of the society's officers sent the present writer a note saying that the membership now (1979) is twenty-five. The chief objective of the SBF is to recognize Masonic authors.

The primary or principal officer is the "Grand Abbot." Headquarters are located wherever he resides. Presently the grand abbot lives in Franklin, Indiana. The secretary general resides in Cresskill, New Jersey.

SOCIETY ESPIRITO SANTO OF THE STATE OF CALIFORNIA (SES). The official name of this fraternal benefit organization is Conselho Supremo Da Sociedade Do Espirito Santo. It was organized in 1895 in Santa Clara, California. Commonly the society's literature refers to itself by the abbreviation of S.E.S.

Over the years the SES has undergone several organizational changes. The first notable change occurred in 1910; the second in 1922; the third in 1962; and the most recent one in 1972. At one time one had to be of Portuguese descent in order to join the society. The present constitution no longer stipulates that members must be Portuguese, although the SES still is very interested in conserving the Portuguese culture and heritage.

As a fraternal benefit organization, the SES offers the usual array of fraternal insurance certificates. It also has available two types of memberships, beneficial and social. All beneficial members are required to be initiated in accordance with the society's ritual. Presently the membership roster reflects about 11,500 members. Since 1972 the society has experienced a slight membership increase. It has even opened an additional lodge in 1976.

The ritual is printed in Portuguese and in English. Like most fraternal rituals, the document contains questions, answers, hymns, pledges, and provision for issuing passwords. The pledge required of every candidate is simple and relatively brief. The pledge is administered by the president of the subordinate lodge.

Fraternally, the SES awards scholarships, sponsors religious Masses for its members, and assists individual members who are sick or affected by natural disasters. Local units carry on various charitable and social activities. Many members serve as volunteers in community projects.

Local units are referred to as "Subordinate Councils." The supreme body is known as the "Supreme Council." The latter council convenes annually as a delegate convention. Headquarters are located in Santa Clara, California.

For more information, see *Constitution and General Laws of the Supreme Council of S.E.S.* (1977). See also *Rituals of the Subordinate Council and Supreme Council* (no date). Both documents are published by the SES.

SONS AND DAUGHTERS OF PROTECTION, THE. Organized in 1896 in Nebraska, this society was founded as a fraternal beneficiary group. The society never had a large membership in its relatively short existence. In 1905 it had 1,825 members. By 1910 the organization seems to have disbanded. Headquarters were located in Lincoln, Nebraska.

SONS OF ABRAHAM, INDEPENDENT ORDER OF. The date of origin for this fraternal benefit society is 1892. It was founded in New York City by three members of the Jewish community. One was a Freemason,* one a member of the Sons of Benjamin,* and the third belonged to the Order of B'rith Abraham.* The society's membership was confined to the city of New York and Brooklyn. Both men and women were eligible for membership. REFERENCE: *Cyc. Frat.*

SONS OF ADAM. Established as a fraternal order by professional men and businessmen in Parsons, Kansas, in 1879, the society had playful elements similar to what the Ku Klux Klan had in the early years of its existence. The order did not survive long, lasting less than fifteen years. REFERENCE: *Cyc. Frat.*

SONS OF BENJAMIN, INDEPENDENT ORDER OF. This Jewish fraternal benefit society was formed in the city of New York in 1877 by individuals who were members of the Order of B'rith Abraham* and other fraternal groups. The society had a secret ritual and other fraternal ceremonies. It also operated lodges exclusively organized for women. Home offices were maintained in the city of New York. REFERENCE: *Cyc. Frat.*

SONS OF HERMANN, ORDER OF (SOH). This fraternal group resulted in response to ethnic and religious prejudice and discrimination that was rather widely practiced in the United States during the 1830s. Supporters of the prejudice eventually formed the Know-Nothing Party in 1852. Since German Americans were frequent recipients of prejudice, some of them banded together in the city of New York in 1840 to protect their German culture and heritage by forming The Order of Sons of Hermann. Reputedly, the name "Hermann" was selected when one of the organization's founders said, in response to the anti-German prejudice, that what was needed was another Hermann, who would conquer the enemies of the Germans. Hermann (the Romans called him Arminius) is a German folk hero, who with his tribal forces, annihilated three Roman legions in the Battle of Teutoberg Forest in 9 A.D. To many Germans he also is the symbol of manhood. In his honor the Germans have erected a tall monument of him near Detmold, Germany. Another statue stands in New Ulm, Minnesota.

The SOH spread to other states. By 1900 the order had over 90,000 members in thirty states, with many states having statewide or grand lodge structures. Presently (1970s), there is really one grand lodge in operation, the Grand Lodge of the Sons of Hermann in Texas. The Texas grand lodge was organized in 1890. In 1921 it became independent of the then-existing National Grand Lodge. The move toward independence was in part prompted by the Texas order's prosperity. In 1921 it had more members and was financially stronger than all other Sons of Hermann lodges in the United States. The Texas SOH also felt independence would provide greater loyalty and pride.

The emblem of the SOH has three symbolic colors: black, red, and gold. Black stands for darkness, ignorance, indifference, and prejudice. Red typifies light and enlightenment, especially as spread by German culture. Gold symbolizes freedom through knowledge and labor. Complementing the three colors on the circular-shaped emblem are the words: HERMANN SONS OF TEXAS, the letters F, L, L, representing friendship, love, and loyalty. The lone star of Texas is in the emblem's center, surrounded by a wreathlike design.

From its very beginning the Sons of Hermann has had a ritual. Although it has an initiation rite, it is not always required of new members. Some become members by means of having taken out insurance with the order. Its burial ritual also is not mandatory. When the burial rite is used, it assures the survivors that the departed "brother" or "sister" has begun a new life in the mansions of the Almighty. Yet, the order does not, like so many other fraternal groups, require belief in a supreme being for membership. Also unlike other orders, the SOH does not give its members degrees.

The SOH has been engaged in benevolent activities from its origin. It still, in a limited way, supports some altruistic programs. There is the Hermann Sons Home for the Aged in Comfort, Texas. Since this home has a capacity of only seventy-five, the order has some of the following requirements for entrance. An applicant must be seventy years or older, in good physical health, a holder of Hermann Sons life insurance certificate of at least $1,000 for at least twenty years, and make the home beneficiary of the first $1,000 in life insurance holdings. The order conducts an extensive youth program, also in Comfort, Texas. Each summer about 2,000 Junior Hermann Sons, ages nine through thirteen, delight in staying at the youth camp for one week. The participants engage in handicraft skills, baseball, swimming, canoeing, tennis, archery, and conducting meetings.

Considerable organizational change has occurred in the SOH. Not only has it become less demanding in requiring the performance of its ritual (as noted), but it also has made other changes. In 1937, the switch was made from German to English in conducting its meetings. That same year membership was opened to individuals of northern European lineage who weren't of German ancestry. Today (1970s), the SOH has Irish, English, and other non-German descendants on its roster. There are no black members in the order. It has moved from a mere benevolent organization, caring for its sick and needy, burying its dead, and caring for widows and orphans, to a highly respectable and financially solvent fraternal insurance society. The membership rolls have been increasing. For instance, from 1965 to 1974, the SOH gained 1,300 members. Apparently the society's organizational change has made the order more attractive.

The Order of the Sons of Hermann in Texas has its grand lodge headquarters in San Antonio, Texas. Over 100 local lodges are spread across the state. In the typical lodge fashion, the SOH calls its officers on the grand level: Grand President, First Grand Vice President, Second Grand Vice President, Grand Secretary-Treasurer, and Grand Physician. The latter's responsibilities include the order's home for the aged. The grand lodge also has three trustees, five finance committeemen, an actuary, and a legal counsel. The grand lodge meets every four years.

Published information on the SOH is scarce. A primary source is the order's monthly periodical, *Hermann Sons News*.

SONS OF ITALY, ORDER OF (OSI). When this order was founded in New York in 1905, only males of Italian descent were permitted to join. Today females may also belong. Members are required to be initiated according to the society's ritual. On formal occasions, such as national holidays and special organizational events, the members dress in colorful regalia.

The society contributes to a number of projects, e.g., the March of Dimes and scholarships for college students. In the summer of 1979 the order made national news when President Carter addressed the society's national convention.

Structurally, the organization operates on three levels: national, state, and local. The national unit is called "Supreme;" the state level now is known as "State." It once was referred to as "Grand." On the local scene the members refer to their order as "Lodge." Headquarters are located in Philadelphia, Pennsylvania.

Additional information may be obtained by reading the society's newspaper, *O.S.I. in America*.

SONS OF NORWAY (SON). Back on January 6, 1895, a group of sixteen Norwegian men met in Minneapolis. They were interested in forming a fraternal benevolent society that would aid fellow Norwegians who were stricken with illness or who had lost a beloved one. As they met, they were encouraged by hearing that other ethnic groups had been quite successful in founding fraternal associations. Thus three days later (January 9) a fraternal organization was born. The organizers decided that the new organization was to be a fraternal lodge in the typical American fashion, namely, with regalia, ritual, and secrecy. One week after the formal date of inception (January 16) the group met to hear a report from its ritual committee. This committee also recommended that three additional officers be elected: a regent, a judge, and a marshall. Previously the order had elected a president, vice-president, secretary, treasurer, three trustees, and a doorkeeper. Of the eighteen charter members, all but two had been residents of the United States for thirteen years or more.

The organization, which chose the name Sons of Norway (*Sönner Af Norge*), was legally incorporated on June 22, 1898. Its formal name on the incorporation document read, "The Independent Order of Sons of Norway." One of the statements in the articles of incorporation revealed that the Sons of Norway had a feeling of ethnic inferiority by stating one of the group's purposes was to see to it that "the Norwegian people in this country may be properly recognized and respected. . . ." Another objective stated that the newly founded lodge would "aid its members and their families in case of sickness and death, by according them financial assistance of such magnitude, and upon such conditions, as may be determined by its by-laws."

The Sons of Norway grew. By 1900 the order had 526 members and four years later it had 2,564 members. From 1905 to 1914 the order spread out its wings, its membership stretching from New York to California. Presently (1978) its roster contains about 40,000 members in 340 local lodges in Canada and the United States. To become a member one must be born Norwegian, of Norwegian descent, or affiliated by marriage.

Through the years the order has had considerable movement toward organizational change. In 1912 the orde merged with the Grand Lodge of the Sons of Norway of the Pacific Coast. That same year the society discontinued using the designation "Head Lodge" and called its national organization "The Supreme Lodge of the Sons of Norway." The year 1912, because of the merger, saw a new constitution adopted at the supreme lodge's convention in Fargo, North Dakota. The new constitution no longer reflected a feeling of ethnic inferiority. Instead one part of the constitution read: "To give our adopted fatherland the fruits of the social and political consciousness of the members, developed in full understanding of the value of the Norse race [sic] and the demands of our new circumstances." In 1950 the SON absorbed the Daughters of Norway.

Like most fraternal lodges, the Sons of Norway was an all-male group. However, by 1916 women could be admitted as members in localities where the Daughters of Norway had no lodge. This exception remained until 1951 when the Daughters of Norway merged with the Sons of Norway. In 1918 the membership was slightly liberalized in terms of ethnic origin. The new rule allowed a candidate "of another nationality, who understands the Norwegian language and is married to a Norwegian who is a member of the lodge . . ." to join. This requirement applied to men and women. Under the old requirement a candidate had to be "Norwegian or of Norwegian descent." Softening the ethnic requirement for membership apparently did not meet much resistance, perhaps because two years earlier (in 1916) the order voted to permit lodges to conduct their meetings in English. Other changes occurred. The Sons gradually adopted better and more accurate actuarial methods in the insurance programs. Although it retained its life insurance program, in 1934 sick and accident insurance policies were discontinued. This action moved the order to place more emphasis on social programs for its members. Organized sports activities, cultural events, and fellowship became an important part of the society's life. Placing a greater accent on being more of a social group did not mean that the order had forsaken all insurance. It did not. Today (1970s) the order offers protection (life insurance) plans, mortgage insurance, pension and retirement plans, juvenile insurance, disability, and hospital benefit plans. In the beginning the order had a "social membership" category (with no voting privileges) for individuals who could not meet health requirements for insurance purposes. The Sons have never permitted the use of alcoholic beverages in lodge halls, bazaars, or picnics.

During the first two decades the order heard considerable criticism of itself. Outsiders referred to the order's lodge meetings as "temples of Norsedom." One historian of the Sons of Norway, Carl G. O. Hansen, said: "Sons of Norway from its very inception, had been viewed with critical eyes by a great many of our [Norwegian] people." The order's secret ritual aroused suspicion. Many Norwegian Lutheran pastors were critical of the order's ritual. Some of the criticism prompted changes in the organization. For example, in 1909 the burial ritual was abolished. This action brought favorable response from the clergy of the conservative Norwegian Synod. since then, the order's ritual has received additional attention. The latest effort was to revise it in 1966, making it less elaborate.

The organization has been quite active in civic and charity endeavors. It erected a statue of Ole Bull (a world-famous Norwegian violinist) in 1897 in Minneapolis' Loring Park. Each year on May 17, Minneapolis citizens see a colorful parade in honor of Norway's Independence Day. In many instances the society was influential in getting Norwegian introduced in public grade schools, high schools, and colleges. The order has supported charities such as hospitals, homes for the elderly, retarded children's homes, and medical research. During World War II it assisted in relief work for Norway. In 1961 a foundation was established to provide continuous support to various charity programs, some of them as far away as Norway.

More recently (since 1956), the order has begun sponsoring junior lodges for young people, providing both boys and girls with colorful regalia. The emblem (in the form of a shield, emblazoned with the North star, the midnight sun, a Viking ship, and the roaring sea) of the junior lodges is the same as that of the Sons of Norway.

The organizational structure resembles that of most fraternal societies. Its national organization is known as the "Supreme Lodge," which elects officers and the directors to the supreme board of the order. Between the supreme and local lodge is the district structure. There are seven districts, encompassing Canada and the United States. National headquarters are housed in a modern, three-storied building in Minneapolis, Minnesota.

Published information on the Sons of Norway may be found by reading C. Sverre Norborg, *An American Saga* (1970); Carol G. O. Hansen, *History of the Sons of Norway* (1944). Valuable information may also be found by consulting back issues of *The Viking*, the order's official magazine.

SONS OF PERICLES, THE ORDER OF (OSOP). Not long after the Order of Ahepa* was formed in 1922, the Ahepans began thinking about creating an organization for young men. Thus in February of 1926 Dr. Alexander Cambadhis and eleven young Greeks created the Order of Sons of Pericles. Two years later the Ahepa Supreme Lodge convention officially recognized the junior group. By 1932 the Sons had entered Canada with their organization.

The Sons of Pericles' order very much bears the imprint of the senior group, the Order of Ahepa. Its young members wear regalia, of which the fez is the most prominent feature. The regalia closely resembles their older "brothers," the Ahepans. The ritual, which was revised in the mid-1960s, also received the guidance of the Ahepans. The order, like Ahepan, conducts its rituals and ceremonies in secret. At its 1937 Supreme Lodge sessions, the Sons accepted the Ahepa ruling that all legislation passed by the Sons needed formal approval by Ahepa. The National (supreme) lodge convenes at the same time and location as does the Order of Ahepa.

The order has not always enjoyed organizational prosperity. During World War II, from 1942 to 1946 there was no national (supreme lodge) organization. Most of the young men were in the military, and the national headquarters had to be disbanded. However, in 1947 at the Ahepa Supreme Lodge convention in Los Angeles it was resolved to restore the national and district offices of the Sons again. By 1977 the order had once again shown signs of growth and prosperity.

Eligibility for membership in the Sons of Pericles requires that candidates are of Greek descent and not older than twenty-one years of age. If an individual joins at age twenty-one, he may remain with the order until age twenty-three. At one time such individuals were permitted to retain their membership in the Sons of Pericles until age twenty-five.

The organization has involved itself in civic affairs. In 1939 it unveiled a memorial in the city of Missolonghi, Greece, to honor the Philhellenes of America, who aided the struggling Greek patriots in the Greek Revolutionary War of 1821, which sought to throw off the Turkish oppression of 400 years. For erecting the memorial, the Sons received the commendation of the United States Senate and House of Representatives. The order has also contributed to various charity programs. In the early 1970s it donated money to the national Multiple Sclerosis Association. For its efforts it received the Hope Award from the association.

Recreationally, the Sons sponsor the National Sons of Pericles Basketball Tournament. This tournament is an annual event. Another form of recreation available for the Sons is in Reading, Pennsylvania, where the Ahepans operate the Sons of Pericles Camp Olympic for their junior order.

The organizational structure in the Sons of Pericles is very similar to that of the Order of Ahepa. On the national scene, the order calls itself the "Supreme Lodge." This group meets annually. Districts ordinarily encompass statewide efforts, and on the local level the group refers to its activities as "Chapters." The officers of the supreme lodge hold the following titles and positions: Supreme President, Supreme Vice President, Supreme Secretary-Treasurer, and five Supreme Governors, who serve as board members. The national structure also has an advisory board, which consists of Ahepans. On the district and chapter levels most of the positions are the same as in the supreme (national) lodge, except the title "Supreme" is not used. The national headquarters are located in Washington, D.C.

Reading materials on the Sons of Pericles, as with the Ahepa, is rather limited. George J. Leber's book, *The History of the Order of Ahepa* (1972) has one chapter on the Sons. It also has some references throughout the book in Leber's discussion on the Order of Ahepa. A Newsletter, *Eleftheri Zoe*, is published jointly with the Maids of Athena,* the junior auxiliary of the Daughters of Penelope.* This newsletter also provides useful information about the Sons of Pericles.

SONS OF POLAND, ASSOCIATION OF THE (ASP). September, 1903, was the date that 338 Poles sent thirty-two delegates to hold their organization's first convention. During the early years of the society's existence, the Sons of Poland attracted and absorbed unaffiliated church, social, and Polish patriotic groups. In 1924 the Polish Military Alliance of the East was the last group to merge with the Sons of Poland. The society's growth was also aided by the support it received from many Roman Catholic priests, who frequently lent their moral and organizing energies.

The association has given considerable aid to its ancestors in Poland.

During World War I it sent aid to starving Polish war victims. And during World War II the society joined the Polish-American Congress and District 5 of the American Relief for Poland to provide assistance to Poland. Since the two world wars, the ASP has also tried to help youth attending college by providing scholarships to worthy Polish-American students, who have been a member of the society for at least two years. Social, fraternal, and civic activities are conducted through the local lodges.

Membership is open to any person who is between sixteen and sixty years of age and is "of good character, by birth, descent and relationship of Polish or Slavonic nationality. . . ." Individuals of non-Polish descent may also join if of the Christian faith and married to someone who is a member of the society. Upon becoming a member, the individual takes an oath, according to the ritual's specification, pledging loyalty to the society's rules and regulations. The current (1979) membership roster lists 13,000.

The official banner of the ASP is a circle with a smaller ring inside, forming a circular border bearing the inscription: STOWARZYSKENIE SYNOW POLSKI. In the center of the circle are the letters SSP. On the left, the circular design is bounded by the American flag, and on the right by the Polish flag.

Local units are called "Lodges," of which the association at the present time has about 100. Somewhat similar to regional structures, the ASP has "Leagues." A league is formed of several lodges in a given city or community. The leagues not only consist of lodges, but also encompass the women's auxiliary groups. The national structure is referred to as the "Supreme Convention." It assembles in convention every four years. Head offices for the ASP are in Jersey City, New Jersey.

Very little material is available on the ASP. The writer based most of his information on the constitution and a mimeographed copy (several pages in length) of the society's history.

SONS OF ST. GEORGE, ORDER OF. This fraternal secret society was composed of Englishmen and their descendants. Apparently, when founded in 1871 in Scranton, Pennsylvania, the society was meant to resist the activities of Molly Moguires. Members were required to believe in a supreme being, have high regard for the Bible, and be loyal to America. The history and martyrdom of St. George served as the bases of the society's ritual. The ladies' auxiliary was named Daughters of St. George. Headquarters were in Chicago, Illinois. REFERENCE: *Cyc. Frat.*

SONS OF SCOTLAND BENEVOLENT ASSOCIATION (SSBA). Only nine years after the Confederation or the Dominion of Canada became a reality in 1867, a group of Scottish-born individuals formed the Sons of Scotland Benevolent Association in Toronto, Ontario, in 1876. By 1880 the society, a fraternal benefit group, was incorporated in the province of Ontario, and by 1937 it received federal incorporation from the Canadian government. The first camp (local unit) was named Robert Burns #1.

As is true of most ethnic fraternal groups, the SSBA not only provides insurance to its members but also seeks to preserve given ethnic values, culture, and traditions. In terms of the society's objectives this means preserving Scottish traditions. Thus the society sponsors a Scottish dancing and piping competition, as one of its several fraternal activities. In public parades the members dress in Scottish kilts.

To become a member of the SSBA one must be "a Scotsman, wife of a Scotsman, Scotswoman, son, daughter or descendant of a Scotsman or Scotswoman, or the wife or husband of a person already a member." The society has five classes of membership: insured, central camp, juvenile, associate, and members at large. The acceptance or rejection of new members is determined by ball ballots. Three or more blackballs cause an individual's application to be rejected. If the applicant is accepted, he must then appear for an initiation rite. Presently (1979) the SSBA has 12,640 members in eighty camps. In 1973 the order had 12,887 members. The SSBA is the largest Scottish fraternal organization in Canada.

Since the SSBA has an initiation ceremony, it might be inferred that the society still has a strong affinity for fraternal ritualism. It does. Members are given annual passwords, and local chapters (called "Subordinate Camps") are in charge of regalia.

The insignia of the SSBA consists of a shield encircled by a garland of maple leaves. On the face of the shield is a lion standing on his hind legs. On top of the shield stands the cross of St. Andrews. The slogan of the society is Lealty—Loyalty—Liberality.

Structurally, the SSBA operates on the local and national level. The local groups, as noted, are known as "Camps." The national organization is called "Grand Camp." It meets in convention every three years. The grand camp headquarters are situated in Toronto, Ontario, Canada.

Additional information may be obtained by acquiring a 45 rpm record that gives the society's history. In addition to the order's constitution, the reader may consult brochures and pamphlets issued by the head office in Toronto. The society also publishes a quarterly periodical, *The Scotian*.

SONS OF TEMPERANCE. This society was founded in New York in 1842, when the temperance reform movement was astir in the United States. The organization was also a fraternal benefit society. Its beneficiary character evolved as it engaged itself in reforming drunkards and trying to prevent others from becoming alcoholics. Membership was open to men and women. The Good Templars* were a spin-off of the Sons of Temperance. The female auxiliary was known as Daughters of Temperance. The Sons of Temperance kept certain features of their organization secret. Its organizational structure was similar to that of other fraternal orders. REFERENCE: *Cyc. Frat.*

SOVEREIGN ORDER OF SAINT JOHN OF JERUSALEM. See Saint John of Jerusalem, Sovereign Order of.

SPARTA, ORDER OF. Established in Philadelphia, Pennsylvania, in 1879, this society was a fraternal benefit order. Its founders were members of the Ancient United Order of Workmen. Only white males between twenty-one and fifty were able to join. Prospective members had to be in good health and "believers in the Christian faith." The society's ritual was based on the ancient history of the Greek city Sparta. Philadelphia, Pennsylvania, served as the headquarters city, while the order was in existence. REFERENCE: *Cyc. Frat.*

STAR OF BETHLEHEM, ANCIENT AND ILLUSTRIOUS (AISB). This order, once known as the Knights of the Star of Bethlehem, was introduced in the United States from England in 1691 by Giles Corey of London. Colonial authorities suppressed it. Over 200 years later it was again brought to the city of New York in 1849 or 1850 by John Bell, who established several commanderies in 1851. Permanent establishment of the order did not really occur until 1869, when the society organized on the state level in Pennsylvania and New York. Between 1878 and 1884 the order completely reorganized with new titles, officers, and organizational name: Ancient and Illustrious Star of Bethlehem.

The AISB was a fraternal benefit order that provided death, sickness, and disability benefits. The society also helped its members find employment in the event they became unemployed. Another objective of the AISB was to perpetuate its traditions.

In terms of its history, the society traced its origin to the first century of the Christian era. More specifically, however, the AISB drew upon the thirteenth century for its tradition. According to the society, the thirteenth century had a monastic order known as the Bethlehemites, whose members wore a five-pointed star on the left breast, in commemoration of the star that appeared over Bethlehem at the time of Christ's birth. In the fourteenth century the order apparently became a semimilitary organization known as the Knights of the Star of Bethlehem. The order spread to various parts of Europe in the fourteenth and fifteenth centuries. In 1571 the order became a benevolent and scientific society in England. In 1813 the order suffered a schism, apparently because some members objected to women being admitted to membership. The schism apparently led to the formation of the Royal Foresters in England.

The ritual of the American order accented the practical teachings on truth, fraternity, and moral law. These elements were reportedly all drawn from the society's ancient past.

Membership in the AISB was open to men, women, and children. The latter formed the order's juvenile department. By the early 1920s the society had about 17,000 members in 250 lodges in the United States and the Canal Zone. The ladies' auxiliary group was known as Eastern Star Benevolent Fund of America. As far as can be determined, the AISB no longer exists today.

The government of the AISB consisted of subordinate lodges, uniformed conclaves, and grand councils. Headquarters were maintained in Detroit, Michigan. REFERENCE: *Cyc. Frat.*

SUNSHINE GIRLS (SG). This is an organization for young girls, sponsored by the Pythian Sisters.* Current information concerning the past and present status of the SG was not received.

SUPREME CAMP OF THE AMERICAN WOODMEN. See American Woodmen, The Supreme Camp of the.

SVITHIOD, INDEPENDENT ORDER OF (IOS). Until recently this was a Swedish fraternal benefit group that was organized in 1881 in Illinois. The society merged with Banker's Mutual Life Insurance, Freeport, Illinois, in 1978.

During the society's existence, it had a fraternal ritual that embodied religious characteristics that made reference to Teutonic gods, such as Belder, Thor, and Odin. The ritual also required a secret oath of every initiate. Lodge sessions were opened and closed with prayer, spoken by the chaplain of the society. The society's headquarters were housed in Chicago, Illinois, until the merger with Bankers' Mutual Life Insurance was effected in 1978.

__ T

TALL CEDARS OF LEBANON OF THE UNITED STATES OF AMERICA (TCOL). What the Shrine is to thirty-second-degree Masons in the Scottish Rite,* the TCOL is to Master Masons (third-degree members) of the Blue Lodge.* Although some Masons received the Tall Cedars of Lebanon degree prior to 1902, the order was not formally chartered until March 18, 1902, in Trenton, New Jersey. Prior to 1902 there is some evidence that the order's roots go back to 1843. In 1846 the Masonic grand lodge in Pennsylvania permitted the conferring of a degree known as the "Tall Cedar Degree." This degree apparently was a type of hazing performance. Then silence concerning this degree again existed until the 1850s, when Dr. Thomas J. Corson in New Jersey conferred the degree. After Corson's death, the degree was perpetuated by others until it resulted in the formal creation of "The Supreme Forest of Tall Cedars of Lebanon of the U.S.A.," in 1902.

The TCOL is a Masonic "side degree" attainable by any Master Mason. As a side degree, the order has no official status in Masonry. The order's name is derived from the cedars of Mount Lebanon that have figured prominently in Masonic legends pertaining to the construction of King Solomon's Temple. Since its inception, the TCOL has been a "fun" order, providing social entertainment and innocent recreation. The group also seeks to promote wider friendship among members of the Masonic order.

Most Masonic side-degree organizations have a ritual with at least one degree. The TCOL order is no exception; it has two degrees: the Royal Court degree and the Sidonian degree.

Membership is open only to third-degree Masons. Women are not eligible. All members wear headgear that is triangular and pyramidical in form. Officers, past officers, and non-officers have different-colored hats. In 1975 membership figures of the order numbered 36,900.

Fraternally, the order says that in all of its meetings "the Masonic spirit is constantly present." Masonry comes first and Cedarism second. Supplementing the society's accent on "fun," it helps support the national Muscular Dystrophy Fund. It also operates a Jerry Lewis Tall Cedar Day Camp in the summer. The watchwords are "FUN, FROLIC, and FELLOWSHIP."

The TCOL loves to participate in public parades; thus it had the Royal Rangers, a militarylike marching unit. A Tuxedo Unit is a formal marching group, requiring all to wear white tuxedos. It also has a chanters, band, and drum corps unit, designed "to keep music flowing."

Local chapters are called "Forests." The national structure is the highest authority and is known as the "Supreme Forest." The principal officer is the Grand Tall Cedar. Headquarters are in Harrisburg, Pennsylvania.

Additional background may be obtained by reading the society's quarterly periodical, *The Cedar Digest*. This magazine is quite professional in design and in its articles. The fraternity's constitution also is helpful in understanding the society.

TEMPLARS OF HONOR AND TEMPERANCE. This fraternal benefit society had a dual focus, benevolency and temperance. The order was a descendant of the Sons of Temperance.* It was found three years after (1845) the birth of the parent order in 1842. Initially, the society was called the Marshall Temperance Fraternity, and later, Marshall Temple, Sons of Honor.

The society had a religiously oriented ritual that was intended for members only. In fact, the society contended that its religious features enabled members to see the order as equal "if not superior, to the Church of Christ." The ritual had six degrees. Much of the ritual was based on the medieval Templars, plus incidents from the life of David and Jonathan, as well as from Damon and Pythias. Some aspects of the ritual revealed Masonic influences. The insignia of the society consisted of a temple, which had a nine-pointed star and three interlaced triangles with another triangle.

The "Supreme Council" had jurisdiction over the "Grand Temples" and "Grand Councils." All members pledged not to drink alcohol or to traffic such products. REFERENCE: *Cyc. Frat.*

TEMPLARS OF LIBERTY. Founded in Newark, New Jersey in 1881, this society had three emphases: fraternal benevolence, patriotism, and anti-Catholicism. Females were eligible for beneficiary membership. The society's ritual was based on incidents and events of the Protestant Reformation. Local units were called "Temples." Most of the society's members resided in the states of New York, New Jersey, and Pennsylvania. Headquarters were in Newark, New Jersey. REFERENCE: *Cyc. Frat.*

TEMPLE OF FRATERNITY. Founded in Syracuse, New York, in 1896, this society devoted much of its time to studying psychic and occult phenomena. The order had a ritual embodying eleven degrees. The society apparently went out of existence in the early 1900s. REFERENCE: *Syc. Frat.*

THETA RHO CLUBS (TRC). This society is the junior order for young women of the Rebekah Assembly.* The society has a ritual that each member is required to go through at the time of initiation. Much of the organization's functions are under the supervision of the Odd Fellows,* the men's fraternal society that also is superior in organizational authority to the Rebekah Assembly.

Although current membership figures were not available to the writer, the membership count in 1970 stood at 13,577. This figure was a decline from 14,150 members in 1969. The 1979 membership has probably decreased some more since 1970.

Additional information can be gleaned from the annual proceedings volume published by the Sovereign Grand Lodge of the Independent Order of Odd Fellows. No scholarly history has been published.

TRAVELERS PROTECTIVE ASSOCIATION OF AMERICA, THE (TPAA). A small group of traveling salesmen gathered in a Chicago hotel in January 1882 to form a cooperative group that would help solve problems confronting the traveling man. By June 24, 1882, in Bellfontaine, Ohio, the concerned travelers effected a group which they called the Travelers Protective Association of the United States. The primary objectives of the newly found group were: (1) to obtain special concessions from hotels, railroads, and other transportation agencies; and (2) to trace grievances of its members. At this time the order had no insurance or benevolent features. By 1889 the TPAA was experiencing financial activities, and by 1890 it was decided that the order could avert organizational doom if it added accident insurance to its objectives. Also in 1890 the order moved from Chicago to St. Louis and changed its name to Travelers Protective Association of America.

At the outset membership eligibility was limited to executives of manufacturing firms and their traveling salesmen, executives of wholesale or jobbing businesses and their sales representatives, and those who sold merchandise for resale. Today (1979) any male between eighteen and fifty-five engaged as a commercial traveler may join. Other occupational groups may be admitted by special review of the Board of Directors of the TPAA. Its 1979 membership roster listed 236,000. This is a substantial increase (22.5 percent) relative to its 1968 enrollment, when the order had 191,000 members.

The TPAA initiation ritual, compared to most fraternal groups—even those primarily engaged in fraternal insurance—is relatively simple and brief. The candidate for membership is not required to take bizarre oaths or obligations. Instead the chairman of the post (local chapter) leads in prayer and reads a discourse about what the order and its faithful members are to accomplish. The chairman also encourages the existing members to assist the new "brothers."

The association has been alert to given problems and issues. For instance, it has been successful in getting laws passed in various states regulating the sanitary conditions of hotels; it has been instrumental in sponsoring and getting driver-training laws enacted in many states; it inaugurated in 1946 an annual Child Accident Prevention Week Program. In 1966 the TPAA constitution was changed to provide for the formation of a community services chairman in each post of the association.

The official emblem of the TPAA is a circle with an inner ring that on its outer border holds the words: The Travelers Protective Association. In the center of the inner ring, the circle is divided into six equal parts with every other part having one letter, T.P.A., respectively.

Like most other fraternal benevolent societies, the TPAA has a national, state, and local organizational structure. On the state level the association refers to its organization as "State Division." The local chapters are known as "Posts." In 1979 the association had 290 posts. The national headquarters are in St. Louis, Missouri.

For additional information see the society's *Articles of Incorporation, Constitution and Bylaws of The Travelers Protective Association* (1978). *Rituals of the Travelers Protective Association of America* (1948) also provides helpful information. The association's annual *Report* gives the details and resolutions of each annual convention.

TRUE KINDRED, SUPREME CONCLAVE (SCTK). According to the Masonic Service Association, the origins of this order in the United States go back to Marquis de Lafayette, when he conferred the True Kindred degree upon George Washington. Washington reportedly also conferred the degree upon his wife, which led to the degree being called the Martha Washington degree. The Supreme Conclave of the True Kindred, however, was not formed and incorporated until December 15, 1905. The latter took place in Illinois. The objectives of the order are to practice fraternalism, promote truth and moral intellectual values, aid and assist its members needing relief, and support charities of various kinds.

The ritual of the SCTK contains four degrees that the order bestows: True Kindred, The Heroine of Jericho, The Good Samaritan, and The Daughters of Bethany degree.

The SCTK is what might be called part of Adoptive Masonry* in that it admits females. Master Masons, their wives, widows, mothers, daughters, sisters, grandmothers, granddaughters, "blood nieces," and half-sisters are eligible for membership, provided that the women are at least eighteen years old.

The order has three levels of administration. The "Conclave" is the local or subordinate unit. The state or regional group is called "Grand Conclave," and the national structure is named "Supreme Conclave."

Additional information may be obtained by consulting the "Masonic Service Association's Rites" (1978). See also Harold V. B. Voorhis, *Masonic Organizations and Allied Orders and Degrees* (1952).

TRUE REFORMERS, THE GRAND UNITED ORDER OF (GUOTR). The founder of this once very successful black fraternal group was the Reverend W. W. Browne. The site of the order's birth was Richmond, Virginia. The date was 1881. The society grew quite rapidly; by 1900 it had 70,000 members. By this time the organization had also contributed about $2,000,000 in benefits and relief. As best as can be determined, the society no longer appears to be in operation today.

TRUE SISTERS, UNITED ORDER OF, INC. (UOTS). This is one of several Hebrew fraternal orders. It was founded in 1846 by Henrietta Bruckman, the wife of a prominent New York physician. Mrs. Bruckman, together with a dozen other women, felt an organization was required to provide assistance to given community wants and the needs of Hebrew housewives. She also obtained support from several men, one of them her husband. The new organization was modeled upon the Independent Order of B'nai B'rith,* which was then three years old. The UOTS claims to be the first women's fraternal and philanthropic organization in the United States.

From its beginning, the UOTS adopted a secret ritual, degrees, regalia, and an emblem. Regarding its secret nature, a UOTS publication recently stated: "The Order was established as a secret society largely because the giving or receiving of charity is traditionally a secret matter so that material assistance can be rendered without humiliation to the recipient." The president of the order is vested with special regalia upon retiring from office. Its official seal is a wreath encompassing the letters UOTS.

The UOTS has undergone a number of organizational changes since 1846. Initially, it was a German-speaking order comprised of Hebrew ladies. The first English-speaking lodge was organized in 1892, and by 1918 the German language was essentially discontinued in all lodges of the UOTS. Other changes resulted. Although the order began largely as a benevolent group that helped its sick members and paid benefits to widows, it now is primarily a philanthropic organization. Since 1947, it has been directing most of its energies to United Order True Sisters, Inc., Cancer Service. Each year $300,000 is given to hospitals and research centers to help fight cancer. More recently it has been sponsoring two postdoctoral fellowships in cancer immunology at the Frederick Research Cancer Center in Frederick, Maryland. In 1966 it opened a clinic for outpatients in New York City. Its United Order True Sisters, Inc., Cancer Service has no salaried workers. The UOTS also contributes aid to a variety of specialized-care hospitals in thirteen states and Israel.

The organizational structure of the UOTS is similar to most fraternals. The national level is referred to as the "Grand Lodge," which is head-quartered in New York City.

For further information, see the published *Proceedings* and the order's official periodical, the *Echo*, which has been published since 1881. Additional information may be obtained by consulting the various pamphlets the order has produced from time to time.

_ U _

UKRAINIAN NATIONAL AID ASSOCIATION OF AMERICA (UNAAA).
Founded in 1914, this ethnic fraternal benefit society has been experiencing an increase in membership. In 1965 the organization had 6,928 members. In 1978 it had more than 8,000 life insurance certificate holders.

In addition to providing fraternal life insurance to its members, the

UNAAA also is very active in lending material and moral support to the Ukrainian people in Europe, as they struggle to regain their independence and freedom. The society also tries to make civic contributions in the various localities where it has local lodges. Like most fraternal benefit groups, the UNAAA awards scholarships to qualified members.

The 8,000 members are primarily found in Pennsylvania, Ohio, Illinois, and Canada. Approximately 170 local lodges are part of the society's grass-roots structure. National conventions are held quadrennially. Headquarters are in Pittsburgh, Pennsylvania.

Additional information may be found by consulting the society's biweekly, *Ukrainian National Word*. Other helpful sources are the publicity brochures and the constitution.

UKRAINIAN NATIONAL ASSOCIATION (UNA). A group of civic-minded Ukrainian immigrants met on February 22, 1894, in Shamokin, Pennsylvania, to organize the Ukrainian National Association. From the very beginning the UNA was a fraternal benefit society. It began with less than 500 founding members. The primary objective of the society was to provide funds for the "relief of destitute families and to cover funeral expenses of members." Like most other fraternal benefit groups, the UNA operated with unsound actuarial methods during its early years. In time, however, the society learned from its trial and error methods. Today it is in a strong financial position, having over 43 million dollars in assets, plus 165 million dollars of insurance in force.

The UNA has always been deeply interested in the status of its people here in the United States as well as in the Ukraine. It has rendered various kinds of assistance to the people of the Ukraine, especially against the Russocommunistic threat. Recently, the society has been encouraged by the American Defense of Human Rights so that it has "aided and defended Ukrainian dissidents imprisoned for monitoring Moscow's infringement of the Helsinki Agreements." In the United States the UNA has "initiated such projects as the erection of the Taras Shevchenko Monument in Washington, D.C., honoring Ukraine's foremost poet and champion of freedom, and the establishment of the Ukrainian Studies Center at Harvard University." The association regularly promotes cultural, educational, social, athletic, and community activities. These are primarily designed to benefit all Ukrainians in Canada and the United States. For members who are college students, the UNA annually awards about $10,000 in scholarships. In 1963 and 1970 the association published *Ukraine: A Concise Encyclopedia*, volumes I and II. The first volume was presented to President Lyndon Johnson.

Also for the benefit and enjoyment of its members (adults and youth), the UNA owns a 400-acre resort called *Soyuzivka*. It is located in the Catskill

Mountains, near Kerhonkson, New York. The resort has a modern year-round spa, offering social and cultural recreation for thousands of Ukrainians every summer. In the summer of 1962 a *Hutzul*-style chapel was built on the resort property. The resort also has a permanent residence for senior retired members.

To join the UNA an individual must be of Ukrainian descent or married to someone who is of Ukrainian background. Those under sixteen years of age belong to the juvenile membership department. The total membership in 1978 was about 81,000 members. This figure represents a slight decline since 1965, when the association had 84,414 members.

The emblem of the UNA consists of three flags: Canadian, American, and Ukrainian. The emblem also portrays two hands clasped in fraternal friendship. The letters U.N.A. are on the lower left side of the insignia, and U.H.C. are on the lower right side.

The UNA still very much retains its ties with the Ukrainian Orthodox Church in the United States of America. Its weekly newspaper, *The Ukrainian Weekly*, and the daily *Svoboda* (in Ukrainian), regularly carry articles on religion. For instance, the April 22, 1979, issue of *The Ukrainian Weekly* carried the following headline: "*Khrystos Voskres*—Christ Is Risen."

Presently (1979) the association has about 465 local groups in Canada and the United States. It also has twenty-nine districts. The highest authority is the national convention, which meets every four years. Main offices are headquartered in Jersey City, New Jersey.

For further information, see the two newspapers cited. Another helpful publication is *Veselka*, a monthly periodical issued in the English and Ukrainian languages. The society published a condensed history in 1964 of its existence, *The U.N.A.: Its Past and Present*.

UKRAINIAN WORKINGMEN'S ASSOCIATION, THE (UWA). A cadre of conscientious men began and founded the Ruthenian National Union in Scranton, Pennsylvania, in 1910. The newly created group had as its objective to provide financial protection for its members who, as Ukranians, were often discriminated against relative to finding and retaining employment.

At the group's first meeting 34 branches were launched. The first convention of the Ruthenian National Union was held in 1911, and by 1918 the name was changed to the Ukrainian Workingmen's Association. Today it is one of the largest Ukrainian fraternal life insurance groups in North America.

From the time that the organization was founded, it permitted Ukrainians, Russians, and other Slavonic people to become members without regard to religious or political affiliation. Those who insisted on debating religious teachings, and clergy, were encouraged to join another group.

Since most Ukrainian immigrants to the United States were unable to afford good insurance, the UWA provided inexpensive policies payable upon death only. Members paid monthly dues, computed on a crude actuarial system. "If death claims exceeded the total intake of dues, then an additional 25 or 50 cents was attached. If a wife (non-member) to the insured died, the husband was guaranteed $400.00 on a $1,000.00 policy ($200.00 on a $500.00 policy) for burial purposes." The basic objective was to have sufficient money to cover funeral expenses.

"Any person of Ukrainian descent in good health, sound of mind and of good character, between the ages of 16 and 65 years . . . if female, not then pregnant with child, is eligible for membership . . . except persons intemperate in the use of alcoholic drinks or addicted to narcotics shall not be admitted to membership. . . ." So reads the constitution of the UWA. Every member is initiated and required to take a pledge in a ritual-oriented setting.

The UWA has a very active scholarship program, supported through its Ivan Franko Scholarship Foundation. Aid also has been dispensed to natural disaster areas and to war relief.

The membership of the UWA had 23,127 members in 275 lodges in Canada and the United States in 1979. In 1965 there were 24,134 members.

On the national (international) level the UWA meets in convention every four years. Between conventions the order has its supreme council of twenty-four members, which administers various policies and business. Each local assembly (lodge) elects delegates to the national convention. The head-quarters are located in Scranton, Pennsylvania.

For additional information see Anthony Batiuk, *Life Insurance in The Ukrainian Workingmen's Association: Its Need and Significance* (n.d.). The *Constitution and By-Laws* (1966) is published in Ukrainian and in English. The UWA publishes a quarterly periodical, *Forum*, which contains news of the organization. A weekly newspaper also is published by the UWA. It goes by the Ukrainian name of *Narodna Volya*.

UNION FRATERNAL LEAGUE. Incorporated in the state of Massachu-setts in 1893, the society admitted both men and women to its membership roster. The society, like so many others, was formed by men who belonged to some of the well-known fraternal orders such as the Ancient Order of United Workmen,* Knights of Honor, and others. In 1916 the order became known as the Catholic Fraternal League. This change in name also meant a change in the orientation of the society, for instance, a Catholic priest would hold the chaplain's office. This order no longer exists today. REFER-ENCE: *Cyc. Frat.*

UNION OF POLISH WOMEN IN AMERICA (UPWA). During World War I a number of Polish women in the Philadelphia, Pennsylvania, area lent their services to the White Cross, Red Cross, Emergency Aid, and Polish Army Mothers. After the war some felt that there was need for a women's organization that would bring the patriotic ladies under one organizational banner. Thus was born the Union of Polish Women in America in Philadelphia on October 17, 1920.

From the society's inception, it has been devoted to fraternal growth along religious, moral, and ethnic lines, with strong affinity to the Roman Catholic Church. Today the UPWA is the largest Polish women's fraternal benefit society in the eastern United States.

The UPWA provides the usual fraternal life insurance benefits and maintains a large social and cultural program for children and adults. The society also seeks to preserve among the Polish women their moral and religious consciousness, as well as to inculcate American patriotism. Partial scholarships and educational loans are given to eligible Americans of Polish descent. The society also helps support religious and ethnic projects.

The UPWA stands for "Unity, Stability, and Prosperity." Its official emblem displays a young woman holding a shield portraying the American eagle, the white Polish eagle, and the letters U.P.W.A., with the founding date of the society.

Membership is open to those of Polish origin or by marriage to someone of Polish background. Individuals from fifteen and a half years of age may join the adult membership category. Present (1979) membership is about 9,500.

Local units are known as "Branches" among the adult ladies. Youth groups are referred to as "Juvenile Circles." Regional structures are called "Districts." The highest authority structure is the convention, which meets every four years. One of the highlights of the convention is the selection of a "convention Queen," who reigns as the UPWA Quadrennial Convention Queen for four years. Between conventions the Supreme Executive Body manages the society's affairs. Head offices are in Philadelphia, Pennsylvania.

Additional information may be acquired by consulting convention manuals, pamphlets, and brochures. The *Fourteenth Quadrennial Convention* publication (1977) has a brief history of the society.

UNION SAINT-JEAN BAPTISTE (USJB). When this fraternal, benevolent group was founded on March 27, 1900, in Woonsocket, Rhode Island, it called itself the Union Saint-Jean-Baptiste d'Amérique. Its purpose was "to unite in a common spirit of brotherhood persons of French origin living in the United States and to promote their collective individual welfare." The society chose the motto: "In Union There Is Strength." In 1968 the name was officially changed to Union Saint-Jean Baptiste.

The USJB has four principal benevolent programs: student aid, promotion of patriotic and cultural activities, aid to the retarded, and Catholic Action.

Many of the society's members serve as volunteers in local hospitals, visit shut-ins, comfort the bereaved, provide meals on wheels, and assist in Catholic parishes. The Saint-Jean Baptiste Educational Foundation provides monies for scholarships. Yearly grants also are made to the Catholic Communications Foundation, which seeks to further understanding of the Catholic faith and doctrine through the mass media.

Membership in the USJB has been declining. In 1968 there were more than 62,000 members, but as of January, 1979, the roster had decreased by 24 percent to 47,000 members. The decline has recently prompted the society to study its insurance methods with the aim of reforming them.

The emblem of the USJB is a circle divided into four equal segments. The top left portion reveals the stars of the American flag, and the bottom left depicts the stripes of Old Glory. The top right segment displays the fleur-de-lis, and the bottom right section portrays the Christian cross.

The constitution of the USJB specifies that all new members are to be initiated. A ritual prescribes the format of the initiation. Officers also are installed according to the society's ritual.

On the national level the USJB meets in convention quadrennially. Its local councils (chapters) elect delegates to the national convention or "National Congress," as the organization calls the convention. Head offices are located in Woonsocket, Rhode Island.

For further reading see the official publication of the society, *L'Union*, a bimonthly newspaper. A mimeographed history of the organization, "A Beautiful Dream Come True," is available from the national headquarters. The constitution of the society also provides helpful insight.

UNITED AMERICAN MECHANICS (UAM). This group was formed by a small coterie of men who were opposed to immigrants coming to the United States. The men met in a grocery store in Philadelphia on July 8, 1845, to form the organization called Union of Workers. The name was soon changed to Order of United American Mechanics (OUAM). Its objectives were to be a patriotic, social, fraternal, and benevolent order, composed of native white male citizens, who would purchase goods only from white businessmen, help native Americans find employment, protect the public school system, aid widows and orphans of deceased members, and defend its members from harmful economic competition by immigrants. The order's formation was an outgrowth of the American Nativist movement, which opposed the German, Irish, and Roman Catholic immigration of the early 1840s. One primary reason for opposing the "foreigners," which led to the OUAM being founded, was that many Americans resented immigrants ("greenhorns") being hired by businesses for lower wages.

According to Albert C. Stevens in his *Encyclopedia of Fraternities* (1907), the OUAM organizational meeting took place on July 4, 1845, with an audience of about sixty individuals. A majority left when they heard that the new group saw would be a secret society. A handful remained. Some of the key organizers were Freemasons.* The name "Mechanics" was chosen because the group saw itself as a secret fraternity of operative mechanics and tradesmen; however, its membership never was entirely composed of mechanics and tradesmen.

The ritual of the OUAM very much bore the influence of Freemasonry, apparently because some of its founders were Masons. In the tradition of Masonry, the ritual was secret, with required vows of secrecy. The emblem included the Masonic square and compass, along with the arm of labor wielding a hammer and the American flag.

The anti-immigration feelings of the OUAM were not confined to this organization in the fraternal arena. For in 1853 the OUAM organized the Junior Order of United American Mechanics* (JOUAM). As a juvenile group, it was to train youths who would later join the OUAM. By 1885 the junior order had become an independent adult group, employing the same objectives and symbols of its parent society. The OUAM also formed auxiliary organizations: the Daughters of Liberty* and the Daughters of America. The latter group was really an affiliate of the JOUAM.

In time the OUAM changed its posture from a Nativist fraternal group to a fraternal society dispensing life insurance. It even changed its name by dropping the word "Order" and simply called itself United American Mechanics. Today the society is part of the Junior Order of United American Mechanics,* the society organized in 1853.

Albert C. Stevens in his *Cyclopedia of Fraternities* (1907) has a rather detailed account of the society up to 1896. The reader may wish to consult Stevens for additional details about the order.

UNITED AMERICANS, ORDER OF. This secret, patriotic order was formed in the city of New York in 1844 as Alpha Chapter No. 1 of the American Brotherhood. Some have suggested that the founders and early leaders had come from Tammany Hall, a patriotic group which produced the Society of Red Men. Others have said that the Order of United Americans helped spawn the Know-Nothing Party of the 1850s. REFERENCE: *Cyc. Frat.*

UNITED ANCIENT ORDER OF DRUIDS. See Druids, United Ancient Order of.

UNITED BROTHERS OF FRIENDSHIP (UBF). This fraternal beneficiary society for blacks was founded in Louisville, Kentucky, in 1861. Its objectives were to provide fraternal care for the sick and to bury the dead. Just after the Civil War the order was reorganized in 1868. In 1875 a national grand lodge was formed. A female auxiliary was founded in 1878 known as Temples of Sisters of the Mysterious Ten.

The UBF, according to Albert C. Stevens, *Cyclopedia of Fraternities* (1907), had 100,000 members by 1892. Kentucky alone had 30,000 members. White persons were eligible to join, and reportedly some did.

The structure of the UBF was similar to that of most American fraternal orders. The society had its subordinate lodges, grand lodges, and a national grand lodge. Headquarters were housed in Jefferson City, Missouri. REFERENCE: *Cyc. Frat.*

UNITED COMMERCIAL TRAVELERS OF AMERICA, THE ORDER OF (OUCTA). This order was founded by Levi C. Pease, a traveling salesman. Pease became dissatisfied with the traveling salesmen's organization in which he held membership and was determined to organize a fraternal secret society for traveling salesmen. In January of 1888, Pease met with five other men in Columbus, Ohio and formed the United Commercial Travelers. The new fraternal order adopted seven objectives: (1) to unite fraternally all commercial travelers; (2) to aid all members and their dependents in financial and material ways; (3) to establish funds to indemnify its members for disability or death from accidental causes; (4) to obtain just and equitable favors for its commercial travelers; (5) to raise the moral and social caliber of its members; (6) to operate as a secret society; and (7) to establish a widow's and orphan's reserve fund. By May 25, 1889, the first grand council was formed in Ohio, and two years later Missouri also organized a grand council (a statewide structure).

The order at one time referred to itself as "the travelers' masonry," apparently because it had a secret ritual devoted to one craft or occupation, reminiscent of operative Freemasonry* prior to 1717. The current (1975) ritual pertaining to the initiation ceremony asks the candidate to vow: "I, . . . , solemnly obligate myself—to assist the needy Brothers—and the dependent widows and orphans—of my deceased brethren—observe and obey the laws of my country—aid in caring for the sick—and burying the dead—Amen." The candidate also promises "upon the faith of an honest man—never to reveal the secrets of this Order,—nor the nature of any confidential business—transacted in my presence within these walls,—to any person not entitled to the same." He further vows, among other things, to "defend the character of woman, and never to violate the chastity of all womanhood. . . ." An older edition read: "I will . . . never violate the chastity of a maiden." The entire ritual consists of five lectures which, the order's publication says, "is full of dignity and beauty and a never-failing source of wonder to the candidates for membership." The ritual and ceremonies of the OUCTA contain a number of religious symbolisms. In the center of the council chamber (lodge room) stands an altar with a Bible placed upon it. A chaplain is one of the council officers, and meetings are opened and closed with prayer.

Since the OUCTA is a secret fraternal group, it also has an officer known as the "Sentinel." He is stationed outside the chamber room door, making sure that nonmembers do not enter.

Membership is open to "any male citizen of the United States, Canada or British possessions in North America, of good moral character, and in good physical and mental condition. . . ." The age range for membership is between eighteen and fifty-five. At one time the OUCTA accepted only white males. Since 1948 it broadened its parameters for membership by also enabling professional and businessmen to join. The order currently (1979) has 226,221 members in 670 local councils in forty-seven states, the District of Columbia, and ten provinces in Canada. Ten years ago the society had about 240,000 members in 680 local councils.

The emblem of the OUCTA is a crescent standing on its horns. Suspended from the crescent is a traveler's suitcase with the letters U.C.T. on the side. The words United Commercial Travelers are embossed on the crescent.

In the tradition of Freemasonry, which has its "fun" organization in the Shrine, the OUCTA also has its "fun" order. This group is known as the Ancient Mystic Order of the Bagmen of Bagdad.*

From the order's inception it was always benevolence-minded. Early in the society's existence, it paid $25 per week to members who were disabled as a result of an accident. Since 1894, it has also paid $5,000 for accidental death. Widow allowances and aid for dependents has also been a feature of OUCTA. In the 1940s the fraternity began providing assistance for needy "brothers." The U.C.T. Fraternal Foundation was established in 1956, which has yielded income for the order's Retarded Children Teachers Scholarship Fund.

The organizational structure of the OUCTA consists of "Councils" on the local level. Five councils in a state or province may apply for a charter to form a grand council. The grand council officers are the same as those of the local councils, except the title of "Grand" is prefixed to each, for instance: Grand Counselor, Grand Past Counselor, Grand Junior, Grand Secretary, Grand Treasurer, Grand Chaplain, Grand Sentinel, and Grand Page. The highest authority is the "Supreme Council." Its officers carry the title of Supreme Counselor, Supreme Junior, and the like. The supreme council offices are located in Columbus, Ohio.

For further information the reader may wish to consult the OUCTA publication, *From The Hearts of Men* (1960), a pamphlet. It gives a thumbnail sketch of the society. The *Constitution, By-Laws and Standing Orders* (1978) provide information relative to the local, state, and supreme councils.

The fraternity also publishes two periodicals. The *Leader* is issued eight times per year; the *Sample Case* appears quarterly. See also *Ritual, The Order of United Commercial Travelers* (1975). *Quick Facts About U.C.T.* (1978) is a helpful booklet too.

UNITED DAUGHTERS OF RECHAB. This was a fraternal or female auxiliary of the Sons of Honadab. The auxiliary was founded in 1845 in Boston, Massachusetts. The society was a total abstinence group. Its motto was "Mercy and Truth are met together." The society was still in existence in 1911 but appears to have become extinct soon after that time.

UNITED FRIENDS OF MICHIGAN. This fraternal benefit group arose in 1889 because of a schism in the Order of Chosen Friends.* From all indications, it appears that the society became extinct some time during the second decade of the 1900s. REFERENCE: *Cyc. Frat.*

UNITED LUTHERAN SOCIETY (ULS). This fraternal benefit traces its roots back to 1893, when the Slovak Evangelical Union (SEU) was founded in Freeland, Pennsylvania. The SEU provided only fraternal insurance for men who were Slovak Lutherans. In 1906 the Slovak women organized their own group, the Evangelical Slovak Women's Union (ESWU). In 1962 these two groups merged to form the United Lutheran society.

Today (1979) the society has a membership of 11,000 in eleven states and Canada. Modern life insurance benefits are available for all members. Headquarters are in Ligonier, Pennsylvania.

UNITED NATIONAL LIFE INSURANCE SOCIETY (UNLIS). The origin of this Portuguese fraternal benefit society goes back to August 6, 1868, when in San Francisco, California, the Portuguese Protective and Benevolent Association of the City and County of San Francisco was founded. In 1875 the society reincorporated. For many years the members of more recent days thought the latter date was really the origin of the society. Four years after the society began it formed a grand council in 1872. In 1921 a supreme council was formed.

With the exception of World War II, the society continued to grow. In 1945 the constitutional bylaws were changed to admit women to membership. The year 1948 saw the society change its name to Benevolent Society of California. In 1957 the society absorbed the *Uniao Portuguesa Continental Do Estado Da California* (UPEC). When this merger was effected, the society took its present name, United National Life Insurance Society.

Three classes of membership are available: active, associate, and honorary. Both males and females are eligible. Presently (1978) the society has about

14,000 members. This figure has remained rather stable during the last ten years.

In 1963 the UNLIS formed the Luso-American Education Foundation, a charitable education corporation that is really independent of the society. It exists to aid qualified students, regardless of race or creed, to help them understand the Portuguese culture by means of providing scholarships to high school students in the state of California. The program of study designed to teach students about Portuguese culture is carried on during the summer.

Local units are known as "Subordinate Lodges." The UNLIS has lodges in California, Connecticut, Massachusetts, Nevada, and Rhode Island. National headquarters are located in Oakland, California.

Further information may be obtained by reading the society's quarterly, *The Luso-American*. Another helpful document published in 1968 is the society's history, commemorating its centennial.

UNITED ORDER OF AMERICANS. At first this fraternal and patriotic benevolent society was known as the United Order of Foresters, which in turn was formerly the Independent Order of Foresters until the name change was made in 1881. Then in the early 1900s the name was changed to United Order of Americans. The society made several revisions of its ritual. Every candidate was asked to take the pledge of secrecy. REFERENCE: *Cyc. Frat.*

UNITED ORDER OF TRUE SISTERS. See True Sisters, United Order of.

UNITED ORDER OF THE GOLDEN CROSS. See Golden Cross, United Order of the.

UNITED SOCIETIES OF THE UNITED STATES (USOTUS). Upon becoming organized in 1903 this group was first known as the United Societies of the Greek Catholic Religion of the United States of America. The society was founded by three ecclesiastical lodges of the Greek Catholic Union, two were from McKeesport, and one from Glassport, Pennsylvania. The initial intentions were not to organize a national fraternal group, but rather to create a group that would locally spread the Greek Catholic religion, foster the Ruthenian national spirit, organize Greek Catholic schools, and offer material assistance, especially to the families of deceased members and those who became sick or disabled. Today the USOTUS is classified as a fraternal benefit society, holding membership in the National Fraternal Congress. The order is licensed to sell fraternal insurance in six states.

To become a member of the USOTUS one must be a practical member "of the One, Holy, Catholic and Apostolic Church of the Greek Catholic or

Latin Rite of which His Holiness, Pope of Rome, is the Visible Head. . . ."
The society, like most fraternal benefit groups, has a beneficiary membership
and a social member category. The former carries an insurance contract,
whereas the latter does not. Every member is asked to take an oath: "I
(name) pledged myself in the name of One god in the Holy Trinity the Blessed
Virgin Mary the Holy Patron of the Lodge and all the Saints, that as a
member of the (Patron Saint's name) lodge of United Societies of U.S.A. I
will regularly and conscientiously observe all the by-laws of the organization.
So help me God. Amen."

Over the past ten years the order has been declining in memberships.
Its 1979 roster had 4,400 members, while in 1968 there were 4,900 enrolled.
The number of subordinate lodges also declined during this period from 190
to 142.

The emblem of the society is an outer and inner ring, forming a circular
border upon which the words "United Societies 1903" appear. In the center
of the inner ring is a Latin cross, and below it is an arclike bank carrying
the words "Of U.S.A."

The USOTUS, which is proud of its Byzantine Catholic heritage, has
loaned money to parishes, helped seminary students, aided college students,
and assisted the sick and needy. The society has also saved several churches
in the past from being sold in sheriff's sales. During the 1930s the USOTUS
came to the defense of some falsely maligned clergy in the Greek Catholic
Church. The society also has published a large variety of prayer manuals,
catechisms, grammars, and liturgical and devotional books. In recent years
the society has discontinued printing ecclesiastical materials. In fact, its
printing operation has been phased out.

Administratively, the USOTUS operates on two levels, the national and
the local. The national convention is the "Supreme Governing Body." It
meets quadrennially. Local groups are referred to as "Subordinate Lodges."
The national headquarters exist in McKeesport, Pennsylvania.

Although the USOTUS for a number of years was engaged in publishing
various ecclesiastical materials, it has very little about its own organization.
The interested reader may wish to consult *The United Societies of the
U.S.A.: A Historical Album* (1978). The order publishes a monthly newspaper, *Prosvita Enlightenment*. The *Constitution and By-Laws* (1979) was
obtained from the national offices.

UNITED TRANSPORTATION UNION INSURANCE ASSOCIATION
(UTUIA). This fraternal benefit society is a relatively new organization
in that it came into being as the result of a merger in 1971. The Order of
Railway Conductors and Brakemen, the Brotherhood of Railroad Trainmen,
the Brotherhood of Locomotive Firemen and Enginemen, and Switchmen's
Union of North America made up the merger. All but the latter group

were fraternal benefit groups since the late 1800s, even though they functioned as labor unions.

Like most fraternal benefit groups, the UTUIA awards scholarships for qualified children and grandchildren of its members. Each year fifty scholarships are awarded, amounting to more than $50,000. This program began in 1973.

Presently (1978) the society has about 240,000 members in some 1,000 subordinate branches that operate on the lodge system, holding meetings every month. The national governing body meets every four years to conduct convention business. Headquarters are in Cleveland, Ohio.

UNITY, ORDER OF. Organized in Philadelphia in 1889, the order provided fraternal benefits based on the assessment plan. Both men and women were admitted to membership. The ritual taught the members that there was strength in unity. The order apparently dissolved in the early 1900s. REFERENCE: *Cyc. Frat.*

UNIVERSAL CRAFTSMEN COUNCIL OF ENGINEERS (UCCE). This society of Freemasons was organized in Chicago in 1894 by a small group of Masonic engineers. In 1903 the society was incorporated in Cleveland, Ohio. Its basic purpose is to work for the enhancement of its members.

True to Masonic tradition, the order has a ritual. The degree bestowed upon the members attempts to accent "the dignity of labor."

Membership is open to Freemasons* who are engineers, for example, chemical engineers, consulting engineers, electrical engineers, or master mechanics. The governing body is named "Grand Council."

Additional information on this order is very sparse. The present report relied mostly on the Masonic Service Association's unpublished manuscript, "Allied Masonic Groups and Rites" (mimeographed, 1978).

V

VASA ORDER OF AMERICA (VOA). This society is named in honor of Sweden's Gustav Vasa, often seen as the George Washington of Sweden. The original name of the order formed in New Haven, Connecticut, in 1896 was "Vasa Orden of America."

The VOA was formed by the coming together of several Swedish sick benefit societies. Its objectives were to educate its members morally, intellectually, and socially and to provide insurance benefits. In order to operate successfully financially the order decided to derive its income from initiation fees, membership dues, donations, and interest earned on money deposits.

From the beginning the VOA adopted a ritual and an initiation ceremony. By 1915, at the society's Minneapolis convention, it had the ritual revised and improved, and by 1923 new rituals were sent out to local lodges for comments. This edition included an English version of the funeral ceremony. The society confers three degrees, one on each organizational level: Local Lodge, District Lodge, and Grand Lodge.

Over the years the VOA has made some organizational and constitutional changes. At one time men and women had separate lodges, but in 1923 the admission requirements were changed to permit "male and female persons of the caucasian race who have reached an age of 16 years, but not exceeding 50 years of age. . . ." Applicants also had to be in good health, of high moral character, able to speak and understand the Swedish language or be descendants of Swedish parents. In 1966 the $10 initiation fee was abolished.

As is true of so many other fraternal orders in the United States, the VOA also has been suffering membership losses. Its all-time high was reached in 1929 when 72,261 members graced the roster. But by 1979 the number had dwindled to 35,000. Several attempts have been made in the 1950s and 1960s to boost the membership rolls, but the results have been poor.

VOA on occasion honors certain persons by making them honorary members of the order. The first honorary members of the order were Crown Prince Gustav Adolf and Crown Princess Louise. Some other honorary members that the society is proud of are Earl and Mrs. Warren, Luther and Mrs. Youngdahl, and Colonel Edwin Aldrin, the second man to walk on the moon.

VOA has several emblems, one for each organizational level: a Vasa Junior League pin, a Junior Club pin, and one that is named Vasa Emblem. The last consists of a Maltese cross that is superimposed on a wreath. A sheaf adorns the top part of the cross and wreath. On the front of the cross are the letters VO, interlaced. The Maltese cross symbolizes charity for the sick; the wreath represents truth; and the sheaf stands for unity.

Each year the VOA provides scholarships for students who are fourteen or older. Near Moline and Rock Island, Illinois, the society operates an archive building in the onetime Swedish village, Bishop Hill, Illinois. The project of providing a permanent home for VOA records and artifacts was begun in 1972. A new building was built in 1974.

Three organizational divisions exist in the Vasa society. Local gatherings are known as "Lodges." The chief lodge officer is called "Chairman." Each local lodge has a chaplain, which is consistent with the society's relatively strong emphasis on the value of its ritual. Regional structures are referred to as "District Lodges." And on the national scene, the VOA follows common fraternal nomenclature by calling the national structure the

"Grand Lodge." The head of the grand lodge is the Grand Master. The grand lodge meets in convention quadrennially. National headquarters of the grand lodge are in Landisville, Pennsylvania.

For additional information, a good one-volume history is available: *Historical Review of Vasa Order of America, 1896-1971* (n.d.). This is a Vasa publication. A fraternal periodical, *The Vasa Star*, is published every month, except August. This magazine provides very good coverage of the society's events and activities.

VERHOVAY FRATERNAL INSURANCE ASSOCIATION. This fraternal beneficiary society was organized in 1886 in Pennsylvania. In the early 1920s the organization had more than 21,000 members. By 1955 when the society merged with the Rakoczi Aid Association to form the William Penn Fraternal Association* it had more than 40,000 adult members. Prior to 1935 the society was known as the Verhovay Aid Association. The society was headquartered in Pittsburgh, Pennsylvania.

VIKINGS, INDEPENDENT ORDER OF (IOV). This fraternal benefit society originated in Chicago, Illinois, in 1896. It was founded by a group of fraternally minded Swedes to provide insurance benefits for its members.

The society, like other fraternal groups, contributes to a number of fraternal programs. Each year it disburses $35,000 to the aged and needy members in its subordinate lodges. In 1977, ten scholarships were awarded to high school seniors who were members of the IOV. Each scholarship was worth $500. Some of the local units have their members visit hospitals and other needy members. Still other local lodges conduct blood donor clinics.

On the social, cultural level the IOV tries to acquaint its members with Scandinavian customs and traditions. Some lodges conduct classes for those interested in learning Scandinavian languages. Others have singers and dancers who put on programs of Scandinavian songs and dances. Still others engage in athletic events such as golfing and bowling.

Membership is open to Swedes or those of Swedish descent. Individuals married to someone of Swedish background may also join. When the order first was founded only Swedish males were eligible for membership. Currently (1978) the membership count stands at approximately 9,500 in sixty-three local lodges. This figure represents a 10 percent decline since the mid-1960s when the society had more than 10,500 members in eighty lodges.

Local units are known as "Lodges." The national body is called the "Grand Lodge." The principal officer is named Grand Chief. The grand lodge convenes every two years. Headquarters are housed in Chicago, Illinois.

Further information may be obtained by consulting brochures and pamphlets that are issued by the IOV. The society's monthly magazine, the *Viking Journal*, also provides helpful information.

WESTERN BEES. When this fraternal benefit group was first founded in 1905, it began as a secessionist group that once had its charter members belong to the Knights of Maccabees. The society was founded in Grand Island, Nebraska. Initially, the new order wanted to call itself Western Maccabees, but the parent order protested to the Nebraska Insurance Department. Thus the name Western Bees was selected. The order never achieved much growth, and by 1911 it merged with the Highland Nobles, an Iowa-based fraternal benefit society. REFERENCE: *Syc. Frat.*

WESTERN CATHOLIC UNION (WCU). On October 16, 1877, about a dozen Catholic laymen met in Quincy, Illinois, to form a fraternal benefit society known as the Western Catholic Union. Its objectives, as was true of other fraternal benefit groups formed in the late 1800s and early 1900s, were to provide aid to widows and orphans of the organization's deceased members. The aid was furnished by insurance that was based on the so-called assessment plan. Today the WCU is a legal reserve fraternal life insurance society.

Membership is confined to Catholics. Each local unit (called a branch) is affiliated with a Catholic parish. Thus a given branch will also bear the name of the parish, e.g., Sacred Heart Branch or St. Antonius Branch. The year 1978 was the best in the history of the society relative to receiving new members. Over 1,000 new enrollees joined the WCU that year. These data indicate that the WCU is growing and prospering. In fact, the society has never experienced any real membership losses. Even in the Great Depression of the 1930s the organization held its own, so to speak.

The society has no ritual, even though it operates on the lodge system. No degrees are offered. Its emblem is a shield with the symbol of a heart overlaid on a cross and anchor. At the bottom part of the shield are two hands clasped together in fraternal friendship. The letters WCU adorn the upper portion of the shield.

During the society's 102 years a number of events have occurred. In 1881 juvenile members were admitted. This was followed by the admission of women in 1912. By 1932 its assets equaled $2,000,000, and today (1979) the assets are in excess of $8,000,000. In 1925 the society built the WCU building. This ten-story structure is the largest building in Quincy, Illinois.

Conscious of its beneficiary obligations, the WCU in 1976 began constructing a retirement home in Quincy, Illinois. In order to build the retirement home the society purchased a Catholic high school and a Presbyterian church. Other buildings were built contiguous to these former edifices. Thus today an entire city block belongs to the retirement complex. At

Christmas time the various districts of the society distribute Christmas food baskets to needy families.

The WCU provides considerable support to the Catholic Church at large. It gives aid to Catholic Communications, which helps underwrite radio and television programs designed to educate Catholics and non-Catholics about the teachings of Catholicism. Annual pilgrimages to Catholic shrines are conducted by the society every year. It also distributes prayer cards and helps in the campaign to "Keep Christ in Christmas."

Fraternally, the group conducts picnics, parties, bus trips, socials, and related activities for its members. Many of these fraternal events are sponsored for the benefit of the youth members.

Administratively, the WCU conducts its business on three levels: the local branch, the district, and the national levels. The national structure is referred to as the "Supreme Council." Its conventions occur quadrennially. Quincy, Illinois, serves as the national headquarters.

The WCU publishes the *Western Catholic Union Record* each month. It provides news of the individual branches and of the society at large. There is no separate history published on the society.

WESTERN FRATERNAL LIFE ASSOCIATION (WFLA). Back in February of 1897, at a special convention, delegates from the western lodges of the Czecho-Slovak Protective Society (CSPS) decided to form a new fraternal benefit society if given inequities were not corrected. The differences were not satisfactorily received, so in June, 1897, the Western Bohemian Fraternal Association (as it was known then) was formed and chartered in Iowa. The new organization began with forty-nine lodges, most of them coming from the CSPS. In 1971 the society changed its name to Western Fraternal LIfe Association.

The WFLA prides itself on being the first Czech fraternal group to accept women on an equal basis with men, to establish a reserve insurance fund, to organize a juvenile department, to form lodges for young adults who preferred the English language, to adopt a table of rates based on age of joining, and to introduce endowment and twenty-payment life certificates.

A variety of contributions have been made by the society. During World War II three giant bombers were purchased through the war bonds that its members bought. Funds were given to the Red Cross and to the USO. The WFLA also continues to support a home for the aged in Chicago, provides scholarship monies to college students, and assists several other charity activities: March of Dimes, Muscular Dystrophy, American Cancer Society, American Heart Association, and Junior Achievement.

Membership is open to men and women who are over fifteen years of age. The maximum age is determined by the laws of each state wherein the WFLA is licensed to operate. All members have to be initiated according to the ritual of the society. Membership does not seem to be limited to Czech descendants. There were a total of 43,471 adult members, plus 8,590 enrollees in the juvenile department, in January of 1979. This figure represents a decline of about 10,000 during the last ten years. As is true in most fraternal benefit societies, the WFLA also has a social membership classification for those who cannot pass the physical examination required for insurance purposes.

A shield portraying a hammer, anvil, plow, and grain sheaf, plus the letters WFLA, and the letters Z.C.B.J., serves as the society's insignia. The letters Z.C.B.J. stand for the organization's name (*Zapadni Cesko-Bratrska Jednota*) in Czech.

The WFLA has lodges in nineteen states. The highest authority is the national convention, which occurs every four years. Delegates are selected for the convention by the society's local lodges. Its board of directors is elected by the seven districts of the society. National headquarters are maintained in Cedar Rapids, Iowa.

For further reading consult the society's monthly magazine, *Fraternal Herald* (*Bratrsky Vestnik*). It provides rather comprehensive coverage of the society's activities. The bylaws are available from the national office in Cedar Rapids, Iowa.

WESTERN SAMARITANS LIFE ASSOCIATION. Organized in 1922 in Illinois, this fraternal beneficiary group admitted both men and women to membership, provided the applicants were white. By 1927 the society had 2,312 members, of which 671 were social members who had no insurance rights. By 1935 there appears to be no evidence of the organization's continued existence.

WESTERN SLAVONIC ASSOCIATION (WSA). Founded in 1908, the society began as a fraternal benefit organization. It still serves this objective by providing even more fraternal benefits than it did in the past. The SWA also continues to have a ritualistic form of work in its meetings and sessions. New members go through a brief initiation ceremony.

As a fraternal benefit group, the WSA provides the usual array of insurance and fraternal projects. Local lodges have their members visit the sick and bereaved. College scholarships are offered to qualified high school graduates. Various recreational activities are also sponsored, ranging from bowling to annual trips to Las Vegas, Nevada. Periodically, trips are taken to Yugoslavia. The trips to Yugoslavia are one way in which the society promotes Slavic heritage and culture. At home in the United States Slavic music, dancing, and movies are frequently offered to the members as part of their local lodge activities.

Membership currently (1978) in the WSA stands at approximately 10,000, a decline from the 13,000 that the society had in 1965. Both males and females may join the organization.

The society has forty-one local lodges in five states. The national convention takes place every four years. Head offices are maintained in Denver, Colorado.

For additional information, see the society's monthly publication, *The Fraternal Voice*. The constitution of the society also provides helpful background.

WHITE SHRINE OF JERUSALEM, ORDER OF THE (WSJ). This group, which has its members profess "belief in the defense of the Christian Religion" [*sic*] was organized in Chicago, Illinois, in 1894 by Charles D. Magee, a Freemason.* Three years later (1897) a schism occurred, largely under the influence of Magee, who founded a rival White Shrine in Grand Rapids, Michigan. However, in 1908 the two orders reunited and formed the Supreme Shrine of the Order of the White Shrine of Jerusalem. The first convention following the merger was held in Chicago in 1909.

The WSJ has a ritual that attempts to create a quasi-Christian atmosphere. Its prayers are said in the name of Jesus Christ. In fact, some prayers even ask for the forgiveness of sins: "Pardon all our sins and deal with us according to Thy mercies, in Jesus Christ, our Lord. Amen." The ritual has one degree known as the "White Shrine of Jerusalem."

Membership requirements since 1953 permit wives, daughters, adopted daughters, mothers, sisters, widows, and half-sisters of husbands, fathers, sons, or brothers who are Master Masons to join the order. Prior to 1953 one had to hold membership in the Order of the Eastern Star.* All must be adults. Only whites are eligible to join. Reportedly, because of the order's purported Christian posture, Jewish Freemasons and their female relatives do not belong to the WSJ. Current (1979) membership is near 180,000 "Sojourners," as the order refers to its members.

Local units are called "Shrines." There were about 845 shrines in 1979. On the international level the order refers to its structure as the "Supreme Shrine." The presiding officer is the Supreme Worthy High Priestess. Headquarters are in Romulus, Michigan.

For additional information, see Harold V. B. Voorhis, "Order of the White Shrine of Jerusalem" in his *The Eastern Star* (1954). The mimeographed copy of "Allied Masonic Groups and Rites" (1978) by the Masonic Service Association is also worthy of note. The order's proceedings are another source for helpful information.

WILLIAM PENN ASSOCIATION (WPA). Back on February 21, 1886, in Hamilton, Pennsylvania, another fraternal benefit organization sprouted in the United States. The society that once was known (until 1971) as the

William Penn Fraternal Association came into being for purposes of providing insurance funds for the aged and sick members, as well as for widows and orphans of deceased members. Another objective at the time of the order's birth was to retain and foster the Hungarian heritage and culture. The founders were primarily Hungarian coalminers who, like most other founders of fraternal benefit societies at that time, knew next to nothing about life insurance. About forty years after its origin the society adopted a sound actuarial basis for its insurance certificates in 1924. In 1923 a juvenile department was formed to accommodate the insuring of those sixteen and under.

Membership in the WPA is open to men and women. Although the society is of Hungarian origin, it has never restricted its membership to those of Hungarian descent. Two classes of membership are available, beneficiary and social. The latter has no insurance with the organization.

The WPA, like all fraternal benefit societies, provides a considerable amount of charity donations, for example, to homes for the aged, youth camps, ethnic groups, Christmas parties for needy youth, and the like. Each year a number of scholarships are awarded to college students. Local branches have numerous members visit the sick and infirm.

In true fraternal fashion, the WPA has a secret ritual, and its members are initiated according to the ritual's format. The insignia of the society is an oval-shaped shield, standing upright. This shield displays the letter "P" in the form of an oil lamp, and a flame rises from its surface. The colors are white, black, and red.

In 1955 the Verhovay Fraternal Insurance Association and Rokoczi Aid Association merged with the WPA. This merger apparently has not averted the decline in memberships. In 1968 the WPA had approximately 80,000 members, whereas its present (1979) number stands at 65,204, a loss of 18 percent during the last decade. These figures, however, do not include the social members, who only enroll on the local level. Hence the WPA has no national record of its social members.

The society has members in sixteen states and the District of Columbia. The national authority resides in the "General Convention," which also elects a board of directors. There is no statewide structure. Local groups are referred to as "Branches," of which there currently (1979) are eighty-five. The national headquarters are situated in Pittsburgh, Pennsylvania.

For additional background the interested reader may consult the society's quarterly publication, *Penn Life*. The society's bylaws and a brief history (mimeographed) are available upon request.

WOMAN'S BENEFIT ASSOCIATION. See North American Benefit Association.

WOODMEN CIRCLE (WC). This once was a prominent female auxiliary of the Woodmen of the World. The society once boasted more than 130,000 woman members. It functioned as a fraternal benefit organization providing insurance for its members. In 1965 the society was absorbed by the Woodmen of the World Life Insurance Society.* When the organization operated independently, it called its local units "Groves."

WOODMEN OF THE WORLD (WOW). When this organization was incorporated in Colorado in 1890 by three members of the Modern Woodmen of America,* it was first named "The Head Camp, Pacific Jurisdiction, Woodmen of the World." In July 1916, the name was changed to "Woodmen of the World." When the WOW was formed in 1890 all but two camps (local units) of the Modern Woodmen in America in the state of Colorado came into the new organization. The constitution of 1976 calls the society "Woodmen of the World and/or Assured Life Association." The society is also known as the "Woodmen of the World (of Colorado)."

The WOW is a fraternal benefit society, holding membership in the National Fraternal Congress of America.* Like many fraternal benefit groups, the WOW has a ritual containing agendas for initiation, installation, and funeral rites. The lodge (camp) floor plan, portrayed in the ritual manual, shows one item quite different from most floor plans of other fraternal societies. In most other lodge rooms an altar stands in the center of the room, but in the WOW camp plan there is a tree stump in place of the altar. The ritual attempts to teach its four "great principles of the Woodmen of the World." The first principle is hospitality; the second is service; the third is loyalty, and the fourth is protection.

Prior to 1928 only men were permitted to join the society. Now women are also admitted, and a division for juvenile members is in existence too. Adult members are admitted on the basis of a ball ballot. The presence of three blackballs bars an individual from membership. Presently (1979) the WOW has 31,000 members in seventy-two lodges (camps). In 1962 the WOW absorbed The Christian Mutual Benefit Association.

As a fraternal benefit society, the order sponsors social and recreational activities such as dinners, dances, bingo parties, picnics, and various athletic events. It awards scholarships, supports Korean and Vietnamese orphans, donates lifesaving equipment to hospitals, and, of course, assists its own members who need temporary material and financial help.

The insignia of the WOW is a circle with an inner ring forming a circular border, which portrays the following inscription: WOODMEN OF THE WORLD. Inside of the inner circle is a square design displaying the letters WOW. Above the square appears the year 1891. At the bottom of the square is the word Colorado.

Local units, as has already been indicated, are known as "Camps." The WOW operates camps in sixteen states. The national structure is called "Head Camp." It meets in convention every four years. The offices of the head camp are located in Denver, Colorado.

For additional information, see *The Pacific Woodmen*, the society's bimonthly periodical. Other helpful sources are the *Ritual of the Woodmen of the World; Constitution and By-Laws of the Woodmen of the World* (1976).

WOODMEN OF THE WORLD LIFE INSURANCE SOCIETY (WOW).

This fraternal benefit society was born under the leadership and impetus of Joseph Cullen Root, who assembled a group of men in the Paxton Hotel in Omaha, Nebraska, in 1890. Root earlier had founded the Modern Woodmen of America in 1883. A few years into the life of the Modern Woodmen brought about a feud between him and the head physician of the society. Both men were expelled, and so Root set out to form a new society, which led him to Omaha, Nebraska.

Root, like so many other founders of fraternal orders in the United States, was a Freemason. He also held membership in the Independent Order of Odd Fellows,* Knights of Pythias,* Ancient Order of United Workmen,* and others. The rituals that Root designed for the WOW showed a decided Masonic flavor. At first Root named the new society Modern Woodmen of the World. A few months later it was changed to Woodmen of the World.

Right from the start, the society issued benefit certificates in denominations of $1,000, $2,000, and $3,000. Members had to be between sixteen and fifty-two years of age. Only white males were eligible. Today (1979) the constitution of the society contains no white clauses relative to membership qualifications. There are, as is commonly true in most fraternal benefit groups, two classes of memberships, beneficiary and social. The latter exists ordinarily because some fail to qualify physically with respect to the insurance requirements. The most recent (1977) constitution states that the minimum age is sixteen years. No maximum is mentioned. The 1979 membership roster had 802,000 members in 4,000 lodges. Part of its membership growth has been facilitated by absorbing the United Order of the Golden Cross in 1962, the Order of Railroad Telegraphers in 1964, and the Supreme Forest Woodmen Circle* in 1965. Also in 1968 the society absorbed the New England Order of Protection.

The society still takes its ritual and secrecy very seriously. Members are initiated according to the ritual's prescriptions, and all beneficiary members are given an annual password. The constitution provides for an Escort, Watchman, and Sentry. Each has specific roles to perform in ritualistic ceremonies.

Relative to insurance benefits, the society provides the typical benefits pertaining to a variety of sicknesses, disaster relief, and orphan assistance. WOW also is active in sponsoring community projects and giving aid to hospitals, rescue squads, and fire departments. Each year the society gives awards to outstanding members who have performed unusual services within local lodges. These are known as "Mr. Woodmen" and "Woman of Woodcraft" awards.

The emblem of the society is a sawed-off tree stump, accompanied by an ax, a mallet (often called "beetle"), and a wedge. Surrounding the emblem are the words: The Family Fraternity, Protection-Service.

On the national level, the society refers to itself as the "Sovereign Camp." It meets in convention every four years. Between conventions the board of directors acts in the supreme capacity. Regional or statewide structures are known as "Jurisdictions" or "Head Camps." There are four different subordinate bodies: camps, courts, groves, and junior units. Camps are composed of "members who have attained the age of sixteen years." Courts have "female members who have attained the age of sixteen years." Groves also are "composed of members who have attained the age of sixteen years." The junior units have members who are under sixteen years of age. The difference between "Camps" and "Groves" is not delineated in the constitution. The national headquarters of the WOW are in Omaha, Nebraska.

For further information see the monthly periodical, *Woodmen of the World Magazine*. The *Constitution and Laws* (1977) also is helpful in understanding the society. A history of the WOW was obtained from the head office in Omaha, Nebraska.

WOODMEN RANGERS AND RANGERETTES (WRR). This is a youth organization sponsored by the Woodmen of the World Life Insurance Society.* It was organized in 1964 by absorbing the Boys of Woodcraft Sportsmen's Clubs and Girls of Woodcraft. Membership is open from ages eight to fifteen for boys and girls. Currently (1979) the group has 115,471 members. The society operates out of the national headquarters in Omaha, Nebraska, where the headquarters of Woodmen of the World also are located.

WORKMEN, ANCIENT ORDER OF UNITED (AOUW). This organization was formed by John Jordan Upchurch in 1868 in Meadsville, Pennsylvania. Upchurch, a mechanic who worked for the Atlantic and Great Western Railroad (now the Erie Railroad), was prompted to organize the AOUW largely because he was dissatisfied with the League of Friendship of the Mechanical Order of the Sun.* He wanted an organization that would be more responsive to the needs of its members. When the AOUW was founded, Upchurch had hoped to form an order that would unite the conflicting interests of labor and management. This goal, however, soon (in

1869) gave way to providing benevolent insurance protection for its members' widows and orphans.

The word "Workmen" was chosen as part of the new order's name because its purpose was to serve and attract men in the mechanical trades. Only two years after the AOUW was formed, however, the order broadened its membership requirements to permit other occupations as well.

Through Upchurch, a Freemason, the AOUW took on a number of Masonic features. Its ritual was secret; the square and compass and the all-seeing eye were organizational symbols. At first there were four degrees, but in 1871 the ritual was revised to work only three degrees. The Bible, as in Masonry, also was an important symbol.

Although most scholars and historians of fraternal insurance credit the AOUW as being the first fraternal group that introduced fraternal insurance at the time of its founding in 1868, the society really did not enter the insurance effort seriously until October 1869. During the society's first year of existence there was as much emphasis on ameliorating unfavorable conditions for workingmen as there was on its insurance fund, which allowed no more than $500 to be paid to the "legal heirs of a deceased member." The real emphasis on fraternal insurance began with Upchurch amending the founding article on insurance on October 6, 1869. The amended article stipulated that each initiated new member pay $1.00 to the insurance fund. After a member died, his beneficiaries received $2,000. Depleted funds were to be restored by each member contributing another $1.00. This procedure was to be repeated each time the fund required restoration. This method was known as the post-mortem plan or the assessment-as-needed plan. If any member failed to pay his $1.00 fee in thirty days, he forfeited his membership in the order. If a subordinate lodge failed to forward the amount of the insurance fund in twenty days, it lost its charter. The change made on October 6, 1869, was approved by the Provisional Grand Lodge.

To offer workingmen life insurance was indeed a novel innovation in the late 1860s, especially when the idea of American insurance was less than twenty years old at that time. Heretofore life insurance really had been available only to businessmen and manufacturers. In addition, other factors made life insurance something less than popular. Religious groups opposed insurance as being sinful and not trusting in God. Then, too, there were numerous bankruptcies of commercial life insurance firms. Ironically, it was the latter that convinced AOUW leaders that life insurance would succeed only in fraternal societies, where overhead expenses would be extremely small.

It should be noted that there is some question whether the AOUW really was the first American fraternal insurance society, primarily because some societies were founded before 1868 which later also had types of insurance programs for their members. The point to be remembered, however, is that while such organizations were formed before 1868, they did not sell insurance until after 1868. (For a more detailed explanation see Myron W. Sackett, *Early History of Fraternal Beneficiary Societies*, 1914.)

The AOUW, compared to numerous other fraternal benefit societies, was quite progressive in its orientation. It was not only the harbinger of fraternal life insurance, but it also took the initiative of calling together a number of fraternal benefit societies in 1886. This action caused sixteen fraternal benefit groups to form the National Fraternal Congress* in that same year. This cooperative association sought to establish uniformity and sound insurance practices among all fraternal benefit societies. The National Fraternal Congress is still in existence today with 121 member societies.

Being the progressively minded organization that it was, the society revised its ritual a number of times. Every revision sought to take into account the changes adopted by the society so that the ritual and the order's objectives would be in harmony. The religious qualities of the ritual were deleted from the revision of 1932.

The watchwords of the AOUW are "Charity, Hope, and Protection." The order, because of its insurance, has always taken great pride in the latter watchword, for having been the pioneer in fraternal insurance, providing protection to its members' widows and orphans in a novel and distinctive manner.

The AOUW, which by 1885 was the largest fraternal benefit society in America, discontinued its supreme lodge structure in 1929. A congress was established in place of the supreme authority. In 1952 the AOUW dissolved or merged with various state societies. Washington is the only state where the society has continued to exist. In other states the order frequently merged or converted to mutual insurance companies. For example, in Massachusetts the AOUW merged with New England Order of Protection. In North Dakota the society converted to a mutual and changed its name to Pioneer Mutual Life Insurance company. In Texas the order went into receivership. Additional changes could be cited.

When the AOUW first was organized, its constitution stated that non-whites were never to join the order. Now, however, membership is no longer limited to white eligibility. The membership presently is very low, with about 3,000 members in the state of Washington. The supreme lodge meets every two years in convention.

For further information, see the volume by Keith L. Yates, *The Fogarty Years* (1972). This is a historical treatment of the AOUW. The order's bimonthly, *AOUW Emblem*, is a helpful source for further information.

WORKMEN'S BENEFIT FUND OF THE UNITED STATES OF AMERICA (WBF). This group was founded in 1884 and incorporated in the state of New York in 1899. The society began as a self-help organization for German-American immigrants. During the life span of the WBF two mergers have resulted: The American Fraternal Insurance Society and the Mutual Benefit Aid Society. The American Fraternal Insurance Society was founded in Chicago, Illinois, by German immigrants who had come from the Volga River area in Russia. The Mutual Benefit Aid Society was also a German-immigrant group based in Chicago. Both groups have merged with the WBF since 1969. The WBF still has a decided German flavor.

As a fraternal benefit society, the WBF provides the usual line of fraternal insurance and benevolencies for its members. For instance, it operates recreation camps, a convalescent home, and a home for the aged. Donations are regularly made to various charities. Scholarships are awarded to worthy student members.

Two types of adult memberships are available, beneficial and social. Individuals under eighteen years of age are classified as juvenile members. The constitution of 1976 does not limit membership to ethnic (German) background. As of December 31, 1978, the society had about 35,000 members. This figure represents a noteworthy decline from 1965, when the society had 53,000 members.

Structurally, the WBF operates on three levels. The local units are known as "Branches." Regional groups are called "Districts." The highest authority is the national convention, which meets quadrennially. The head office is found in Brooklyn, New York.

No published history exists regarding the WBF, although the society's bimonthly publication, *Solidarity*, provides helpful insights into the organization. The constitution is published by the Brooklyn office.

WORKMEN'S CIRCLE, THE (WC). The 1880s and 1890s saw about 40,000 Jews migrate to the United States from eastern Europe. Most of them settled in the larger American cities. Their manners, appearance, and poor economic status threatened the American image. Most of them lived in segregated areas of the cities.

In 1900 a group of concerned working-class Jews met in Manhattan, New York, on September 4th and 5th to organize a Jewish fraternal benevolent society known as "Central Farband of Workmen's Circle Branches." Before the national group was formed in 1900, there were local groups in existence since at least 1894 that called themselves Workmen's Circle. The newly formed order in 1901 stated its reason for coming into existence in the following words: "The continuous poverty and frequent illness, which are especially burdensome for the worker, have brought us together within the Workmen's Circle so that through our unity we may be of mutual assistance to each other."

By 1910 the WC had become a success. It had attained a membership of 36,866 and carried almost 12 million dollars of insurance on its members. It also had a reasonable reserve fund of one-quarter million dollars. With its success came the fear, on the part of some, that the order would attract "strange elements, those who do not belong to the working class." By 1925 the WC had 85,000 members. This year essentially was the zenith point of the organization. Beginning with the late 1920s the order began losing members. Its present (1979) membership is about 55,000, compared to 65,000 members in the late 1960s. This is a loss of 15 percent in a period of about ten years.

Throughout the WC's lifespan, it has been a keen advocate of social legislation. The Society has been very supportive of Franklin D. Roosevelt's New Deal, Truman's Fair Deal, Kennedy's New Frontier, and Johnson's Great Society.

To enhance the WC's fraternalism, the order has a Workmen's Circle Hymn. The first stanza reads:

> Mid the blaze of a world commotion,
> The light of true freedom we sought.
> Here at home and far over the ocean,
> To the forge of our vision we brought
> The fire of our love and devotion,
> And our own Workmen's Circle we wrought.

The refrain reads:

> A timeless bond unites us,
> A ring of tempered steel.
> One radiant beacon lights us
> To peace and common weal.
> Stand all for one and one for all,
> The working class ideal.

The WC maintains three homes for the elderly, in Pennsylvania, New Jersey, and New York. Since 1958 the WC has maintained a network of secular Yiddish schools in Canada and the United States. Presently (1979) it has thirty-three such schools. The society has also given support to rehabilitation training programs.

The WC believes that with its new and improved insurance benefits it will experience membership increases. In 1971 some 5,000 new members were gained. The society now offers a wide range of life, as well as accident and health insurance. It also offers insurance for general practitioners, surgeons, and medical specialists.

On the national level, which includes Canada, the WC meets in convention biennially. Delegates are chosen by regional groups known as "Convention Territories" or "Territorial Conferences." Local chapters are called "branches." The headquarters of the WC (*Der Arbeter Ring* in Yiddish) are in the city of New York.

Additional information on the WC may be obtained by reading Judah J. Shapiro, *The Friendly Society: A History of the Workmen's Circle* (1975). *The Workmen's Circle Call*, a quarterly magazine, published by the WC, provides news about the society.

YE ANCIENT ORDER OF CORKS. See Corks, Ye Ancient Order of.

YELLOW DOGS, ORDER OF (OYD). While the society originated in the southern part of the United States, it was first introduced in the northern states in 1923, according to Arthur Preuss in his *Dictionary of Secret and Other Societies* (1924). The order called its local units "Kennels." Initiation rites were performed on all new members. The writer was unable to ascertain when the order became extinct.

YEOMEN, BROTHERHOOD OF AMERICAN (BAY). Organized in 1897, this fraternal benefit society began, as did most fraternal insurance groups, with the assessment plan. By 1817, however, the BAY made considerable changes in its efforts to achieve solvency. Fifteen years after it began to work seriously to become completely solvent, the BAY left its fraternal moorings in 1932 by converting to a mutual life company, adopting the name of Mutual Life Insurance Company.

The BAY, while it was a fraternal benefit group, had attained a membership of 215,000 members by 1923. About 7,500 of this roster were social (nonbenefit) members. It had in 1923 about 3,200 subordinate units in Canada and the United States. Women were admitted along with male members. For the youth the society operated a juvenile insurance department. By 1927 its membership had dropped to 153,586.

In typical fraternal fashion the BAY had a ritual with signs, passwords, and oaths. Its lodge room (called "Homestead") had an altar in the center of the meeting. The ritual also contained hymns and prayers. The latter were commonly spoken by a chaplain. The initiation rite, among other emphases, accented the Magna Carta and the English language as man's two greatest achievements.

In 1906 the order experienced a schism when John E. Paul and Clarence B. Paul, who were relieved of their offices in the BAY, formed the Homesteaders* society. The new organization copied a number of characteristics from the BAY.

Local units, as already noted, were called "Homesteads." The national structure was known as "Castle," and its headquarters were maintained in Des Moines, Iowa.

Additional information concerning the BAY may be found by consulting back issues of *The Yeoman Shield*, a former publication of the society. A short history of the society appeared in the *Fraternal Monitor*, 32 (January 1922). See also Arthur Preuss, *A Dictionary of Secret and Other Societies* (1924).

YORK RITE SOVEREIGN COLLEGE, THE (YRSC). This body is an appendant order of Freemasons* that was founded by Richard W. Lewis, Past Grand High Priest of the Grand Chapter of Royal Arch Masons* in Michigan. Lewis organized the new structure in January 6, 1957, in Detroit, Michigan. One recent Masonic publication states that Lewis had hoped the organization "would become a kind of Supreme Council for the York Rite; but it has not met with approval of all bodies of that Rite."

The YRSC lists six purposes in its literature:

(a) To foster a spirit of cooperation and coordination among each of the Bodies of York Rite Masonry.
(b) To assist in worthy efforts to improve the ritualistic and dramatic presentation of York Rite work.
(c) To conduct an education program in order to inculcate a greater appreciation of the principles, ideals and programs of York Rite Masonry.
(d) To strengthen York Rite Masonry in every possible manner.
(e) To build up a love of country and to aid and support genuine Americanism.
(f) To reward outstanding service to York Rite Masonry by awards, honors and other methods of proper recognition.

Membership in the YRSC is by invitation only; moreover, only those who are members of York Rite* Masonic bodies are eligible. As of June 30, 1978, the order had 5,000 members in fifty-seven colleges (organizational units). Since the founding of the order, it has shown a slow but steady increase in membership. Regarding the selection of new members, the order requires that "No member shall reveal to any person being considered for membership or any other non-member the fact that a particular person might be, is being, or has been proposed for membership until after a favorable note. . . ."

In true Masonic tradition, the YRSC has a secret ritual that contains the formulations for the following degrees and honors: Order of Knight Postulant, Order of Knight of York, and the York Rite Purple Cross. The insignia of the order is a pentagonal design that displays the letters C, Y, C, C, L,— one in each corner (angle) of the pentagon. In the center of the pentagon is a seven-pronged design, which in turn has a nine-cornered star-like pattern superimposed upon it. The pentagon is encircled by a wreath that holds the Masonic square and compass on the lower part of the wreath.

The fifty-seven "Colleges" are the order's basic organizational units. In some states there are several, and in other states there is only one college. The colleges are located in Canada as well as in the United States. The highest authority structure is the "General Assembly," which meets annually. Head offices are in Detroit, Michigan.

Additional information on the YRSC may be gained by consulting the order's monthly periodical, *The York Rite Crusader*. The annual *Proceedings* are available from the head offices. In addition to the constitution and bylaws, the interested reader may benefit by obtaining a short publication, *A Preview of York Rite*, published by the YRSC.

___ Z ___

ZIVENA BENEFICIAL SOCIETY (ZBA). Organized in 1891, when fraternal societies were being formed all over the United States, the ZBA began as a fraternal beneficiary society. The membership of this organization has never been very large. For instance, by 1927, when many fraternal groups reached their highest memberships, the ZBA had 7,277 members. In 1965 it had 4,357, and by 1977 the roster contained about 2,500 members.

Like most fraternal benefit groups, the society awards scholarships to eligible members. Aid is given to the aged and handicapped who belong to the organization. Civic and charitable organizations regularly receive donations from the ZBA.

The society is licensed to sell fraternal insurance in only four states: Illinois, New York, Ohio, and Pennsylvania. The national convention meets quadrennially. Ligonier, Pennsylvania, is the ZBA's headquarters city.

The writer knows of no really helpful sources, as the society did not respond to the author's request for information. The present sketch primarily was based on a brief report in *Statistics, Fraternal Benefit Societies* (1977).

CHRONOLOGY

Following is a chronological catalog of the fraternal organizations discussed in the present volume. The reader will note that the last two decades of the nineteenth century and the first two decades of the twentieth century experienced the birth of most fraternal benefit and fraternal secret societies.

1717
Freemasonry (Ancient Free and Accepted Masonry)

1730
Free and Regenerated Palladium

1769
Knights Templar

1775
Prince Hall Freemasonry

1797
Royal Arch Masonry, International General Grand Chapter of

1801
Ancient and Accepted Scottish Rite of Freemasonry for the Southern Jurisdiction of the United States of America, The Supreme Council 33°, Mother Supreme Council of the World

1813
Ancient and Accepted Scottish Rite of Freemasonry for the Northern Masonic Jurisdiction of the United States of America
Ancient Order of Foresters

1819
Independent Order of Odd Fellows

1830
Loyal Orange Association (Canada)
United Ancient Order of Druids

1834
Improved Order of Red Men

1835

Independent Order of Rechabites

1836

Ancient Order of Hibernians in America

1840

Order of Sons of Hermann

1842

Sons of Temperance

1843

B'nai B'rith International
Grand United Order of Odd Fellows in America

1844

American Brotherhood
Order of United Americans

1845

Templars of Honor and Temperance
United American Mechanics
United Daughters of Rechab

1846

United Order of True Sisters, Inc.

1847

Independent Order of Good Samaritans and Daughters of Samaria

1849

Free Sons of Israel

1850

American Protestant Association
Brotherhood of the Union
Independent Order of Red Men
International Order of Good Templars
Knights of Jericho

1851

Ancient and Illustrious Star of Bethlehem
International Association of Rebekah Assemblies

1852

Order of the Heptasophs

1853

Junior Order of United American Mechanics of the United States of America, Inc.

1854

Czechoslovak Society of America

1856

Grand United Order of Galilean Fishermen

1857

Order of Eastern Star

1858

Rosicrucian Fraternity

1859

Order of B'rith Abraham
Order Knights of Friendship

1861

United Brothers of Friendship

1863

The Locomotive Engineers Mutual Life and Accident Insurance Association

1864

Knights of Pythias

1865

Ancient Order of Freesmiths
Knights of the Ku Klux Klan
North American Swiss Alliance
Slovak Gymnastic Union Sokol of the United States of America

1867

Benevolent and Protective Order of Elks
Order of Patrons of Husbandry (The Grange)

1868

Ancient Order of United Workmen
Catholic Family Life Insurance
Independent Order of Mechanics
Knights of Pythias of North America, Europe, Asia, and Africa
St. Patrick's Alliance of America
Ye Ancient Order of Corks

1870

The Ancient and Illustrious Order Knights of Malta
Knights of the Red Cross of Constantine
P.E.O. Sisterhood
The Royal Templars of Temperance

1871

Ancient Order of Knights of the Mystic Chain
Order of Sons of St. George

1872

Ancient Arabic Order of the Nobles of the Mystic Shrine
Artisans Order of Mutual Protection
Independent Order of Immaculates of the United States of America
International General Grand Council of Royal and Select Masters
International Order of Twelve of Knights and Daughters of Tabor
Knights of the Golden Eagle
Masonic Life Association

1873

Degree of Honor Protective Association
Knights of Honor
The Order of Amaranth
Order of the American Union
Polish Roman Catholic Union of America

1874

German Order of Harugari
Independent Order of Foresters

1875

Native Sons of the Golden West

1876

Sons of Scotland Benevolent Association
United Order of Golden Cross

1877

Catholic Knights of America
Independent Order of Sons of Benjamin
Order of Shield of Honor
Royal Arcanum
Western Catholic Union

1878

American Legion of Honor
The Catholic Aid Association
Elks Mutual Benefit Association
Improved Order of Heptasophs
The Maccabees
Order of Mutual Protection
Order of Scottish Clans
The Royal Order of Scotland
United Order of Pilgrim Fathers

1879

Canadian Foresters Life Insurance Society
Catholic Association of Foresters
Czech Catholic Union
Equitable Aid Union of America
The Home Circle

Iowa Legion of Honor
Knights and Ladies of the Golden Rule
Knights of St. John
Knights of the Red Cross
National Haymakers' Association
Order of Chosen Friends
Order of Scottish Clans
Order of Sparta
Sons of Adam

1880

Patriarchal Circle of America
Polish National Alliance of the United States of North America
Portuguese Union of the State of California
Societas Rosicruciana in Civitatibus Foederatis

1881

Benevolent Order of Buffaloes
Catholic Knights of St. George
The Danish Brotherhood in America
The Danish Sisterhood
Fraternal Legion
Golden Star Fraternity
The Grand United Order of True Reformers
Independent Order of Svithiod
Knights and Ladies of Honor
Loyal Knights and Ladies
National Union Assurance Society
Order of Iron Hall
Templars of Liberty

1882

Independent Order of Mystic Brothers
Knights of Columbus
Royal Society of Good Fellows
The Travelers Protective Association of America

1883

Baptist Life Association
Catholic Order of Foresters
Modern Woodmen of America
Mosaic Templars of America
Royal League

1884

American Insurance Union
Bavarian National Association of North America
Free and Regenerated Palladium
Knights and Ladies of the Golden Star
Northwestern Legion of Honor
Workmen's Benefit Fund of the United States of America

1885

Catholic Knights Insurance Society
Fraternal Mystic Circle
The Degree of Pocohontas
Grand Fraternity
Legion of the Red Cross
Masonic Relief Association of the United States and Canada

1886

Lithuanian Alliance of America
National Fraternal Congress of America
National Order of Videttes
Native Daughters of the Golden West
Order of Golden Circle
Protected Home Circle
Verhovay Fraternal Insurance Association
William Penn Association

1887

American Protective Association
Canadian Order of Chosen Friends
Independent Order of B'rith Abraham
New England Order of Protection
Polish Falcons of America

1888

American Order of Druids
Knights of the Ancient Essenic Order
Knights of the Blue Cross of the World
Loyal Order of Moose
Loyal Women of American Liberty
Modern Order of Chaldeans
Order of Pente
Rathbone Sisters of the World
Sexennial League
The Order of United Commercial Travelers of America

1889

First Catholic Slovak Union of the United States of America and Canada
Knights of the Globe
Lithuanian Catholic Alliance
National Fraternal Union
Order of Equity
Order of Unity
Royal Neighbors of America
Supreme Council Grottoes of North America
United Friends of Michigan

1890

Ahavas Israel
Brotherhood of America

Fraternal Aid Union
Independent International Order of Owls
Loyal Christian Benefit Association
Loyal Knights of America
National Slovak Society of the U.S.A.
Order of Home Builders
Order of the Continental Fraternal Union
Polish Union of America
Social Order of the Beauceant
Woodmen of the World
Woodmen of the World Life Insurance Society

1891

Ancient Arabic Order of the Nobles of the Mystic Shrine
Canadian Fraternal Association
The Catholic Knights of Ohio
Catholic Workman
Daughters of America
Home Palladium
Modern Knights' Fidelity League
National Protective Life Association
Order of Aegis
Zivena Beneficial Society

1892

First Catholic Slovak Ladies Association
Greater Beneficial Union of Pittsburgh
Greek Catholic Union of the United States of America
Mystic Workers of the World
Independent Order of Sons of Abraham
International Order of Hoo-hoo
Knights and Ladies of Security
Loyal Mystic Legion of America
North American Benefit Association
Pioneer Fraternal Association

1893

American Benefit Society
Ancient Egyptian Arabic Order of Nobles of the Shrine
Daughters of Isis
Knights and Ladies of Azar
National Fraternity
Pennsylvania Slovak Catholic Union
Royal Benefit Society
Union Fraternal League

1894

American Hungarian Catholic Society
American Knights or Protection
Ben Hur Life Association
Catholic Women's Fraternal of Texas K.J.Z.T.

Croatian Fraternal Union of America
Dramatic Order Knights of Khorassan
Freeman's Protective Silver Federation
The Gleaner Life Insurance Society
Imperial Order of Muscovites
National Benefit Society
Order of the Golden Rod
Order of the White Shrine of Jerusalem
Royal Tribe of Joseph
Ukrainian National Association
Universal Craftsmen Council of Engineers
The Workmen's Circle

1895

The Alliance of Poles
Ancient Mystic Order of Bagmen of Bagdad
Ancient Order of Sanhedrims
Court of Honor
Improved Order of Knights of Pythias
Italo American National Union
Knights of Equity
Knights of the Loyal Guard
North American Union Life Assurance Society
Order of the Daughters of Scotia
Order of the Little Red School House
Protestant Knights of America
Russian Orthodox Catholic Mutual Aid Society of the U.S.A.
Sons of Norway

1896

American Order of United Catholics
Association Canado-Americaine
Columbian League
Dames of Malta
Hungarian Reformed Federation of America
Imperial Mystic Legion
Loyal American Life Association
Modern American Fraternal Order
Occidental Mutual Benefit Association
Order of Shepherds of Bethlehem
Royal Highlanders
Slavonic Benevolent Order of the State of Texas
Sons and Daughters of Protection
Temple of Fraternity
Vasa Order of America

1897

Brotherhood of American Yeomen
Daughters of Isabella
Equitable Reserve Association
Fraternal Tribunes
Independent Order of Chosen Friends

Modern Brotherhood of America
Modern Samaritans
Neighbors of Woodcraft
New Era Association
Order of Americus
Prudent Patricians of Pompeii of the United States of America
Western Fraternal Life Association

1898

American Fraternal Congress
American Fraternal Union
American Postal Workers Accident Benefit Association
Fraternal Order of Eagles
Improved Benevolent and Protective Order of Elks of the World
Ladies' Pennsylvania Slovak Catholic Union
Modern Order of Praetorians
Order of Iroquois
Polish Women's Alliance
Sociedade Portuguesa Rainha Santa Isabel

1899

Arctic Brotherhood
Daughters of Scotland
North Star Benefit Association
Polish Beneficial Association

1900

Mutual Guild of Grand Secretaries
Russian Brotherhood Organization of the U.S.A.
Supreme Ladies' Auxiliary Knights of St. John
Union Saint-Jean Baptiste

1901

Associated Fraternities of America
National Fraternal Society of the Deaf
Presbyterian Beneficial Union
Serb National Federation
The Supreme Camp of the American Woodmen

1902

Aid Association for Lutherans
Alliance of Transylvanian Saxons
Ancient Order of Shepherds
Beavers Reserve Fund Fraternity
Daughters of Independent, Benevolent, Protective Order of Elks of the World
National Fraternal League
Tall Cedars of Lebanon of the United States of America

1903

American Stars of Equity
Association of the Sons of Poland
Catholic Daughters of America

Polish National Alliance of the United States of North America
United Societies of the United States

1904

International Geneva Association
International Order of Alhambra
Modern Romans
Order of Owls
Slovene National Benefit Society

1905

Ancient Egyptian Order of Sciots
Ancient Order of Pyramids
Brith Sholom
The National League of Masonic Clubs
Order of Golden Links
Order of Sons of Italy
Slovak Catholic Sokol
Supreme Conclave True Kindred

1906

The Homesteaders

1907

Benevolent Order of Bereans
National Home Guard
Pythian Sisters
Russian Orthodox Catholic Women's Mutual Aid Society

1908

American Workmen
Bnai Zion
Concordia Mutual Life Association
Polish National Union of America
Sovereign Order of Saint John of Jerusalem
Western Slavonic Association

1909

American Home Watchmen
Conference of Grand Masters of Masons in North America
Knights of Peter Claver

1910

The Fraternal Order Orioles
The Ukrainian Workingmen's Association

1911

Federation Life Insurance of America
Fraternal Order of Beavers
Fraternal Order of Clover Leaves
George Washington Masonic National Memorial Association

Loyal Order of Buffaloes
Patriotic and Protective Order of Stags of the World
Royal Order of Jesters
Royal Order of Lions

1912

Benevolent and Protective Order of Elks of Canada
Knights of Luther
Order of Ancient Oaks
Order of Bugs
Order of Houn' Dawgs
Order of Red Eagles
Providence Association of Ukrainian Catholics in America

1913

Supreme Temple Daughters of the Nile
Improved Order of Deer
Mutual Benefit Association of Rail Transportation Employees, Inc.
Police and Firemen's Insurance Association

1914

Ladies Oriental Shrine of North America
National Order of Cowboy Rangers
Ukrainian National Aid Association of America
Women of the Moose

1915

American Brotherhood U.S.A.
Fraternal Order of Police
Order of Royal Purple
The Rosicrucian Order (also known as the Ancient, Mystical Order Rosae Crucis)

1916

The Beavers National Mutual Benefit
Pancretan Association of America

1917
Lutheran Brotherhood
Modern Knights of St. Paul
Supreme Emblem Club of the United States of America

1918
National Sojourners, Inc.

1919

Daughters of Mokanna
Masonic Service Association
National Defenders
Order of De Molay
Shrine Directors Association of North America

1920

Loyal Sons of America
Order of Camels
Union of Polish Women in America

1921

Croatian Catholic Union of the United States of America
High Twelve International
International Order of Job's Daughters
Odd Fellows, Junior Lodge
Order of the Bath of the United States of America

1922

The Antlers
International Order of Rainbow Girls
The Order of Ahepa
The Order of Sons of Pericles
Western Samaritans Life Association

1923

American Krusaders
American Order of Clansmen
Heroes of '76
Hooded Ladies of the Mystic Den
Kamelia
Knights of the Flaming Circle
Knights of the Invisible Colored Kingdom
Knights of Liberty
Loyal Ladies of the Royal Arcanum
Order of Anti-Poke-Noses
Order of Knight Masons
Order of Yellow Dogs

1924

Ancient Mystic Order of Samaritans

1925

Columbian Squires
Daughters of the Eastern Star
Junior Catholic Daughters of America
Order of Golden Key
Portuguese Continental Union of the United States of America

1926

Supreme Emblem Club of the United States of America

1928

The Philalethes Society

1929

Daughters of Penelope

National Federated Craft
Order of Golden Chain

1930

Association of Lithuanian Workers
The Convent General Knights of the York Cross of Honour
The Maids of Athena
Mennonite Mutual Aid Association

1931

National Mutual Benefit
Russian Independent Mutual Aid Society

1932

Grand College of Rites of the United States of America
The Grand Council of Allied Masonic Degrees of the United States
The Society of Blue Friars

1934

Holy Order of Knights Beneficent of the Holy City

1946

Order of Desoms

1948

International Supreme Council of World Masons, Inc.

1949

The Order of the Constellation of Junior Stars

1952

Degree of Anona
Degree of Hiawatha

1957

Federation of Masons of the World
The York Rite Sovereign College

1962

United Lutheran Society

1964

Woodmen Rangers and Rangerettes

1966

National Travelers Club for Masons

1971

United Transportation Union Insurance Association

1972

Lutheran Life Insurance Society of Canada

GEOGRAPHIC HEADQUARTERS

Most fraternal organizations discussed on the preceding pages of the present volume have national headquarters. This catalog indicates in what state or province a given group has or had (if no longer active) its head offices.

California

Ancient Egyptian Order of Sciots
Ancient Order of Foresters
Degree of Pocahontas
Knights of Pythias
Mutual Guild of Grand Secretaries
Native Daughters of the Golden West
Native Sons of the Golden West
Pancretan Association of America
Portuguese Union of the State of California
The Rosicrucian Order
Social Order of the Beauceant
Sociedade Portuguesa Rainha Santa Isabel
Society Espirito Santo of the State of California
United National Life Insurance Society

Colorado

The Supreme Camp of the American Woodmen
Western Slavonic Association
Woodmen of the World

Connecticut

Columbian Squires
Daughters of Isabella
Knights of Columbus
Loyal Ladies of the Royal Arcanum
Independent Order of Owls

District of Columbia

Ancient and Accepted Scottish Rite of Freemasonry for the Southern Jurisdiction of the U.S.A.
B'nai B'rith International
Hungarian Reformed Federation of America

Independent Order of Rechabites
The Maids of Athena
National Sojourners, Inc.
The Order of Ahepa
Order of Eastern Star
Order of Patrons of Husbandry
Order of Sons of Pericles

Delaware

Order of Knight Masons

Florida

Shrine Directors Association of North America

Illinois

American Slovenian Catholic Union
Ancient Arabic Order of the Nobles of the Mystic Shrine
Ancient Order of Shepherds
Benevolent and Protective Order of Elks
Catholic Knights and Ladies of Illinois
Catholic Order of Foresters
Concordia Mutual Life Association
Czechoslovak Society of America
The Danish Sisterhood
Home Forum Benefit Order
Independent Order of Svithiod
Independent Order of Vikings
Italo American National Union
Knights of the Red Cross of Constantine
Knights Templar
Loyal American Life Association
Loyal Order of Moose
Modern Woodmen of America
National Fraternal Congress of America
National Fraternal Society of the Deaf
North American Union Life Insurance Association Society
North Star Benefit Association
Order of Sons of St. George
Polish National Alliance of the United States of North America
Polish Roman Catholic Union of America
Polish Women's Alliance
Royal League
Royal Neighbors of America
Russian Independent Mutual Aid Society
Slovene National Benefit Society
Supreme Council Grottoes of North America
Western Catholic Union
Women of the Moose

Indiana

Ancient Mystic Order of Bagmen of Bagdad
Ben Hur Life Association

Croatian Catholic Union of the United States of America
Daughters of Isis
Fraternal Order of Police
Knights and Ladies of Honor
Mennonite Mutual Aid Association
National Federated Craft
Police and Firemen's Insurance Association
Royal Order of Lions

Iowa

Brotherhood of American Yeomen
Dramatic Order Knights of Khorassan
Iowa Legion of Honor
P.E.O. Sisterhood
Royal Order of Jesters
Western Fraternal Life Association

Kansas

International Association of Rebekah Assemblies
Modern Knights' Fidelity League
Occidental Mutual Benefit Association

Kentucky

Knights and Ladies of the Golden Rule
International General Grand Chapter of Royal Arch Masons

Louisiana

Knights of Peter Claver
Order of the Heptasophs

Manitoba

The Benevolent and Protective Order of Elks of Canada
Pioneer Fraternal Association
Order of Royal Purple

Maryland

Conference of Grand Master of Masons in North America
Hooded Ladies of the Mystic Den
Improved Order of Heptasophs
Independent Order of Mechanics
Independent Order of Odd Fellows
International Order of Alhambra
Masonic Service Association
Order of Shield of Honor
The Philalethes Society
The Royal Order of Scotland

Massachusetts

Ancient Accepted Scottish Rite of Freemasonry for the Northern Masonic Jurisdiction of the
    United States of America
Catholic Association of Foresters

International Order of Hoo-Hoo
Loyal Knights and Ladies
Order of Scottish Clans
Portuguese Continental Union of the United States of America
Royal Arcanum
United Order of Pilgrim Fathers

Michigan

Ancient and Illustrious Star of Bethlehem
Ancient Egyptian Arabic Order of Nobles of the Shrine
The Gleaner Life Insurance Society
International Supreme Council of World Masons, Inc.
Ladies of Maccabees of the World
The Maccabees
Modern Romans
New Era Association
North American Benefit Association
Order of Red Eagles
The Order of the Daughters of Scotia
Order of the White Shrine of Jerusalem
Prudent Patricians of Pompeii of the United States of America
United Friends of Michigan
The York Rite Sovereign College

Minnesota

American Fraternal Union
The Catholic Aid Association
Catholic Workmen
Degree of Honor Protective Association
Lutheran Brotherhood
Modern Samaritans
Sons of Norway

Missouri

Ancient Order of Pyramids
Catholic Knights of America
The Order of De Molay
National Benefit Society
Patriotic Protective Order of Stags of the World
Royal Tribe of Joseph
The Travelers Protective Association of America
United Brothers of Friendship

Nebraska

The Danish Brotherhood in America
International Order of Job's Daughters
Loyal Mystic Legion of America
Royal Highlanders
The Sons and Daughters of Protection
Western Bees
Woodmen of the World Life Insurance Society
Woodmen Rangers and Rangerettes

New Hampshire

American Postal Workers Accident Benefit Association
Association Canado-Americaine

New Jersey

Association of the Sons of Poland
Knights and Ladies of the Golden Star
The Order of Amaranth
Order of the Bath of the United States of America
Order of Golden Chain
Order of Shepherds of Bethlehem
St. Patrick's Alliance of America
Slovak Catholic Sokol
Societas Rosicruciana in Civitatibus Foederatis
The Society of Blue Friars
Supreme Emblem Club of the United States of America
Templars of Liberty
Ukrainian National Association

New York

Ancient Order of Hibernians in America
Association of Lithuanian Workers
Baptist Life Association
Bnzi Zion
Catholic Daughters of America
The Convent General Knights of the York Cross of Honour
Daughters of Mokanna
Free Sons of Israel
German Order of Harugari
The Homesteaders
Independent Order of Good Samaritans and Daughters of Samaria
Independent Order of Sons of Benjamin
International Geneva Association
Knights of Liberty
The National League of Masonic Clubs
National Protective Life Association
Order of B'rith Abraham
Polish Union of America
Royal Benefit Society
Independent Order of Sons of Abraham
Sons of Temperance
Supreme Ladies' Auxiliary Knights of St. John
United Order of True Sisters, Inc.
Workmen's Benefit Fund of the United States of America
The Workmen's Circle

North Carolina

Daughters of Independent, Benevolent, and Protective Order of Elks of the World
The Grand Council of Allied Masonic Degrees of the United States
Improved Benevolent and Protective Order of Elks of the World

Ohio

The Alliance of Poles
Alliance of Transylvanian Saxons
American Hungarian Catholic Society
The Catholic Knights of Ohio
Czech Catholic Union
Daughters of America
First Catholic Slovak Ladies Association
First Catholic Slovak Union of the United States of America and Canada
Knights of St. John
The Locomotive Engineers Mutual Life and Accident Insurance Association
Loyal Christian Benefit Association
National Union Assurance Society
North American Swiss Alliance
The Order of United Commercial Travelers of America
United Transportation Union Insurance Association
Universal Craftsmen Council of Engineers

Oklahoma

International Order of Rainbow Girls

Ontario

Canadian Foresters Life Insurance Society
Canadian Fraternal Association
The Independent Order of Foresters
Loyal Orange Association (Canada)
Lutheran Life Association Insurance Society of Canada
Sons of Scotland Benevolent Association

Oregon

Neighbors of Woodcraft

Pennsylvania

American Home Watchmen
The Ancient and Illustrious Order Knights of Malta
Artisans Order of Mutual Protection
Brith Sholom
Catholic Knights of St. George
Croatian Fraternal Union of America
Dames of Malta
The Fraternal Order Orioles
Grand United Order of Odd Fellows in America
Greater Beneficial Union of Pittsburgh
Greek Catholic Union of the United States of America
Independent Order of Puritans
National Council of Junior Order of United American Mechanics of the United States of
    America
Knights of the Golden Eagle
Ladies Pennsylvania Slovak Catholic Union
League of Friendship Mechanical Order of the Sun
Lithuanian Catholic Alliance

Loyal Christian Benefit Association
Mutual Benefit Association of Rail Transportation Employees, Inc.
National Fraternity
National Haymakers' Association
National Slovak Society of the U.S.A.
Order Knights of Friendship
Order of Americus
Order of Home Builders
Order of Iroquois
Order of Pente
Order of Sons of Italy
Order of Sparta
Order of the Builders
Pennsylvania Slovak Catholic Union
The Polish Beneficial Association
Polish Falcons of America
Polish National Union of America
Presbyterian Beneficial Union
Protected Home Circle
Providence Association of Ukrainian Catholics in America
Pythian Sisters
Russian Brotherhood Organization of the U.S.A.
Russian Orthodox Catholic Mutual Aid Society of the U.S.A.
Russian Orthodox Catholic Women's Mutual Aid Society
Serb National Federation
Sexennial League
Tall Cedars of Lebanon of the United States of America
Ukrainian National Aid Association of America
Ukrainian Workingmen's Association
Union of Polish Women in America
United Lutheran Society
United Societies of the United States of America
Vasa Order of America
Verhovay Fraternal Insurance Association
William Penn Association
Zivena Beneficial Society

Rhode Island

Union Saint-Jean Baptiste

Saskatchewan

The Benevolent and Protective Order of Elks of Canada

South Dakota

Masonic Relief Association of the United States and Canada

Tennessee

Independent Order of Immaculates of the United States of America

Texas

Catholic Women's Fraternal of Texas K.J.Z.T.
Independent Order of Red Men

Modern Order of Praetorians
Order of Sons of Hermann
Slavonic Benevolent Order of the State of Texas

Virginia

Ancient Order of Sanhedrims
George Washington Masonic Memorial Association
Grand College of Rites of the United States of America
Heroes of '76

Washington

Ancient Order of United Workmen

West Virginia

Ancient Mystic Order of Samaritans

Wisconsin

Aid Association for Lutherans
The Beavers National Mutual Benefit
Catholic Family Life Insurance
Catholic Knights Insurance Society
Equitable Reserve Association
Federation Life Insurance of America
National Fraternal League
National Mutual Benefit
Sloga Fraternal Life Insurance Society

FRATERNAL ORGANIZATIONS BY ETHNIC AFFILIATION

Many fraternal groups are organized along ethnic lines. The following appendix indicates the various ethnic categories and their respective societies.

Black
Ancient Egyptian Arabic Order of Nobles of the Shrine
Daughters of Isis
Daughters of Independent, Benevolent, Protective Order of Elks of the World
Grand United Order of Galilean Fishermen
Grand United Order of Odd Fellows in America
Heroines of Jericho
Improved Benevolent and Protective Order of Elks of the World
Independent Order of Good Samaritans and Daughters of Samaria
International Order of Twelve Knights and Daughters of Tabor
Knights of Peter Claver
Knights of Pythias of North America, Europe, Asia, and Africa
Knights of the Invisible Colored Kingdom
Mosaic Templars of America
Order of Golden Circle
Prince Hall Freemasonry
Prince Hall Grand Chapter of the Eastern Star

German
Alliance of Transylvanian Saxons
Bavarian National Association of North America
German Order of Harugari
Improved Order of Knights of Pythias
Order of Sons of Hermann

Greek
Daughters of Penelope
Greek Catholic Union of the United States of America
The Maids of Athena
The Order of Ahepa
The Order of the Sons of Pericles

Hungarian
American Hungarian Catholic Society
Hungarian Reformed Federation of America
William Penn Association

Italian

Italo American National Union
Order of Sons of Italy

Lithuanian

Lithuanian Alliance of America
Lithuanian Catholic Alliance
Association of Lithuanian Workers

Portuguese

Portuguese Continental Union of the United States of America
Portuguese Union of the State of California
Sociedade Portuguesa Rainha Santa Isabel
Society Espirito Santo of the State of California

Polish

The Alliance of Poles
Association of the Sons of Poland
Polish Beneficial Association
Polish Falcons of America
Polish National Alliance of Brooklyn, U.S.A.
Polish National Alliance of the United States of America
Polish National Union of America
Polish Roman Catholic Union of America
Polish Union of America
Polish Women's Alliance
Union of Polish Women in America

Russian

Russian Brotherhood Organization of the U.S.A.
Russian Independent Mutual Aid Society
Russian Orthodox Catholic Women's Mutual Aid Society of the U.S.A.
Russian Orthodox Catholic Women's Mutual Aid Society

Scandanavian

The Danish Brotherhood in America
The Danish Sisterhood
Independent Order of Svithiod
Independent Order of Vikings
Sons of Norway

Slavonic

American Fraternal Union
American Slovenian Catholic Union
Croatian Catholic Union of the United States of America
Croatian Fraternal Union of America
Czech Catholic Union
Czechoslovak Society of America
First Catholic Slovak Ladies Association
First Catholic Slovak Union of the U.S.A. and Canada
Ladies Pennsylvania Slovak Catholic Union

National Slovak Society of U.S.A.
Pennsylvania Slovak Catholic Union
Presbyterian Beneficial Union
Serb National Federation
Slavonic Benevolent Order of the State of Texas
Slovak Catholic Sokol
Slovak Gymnastic Union Sokol of the United States of America
Slovene National Benefit Society
United Lutheran Society
Western Fraternal Life Association
Western Slavonic Association

Ukrainian

Ukrainian National Aid Association of America
Ukrainian National Association
The Ukrainian Workingmen's Association

FRATERNAL ORGANIZATIONS BY RELIGIOUS AFFILIATION

A number of the fraternal societies in the present volume reflect religious or denominational ties. There are four religious clusters. A denomination represented by only one fraternal organization is not listed in the present appendix.

Jewish

B'nai B'rith International
Bnai Zion
Brith Sholom
Free Sons of Israel
Independent Order of B'rith Abraham
Order of B'rith Abraham
The Workmen's Circle

Lutheran

Aid Association for Lutherans
Concordia Mutual Life Association
Knights of Luther
Lutheran Brotherhood
Lutheran Life Insurance Society of Canada
United Lutheran Society

Orthodox Catholic

Greek Catholic Union of the United States of America
Russian Orthodox Catholic Mutual Aid Society of the U.S.A.
Russian Orthodox Catholic Women's Mutual Aid Society

Roman Catholic

American Hungarian Catholic Society
American Order of United Catholics
American Slovenian Catholic Union
The Catholic Aid Association
Catholic Association of Foresters
Catholic Daughters of America
Catholic Family Life Insurance
Catholic Knights and Ladies of Illinois

Catholic Knights Insurance Society
Catholic Knights of America
The Catholic Knights of Ohio
Catholic Knights of St. George
Catholic Order of Foresters
Catholic Women's Fraternal of Texas K.J.Z.T.
Catholic Workmen
Columbian Squires
Croatian Catholic Union of the United States of America
Czech Catholic Union
Daughters of Isabella
First Catholic Slovak Ladies Association
First Catholic Slovak Union of the United States of America and Canada
Knights of Columbus
Ladies Pennsylvania Slovak Catholic Union
Lithuanian Catholic Alliance
Loyal Christian Benefit Association
Pennsylvania Slovak Catholic Union
Polish Roman Catholic Union of America
St. Patrick's Alliance of America
Slovak Catholic Sokol
Western Catholic Union

INTERRELATED FRATERNAL ORGANIZATIONS

A few of the major fraternal orders have allied organizations. These allied relationships sometimes are youth groups; sometimes they are female auxiliaries. The following appendix lists several groups of allied societies. The reader will note that Freemasonry has the largest number of allied organizations.

Elks

The Antlers
Benevolent and Protective Order of Elks
The Benevolent and Protective Order of Elks of Canada
Improved Benevolent and Protective Order of Elks of the World
Daughters of Independent, Benevolent, Protective Order of Elks of the World
Elks Mutual Benefit Association
Order of Royal Purple

Masonic (White)

Ancient and Accepted Scottish Rite of Freemasonry for the Northern Masonic Jurisdiction of the United States of America
Ancient and Accepted Scottish Rite of Freemasonry for the Southern Jurisdiction of the United States of America
Ancient Arabic Order of the Nobles of the Mystic Shrine
Ancient Egyptian Order of Sciots
Ancient Order of Knights of the Mystic Chain
Conference of Grand Masters of Masons in North America
The Convent General Knights of the York Cross of Honour
Daughters of the Eastern Star
Daughters of Mokanna
Daughters of the Nile, Supreme Temple
Federation of Masons of the World
Free and Regenerated Palladium
Freemasonry, Ancient, Free and Accepted Masons
George Washington Masonic National Memorial Association
Grand College of Rites of the United States of America
Grottoes of North America
Heroes of '76
Heroines of Jericho

High Twelve International
Independent International Order of Owls
International General Grand Chapter of Royal Arch Masons
International General Grand Council of Royal and Select Masters
International Order of Job's Daughters
International Order of Rainbow Girls
International Supreme Council of World Masons, Inc.
Knights of the Globe
Knights Templar
Ladies Oriental Shrine of North America
Masonic Life Association
Masonic Relief Association of the United States of America and Canada
Masonic Service Association
Mutual Guild of Grand Secretaries
The National League of Masonic Clubs
National Sojourners, Inc.
National Travelers Club for Masons
The Order of Amaranth
Order of the Bath of the United States of America
Order of the Builders
The Order of the Constellation of Junior Stars
The Order of De Molay
Order of Desoms
Order of Eastern Star
Order of Golden Key
Order of Knight Masons
The Order of the White Shrine of Jerusalem
The Philalethes Society
Royal Order of Jesters
The Royal Order of Scotland
Shrine Directors Association of North America
Social Order of the Beauceant
Tall Cedars of Lebanon of the United States of America
Ye Ancient Order of Corks
The York Rite Sovereign College

Odd Fellows

Ancient Mystic Order of Samaritans
Grand United Order of Odd Fellows in America
Independent Order of Odd Fellows
International Association of Rebekah Assemblies
Imperial Order of Muscovites
Junior Lodge Odd Fellows
Oriental Order of Humility and Perfection
Theta Rho Clubs

Pythians

Improved Order of Knights of Pythias
Junior Order of Princes of Syracuse
Knights of Pythias
Knights of Pythias of North America, Europe, Asia, and Africa

Pythian Sisters
Rathbone Sisters of the World
Sunshine Girls

Red Men

Degree of Anona
Degree of Hiawatha
Degree of Pocahontas
Improved Order of Red Men
Independent Order of Red Men
National Haymakers' Association

INDEX

Page numbers in **boldface** indicate the location of the main entry.

Alvin J. Schmidt is Professor of Sociology at Concordia Theological Seminary, Fort Wayne, Indiana. He is the author of *Oligarcy in Fraternal Organizations*, as well as articles in the *Journal for the Scientific Study of Religion*, *Phylon*, *Journal of Voluntary Action Research*, and other publications.

Nicholas Babchuk is Professor of Sociology at the University of Nebraska, Lincoln. He has published extensively on the subject of voluntary associations. Dr. Babchuk is a past president of the Midwest Sociological Society and has been on the board of the Association of Voluntary Action Scholars. He is an editorial board member on several journals and is currently engaged in research dealing with the social participation of the elderly.